Gastroenterology

D1329291

Concise Medical Textbooks

BIOCHEMISTRY
S. P. Datta and J. H. Ottaway

CARDIOLOGY
D. G. Julian

COMMUNITY HEALTH, PREVENTIVE MEDICINE AND
  SOCIAL SERVICES
J. B. Meredith Davies

DERMATOLOGY
E. Lipman Cohen and J. S. Pegum

EMBRYOLOGY
M. B. L. Craigmyle

GASTROENTEROLOGY
I. A. D. Bouchier

MEDICAL MICROBIOLOGY
C. G. A. Thomas

OPHTHALMOLOGY
Kenneth Wybar

PAEDIATRICS
John Apley

PATHOLOGY
J. R. Tighe

PHARMACOLOGY
R. G. Penn

PSYCHIATRY
E. W. Anderson and W. H. Trethowan

RENAL MEDICINE
Roger Gabriel

Gastroenterology

Second edition

Ian A. D. Bouchier

MD, FRCP (Lond), FRCP (Edin)
Professor of Medicine,
University of Dundee, Scotland

BAILLIÈRE TINDALL • LONDON

First published 1973
Second edition 1977

A BAILLIÈRE TINDALL book published by
Cassell & Collier Macmillan Publishers Ltd
35 Red Lion Square, London WC1R 4SG
and at Sydney, Auckland, Toronto, Johannesburg
an affiliate of
Macmillan Publishing Co. Inc.
New York

© 1977 BAILLIÈRE TINDALL
a division of Cassell & Collier Macmillan Publishers Ltd

All rights reserved. No part of this publication may be
reproduced, stored in a retrieval system or transmitted in
any form or by any means, electronic, mechanical, photocopying
or otherwise without the prior permission of Baillière Tindall,
35 Red Lion Square, London WC1 4SG

ISBN 0 7020 0659 9

Printed Offset Litho in Great Britain by
Cox & Wyman Ltd,
London, Fakenham and Reading

Contents

Chapter		Page
	Preface	vii
1	Oesophageal Disease	1
2	Hiatus Hernia	17
3	Peptic Ulcer	22
4	Other Gastric Disorders	63
5	Malabsorption Syndromes	74
6	Appendicitis	120
7	Crohn's Disease	125
8	Ulcerative Colitis	136
9	Vascular Injury to the Bowel	149
10	Intestinal Tumours	158
11	Other Bowel Disorders	175
12	Minor Anal Conditions	204

13   Cirrhosis of the Liver   212

14   Viral Hepatitis   266

15   Other Liver Disorders   281

16   Pancreatic Disease   302

17   Biliary Tract Disease   329

18   Infections and Infestations   350

     Index   367

Plate section between pp. 182 and 183

Preface to the Second Edition

The preparation of a second edition of *Gastroenterology* has provided the opportunity to make a number of changes to the text. The helpful suggestions of friends have been incorporated and a number of sections has been updated and altered, particularly that of the gastro-oesophageal junction, peptic ulcer disease, gastrointestinal hormones, viral hepatitis and of course various aspects of therapy. I had hoped that the revision would not increase the length of the text. Unfortunately I succumbed to the temptation to add rather than delete and the monograph has grown. But I hope that it retains a uniformity and cohesion which will enable the reader to obtain readily a perspective of modern gastroenterological thought and practice. I have taken the opportunity to include a small selection of radiographs for some of which I am indebted to Dr D. Clarke.

For a fuller introduction to the book the reader is referred to the preface to the first edition which appears overleaf.

Dundee
March 1977   *Ian A. D. Bouchier*

From the Preface to the First Edition

Digestive diseases are an important cause of morbidity in our community today. It has been estimated that one-half of the population of the United States of America has digestive complaints and that the economic loss to the nation amounts to 8 billion dollars annually. The greatest impact of gastrointestinal disorders is on the health of the middle aged and this has important consequences for the community in general and the family in particular.

There are many textbooks on the subject of gastroenterology. Why add yet another? First, in a field which is expanding rapidly there will always be something new to say. A second and more important reason is the need for a concise text by one author which presents a unified approach to the subject and which reflects his own attitudes towards it. The briefer text by the single author provides the opportunity for the writer to present his concept of the specialty as a whole. This presentation is therefore essentially personal but also, I hope, balanced and coherent.

The discipline of gastroenterology has gained from many advances in the last decade and it is currently experiencing an exciting expansion of knowledge. This is the result of enthusiastic and frequently successful attempts to link physiological and biochemical information to the clinical situation. Increasingly clinical gastroenterology is being practised according to sound and established scientific principles. Significant advances, for example, have been made in the isolation, characterization and synthesis of a number of gastrointestinal hormones. It is now possible to use biologically active synthetic fractions of gastrin to stimulate parietal cells to secrete acid and the measurement of serum gastrin activity is of considerable diagnostic value in certain circumstances.

The wider role of the gut in the homeostasis of the body is accepted and is well exemplified by protein metabolism. Albumin is synthesized in the liver and normally enters the gastrointestinal tract where it undergoes digestion with reabsorption and reutilization of the breakdown products. The syndrome of protein-losing enteropathy is an exaggeration of this process. The gut makes an important contribution to the serum immunoglobulin levels and there is a greater awareness that immunoglobulin deficiency states may accompany various gastrointestinal disorders. Indeed, the impact of immunology on gastrointestinal disease has been most significant from a consideration of both the pathogenesis and the diagnosis of a variety of abdominal disorders.

Diagnostic methods have improved considerably, leading to more accurate documentation of established diseases and the delineation of new clinical syndromes. Gastrointestinal radiology has become more precise with the introduction of techniques such as hypotonic duodenography, percutaneous transhepatic cholangiography and selective arteriography. Isotopic scanning of the intra-abdominal organs is being used with increasing frequency and effect. The introduction of fibreoptic systems and the wider use of photography have added a new dimension to diagnosis and are of much value in the training of gastroenterologists.

This book attempts to reflect the synthesis of physiology and biochemistry which is the aim of modern clinical gastroenterology. Intentionally therefore, no formal separation is made between physiology and pathology, between the laboratory bench and the hospital bed; but the reader will be reminded constantly of the normal function when attempting to understand the characteristics and effects of a disease process and the investigations required for a diagnosis to be made. The able practice of gastroenterology must involve the close cooperation of a number of disciplines and I hope that this belief is reflected in these pages.

Because of the limitations of space I have introduced only selected aspects of paediatric gastroenterology and I have dealt but briefly with the vast subject of gastrointestinal infections and infestations, the number of pages allocated in no way reflecting the importance of the subject.

1   Oesophageal Disease

The oesophagus is the tube which extends from the pharynx to the stomach. It conveys food from the mouth to the stomach and it has barriers at the oesophageal inlet and in the region of the oesophagogastric junction.

Upper Oesophageal Sphincter

The upper 3 cm are normally closed by the action of the cricopharyngeal muscle aided by the upper fibres of the smooth muscle of the oesophagus. This upper oesophageal sphincter opens during swallowing, regurgitation, vomiting and belching.

Lower Oesophageal Sphincter

The lower oesophageal sphincter mechanism protects against gastric regurgitation and this, too, is normally held in the closed position. There have been many suggestions regarding the nature and mechanism of the barrier between the oesophageal and gastric lumens: an intrinsic sphincter mechanism at the oesophagogastric junction, the pinchcock action of the crura of the diaphragm, the valve-like effect of the oblique entry of the oesophagus into the stomach, the mucosal rosette formed by gastric mucosal folds and the effect of the positive intra-abdominal pressure upon the flaccid intra-abdominal portion of the oesophagus. Despite the inability to define precisely an anatomical site for the sphincter mechanism it is widely accepted that such a sphincter exists functionally. It is characterized by a zone (2–5 cm long) of increased pressure usually between 15 and 30 mmHg (2 and 4 kPa).

There are both neural and hormonal influences on the lower oesophageal sphincter. Neither cervical nor intra-abdominal vagotomy affects resting sphincter pressure but the pressure is increased following α-adrenergic stimulation. Probably of more significance is the role of hormones. Pharmacological doses of gastrin will increase sphincter pressure; the pressure is decreased by secretin, cholecystokinin and glucagon. The precise physiological role of these hormones is uncertain. Thus, although alkalinization of the stomach increases sphincter tone, the relationship to endogenously released gastrin is not clear. An increase in lower oesophageal sphincter pressure can be induced by cholinergic agents, metoclopramide, antacids, α-adrenergic stimulators, gastrin and protein ingestion. A decrease in pressure accompanies the use of anticholinergic drugs, secretin, glucagon, cholecystokinin, chocolate, coffee, fat, ethanol and smoking. Carminatives, which are volatile oily extracts from plants such as garlic, onion and peppermint, have a relaxing effect permitting belching thereby reducing gastric distension. Belching is the reflux of gas through the lower oesophageal sphincter and is accompanied by the opening of the oesophagogastric barrier to form a common cavity with the stomach while at the same time there is contraction of the abdominal musculature.

Dysfunction of the lower oesophageal sphincter occurs in a variety of conditions. Sphincter pressures less than 10 mmHg above intragastric pressure are frequently found in gastro-oesophageal reflux and in scleroderma. Despite high serum gastrin levels the sphincter pressure is normal or even reduced in pernicious anaemia, but patients rarely have symptoms of heartburn. The Zollinger–Ellison syndrome is characterized by increased resting lower oesophageal sphincter pressures (25–35 mmHg; 4–5 kPa) has been related to the elevated circulating endogenous gastrin. There are no accompanying symptoms.

The body of the oesophagus is normally relaxed under basal conditions and contracts in response to distension or swallowing. Material is normally conveyed along the oesophagus in an aboral direction by oesophageal peristalsis, but the nature of the oesophageal response depends upon the character of the stimulus. Two types of peristaltic wave normally occur, known as the primary and secondary peristaltic waves. Primary peristalsis is initiated by swallowing; it starts in the pharynx and sweeps down to the oesophagogastric junction. Secondary peristalsis depends upon local stimulation in the oesophagus and is conveniently thought of as the mechanism whereby it is cleared of particles left behind after the primary peristaltic wave. After the initiation of either the primary or secondary wave there is a fall in the lower oesophageal pressure and this precedes the arrival of the peristaltic wave. The resting pressure in the oesophagus is less than atmospheric. Thus when a patient swallows a wave of positive pressure sweeps down the oesophagus and the oesophagogastric sphincter relaxes, the relaxation preceding the arrival of the peristaltic wave. Non-peristaltic or 'tertiary' contractions are found in the elderly and in certain disease states. They are ring-like contractions most marked in the distal third of the oesophagus. It is probable that anti- or reversed peristalsis does not occur in the human oesophagus.

The characteristic symptoms of oesophageal disease or dysfunction are dysphagia, heartburn and regurgitation. Dysphagia is the complaint of food sticking in the oesophagus and accompanies most oesophageal diseases. It is necessary to inquire regarding the duration of the dysphagia, whether it is episodic, continuous or worsening, whether it is for solids only or for fluids as well and whether it is influenced by emotion. The retrosternal site at which the patient feels that the food sticks is poorly correlated with the actual site of the lesion. Heartburn is a retrosternal burning sensation which usually moves in a wave-like manner towards the throat. It usually indicates gastro-oesophageal reflux. There are probably two mechanisms for the oesophageal pain which act singly or together: oesophageal spasm and oesophagitis. Oesophageal pain may be similar in all respects to cardiac pain so that the clinical distinction may prove very difficult.

Achalasia of the Cardia

Achalasia of the cardia is an uncommon disorder of oesophageal motility in which there is abnormal ineffective peristalsis in the body of the oesophagus. This is associated with the failure of the lower oesophageal sphincter to relax in response to a swallow. Degeneration of the myenteric nerve plexus results in feeble, simultaneous tertiary contractions throughout the oesophagus, while denervation of the lower oesophageal (cardiac) sphincter is responsible for the failure of the sphincter to relax. The resting lower oesophageal pressure is elevated to 40–60 mmHg (5–8 kPa).

The condition is chronic and progressive. The length of history is variable, but usually from 2 to 5 years. The major complaints are dysphagia, a choking sensation when attempting to swallow liquids and solids, regurgitation of undigested food and precordial pain. The dysphagia may be more marked under emotional stress. Many patients learn to swallow by trick manoeuvres; often they are able to drink a pint of beer with ease while a sausage roll sticks. Occasionally the first presentation is acute oesophageal obstruction. Regurgitation of food, particularly at night, and recurrent pneumonia are other manifestations of the disease. Weight loss is mild and anaemia uncommon.

A barium swallow will show variable dilatation of the oesophagus with an air fluid level, lack of peristalsis and numerous sluggish tertiary contractions—the 'bag of worms' appearance. The failure of the cardiac sphincter to relax gives a smooth 'beaklike' appearance in the region where the oesophagus passes through the diaphragm. Oesophageal pressure studies confirm the abnormal contractions, the elevated resting lower oesophageal sphincter pressure and the failure of the oesophagogastric sphincter to relax. The intramuscular injection of 1–10 mg methylcholine chloride during radiography or manometry will cause marked muscular contractions, and this has been used as a diagnostic test. Oesophagoscopy is difficult because of the dilated organ and much food residue. It must be performed with caution but the procedure is useful to assess whether or not malignant change has occurred. The incidence of oesophageal cancer in achalasia varies from 3 to 8% and the development of malignancy should be suspected if increasing dysphagia, weight loss, oesophageal bleeding and anaemia occur. Failure to cleanse the oesophagus adequately prior to oesophagoscopy is an important reason for failure to detect malignant degeneration.

The differential diagnosis is between cancer of the oesophagus, diffuse oesophageal spasm, benign oesophageal stricture and, in South American countries, Chagas' disease.

The treatment of achalasia of the cardia is either by hydrostatic dilatation using bougies or expanding bags (Plummer bag, Negus bag, Mosher bag, Browne–Hardy bag) or by surgical oesophagomyotomy (the Heller operation) or some modification of it. There is relatively little difference between the results achieved by these two methods of treatment but the Heller operation is recommended when the oesophagus is very tortuous, when there has been failure of dilatation and in children. The two complications which detract from the good results obtained by the various procedures are recurrence of the oesophageal obstruction and reflux oesophagitis. Even when treatment is accompanied by a satisfactory clinical state the oesophageal contractions remain abnormal.

Lower Oesophageal Ring

This clinically important lesion has been the source of confusion for many years. There is still no general agreement over the definition or nature of the ring; it is probable that there are two morphologically distinct rings. The mucosal ring (Schatski ring) is more frequent and is a 'membranous ridge of mucosa projecting into the lumen of the lower oesophagus in an annular fashion'. The ring is located at or close to the squamocolumnar epithelial junction. It is believed that a hiatus hernia is an integral part of the mucosal ring and therefore the presence of such a ring constitutes evidence of a hiatus hernia. Less commonly a broader muscular ring may be seen. This occurs proximal to the site of the mucosal ring and is covered by squamous epithelium. The muscular ring coincides with the position of the lower oesophageal sphincter.

Both sexes are equally affected. The ring may be symptomless and when symptoms occur they usually present after the age of 50 years. The characteristic feature is episodic, brief dysphagia and it is believed that the lower oesophageal ring is the commonest cause for dysphagia. Both solids and fluids may give rise to difficulty and the obstruction may be sudden and complete. Hurried eating or tension may precipitate the dysphagia and these patients are often mislabelled as neurotic. There is a correlation between the size of the ring and the degree of symptoms. The dysphagia only occasionally becomes progressive and any deterioration in health is rare. Heartburn and chest pain are uncommon. The diagnosis is established by the history of episodic dysphagia and the radiological demonstration of a ring-like narrowing in the lower oesophagus. The ring is difficult to identify at oesophagoscopy.

The differential diagnosis lies between diffuse oesophageal spasm, achalasia of the cardia and oesophageal cancer.

The management is based on reassurance for the patient, who is also advised to chew food well and to eat in a relaxed and unhurried fashion. Anticholinergic therapy is of limited value. Hydrostatic dilatation of the ring has been recommended; alternatively various surgical manoeuvres have been tried, such as repair of the hiatus hernia, digital dilatation of the ring or even excision of the ring.

Upper Oesophageal Web

Webs may be found throughout the oesophagus but are classically found in the postcricoid region near the cricopharyngeus muscle. The condition is usually seen in females over the age of 50 years. The webs may be symptomless or they may be associated with dysphagia and anaemia. The Plummer–Vinson syndrome, also called the Paterson–Brown–Kelly syndrome or sideropenic dysphagia, is the association of dysphagia in middle-aged women with iron deficiency, koilonychia, glossitis, angular stomatitis and postcricoid webs. However, many middle-aged females with postcricoid dysphagia do not have webs; some patients with webs do not have dysphagia and as many as 50% of patients with webs will have no evidence of anaemia or iron deficiency. Thus the concept of the Plummer–Vinson syndrome is uncertain, and there seems little purpose in retaining it. There is an association between upper oesophageal webs and thyroid antibodies and thyroid disease, particularly myxoedema. It has been claimed that there is an association between upper oesophageal webs and postcricoid cancer but this is not generally accepted.

The diagnosis is established by barium swallow when the web will be seen as a filling defect arising at right angles from the anterior wall of the oesophagus in the postcricoid region. Cineradiology is frequently very informative. The web is rarely seen with the oesophagoscope, probably because it is usually ruptured during the procedure. The patient loses the dysphagia after oesophagoscopy and may be labelled neurotic.

The differential diagnosis includes motor disorders of

the oesophagus, scleroderma, pharyngeal pouch and cancer.

The treatment is oesophagoscopy and rupture of the web. Treatment of an associated iron deficiency is advised, but will not necessarily lead to the disappearance of either the web or the dysphagia.

Diffuse Oesophageal Spasm

Diffuse oesophageal spasm is a disorder characterized by dysphagia and abnormal oesophageal motility. It may occur as a primary disorder or, as a secondary phenomenon in achalasia, cancer of the oesophagus, or in neuromuscular disorders. The condition usually affects the older age groups. The clinical features are dysphagia with or without retrosternal discomfort or pain and the latter may be severe enough to cause confusion with cardiac disease. There is difficulty in swallowing fluids and solids, and cold drinks, meat and bread are frequently troublesome. The swallowing difficulty may be worse under conditions of stress and tension and the patients are readily labelled neurotic. The disorder is mild and intermittent and weight loss and malnutrition are rare. The barium swallow appearances are characteristic: the oesophagus is of normal calibre; hyperactive tertiary contractions are present and normal peristalsis is absent in the lower half of the organ. These appearances have given rise to terms such as corkscrew oesophagus, curling, pseudo-diverticulosis and the rosary bead appearance. The lower oesophageal sphincter functions normally. Manometric studies demonstrate simultaneous and repetitive high pressure waves with normal lower oesophageal sphincter function.

The condition is benign and the majority of the patients show no deterioration in health. At one extreme are those rare patients who appear to progress from diffuse oesophageal spasm to achalasia of the cardia; at the other are the elderly patients with no symptoms but who are found to have gross tertiary contractions on barium swallow (presbyoesophagus).

The differential diagnosis includes achalasia of the cardia, scleroderma of the oesophagus, cancer and oesophagitis.

Treatment is mainly reassurance of the patient. Dietary manipulations may help, such as avoiding cold or 'fizzy' drinks. Topical viscous anaesthetic agents and anticholinergic drugs may be tried but they are seldom of lasting benefit. If the symptoms are severe pneumatic dilatation may be useful while long oesophagomyotomy and Heller's operation have been used to advantage in some patients with severe symptoms.

Other Disorders of Oesophageal Motility

Diabetes Mellitus

Diabetics may develop a neuropathic gastroenteropathy which is believed to be the consequence of degeneration of the autonomic nerves (p. 187). The oesophagus, small bowel and gall bladder may be affected. The patient may develop dysphagia and there will be absence or diminution of the primary peristaltic wave, delay in oesophageal emptying and the presence of tertiary contractions.

Alcoholism

Disturbance of oesophageal motility may occur in chronic alcoholics with peripheral neuropathy. Abnormal oesophageal peristalsis in the distal oesophagus may be demonstrated, although the patients are usually free of symptoms.

Scleroderma (p. 185)

Dysphagia may be a prominent feature in scleroderma and results from two mechanisms. First, there may be feeble, simultaneous contractions in the upper and middle thirds of the oesophagus and eventually the smooth muscle destruction may progress to involve the whole of the oesophagus; secondly, there may be destruction of the lower oesophageal sphincter with free reflux, so that oesophagitis and stricture formation may supervene.

Myotonia Dystrophica

Myotonia dystrophica is associated with reduction in the amplitude and prolonged duration of the upper oesophageal contractions and motility disorders have been recorded in multiple sclerosis and myasthenia gravis.

Oesophagitis

Oesophagitis may result from reflux of gastric contents, infection of the oesophagus or the ingestion of corrosive agents.

REFLUX OESOPHAGITIS

Reflux oesophagitis is associated with reduced lower oesophageal sphincter pressure; the incompetent sphincter mechanism enables gastric contents to reflux into the oesophagus. The basic defect is uncertain but may be the combination of abnormal sphincteric smooth muscle and a deficient endogenous production of gastrin. Prolonged gastric intubation permits reflux as does sclerodermatous involvement of the oesophagus. The presence or absence of a hiatus hernia is irrelevant to the development of gastro-oesophageal reflux.

The main symptom is that of heartburn: retrosternal burning pain arising in the epigastrium and travelling towards the throat. This is accompanied by a sour or bitter taste in the mouth. The symptoms are aggravated by bending or lying down after a large meal. Acute pain similar in all respects to that of myocardial infarction occurs when there is severe oesophagitis. The severity of the reflux symptoms, the ease with which reflux occurs and the degree of oesophagitis are poorly correlated. Complications include mild iron deficiency anaemia and the development of a stricture (Plate I. Fig. 1) which is suggested by dysphagia for solids and eventually fluids, and anorexia and weight loss. At this stage heartburn may not be a feature. Aspiration of gastric contents causes nocturnal coughing, aspiration pneumonitis and lung abscess.

Patients are evaluated by oesophagoscopy which will reveal a reddened, oedematous mucous membrane with white slough. A biopsy is necessary. A barium swallow is usually requested to demonstrate reflux but failure to demonstrate retrograde flow of barium does not rule out the condition because this technique is relatively insensitive for demonstrating reflux. Other tests of use include oesophageal manometry and pH measurement, the Bernstein acid perfusion test and the acid reflux test. The acid perfusion test indicates the sensitivity of the oesophagus to an infusion of 0.1N HCl; the test of acid reflux measures the change in oesophageal pH following the installation of 0.1N HCl into the stomach.

The differential diagnosis includes cancer of the oesophagus, scleroderma and achalasia of the cardia.

The initial management includes wearing loose clothing, that of weight loss, elevation of the head of the bed by 10–15 cm and the frequent use of antacid preparations preferably in the liquid form (p. 33). Antacids both neutralize acid in the oesophagus and increase the lower oesophageal sphincter pressure. An alginate/antacid compound (Gaviscon) is helpful on occasions. Anticholinergic agents are contraindicated because they lower sphincter tone. The patient should not bend after meals. Foods to be avoided include fat, chocolate, coffee and alcohol. Patients are encouraged to stop smoking. Metoclopramide tablets, 10 mg thrice daily may be of help possibly acting by stimulating the oesophagus to clear itself of acid. Failure to respond to these measures or the development of a complication is an indication for surgical intervention. The goal of modern anti-reflux operations is to re-create the intra-abdominal segment of the oesophagus and then suture the stomach around this segment. Three procedures are in common use: the Belsey repair, the Hill repair and the Nissen fundoplication. The operations are successful in 85–90% of patients and the resting lower oesophageal pressures return to normal.

CORROSIVE OESOPHAGITIS

About 75% of acute corrosive oesophagitis is caused by the ingestion of strong caustic solutions. These cause more trauma than alkali in the solid form. The patient will have a burnt mouth, much salivation and retrosternal and epigastric pain. Varying degrees of shock are present. Of the patients who survive the acute episode 25–50% develop strictures.

The management is first the treatment of the shock and second the prevention of stricture formation. If the patient has a lye burn and can swallow, citrus juice is of value during the first few hours. Olive oil is soothing. Oesophago-scopy should be performed under a general anaesthetic within 48 hours. A plastic tube can be introduced at this time and it will serve both for feeding and as a splint. It should be replaced regularly. The patient is given anti-biotics for 4–8 weeks and prolonged steroid administration is recommended until the inflammatory reaction has sub-sided. If a stricture supervenes the patient can be taught self-bouginage with Hurst's mercury bougies. Extensive oesophageal burns may require replacement of the oeso-phagus by a colon transplant.

OESOPHAGEAL MONILIASIS

Oesophageal moniliasis should be suspected in debilitated patients and patients on antibiotics or corticosteroids who complain of difficulty or painful swallowing, or retrosternal pain. The oesophageal moniliasis is not necessarily associated with oral thrush. The mucosa has a nodular appearance on the barium swallow which may be confused with oesophageal varices. The patients respond to oral nystatin therapy which may be combined with liquid antacids and local anaesthetic agents.

LOWER OESOPHAGUS LINED BY COLUMNAR EPITHELIUM

Columnar epithelium may replace the squamous epithelium of the lower oesophagus and extend either as an upgrowth from the cardia or as isolated island of tissue. The majority of subjects are probably asymptomatic. However, if reflux occurs the columnar epithelium reacts with the formation of deep penetrating ulcers (Barrett's ulcer), in contrast to the superficial inflammation which occurs in the squamous epithelium, and these behave like gastric ulcers. The diagnosis can be made by oesophagoscopy and a biopsy is essential. The presence of a deep oesophageal ulcer on the barium swallow should raise the suspicion of this entity. The ulcer is treated by surgical resection.

Emetogenic Injury to the Oesophagus and Stomach

Lacerations of the lower oesophagus and gastric fundus may occur during violent retching and vomiting. The mechanism is probably the sudden increase in intraluminal pressure associated with emesis but such pressure changes and the subsequent injury can follow coughing, straining at stool, childbirth, epileptic seizures and blunt trauma. The condition is more likely to occur in alcoholics and patients with hiatus hernia. When the laceration involves the mucosa the patient may vomit blood and the sequence of prolonged retching or vomiting followed by haematemesis is known as the Mallory–Weiss syndrome. However, a mucosal tear should be suspected in any patient presenting with haematemesis even in the absence of a history of prolonged vomiting. Endoscopy is essential to establish the diagnosis, which cannot be made radiologically. The use of flexible glass fibre endoscopes with movable tips has greatly enhanced the diagnostic potential because most tears involve the gastric fundal mucosa in the region of the cardia. In the majority of patients the bleeding is minor and can be controlled by supportive medical therapy.

Rarely the lower oesophagus ruptures and this condition has been termed 'Boerhaave's syndrome'. Typically the patient vomits after a heavy meal and then develops lower chest pain, shock and the signs of an effusion or pneumothorax. The prognosis is poor unless early reparative surgery is undertaken.

Cancer of the Oesophagus

Cancer of the oesophagus is usually of the squamous cell variety and an adenocarcinoma is frequently the manifestation of an upward extension from a primary growth in the gastric fundus. The disease affects mainly the elderly and occurs more often in alcoholics and cigarette smokers. Oesophageal cancer may complicate achalasia of the cardia and occurs in families with tylosis. There are marked geographic variations in incidence and the disease is extremely common in certain areas of Russia, China and South Africa. Three sites are mainly affected: the lower segment, the level of the aortic arch and the postcricoid region. The growth spreads early to involve lymph nodes and direct spread to the bronchi and other mediastinal tissues occurs.

The major presenting symptom is dysphagia. This is usually painless and progressive, commencing with solid food and progressing until the patient is unable to swallow fluids. Occasionally the first manifestation is sudden and complete oesophageal obstruction or retrosternal pain. Increased salivation may be prominent. Eventually regurgitation, bleeding and weight loss dominate the clinical picture.

The differential diagnosis is mainly between benign oesophageal stricture and achalasia and the correct diagnosis is established after radiological, endoscopic and histological examinations. The barium swallow shows the site of the obstruction (Plate I. Fig. 2). The narrowing is irregular and of variable length. It is not possible to predict the extent of the growth from the length of the stricture because the oesophagus distal to the growth is not adequately filled with barium. Unfortunately in up to 25% of patients the barium meal may provide misleading information. Oesophagoscopy indicates the area of narrowing and may show either an ulcerating or a proliferative growth. Any associated oesophagitis makes it difficult to recognize the underlying cancer. Similarly, a biopsy may miss the malignant tissue and a negative biopsy reporting only inflammatory changes does not exclude oesophageal cancer. Exfoliative cytology is helpful and in some departments has proved more accurate than a biopsy.

Treatment is difficult and unrewarding. Half the patients are unsuitable for radical surgery when first seen and therapy is usually palliative, being aimed at enabling the patient to swallow. Some form of tube, such as a Souttar's tube, Mousseau–Barbin tube or Celestin tube, may be inserted, but these have the hazard of slipping and the disadvantage of becoming blocked by either food or growth. Radiotherapy may be used and is of particular benefit in growths of the middle and upper oesophagus. Modern supervoltage X-ray therapy and cobalt therapy have made it possible to treat tumours accurately without damage to surrounding tissues. Radiotherapy and surgery are often used in combination. If the condition of the patient is satisfactory and the extent of the tumour is limited an oesophagectomy can be undertaken with the right colon being used for oesophageal substitution being brought up either by a subcutaneous or retrosternal technique. Growths in the lower oesophagus are suited to this operation but lesions in the middle third of the oesophagus and the postcricoid region can also be resected. Alternatively oesophagogastrostomy or oesophagojejunostomy may be used for cancers involving the lower part of the oesophagus and the cardia. The long-term results of oesophagectomy are poor and the 5-year survival rate is under 5%.

Further Reading

Atkinson, M. (1962) Mechanisms protecting against gastro-oesophageal reflux. *Gut*, **3**, 1–15.

Barrett, N. R. (1964) Achalasia of the cardia. *Br. med. J.*, **i**, 1135–1140.

Castell, D. O. (1975) Physiology and pathophysiology of the lower oesophageal sphincter. *Ann. Otol. Rhinol and Laryngol.*, **84**, 569–576.

Chisholm, M. et al. (1971) A follow-up study of patients with postcricoid webs. *Q. Jl. Med.*, **40**, 409–420.

Fleshler, B. (1967) Diffuse esophageal spasm. *Gastroenterology*, **52**, 559–564.

Goyal, R. K. et al. (1970) Lower esophageal ring. *New Engl. J. Med.*, **282**, 1298–1305, 1355–1362.

Ingelfinger, F. J. (1958) Esophageal motility. *Physiol. Rev.*, **38**, 533–583.

Lipshutz, W. H. et al. (1974) Normal lower oesophageal sphincter function after surgical treatment of gastro-oesophageal reflux. *New Engl. J. Med.*, **291**, 1107–1110.

Nanson, E. M. (1966) Treatment of achalasia of the cardia. *Gastroenterology*, **51**, 236–241.

Seaman, W. (1967) The significance of webs in the hypopharynx and upper oesophagus. *Radiology*, **89**, 32–38.

Thompson, N. W. et al. (1967) The spectrum of emetogenic injury to the oesophagus and stomach. *Am. J. Surg.*, **113**, 13–26.

2   Hiatus Hernia

Herniation of the stomach through the oesophageal hiatus into the thorax is the commonest form of diaphragmatic herniation, all other varieties being infrequent. There are 3 types of hiatus hernia: sliding (accounting for 75% of hiatus hernias), rolling or paraoesophageal (20%) and mixed, which is a combination of the other two varieties. In another classification there are four types of hiatus hernia: Type I equivalent to a sliding hiatus hernia; Type II, the paraoesophageal variety; Type III or mixed variety and Type IV in which Type I or II is combined with the presence of other intra-abdominal organs in the chest.

In a sliding hiatus hernia the oesophagogastric junction moves through the oesophageal hiatus in the diaphragm. Normally the oesophagus enters the stomach on the lesser curvature aspect but in a sliding hiatus hernia the oesophagus meets the centre of the stomach. In a paraoesophageal hernia the oesophagogastric junction is placed normally but the greater curve of the stomach herniates into a peritoneal sac which passes through the oesophageal hiatus.

The aetiology of hiatus hernia is unknown. Obesity, pregnancy and ascites, by increasing the intra-abdominal pressure, may be factors; it is also possible that in afflicted persons the oesophageal hiatus is abnormally wide. Shortening of the longitudinal muscle of the oesophagus has been implicated, but a shortened oesophagus is probably the result and not the cause of the herniation.

Sliding Hiatus Hernia

Movement of the oesophagogastric junction through the oesophageal hiatus is probably common and may occur in up to 33% of otherwise normal adults, increasing to 50% in the aged. However, in the majority of individuals the hernias are not clinically significant. The characteristic symptoms are heartburn and regurgitation and these occur particularly when the patient bends, stoops or lies down. Hence the symptoms are often worse at night or when the patient gardens. At a later stage respiratory symptoms due to 'spill over', aspiration pneumonitis and dysphagia may supervene. Heartburn developing during pregnancy may be a manifestation of a sliding hiatus hernia. This form of herniation may cause persistent vomiting in the neonate. Once dysphagia ensues the heartburn disappears in many patients and this sequence is very suggestive of the development of an oesophageal stricture.

Earlier beliefs that herniation of the oesophagogastric junction into the chest caused reflux have given way to the concept that reflux does not occur from the herniation per se but is related to the function of the sphincter, regardless of the position of the oesophagogastric junction. The symptoms of a sliding hiatus hernia are related to diminished lower oesophageal sphincter tone rather than the presence of the hernia in the chest. This would explain why some individuals with 'characteristic symptoms' of a sliding hiatus hernia do not have demonstrable herniation, whereas other patients with a hiatus hernia are symptom-free. Bleeding from an associated oesophagitis is a frequent complication; usually the bleeding is mild and chronic and causes an iron deficiency anaemia. There is no evidence of increased gastric acid secretion in patients with sliding hiatus hernia.

The diagnosis is established by a radiological examination (Plate II. Fig. 1), and a variety of techniques are described to demonstrate the hernia, most of which depend upon elevating the intra-abdominal pressure. The hernia may be suspected if a fluid level is seen behind the cardiac shadow on a plain radiograph of the chest. Endoscopic examination is not an accurate method of determining the position of the oesophagogastric junction but manometric techniques may be of help. Consideration of a sliding hiatus hernia enters into the differential diagnosis of heartburn, dysphagia and iron deficiency anaemia.

The management of a symptomatic sliding hiatus hernia, initially at least, is by medical methods and is similar to that for oesophageal reflux (see page 10). The patient should first be advised to lose weight, to avoid tight clothing, to take antacids after meals, to elevate the head of the bed so as to avoid reflux and finally to avoid taking a meal within 3 hours of going to bed. The use of viscous antacid preparations has been recommended. Anticholinergic preparations are contraindicated because they cause gastric stasis, thereby increasing any oesophageal reflux. The introduction of the above regimen generally results in considerable relief of symptoms and the patient may be maintained reasonably well if not entirely free of symptoms. The natural history of the condition appears such that a large number of patients improve and may even lose their symptoms; it is only a minority of patients who require surgery. Surgical management comprises reduction of the hernia, the creation of an intra-abdominal segment of oesophagus and a refashioning of the oesophagogastric junction. The stomach is partially sutured around the intra-abdominal oesophagus and then either to the undersurface of the diaphragm (Belsey repair) or the preaortic fascia (Hill repair). In the Nissen fundoplication procedure the stomach is wrapped completely around the oesophagus. These operations are highly successful and are accompanied by restoration of lower sphincter tone and the relief of symptoms.

OESOPHAGEAL STRICTURE

The surgical methods outlined above are reported to be effective for strictures accompany hiatus hernia and oesophageal reflux. Little or no pre-, intra-, or postoperative dilatation is necessary, the only prerequisite for success being an effective anti-reflux operation. Procedures of such magnitude as oesophageal resection with jejunal or colonic interposition, and oesophagogastrostomy with or without vagotomy and antrectomy are rarely, if ever, necessary.

Paraoesophageal Hernia

These less common hernias usually produce few symptoms. A feature is retrosternal pain occurring during a meal, relieved by standing and walking about. A gastric ulcer may develop at the site of constriction in the herniated portion of the stomach and this may present with pain or, not infrequently, massive gastrointestinal bleeding. The features of oesophageal reflux are uncommon (Plate II. Fig. 2). The diagnosis is established by a barium meal. The treatment is surgical reduction and repair of the hernia orifice.

Other Diaphragmatic Hernias

Herniation through the foramen of Morgagni results in a central, but not always symmetrical, retrosternal hernia. Herniation through the foramen of Bochdalek causes a posterolateral hernia through the diaphragm. The hernias present in the neonatal period as an acute abdominal or thoracic emergency, or in childhood, when the clinical picture will vary depending on the abdominal structures involved, the presence of intestinal obstruction and the degree of compression of the intrathoracic structures. Surgical intervention is always necessary.

Further Reading

Kramer, P. (1969) Does a sliding hiatus hernia constitute a distinct clinical entity? *Gastroenterology*, **57**, 442–448.
Larrain, A. et al. (1975) Surgical correction of reflux. *Gastroenterology*, **69**, 578–583.

3   Peptic Ulcer

Gastric Function

In the stomach the food undergoes mixing and initial digestion and absorption occurs and will be carried further in the small intestine. The main gastric glands are the chief cells which secrete pepsin, the parietal cells which secrete hydrochloric acid and the pyloric glands which produce the hormone gastrin. The mucosal cells are constantly being shed into the lumen of the stomach to be replaced by cells originating from the base of the gastric pits. The process of migrating up the wall of the gland to the mucosal surface takes from 2 to 6 days. There is frequent division of the gastric surface epithelial cells but this is less common in the parietal and chief cells.

GASTRIC EMPTYING AND MOTILITY

The stomach pumps its contents into the duodenum, the pump mechanism comprising the distal portion of the gastric antrum, the pylorus and possibly the duodenal bulb. Peristaltic contraction waves sweep from the cardia to the pylorus, increasing in magnitude as the antrum is approached. The gastric antrum, pylorus and duodenal bulb work and act as a unit and the frequency of antral and pyloric contractions during gastric emptying is 3/minute. The normal stomach empties the major portion of a liquid or solid meal in an exponential fashion so that a certain percentage of the gastric contents empties per unit time. Liquids are emptied faster than solids. The body may regulate emptying of liquids and the antrum solids. The gastroduodenal pump mechanism is subjected to inhibitory impulses arising from the wall of the duodenum and upper jejunum. The rate of gastric emptying depends upon the osmotic pressure, pH and chemical composition of the material reaching the duodenum. Hyperosmolar substances, acids and fats delay gastric emptying. Gastrin, secretin and cholecystokinin inhibit gastric motility but there is little evidence that they have a physiological role in gastric emptying. It is possible that the major influence of food is via the inhibitory enterogastric reflex. However, the neural control of gastric emptying is complex which explains the variable results which follow vagotomy. These depend upon the nature of the food and whether vagotomy is truncal or a proximal gastric vagotomy. The rate of gastric emptying in patients with uncomplicated duodenal ulcers is more rapid than normal; patients with gastric ulceration may empty the stomach normally but in antral ulceration there is delayed gastric emptying. Gastric emptying is frequently delayed in gastric cancer.

ACID SECRETION

The acid output of the parietal cell mass depends upon the interaction of the cephalic phrase mediated via the vagus nerve, the gastric phase mediated via the hormone gastrin and the intestinal phase in which there is stimulation of acid secretion by an as yet unidentified hormonal mechanism. It is believed that histamine serves as the final common local chemostimulator of the parietal cells acting on H_2-receptor sites. Histamine is known to stimulate adenyl cyclase, the enzyme that forms cyclic AMP. The maximum acid output of the stomach depends upon the size of the parietal cell mass and it is believed that each individual cell responds maximally to the stimulus, be it vagus or gastrin. There is a circadian rhythm in acid output, the rate of secretion being greater in the evening than during the morning. The vagus nerves transmit psychogenic stimuli directly to the acid-secreting mucosa and in addition the nerves are distributed to the pyloric gland area influencing the release of gastrin. Basal acid output is believed to result from vagal activity between meals.

Gastrin is produced by the argyrophil cells in the pyloric antral area and the proximal duodenum, called G cells. It is the most important humoral agent involved in the regulation of gastric acid secretion and also exerts a trophic effect on the parietal cell mass. All the physiological activities of gastrin are possessed by the carboxyl-terminal tetra-peptide (Try, Met, Asp, Phen NH_2). Gastrin is probably synthesized as the 34-amino acid molecule, G-34 or 'big gastrin' and converted enzymatically into smaller fragments: G-17 or little gastrin and G-13 or mini-gastrin. Gastrin can also be demonstrated in normal pancreatic islet cells. Sensitive radioimmunoassays have been developed for gastrin and normal fasting serum values are 50 pg/ml with an upper limit rarely greater than 200 pg/ml. Gastrin secretion occurs in response to antral distension, protein ingestion, the presence of peptides and amino acids, particularly glycine, in the stomach, vagal stimulation and calcium. Thus serum gastrin levels rise after a meal. Gastrin release is inhibited by antral and duodenal acidification and by micellar lipid emulsions in the small intestine. Both secretin and cholecystokinin inhibit acid output. There are a number of synergistic mechanisms whereby food stimulates acid output: antral distension, the buffering effect on gastric acid and the presence of protein, all of which serve to increase the output of gastrin by the pyloric gland area. Serum gastrin values are elevated in the Zollinger–Ellison syndrome (gastrinoma) and antral G-cell hyperplasia where there is also acid hypersecretion, and in pernicious anaemia and atrophic gastritis where gastric acid output is absent or reduced. Gastrin is degraded in the kidney and elevated levels occur in chronic renal disease.

Gastric acid output may be measured in a number of ways, but the most widely used clinical tests are the measurement of the basal 1 hour acid output followed by the maximal acid output during the hour following a recognized stimulus to acid secretion. The stimulus used in clinical practice is pentagastrin (6 μg/kg body weight s.c.). For clinical purposes the acid output is expressed best as mmol/hour. The range of gastric acid output in normal subjects and patients with duodenal ulcer, gastric ulcer and gastric cancer is shown in Table I. The value of acid studies in clinical practice is limited as the measurement is rarely of critical diagnostic significance in the individual patient.

TABLE I. *Acid Output in Health and Disease*

Subject	Basal Acid Output (mmol/hour)	Maximal Acid Output (mmol/hour)
Normal	2.0 ± 2.0	18.0 ± 8.0
Duodenal ulcer	4.0 ± 4.0	34.0 ± 13.0
Gastric ulcer	1.2 ± 1.5	14.0 ± 10.0
Gastric cancer	0.3 ± 1.0	2.5 ± 3.5

Intrinsic factor is a glycoprotein of molecular weight 50 000 which is secreted by the normal stomach from the parietal cells. Intrinsic factor output thus parallels acid output and is increased by vagal stimulation and histamine infusion.

Human gastric juice contains a number of proteases produced by the chief cells and which differ in their pH optima. Increased protease secretion occurs in response to vagal stimulation, histamine and gastrin. Pepsin may be regarded as a gastric juice protease which is active at an acid pH. A gastric juice lipase is present in man but its physiological role has yet to be defined. Many other enzymes may be detected in gastric secretions and the lysozomal enzyme β-glucuronidase has achieved prominence for its possible diagnostic role in patients with gastric cancer. All the components of the plasma proteins are found in the gastric secretions. The desquamated cells contribute DNA to gastric juice.

The surface of the gastric mucosa is covered by a layer of 'mucus'. The precise chemical composition of this material remains uncertain but it appears to be a glycoprotein in which the terminal sugar residues have characteristic blood group specificity. It is thought that the newly secreted glycoprotein forms a gelatinous protective covering for the gastric mucous membrane and this is known as the glycocalyx. Normally gastric glycoprotein is resistant to the action of pepsin but degradation occurs under the influence of agents such as the bile acids, alcohol, and salicylates so that the mucus ceases to perform its protective function.

Aetiology

Peptic ulceration is among the commonest of gastrointestinal disorders and affects up to 10% of the community at any one time. The disease is of considerable economic importance. It occurs more commonly in patients of blood group O. Although it is customary and convenient to consider both gastric and duodenal ulcers under the same grouping there is much evidence to indicate that the two forms of ulceration may have different causes. Gastric ulcers, while less common than duodenal ulcers, are more frequent in females and occur in an older age group. Patients are commonly poor, alcoholic and debilitated. Duodenal ulceration is associated with gastric hypermotility and an increased gastric acid output accompanies an increased parietal cell mass. Furthermore there are differences in clinical presentation, and response to medical and surgical therapy.

AETIOLOGY OF GASTRIC ULCERS

There have been many theories to account for gastric ulceration but no single mechanism has found universal acceptance. Because patients with gastric ulcers tend to have reduced acid output it is suggested that the 'protective mechanism' of the gastric mucous membrane, such as mucus, is deficient or abnormal and this leads to lowered mucosal resistance. Mucosal metaplasia is also accompanied by a reduction in mucosal resistance. Ulcers tend to be associated with and occur in an area affected by atrophic or chronic gastritis. The majority of the ulcers occur in the pyloric gland area at the junction with the parietal cell area. An apparent association between calcification of the aorta and gastric ulceration has led to the suggestion that athero-sclerosis causes arterial insufficiency of the stomach and that ulcers result. It has been suggested that some degree of gastric atony with delayed gastric emptying and prolonged contact with food in the antrum causes excessive release of gastrin followed by gastric hypersecretion and gastric ulceration. While such a mechanism may not apply to all gastric ulcers it may well play a role in those gastric ulcers associated with a duodenal ulcer for in this situation the duodenal ulcer invariably precedes the gastric ulcer. The association is observed in up to 30% of ulcers in the stomach. Gastric ulcers can be separated into those in the prepyloric area, which tend to be accompanied by a large acid output comparable to that found in duodenal ulcers, and those ulcers nearer the body of the stomach in which the acid output may be low. This difference in acid secretion reflects the proportion of pyloric gland to parietal cell area in the gastric mucosa; the nearer the ulcer is to the pylorus the larger the parietal cell mass and therefore the greater the acid output.

There is much evidence that an increased reflux of bile occurs into the stomach of patients with gastric ulcers. Whether this event reflects an abnormality of the pyloric sphincter mechanism is not known. The gastric mucosa is exposed to an increased concentration of bile acids which increase the back diffusion of hydrogen ions from the gastric lumen into the mucosal cells. This reversed movement of the hydrogen ions results first in histamine release, mucosal injury and gastritis, and secondly in a reduced hydrogen ion content in the gastric juice. This may be another explanation for the relatively low acid output observed in patients with gastric ulcers.

AETIOLOGY OF DUODENAL ULCERS

It is widely held that an important factor in the development of duodenal ulcers is excessive gastric acid secretory capacity and that this is a reflection of an increased number of parietal cells. The reason for the increased parietal cell mass remains obscure. Ulcer individuals appear to have an increased release of gastrin following a meal although fasting serum gastrin levels are no different from non-ulcer persons. There is also reduced suppression of gastrin release at low pH and a relatively increased acid output at low pH values; there is increased sensitivity to pentagastrin. Patients with duodenal ulcer have more acid in the proximal duodenum than normal subjects. This is in part related to increased gastric acid output and in part the consequence of an increased rate of gastric emptying. The effect is to reduce the buffering effect of meals. There is also some evidence that the low duodenal pH might be due to an inappropriately low secretion of bicarbonate by the pancreas relative to the amount of intraluminal acid. The resistance of the duodenal mucosa is not at fault neither does vagal overactivity seem important. There is little to support the concept that duodenal ulcer subjects are emotionally intense, driving, ambitious individuals who work under great pressure and tension.

Incidence

Peptic ulcer disease is common but the frequency has declined over the past decade, the decrease being more marked for gastric than duodenal ulcers. Both are becoming common in the elderly and duodenal ulceration has joined gastric ulcers as a disease of the socially underprivileged. Claims have been made for the association of peptic ulceration with a number of diseases. There is an increased frequency of duodenal ulcers in patients with chronic renal failure undergoing maintenance haemodialysis or transplantation (p. 189). Peptic ulcers may be more frequent in cirrhosis of the liver, hyperparathyroidism and chronic lung disease. There is less convincing evidence for association with rheumatoid arthritis, chronic pancreatitis and gall stone disease. Although it has been held that adreno-corticosteroid therapy is associated with the development of peptic ulceration and an increased tendency for these ulcers to bleed or perforate, a recent critical review suggests that this is not so, and that corticosteroids are not ulcerogenic. Chronic (but not acute, sporadic) ingestion of salicylates is associated with gastric but not duodenal ulcers. The other anti-inflammatory agents phenylbutazone and indomethacin have also been implicated in peptic ulceration. Peptic ulcers are an important component of the multiple endocrine adenoma complex (p. 49). Acute gastric or duodenal ulceration may follow severe stress, particularly burns (p. 48).

All age groups are affected, with the maximum incidence between the ages of 30 and 60 years. Over 80% of peptic ulcers occur in males. There is evidence of a hereditary predisposition to peptic ulceration and one type of ulcer tends to occur in members of the same family. Persons who are blood group O and non-secretors are more liable to duodenal ulcers. There is an association between blood group O and bleeding and perforation. However, this association between blood group and secretor status does not hold for ulcers in the body of the stomach. There is a positive association between cigarette smoking and peptic ulceration.

Clinical Features

Abdominal pain or discomfort is the characteristic feature of peptic ulceration. It is of a dull burning nature and felt in the epigastrium. It may radiate to the right or left of the midline; radiation in an anteroposterior direction is usually an indication that the ulcer has penetrated the pancreas. The pain usually has a relationship to meals; in gastric ulceration the pain occurs shortly after eating and frequently within an hour of the meal; the pain may be relieved by vomiting. Such patients tend to be afraid to eat and lose their appetite. They induce vomiting and show some loss of weight. The pain of duodenal ulceration occurs 2.5–3 hours after eating; it is often interpreted as 'hunger pains' and the patient is able to obtain relief by eating. There is no loss of appetite or weight. Characteristically the pain of a duodenal ulcer wakens the patient in the middle of the night. The pain in both gastric and duodenal ulcers is relieved by the ingestion of antacids. Another characteristic is a tendency for the pain to be periodic: the patient will have many months which are painfree and then for no accountable reason have a return of pain. The reason for the periodicity is not known but it does not necessarily indicate that the ulcer is healing.

Heartburn and waterbrash (the sudden flow of clear fluid into the mouth) may also occur; however, the latter complaint is not confined to duodenal ulcer disease. Flatulence, belching and an alteration in bowel habit may be present.

There are few signs of uncomplicated ulcer disease. Epigastric tenderness may be observed and while this may be to the left of the midline in gastric ulcers and to the right in duodenal ulceration the sign is not sufficiently constant to be of diagnostic value.

Diagnosis

While the diagnosis of peptic ulcer may be suggested from the history the clinical distinction between gastric and duodenal ulcers cannot be made with confidence and the site of the ulcer will only be established by a barium meal. The majority of gastric ulcers are situated on the lesser curve of the stomach in the antral and prepyloric region. The ulcer is recognized as a niche of barium which protrudes beyond the line of the stomach wall. The ulcers tend to be oval or round with a smooth outline (Plate III). The size of the ulcer crater varies greatly and some of the largest ulcers are on the greater curve in elderly patients. Other features are oedema and mucosal folds which radiate towards the ulcer crater. Gross scarring and contraction may distort the stomach into an 'hour-glass' appearance but this is rarely seen.

Duodenal ulcers are recognized as an ulcer niche or as a fleck of barium, depending upon the angle of the film (Plate IV). Compression of the duodenal bulb during the barium examination is a valuable technique for demonstrating the crater. There may be oedema, spasm or contraction of the duodenal bulb. Marked contraction of the bulb produces a cloverleaf appearance which makes it very difficult to recognize radiologically whether an active ulcer is present. When there is gross scarring and distortion of the pyloroduodenal region it may be impossible to decide whether the ulcer is duodenal or gastric in origin. The presence of a postbulbar ulcer is readily missed and that portion of the duodenum which bends to form the second part must be submitted to careful radiological examination.

The routine barium meal achieves an accurate diagnosis in about 80% of gastric and only 60% of duodenal ulcers. The introduction of a double contrast technique has improved the accuracy of the barium examination. But the most significant advance in the past decade has been the widespread use of fibreoptic endoscopy which permits ready visualization of the stomach and duodenum. Both end-viewing and side-viewing instruments are employed. It is probable that the skilled endoscopist can achieve a higher diagnostic rate than can the radiologist; but radiology and endoscopy are not in competition and the best results are obtained when both are used in sensible cooperation. An ulcer is recognized as an area of grey-white slough having sharp, discrete margins, a clean smooth base, normal surrounding mucosa and radiating mucosal folds. Acid studies are of no value in either the diagnosis of peptic ulceration or the distinction between gastric and duodenal ulcers. This is because of the considerable overlap between both the basal and the stimulated acid output in normal, gastric ulcer and duodenal ulcer populations so that in any individual the significance of the acid output cannot be assessed.

The differential diagnosis includes hiatus hernia, gastritis, cancer of the stomach, gall bladder and pancreatic disease and cancer of the colon. The early symptoms of pregnancy must not be forgotten nor must pulmonary tuberculosis. The distinction between a benign and malignant ulcer of the stomach may be a problem. An ulcerated cancer should be suspected clinically when there is marked weight loss or an abdominal mass; on barium studies the ulcer niche is seen within the confines of the gastric silhouette, the gastric contractions do not pass through the ulcer, the base is nodular, the margins rolled, and the mucosal folds are thickened and irregular. A valuable sign that an ulcer is benign is the presence of a radiotranslucent line traversing the crater of the ulcer. Complete healing of an ulcer both clinically and radiologically is an indication that the ulcer is benign, but the problem is what constitutes healing and how long it is necessary to wait: 6 weeks is the usual time recommended but this may be too short a period and many benign ulcers are not fully healed within this time. Complete restoration of the gastric contour does not necessarily occur and careful radiology may demonstrate a flat area or dimple with radiating folds. The ulcer may be recognized to be malignant at endoscopy and at this time a biopsy can be obtained. Because of sampling errors it is essential that these are taken from more than one site in the ulcer and sampling from 3 or 4 areas is recommended. The location and size of the ulcer has little diagnostic significance. Cytological examination is helpful. Gastric acid studies are of little value in determining the character of a gastric ulcer; although histamine-fast achlorhydria is considered to be diagnostic of a cancer it is so rare an observation as to be unhelpful.

For practical purposes all duodenal ulcers can be considered to be benign.

Treatment

MEDICAL

In the absence of any certain mechanism for peptic ulceration or clear differentiation between the pathogenesis of duodenal and gastric ulcers the treatment tends to be similar for all ulcers. The aim is to relieve symptoms and promote healing but while the former is easy to achieve few drugs cure ulcers.

Antacids

Antacids effectively produce symptomatic relief but do not promote ulcer healing; nonetheless they form the mainstay of medical management. The goal of therapy is to reduce the amount of gastric acid. This both limits the acid load on the duodenum and, if the gastric contents are brought to a pH greater than 6, inactivates pepsin. Because the rate of gastric emptying is a major determinant of antacid effectiveness a better buffering effect is achieved by frequent small doses than infrequent large doses.

There are a large number of antacid preparations available. One of the best combinations is that of magnesium hydroxide (600 mg) plus aluminium hydroxide (600 mg) which is effective, palatable and does not have an excessive tendency to cause diarrhoea. The mixture is given half to one hour after meals to obtain the maximum period of retention in the stomach. This may also be achieved by frequent snacks or anticholinergic therapy. Usually 4 to 5 doses of 10–15 ml of the magnesium–aluminium hydroxide mixture is adequate. If this fails to relieve pain the frequency of the dosage may be increased to every hour and may even be supplemented by 4 to 8 doses of aluminium hydroxide.

Other antacid preparations which may be used are magnesium trisilicate which is a less potent buffer than the hydroxide, calcium carbonate which is effective but has the hazard of excess calcium absorption, and sodium bicarbonate which is the most effective but prone to induce sodium overload. Antacid therapy is maintained for 6 weeks after which it is reduced and discontinued if the patient is pain-free. Thereafter patients can be instructed to use small doses of antacids as required for the occasional episode of abdominal discomfort to which ulcer subjects appear prone. There is no difference in the prescription of antacids for gastric or duodenal ulcers.

No antacid is free from hazard or unwanted side-effects. Magnesium salts cause diarrhoea while constipation is an effect of aluminium preparations. Calcium carbonate can induce hypercalcaemia and renal failure, and sodium bicarbonate may be accompanied by sodium overload and a metabolic alkalosis. Excessive use of either of these two agents together with large quantities of milk may result in alkalosis, hypercalcaemia, metastatic calcification and uraemia, the 'milk–alkali' syndrome. Aluminium hydroxide in large amounts is associated with phosphate depletion manifesting as muscle weakness, bone reabsorption and hypercalcuria.

Anticholinergic Drugs

It is improbable that anticholinergic agents alone effect healing, but they can be used to supplement the symptomatic effects of antacids. It is particularly helpful to add anticholinergics at bed time if nocturnal pain is present or if there has been no response to vigorous antacid therapy. There are very many anticholinergic preparations available and an effective example is dicyclomine hydrochloride, 10–20 mg three to four times daily, or given as a single 20 mg dose at night. Unwanted side-effects of all preparations include dry mouth, hesitancy of micturition and paralysis of accommodation. Anticholinergics are to be avoided in patients with gastric ulcer, gastric outflow obstruction and oesophagitis.

Carbonoxelone Sodium

There is convincing evidence that this drug which is derived from liquorice promotes the healing of gastric ulcers. An unequivocal beneficial effect on duodenal ulcers has been less easy to demonstrate. When used for gastric ulceration the dose is 100 mg thrice daily orally for 1–2 weeks followed by 50 mg thrice daily for up to 6 weeks. In duodenal ulceration the drug is given in the form of a timed release capsule (Duogastrone) in a dose of 4 daily for 6 weeks. The side-effects of carbonoxelone include salt and water retention, hypertension and hypokalaemia.

H_2-Receptor Antagonists

The development of these agents which are able to inhibit almost completely basal and stimulated acid output has been one of the most significant advances in peptic ulcer therapy. The drug under current evaluation is cimetidine. It is of symptomatic value as well as promoting healing of gastric and duodenal ulcers. It remains to be established what the optimal dose of H_2-receptor antagonists is, whether there are unwanted side-effects and for how long therapy should be continued.

Other Agents

A number of other agents are available, some of which appear to have beneficial effects. Preparations derived from liquorice from which glycyrrhizinic acid has been removed (Caved S, Ulcedal), and geranyl farnesyl acetate (Gefarnate) promote the healing of gastric ulcers but their effect on duodenal ulcers is less certain. Colloidal bismuth (De-Nol) is a safe and effective preparation for both gastric and duodenal ulcers. There is no evidence to support the use of either sedatives or tranquillizers in the management of peptic ulcers.

The role of dietary manipulations is controversial. Frequent small meals help relieve pain, aid acid neutralization in the stomach and probably enhance the effects of antacids. There is little justification in the use of bland, milk-rich 'gastric' diets and they can be abandoned. Patients should eat a normal balanced diet omitting only strong condiments and spices. Alcohol should be taken in moderation and not on an empty stomach. The patient is strongly advised to stop smoking.

Most patients can be commenced and maintained on therapy as outpatients and only require hospital admission in the event of symptoms persisting. Therapy is discontinued once symptoms disappear. Duodenal ulceration requires no subsequent barium study since the cap will probably be deformed and little information gained about activity. Duodenoscopy is of value. The healing of gastric ulcers can be judged radiologically or preferably endoscopically and this must be shown to occur within 6 weeks. If the ulcer is still present the patient is admitted to hospital for a further 3 weeks of ulcer treatment and if still demonstrable the patient is advised to undergo surgical treatment whether or not symptoms are present. This is in order that malignant ulceration is not managed as a benign peptic ulcer. There is little to support the view that all large gastric ulcers should be removed surgically because they heal poorly on medical therapy; indeed the speed of healing of a gastric ulcer is inversely related to its size.

Persistent pain or troublesome vomiting are the usual reasons for admitting patients with duodenal ulcers to hospital and the majority of patients manage perfectly well on outpatient treatment which induces relief from pain within a few days. Hospital therapy can take the form of strict bed rest and if pain persists the intragastric adminis-tration of milk (1–2 litres daily) with or without antacids is often of value.

Gastric irradiation is occasionally employed when the patient remains symptomatic but is unsuitable for surgery. A daily dose of 150 rads is given as two 5-day courses separated by 2 days.

There is no evidence that long-term antacid, or anti-cholinergic or dietary management aids in keeping the ulcer healed. Probably the most effective measure is to stop smoking.

The long-term outcome of medically treated ulcers is not known. The incidence of recurrence for gastric ulcers is variously between 30% and 80%; and a second recurrent ulcer may occur in up to 40% of patients whose first recurrent ulcer has healed satisfactorily. Consequently nearly half of all diagnosed gastric ulcers eventually come to surgery. Duodenal ulcers probably have a slightly lower chance of healing than gastric ulcers. It appears that the male sex and long duration of symptoms are of poor prognostic significance for healing.

SURGICAL

Surgical therapy for peptic ulceration is undertaken if the symptoms are recurrent and fail to respond to medical therapy. Surgery is also indicated for complications of the disease such as haemorrhage, penetration, perforation or obstruction. In the case of gastric ulcers a further recommendation for surgery will be failure of the ulcer to heal after adequate medical therapy. The operation of choice for gastric ulcers is a Billroth I gastrectomy in which a partial gastrectomy is undertaken with a gastroduodenal anastomosis (Fig. 1). The main aim is to excise a good

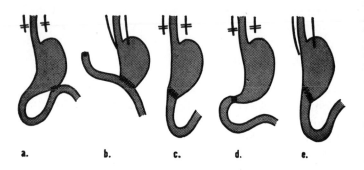

Fig. 1. The various types of operation used in peptic ulcer disease: *a*. Vagotomy and gastroenterostomy; *b*. Subtotal gastrectomy and gastrojejunostomy; *c*. Vagotomy with antrectomy and gastroduodenal anastomosis; *d*. Vagotomy and pyloroplasty; *e*. Partial gastrectomy and gastroduodenal anastomosis.

portion of the stomach, including the antrum and the ulcer. Equally satisfactory results are given by vagotomy plus some form of gastric drainage procedure, but this has the disadvantage of leaving the ulcer in situ. Because of the danger of missing a cancer it is recommended that at such operations an adequate four-quarter biopsy of the ulcer is taken. If a duodenal ulcer is present as well as a gastric ulcer the surgical treatment is as for duodenal ulceration.

The decision when to advise surgery for the uncomplicated duodenal ulcer which has not healed is not always easy. There is no evidence that the patient who 'earns' his operation by going for a long period with uncontrolled pain is any less likely to develop postgastrectomy problems. Thus on the one hand it is probably inadvisable to resort to surgery in a patient with a very short history, while on the other hand there is no purpose in delaying the decision to operate in a patient with a proven ulcer which has recurred a number of times.

There are a variety of operations in current use (Fig. 1). Many surgeons now employ either a truncal vagotomy and antrectomy, or a truncal vagotomy and a drainage procedure such as gastroenterostomy or pyloroplasty. The use of the distal 2/3 or 3/4 gastrectomy with closure of the duodenal stump and a gastrojejunostomy (Billroth II anastomosis) is less favoured although adequately controlled clinical trials have demonstrated that operations involving the removal of a portion of the stomach are not necessarily accompanied by a greater incidence of postgastrectomy problems. Thus there appears to be little to choose between the various operations. Vagotomy and pyloroplasty is probably the safest operation but there is a slightly higher rate of recurrent ulceration than with vagotomy and antrectomy. There is little justification for performing a 3/4 partial gastrectomy if an adequate vagotomy has been performed.

Preoperative acid secretory studies are of no value in planning surgical treatment. Postoperative gastric secretory studies enable a judgement to be made on the effectiveness of the vagotomy and serve as a guide to future therapy. Such studies may be either the pentagastrin test or an insulin response test.

The suggestion that denervation of the small intestine and biliary tree following a truncal vagotomy might be responsible for diarrhoea led to the introduction of modifications of the vagotomy technique. In a selective vagotomy only the stomach is denervated. Highly selective (proximal gastric) vagotomy is a further refinement in which only the parietal cell mass is denervated. The results of these newer techniques await evaluation but early reports are promising. These procedures call for the highest quality surgical technique but have the advantage of causing the least possible disturbance to the anatomy and physiology of the stomach.

Complications of Peptic Ulcer Disease

HAEMORRHAGE

Bleeding from a peptic ulcer is an important and potentially life-threatening complication. While there are no definite figures for the frequency of gastrointestinal bleeds in ulcer patients there can be little doubt that bleeding from acute or chronic peptic ulcers is the most important cause of upper gastrointestinal bleeding. The haemorrhage may present as the vomiting of fresh blood in varying quantities; there will be melaena and varying degrees of shock, with pallor, sweating, tachycardia and hypotension. Rarely the first sign of the bleed is the passage of bright red blood per rectum. The patient may present with melaena and no vomiting; this does not indicate a duodenal ulcer. Lesser degrees of bleeding will cause the vomiting of altered blood—'coffee-ground vomit'. When the bleeding is chronic and small in amount the patient may not complain of gastric symptoms or bleeding but will present with, or be found to have a chronic iron deficiency anaemia. About one-third of patients give a previous history of gastrointestinal bleeding. Some patients will have a history of exacerbations of the peptic ulcer pain prior to the bleeding and the pain is relieved once the bleeding has occurred. A great many patients report having taken drugs before the bleeding episode. This makes for difficulties in the interpretation of the cause of the bleeding and implies that, even if there is a history of drug ingestion, the patient should still be investigated fully for the cause of the bleeding. Complications include heart failure, myocardial infarction and cerebrovascular thrombosis. Much blood in the bowel of an elderly patient will elevate the blood urea concentration.

The outcome of the bleed depends on many factors. The great majority of haemorrhages are not life-threatening and only very few patients will bleed sufficiently vigorously within the first 12 hours to threaten exsanguination. Unfavourable features include the loss of a large volume of blood, evidence of associated disease particularly cardiac, renal or pulmonary, the age of the patient (death is rare below the age of 55 years but the mortality rate increases over the age of 55 years) and the nature of the lesion (bleeding gastric ulcers have a poorer outlook than bleeding duodenal ulcers). A history of a previous bleed does not influence the prognosis for the immediate event unless the current episode has been preceded by 4 or 5 episodes within the previous few weeks, or the patient has a background of chronic anaemia.

Attempts should be made to locate the source of the bleeding as soon as possible. The necessary diagnostic methods are undertaken once the condition of the patient is satisfactory and this is usually within the first 24 hours of admission following the initiation of appropriate resuscitative methods. The two essential diagnostic techniques are a barium meal and endoscopy. The timing and order of these will depend upon circumstances. Endoscopy, which may include oesophagoscopy, gastroscopy and duodenoscopy, is a simple procedure using flexible fibreoptic instruments and can be performed in the ward if necessary. The endoscopy should probably precede the barium studies because lesions such as oesophagitis, gastritis and the Mallory–Weiss syndrome will only be diagnosed by endoscopy. Such lesions account for up to 25% of all the causes of upper gastrointestinal haemorrhage. Other disadvantages of an emergency barium meal are that the interpretation of the radiographs may be made difficult by the presence of blood in the stomach and an ulcer filled with blood clot may be easily missed. Angiography has proved valuable in skilled hands when the patient is actively bleeding, extravasation of dye into the gut lumen is seen.

The diagnosis will be simple when there is a long history of typical ulcer pain. On the other hand, a gastrointestinal bleed may be the first symptom of a peptic ulcer. A good history and physical examination is always rewarding and is particularly helpful when considering the uncommon causes of gastrointestinal haemorrhage. The commonest causes of upper gastrointestinal bleeding are duodenal ulcer, gastric ulcer, acute gastritis (this term includes acute gastric ulcers and acute gastric erosions), hiatus hernia and oesophageal varices. Less common conditions are gastric tumours, Mallory–Weiss syndrome, leukaemia and aortic aneurysms. The relative frequency of these different diseases will differ from community to community and from hospital to hospital. In general, peptic and more particularly duodenal ulceration is the most frequent cause.

After all the common causes have been excluded there are a variety of rare causes, the chief significance of which is that the diagnosis can frequently be made by a careful examination of the skin and mucous membranes. This includes hereditary haemorrhagic telangiectasia, pseudo-xanthoma elasticum, Ehlers–Danlos syndrome, polyarteritis nodosa, atrophying papalosis of Degos, Peutz–Jeghers syndrome and a variety of other forms of arterial, venous and capillary malformations.

It is usual for patients with upper gastrointestinal bleeding to be admitted to a medical ward but the treatment should involve constant consultation and cooperation between the medical and the surgical teams. The initial management includes an assessment of blood loss and shock and the restoration of the blood volume when necessary. A sample of blood is taken for haemoglobin, haematocrit, smear, blood group and cross-match. This is followed by the administration of intravenous saline or a plasma expander depending upon the severity of the haemorrhage. Before a plasma expander is given it is necessary to ensure that serum is available for cross-matching of blood. The initial insertion of a venous catheter to monitor the central venous pressure is favoured by some authorities, thereby preventing overtransfusion and enabling recurrent bleeding to be detected early. Whether or not a nasogastric tube is used is debatable. There are a number of points in its favour: the stomach can be aspirated and cleared of clot and the occurrence and speed of further bleeding can rapidly be identified. The tube should be aspirated by hand. The routine administration of morphine is not recommended but mild sedation is given if the patient is very anxious.

In the event of severe persistent bleeding it may not be possible to embark upon any diagnostic procedures and it becomes necessary for the patient to proceed directly to surgery. This is most unusual for the bleeding usually slackens and stops and it is during this period that the necessary diagnostic steps are taken. The surgical procedure is simplified and the outcome improved if the cause of the bleeding is established prior to operation. If bleeding does not recur the patient is managed conservatively and placed on medical treatment for the ulcer. Elective surgery may be required at a later stage. The occurrence of a single bleed from an ulcer is not, per se, an indication for surgical intervention. Local gastric hypothermia has not found general acceptance as a method of dealing with upper gastrointestinal bleeding.

If the bleeding recurs within hours or a few days then surgery will be considered. The decision to operate depends on many circumstances. In patients over the age of 50 years and particularly if the ulcer is in the stomach the operation is not delayed; in younger patients who tolerate blood loss better the operation may be delayed in order to give the patient an opportunity to stop bleeding spontaneously and so possibly avoid an operation. Another factor which will influence the decision is the rarity of the blood group and the availability of blood.

The surgical procedure depends on individual preferences. There is at present a move towards vagotomy and pyloroplasty, with oversewing of the ulcer as the treatment for both gastric and duodenal ulcers. This operation is particularly recommended when the lesion is small or when the patient is severely ill for it carries less of a risk than the more extensive gastric resections. Partial gastrectomy or vagotomy and hemigastrectomy are also in common use but carry an appreciable mortality. In general conservative surgery is favoured for a duodenal ulcer while some surgeons still perform a gastrectomy for a bleeding gastric ulcer because of the fear of malignancy.

Some 70% of patients will stop bleeding spontaneously. The immediate prognosis depends upon the age of the patient, the nature of the lesion and the type of operation used. Factors acting unfavourably include over- or under-transfusion, poor timing of surgery and inferior surgical technique. The overall mortality approaches 10% for gastric ulcer and is half this for a duodenal ulcer. Nearly 25% of non-surgically treated patients will subsequently have a further bleed. However there is also evidence that a minority of patients who have undergone surgery will rebleed, the haemorrhage relapse rate for operated duodenal ulcers being from 5 to 27% in different series.

GASTRIC OUTFLOW OBSTRUCTION

The term 'gastric outflow obstruction' is used in preference to pyloric obstruction or pyloric stenosis because in chronic pyloroduodenal disease it may be difficult to distinguish whether the ulceration is in the prepyloric area, the pyloric canal or the duodenum, and furthermore the obstruction is frequently due to oedema and not the result of irreversible scarring.

The cardinal feature of this complication of ulcer disease

is vomiting. Initially when gastric muscular tone is good the vomiting is frequent and occurs soon after meals so that the vomitus contains recently ingested food. Subsequently gastric atony develops and the vomiting becomes less frequent, eventually occurring only once a day. At this stage the vomitus is of a large volume and unpleasant in character. It will contain undigested food recognized from meals eaten some days previously. Characteristically the vomitus contains no bile. The patient has anorexia, loss of weight and is constipated. Physical examination may confirm a distended stomach and a succession splash may be detected. The prolonged vomiting results in loss of hydrochloric acid, sodium and potassium and a metabolic alkalosis may develop. The hypochloraemia induces an accelerated sodium–potassium and sodium–hydrogen exchange in the kidney. The altered tubular function results in a rise of the bicarbonate threshold and a negative potassium balance. There may be evidence of tetany.

The gastric outflow obstruction can be demonstrated in a number of ways. An early morning volume (gastric contents after an overnight fast) greater than 150 ml is suggestive of obstruction, particularly if food particles are present. The standard method of demonstrating the obstruction is by a barium meal. A dilated stomach is seen and it contains increased fluid and food residue. Gastric emptying may be delayed for 5 hours or longer. A number of techniques using radioactive materials and nonabsorbable markers are available to assess gastric emptying.

The differential diagnosis is from other causes of gastroduodenal obstruction, including adult pyloric stenosis, ectopic pancreas, duplication cyst, tumours and arteriomesenteric occlusion of the duodenum. The presence of bile in the vomit is of help to localize the site of obstruction but the main diagnostic techniques are the barium meal and endoscopy.

It must not be assumed that the presence of gastric outflow obstruction automatically implies the need for surgical intervention. The institution of gastric suction and decompression, intravenous infusion to restore the fluid and electrolyte balance (particularly chloride) and to supply calories, may effect the restoration of gastric muscular tone. If the basis for obstruction is active inflammation and oedema it is possible that the episode may subside and the underlying ulcer can then be treated by medical means. Antispasmodic agents are contraindicated. The majority of patients, however, require surgery. The stomach must be decompressed and washed out regularly for the week before the operation. In this way recovery is enhanced and the period of atony and postoperative gastric stasis reduced. The operation of choice is some form of gastric resection but there are reports favouring vagotomy and drainage for pyloric obstruction due to duodenal ulceration. Whether a pyloroplasty or a gastroenterostomy is performed will depend upon the state of the duodenum.

PERFORATION

Perforation is commoner in males than females. The majority of perforations complicate anterior duodenal ulcers and the perforation is usually into the peritoneal cavity but may be into the lesser sac. The clinical features are characteristic: sudden severe abdominal pain which may be local or general. This is followed by a brief period of improvement in the clinical condition to be succeeded by the development of generalized peritonitis. The patient presents in varying degrees of shock. The abdomen is tender and rigid and an ileus is usually present. Reduced liver dullness may be detected clinically. The diagnosis is confirmed radiologically by the demonstration of air under the diaphragm. The condition may be missed in the elderly or the patient on corticosteroid therapy for in such patients the leak is often silent and painless.

The differential diagnosis includes the many causes of acute abdominal pain, among them acute pancreatitis, acute cholecystitis, acute appendicitis, myocardial infarction and porphyria.

The treatment of a perforated peptic ulcer is resuscitation followed by early surgery. The patient is rehydrated with intravenous fluids and monitoring of the central venous pressure is of value. Adequate analgesia is required and a broad-spectrum antibiotic is given. The nature of the operation depends upon the clinical state of the patient and the experience of the surgeon. The simplest procedure is suture of the perforation which is then oversewn with an omental patch. Biopsies must be taken from a gastric ulcer. The ulcer symptoms may be expected to recur some time after such an operation and therefore many surgeons attempt a definitive ulcer operation when dealing with the perforation. Simple closure of the ulcer can be combined with vagotomy and a drainage operation. Emergency gastrectomy may be undertaken for a gastric ulcer if there is associated bleeding, pyloric stenosis or any suspicion of malignancy. The mortality in large series is less than 5%.

PENETRATION

The usual site for a penetration is from a posterior duodenal ulcer to involve the pancreas. However, peptic ulcers may penetrate into other organs, including the liver, colon and exceptionally the anterior chest or abdominal wall. The clinical features suggestive of penetration include an alteration in the character of the ulcer-type pain which becomes continual. There is no longer periodicity, a relationship to meals or relief from antacid therapy. Characteristically the pain of pancreatic penetration is felt deep in the epigastric region passing directly 'through' to the back. The ulcer which has penetrated does not respond to medical measures and requires definitive surgery.

MALIGNANCY

For practical purposes all duodenal ulcers can be regarded as being benign. Gastric ulcers rarely, if ever, undergo malignant change. The problem from a clinical point of view is how often an ulcer in the stomach is malignant; the published figures vary from 1 to 18% with an average of 10%. The difficulty is to recognize that an ulcer is malignant. With increasing accuracy in the use of radiological, endoscopic, cytological and biopsy techniques distinction between benign ulcers and ulcerating cancers is becoming more feasible. Nevertheless because the differentiation cannot always be made with certainty it is generally advised that any gastric ulcer which does not heal within 6 weeks of adequate medical therapy should be removed surgically. Undoubtedly this policy results in the excision of a great number of benign ulcers but the precaution ensures the early detection and removal of ulcerating cancers with, hopefully, an improvement in the prognosis. A Billroth I operation is performed with removal of adjacent omental tissue. If the malignant ulcer is near the cardia a total gastrectomy may be required.

Other Forms of Peptic Ulcer

STRESS ULCER

Peptic ulcers associated with stress are usually acute, multiple, superficial and affect the fundus and body of the stomach. They are most often found in patients with burns ('Curling's ulcer') of whom 25% may have such ulcers, but they also occur following trauma, sepsis, hypotension and renal and respiratory failure. The pathogenesis is obscure but may be related to acid damage of an ischaemic mucosa.

The ulcers usually present with sudden severe bleeding. Treatment is difficult and unsatisfactory. Nasogastric aspiration and blood replacement is effective in 50% of patients but rebleeding is common. Gastric lavage with cold water or an adrenaline solution is seldom of benefit. Coeliac artery catheterization with vasopressin infusion is hazardous. It is possible that H_2-receptor antagonists may be of value; but surgery is necessary if bleeding is uncontrolled or recurrent. The usual operation is vagotomy and antrectomy, or a subtotal gastrectomy. The postoperative morbidity is high and the mortality varies between 20% and 70%.

CUSHING'S ULCER

Cushing's ulcers occur in association with intracranial trauma or a brain tumour or following craniotomy. They are usually deep and penetrating and appear to be related to increased gastrin secretion.

MULTIPLE ENDOCRINE ADENOMA SYNDROME

This is a group of disorders which are inherited in an autosomal dominant manner and characterized by adenomas in more than one endocrine gland. Two types of syndrome are described. In Type I there are adenomas affecting the pituitary, the parathyroids and the pancreatic islets of Langerhans; there may also be multiple lipomas and the carcinoid syndrome. Peptic ulceration occurs in 18–48% of patients. The ulcers are multiple and in atypical sites which has led to the suggestion that these patients have the Zollinger–Ellison syndrome; and indeed, many do have gastrinomas with raised serum gastrin levels. However, hypercalcaemia, the manifestation of hyperparathyroidism, also evoke raised gastrin levels, an increase in gastric acid output and peptic ulceration.

The uncommon Type II syndrome is the association of medullary cancer of the thyroid gland, bilateral phaeochromocytomas and adenomas of the parathyroid glands. In some kindreds neuromas and neurofibromas are an added feature. One-third of all the patients with this syndrome present with severe diarrhoea. The patients usually have raised circulating calcitonin levels with variable serum calcium concentrations but it is thought that the diarrhoea is related to an increased production of prostaglandins.

ZOLLINGER–ELLISON SYNDROME

This entity comprises pancreatic islet cell tumours or 'gastrinomas', gastric acid hypersecretion and multiple recurrent peptic ulcers. The tumours in the pancreatic islets are related to neither the α nor the β cells but to the δ argyrophil-metachromatic cells, D cells. About 60% are malignant at the time of diagnosis and two-thirds have already spread to the liver or regional lymph nodes. There is an extrapancreatic localization in 10% of tumours and in a further 10% the lesion is a diffuse islet cell hyperplasia affecting the whole pancreas. Normally the syndrome is not familial unless it forms part of the MEA type 1 syndrome.

The tumours produce gastrin and therefore the parietal cells are under continual maximal secretory stimulation. There is an associated increased parietal cell mass and gastric acid hypersecretion. The excessive acid output is responsible for peptic ulceration and steatorrhoea. Ulcers are usually present in the duodenal bulb but may occasionally be gastric. Characteristically the ulcers are atypically situated in the second, third or fourth parts of the duodenum and in the jejunum. Fat malabsorption and diarrhoea may be striking features and have multiple causes which include inactivation of pancreatic lipase by an abnormally low duodenal pH, less than 2.0 (normal 6.8); precipitation of bile salts, mainly glycocholate, which results in defective micelle formation; mucosal damage; and intestinal hurry. The low intraluminal pH is a marked stimulus to intestinal and colonic contractions. Vitamin B_{12} absorption may be impaired because of the low intestinal pH. The patient may present as a problem of recurrent stomal ulceration after surgery for apparently uncomplicated duodenal ulcer disease.

The excessive circulating gastrin evokes a high basal acid secretion. Several indices of gastric acid secretion have been suggested as diagnostic of the syndrome but none have proved reliable, including a basal gastric acid output of 15 mmol/hour and a basal acid output/maximal acid output ratio of more than 0.6. It has been shown that 10% of patients with 'idiopathic' uncomplicated duodenal ulcers will have acid secretory values within the Zollinger–Ellison range.

The diagnosis is established with certainty by demonstrating increased serum gastrin levels. Gastrin concentrations vary from day to day but are usually greater than 200 pg/ml and often as high as 350 000 pg/ml. It is necessary to exclude other causes of raised serum gastrin concentrations including Addisonian pernicious anaemia and retained antral segment following gastric surgery, but this is generally easy. A rare cause of fasting and postprandial hypergastrinaemia and peptic ulceration is antral G-cell hyperplasia. The diagnosis of the Zollinger–Ellison syndrome may be suspected at the time of a barium meal: there are prominent gastric folds, an excess of gastric secretions, dilution of barium in the upper small bowel giving a flocculated appearance, dilatation of the duodenum, and large often multiple ulcer craters in the duodenum and upper small intestine. Gastric and oesophageal ulcers are less common. The tumours are difficult to locate by pancreatic angiography or by pancreatic scanning with ^{75}Se-selenomethionine.

The treatment of choice is total gastrectomy and excision of the tumour if possible. Any other form of gastric surgery is associated with recurrent upper gastrointestinal ulceration which is frequently fatal. Islet cell tumours grow slowly and the patient with metastases who has undergone total gastrectomy may survive a number of years. In some patients total gastrectomy is followed by the regression or even complete disappearance of the metastases. Medical treatment is quite unsatisfactory although large doses of antacid and anticholinergic preparations may provide some symptomatic relief. It is probable that the H_2-receptor antagonists will have a useful role in the management of these patients.

It will be appreciated that at times the diagnosis of a duodenal ulcer as being of the 'ordinary' variety may be very difficult. Thus there are those ordinary, common duodenal ulcers with marked hypersecretion of acid; there is the duodenal ulcer which arises as an association with non-β pancreatic islet cell tumours; there are duodenal ulcers which appear to be associated with β cell tumours (insulinomas); there are duodenal ulcers complicating parathyroid tumours; and there are duodenal ulcers which are found in association with the multiple endocrine adenoma syndrome. It is probable that only 3% of patients with the Zollinger–Ellison syndrome fall into the category of multiple endocrine adenomas. It is necessary in all patients with duodenal ulcer to obtain a careful family history and a high index of suspicion is necessary to detect those clinical syndromes which fall on the fringe of the great number of 'ordinary' duodenal ulcers.

Postgastrectomy Problems

The term 'postgastrectomy syndrome' is used for symptoms which follow gastric surgery and includes those arising after vagotomy and drainage operations. Significant symptoms probably develop in under 15% of patients who undergo gastric surgery.

Some alteration in gastrointestinal function is inevitable after operations on the stomach and must be accepted as the price to be paid for relief from those symptoms for which the operation was undertaken. Many patients have early satiation, the quantity of food which satisfies depending upon the size of the gastric remnant. Patients fail to gain weight following gastric surgery, those at risk being patients who were malnourished before the operation. This applies particularly to patients with a gastric ulcer. The weight loss is seldom related to significant malabsorption.

RECURRENT PEPTIC ULCERATION (STOMAL ULCER, ANASTOMOTIC ULCER)

Recurrent ulceration usually occurs in the jejunal anastomotic segment (stomal ulcer) but is also encountered at the suture line or in the stomach. It is reported in 5% of patients after ulcer surgery and 95% of recurrent ulcers are found in patients who have undergone surgery for duodenal ulcers. The risk of recurrent ulceration in duodenal ulcer patients is 3–10% but only 2% following operation for a gastric ulcer. The mechanism of these ulcers is variable and includes the provision of a simple gastroenterostomy alone, an incomplete vagotomy, inadequate gastric resection, a long afferent loop in a Billroth II anastomosis, poor antral drainage, and hypersecretion of gastric acid which may accompany the Zollinger–Ellison syndrome, hypercalcaemia and retained gastric antrum in a Billroth II anastomosis.

Patients present with recurrence of epigastric pain which has no periodicity or relationship to food. The diagnosis is usually made by endoscopy. Barium studies can also be undertaken although the radiological interpretation of a postoperative stomach can be extremely difficult. It is for this reason that many surgeons advise routine radiological assessment about 6 weeks postoperatively so that folds and puckering can be identified and not confused with ulceration should a barium meal subsequently become necessary. The radiological signs of a stomal ulcer are an ulcer niche and persistent deformity or stenosis. The niche can be distinguished from postoperative deformity by its constancy and lack of mucosal folds, but the accuracy of a radiological diagnosis is only around 60%. The commonest site is in the jejunum opposite the stoma, or a centimetre or two down the efferent jejunal loop. There is no convincing evidence that preoperative acid studies permit the prediction of those patients who are at risk to develop stomal ulcer. Acid studies on the postoperative stomach are very difficult to undertake and interpret, so that the conventional pentagastrin test is of little value. It appears that patients at risk of developing a stomal ulcer are of blood group O who do not secrete blood group substances in the body fluids.

An insulin (Hollander) test may be performed to test vagal activity after a vagotomy has been attempted. The test is performed by collecting a basal 1 hour acid output followed by the i.v. administration of 20 units soluble insulin and a collection of gastric secretions is made in 15 minute samples over 2 hours. If the blood sugar is greater than 50 mg/100 ml (2.7 mmol/litre) the test is discarded. A positive test is defined as one in which acid is secreted in the presence of hypoglycaemia and implies that the vagi are intact. Insulin tests should not be undertaken within the first 12 months after the operation because during this time a negative response may change to a positive.

The differential diagnosis of a stomal ulcer includes the development of postoperative gastritis, pancreatitis and gall stone disease. The patient should be screened for the Zollinger–Ellison syndrome.

In the majority of patients the only effective therapy is further surgery. The nature of the operation will depend on the original surgical procedure, the site of the ulcer and the clinical state of the patient. Usually a definitive acid-reducing operation is required such as vagotomy, or gastric resection, or vagotomy combined with resection. Satisfactory results are obtained in 66% of patients with a mortality of 4% and further recurrence in 13%. Non-surgical management comprises the withdrawal of possible ulcerogenic drugs and a strict ulcer regimen (p. 33). This is helpful in only one-third of patients and is accompanied by a mortality of 11%. Gastric irradiation (p. 37) may be tried and it is probable that the H_2-receptor antagonists will have a therapeutic role.

BILIOUS VOMITING

This complication has been called the afferent loop syndrome but this is probably misleading. An acute afferent loop syndrome is rare and usually occurs during the first 3 weeks after a partial gastrectomy. There is acute obstruction of the afferent loop and the patient experiences intense epigastric pain followed by vomiting of bile-free fluid and eventually a state of shock and collapse ensues. The management is the surgical relief of the obstruction which is usually the consequence of internal herniation of the afferent loop.

The term chronic afferent loop syndrome was introduced to describe the situation when patients develop postcibal epigastric discomfort or pain associated with vomiting of heavily bile-contaminated material. In severe cases there is considerable debility and weight loss. It is probable that this syndrome is not the consequence of afferent loop obstruction but rather the result of the regurgitation of bile and other duodenal secretions into the stomach. This may follow not only a partial gastrectomy but also the various gastric drainage procedures. This complication affects between 9–14% of patients following ulcer surgery. Marked gastritis develops but it does seem that there is considerable individual variation in the reaction of the gastric mucous membrane to bile. Radiological examination and particularly gastroscopy will help to establish the diagnosis. When the symptoms are troublesome it will be necessary to refashion the anastomosis and the operations currently favoured are either a Roux-en-Y conversion or

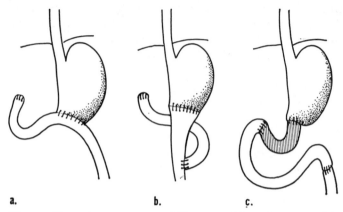

a.   b.   c.

Fig. 2. Operations to correct bilious vomiting after a partial gastrectomy: *a*. Partial gastrectomy with a gastrojejunal anastomosis. This can be converted into either a Roux-en-Y anastomosis (*b*) or a jejunal loop interposition (*c*).

jejunal loop interposition (Fig. 2). Non-surgical measures such as elevation of the head of the bed, antacids, cholestyramine and metoclopramide are seldom of more than temporary benefit.

DUMPING

Many patients experience some degree of epigastric discomfort after eating and this is related to distension of the residual gastric pouch. These symptoms must be clearly distinguished from the dumping syndrome in which, in addition to epigastric fullness and discomfort, there are borborygmi, cramps and vasomotor symptoms such as weakness, dizziness, pallor, palpitations, sweating and faintness. The symptoms occur either immediately after a meal or within 20–30 minutes of eating and last for 20–60 minutes. They are relieved by lying down. The incidence of the syndrome is uncertain but it may occur in up to 30% of patients during the first few months after the operation; the symptoms usually subside within the first year and less than 5% of patients are seriously incapacitated. Dumping may occur after a partial gastrectomy or a drainage operation. The mechanism is not clear and has been ascribed to jejunal distension, loss of gastric support, gastric stretching, jejunal hyperperistalsis, potassium depletion, anaemia, sequestration of the blood volume following jejunal hyperosmolarity and release of serotonin into the general circulation.

The management of the syndrome includes advice to eat small meals at frequent intervals; the meals should have a low carbohydrate content. Lying down after a meal alleviates symptoms. Many drugs have been tried, including anticholinergic agents, serotonin antagonists, tolbutamide and propranalol. In intractable situations further surgery to refashion the anastomosis has been tried but the results are not always satisfactory.

Delayed Hypoglycaemia

This condition has been called 'late dumping' but this term should be abandoned as the condition is not related to the dumping syndrome. Symptoms of sweating, tremor, tachycardia and faintness occur 2–4 hours after a meal and are due to reactive hypoglycaemia. The condition may be avoided by eating small meals low in carbohydrate and, in contrast to the dumping syndrome, symptoms are alleviated by the ingestion of food.

Haematological Changes

Anaemia after gastric surgery develops in 50–60% of patients and varies according to the time elapsing after the operation, the sex (more frequent in females), the type of anastomosis (more frequent after partial gastrectomy) and the indication for the operation (more frequent after operations for gastric ulcer). Iron deficiency is the commonest cause for the anaemia. The deficiency is due to decreased iron absorption after gastric surgery and factors such as the lack of acid and pepsin and intestinal hurry are implicated. An inadequate intake of iron may also play a role but blood loss after surgery is rarely a cause. Deficiency of folic acid is also frequent if looked for, although megaloblastic anaemia is less common than iron deficiency states. The mechanism for the folate deficiency is not entirely clear but inadequate dietary intake is important. A megaloblastic anaemia caused by vitamin B_{12} lack is uncommon and is the consequence of impaired secretion of intrinsic factor. This is related to the extent of the gastric resection and the degree of gastric atrophy which follows the gastric surgery. This vitamin B_{12} lack is more frequent in patients who have undergone surgery for gastric ulcer. A small number of patients develop vitamin B_{12} deficiency because of bacterial overgrowth in the anastamotic loop of the jejunum.

The development of significant anaemia may be prevented by having patients undergo an annual blood test after gastric surgery. Should anaemia develop the peripheral blood morphology, serum iron, folate and vitamin B_{12} levels are assessed and the appropriate therapy instituted. The routine administration of haematinics after gastric surgery has been suggested but is not in general use.

MALNUTRITION

While some loss of weight and a mild anaemia are common after gastric surgery significant malnutrition is infrequent. Severe protein malnutrition which presents as a kwashiorkor-like syndrome rarely occurs and is associated with bacterial infection within a long afferent loop. In about 40% of patients there is mild steatorrhoea following gastric surgery, whether this be some form of gastric resection or a vagotomy and drainage procedure. The mechanism for this is complex and includes rapid gastric emptying, bypassing of the duodenal mucosa so that there is failure to stimulate the pancreas adequately, poor mixing of food with the pancreaticobiliary secretions and bacterial overgrowth in the upper jejunum. After vagotomy there is decreased pancreatic sensitivity to cholecystokinin–pancreozymin. The steatorrhoea is seldom troublesome enough to cause symptoms and in general it is not responsible for diarrhoea.

There have been many reports of osteomalacia and osteoporosis after gastric surgery, particularly partial gastrectomy. Unfortunately the frequency of bone disease after the operation remains controversial: first, because of the difficulty, in the absence of a bone biopsy, of making a precise diagnosis of the presence and nature of bone disease, and secondly because of the variations in the patient populations that have been studied. The most widely used screening test is the serum alkaline phosphatase which is used as a guide to osteomalacia but it has not yet been resolved whether elevated levels indicate evidence of metabolic bone disease or whether they are unrelated to the operation. It is probable that, in the absence of Paget's disease, an elevated serum alkaline phosphatase level is due to overt or subclinical osteomalacia. A reduced 24-hour urinary calcium excretion is also a sensitive indicator of osteomalacia. Clinical features include proximal muscle weakness, slight muscle wasting and bone pain and tenderness. The likely mechanism is deficient intake of vitamin D but it is possible that malabsorption of calcium and vitamin D may play a part.

Gastric surgery is not associated with significant alterations in jejunal mucosal morphology. However, occasionally the operation is followed by the development of clinically significant lactase deficiency or coeliac disease. There is an increased frequency of pulmonary tuberculosis after gastric surgery, the patients at particular risk being those operated upon for gastric ulcer who had evidence of previous pulmonary tuberculosis. The development of tuberculosis in these patients can usually be related to vomiting and malnutrition following the operation. Partial gastrectomy should be avoided in ulcer patients with a past history of pulmonary tuberculosis and a less radical procedure used.

Diarrhoea

Increased frequency of bowel actions is common after gastric surgery but is rarely troublesome. The symptom does not correlate with the presence or degree of steatorrhoea. In less than 5% of patients there is profuse, watery, intractable diarrhoea which presents a problem to the patient and clinician. The aetiology of this diarrhoea is unknown but one theory relates the diarrhoea to an excess of faecal bile acids in these patients. The management includes having frequent small meals, using methylcellulose water-absorbing compounds, and codeine phosphate, a course of antibiotic therapy and advice to avoid those items in the diet known to aggravate the diarrhoea. It is possible that use of the bile acid binding agent, cholestyramine in daily doses of 4–12 g may be of benefit in some patients. There is no evidence that selective vagotomy reduces the frequency of the complication. In the assessment of such patients it is necessary to exclude Zollinger–Ellison syndrome, inadvertent gastroileostomy, gastrojejunocolic fistula, sensitivity to gluten or carbohydrates and gross bacterial contamination of the upper small bowel.

Cancer of the Gastric Remnant

There is a slightly increased hazard of cancer developing in the portion of the stomach remaining after gastric resection, and the risk is greater in those patients having been operated upon for gastric ulcers. Symptoms develop some 20 years after the initial operation and include loss of weight, dysphagia and gastric outflow obstruction.

SURGICAL COMPLICATIONS

There are a number of surgical complications which occur in the immediate postoperative period. These include leakage from the duodenal stump, herniation and obstruction of the afferent loop and delayed gastric emptying. A delay in the emptying time of the stomach or gastric remnant is probably a regular event if looked for during the first weeks after gastric surgery. When truncal vagotomy is combined with pyloroplasty gastric emptying may be delayed but gradually returns to normal. There is considerable variation in the time taken for gastrointestinal function to return to normal following an operation. It is only the occasional patient in whom vomiting, distension, pain and fluid and electrolyte imbalance supervene. Factors involved include stomal oedema and a stoma which has been fashioned too narrowly, but in many cases no adequate explanation is apparent. A period of intravenous fluid administration and gastric suction will frequently enable gastric tone to recover so that emptying will be adequate if somewhat delayed. If this approach fails it will be necessary to refashion the anastomosis.

Subdiaphragmatic vagotomy does not affect oesophageal motility but temporary dysphagia is an occasional complication during the first few postoperative weeks. Heartburn may develop after gastric surgery.

Further Reading

Alexander-Williams, J. (1973) Sequelae of peptic ulcer surgery. *Br. J. Hosp. Med.,* August, 167–172.

Ballard, J. S. et al. (1965) Familial multiple endocrine adenoma-peptic ulcer complex. *Medicine, Baltimore,* **43**, 481–516.

Baron, J. H. (1970) The clinical use of gastric function tests. *Scand. J. Gastroent.,* Suppl. 6, 9–46.

Cooke, A. R. (1975) Control of gastric emptying and motility. *Gastroenterology*, **68**, 804–816.

Duthie, H. L. (1967) Surgical treatment of upper alimentary bleeding. *Br. med. J.*, **ii**, 790–792.

Edwards, F. C. and Coghill, N. F. (1968) Clinical manifestations in patients with chronic atrophic gastritis, gastric ulcer, and duodenal ulcer. *Q. Jl Med.*, **38**, 337–360.

Forrest, J. A. et al. (1974) Endoscopy in gastrointestinal bleeding. *Lancet*, **ii**, 394–397.

Hoare, A. M. (1975) Comparative study between endoscopy and radiology in acute upper gastrointestinal haemorrhage. *Br. med. J.*, **i**, 27–30.

Ivey, K. T. (1975) Anticholinergics: do they work in peptic ulcer? *Gastroenterology*, **68**, 154–166.

Johnston, D. (1974) Highly selective vagotomy. *Gut*, **15**, 748–757.

Morrissey, J. F. and Barreras, R. F. (1974) Antacid therapy. *New Engl. J. Med.*, **290**, 550–554.

Pruitt, B. A. jr et al. (1970) Curling's ulcer: a clinical pathology study in 323 cases. *Ann. Surg.*, **172**, 523–539.

Stabile, B. E. and Passaro, E. jr (1976) Recurrent peptic ulcer. *Gastroenterology*, **70**, 124–135.

Walsh, J. H. and Grossman, M. I. (1975) Gastrin. *New Engl. J. Med.*, **292**, 1324–1333; 1377–1384.

Wise, L. and Ballinger, W. F. (1974) The elective surgical treatment of chronic duodenal ulcer; a critical review. *Surgery, St Louis*, **76**, 811–826.

Wormsley, K. G. (1974) The pathophysiology of duodenal ulceration. *Gut*, **15**, 59–81.

Gastritis

The clinical documentation and histological definition of gastritis presents many difficulties and there is no general agreement about the various syndromes which are included in the broad classification of gastritis. The subject may conveniently be discussed under the headings of acute gastritis, chronic gastritis and gastric atrophy.

ACUTE GASTRITIS

The term 'acute gastritis' can be used to include the syndromes of acute gastric erosions, acute gastric ulcers, erosive gastritis and acute haemorrhagic gastritis. Thus the pathology will vary from acute inflammation of the gastric epithelium, with infiltration by polymorphonuclear leucocytes and destruction of the superficial epithelial cells, to superficial ulceration of the mucosa or multiple discrete superficial bleeding lesions. The aetiology is frequently obscure. Drugs which may cause gastritis include alcohol, aspirin, phenylbutazone, indomethacin and corrosives. The reflux of bile might be important. Aspirin probably causes mucosal damage by destroying the surface lipid–protein layer of the gastric cells. As a result mucosal permeability is abnormal and back diffusion of hydrogen ions into the cell occurs while sodium escapes into the gastric lumen. This damages the mucosa further, while the escape of hydrogen ions results in a deficit of acid in the gastric secretions. The role of aspirin in gastrin mucosal damage has been questioned recently. A report from the Boston Collaborative Drug Surveillance Program suggests that the use of aspirin for 4 or more days a week is associated with a risk of upper gastrointestinal bleeding and gastritis but not when the drug is used less regularly. Similarly, a recent survey of the literature has questioned the association between adrenocorticosteroid administration and gastritis, peptic ulceration and upper gastrointestinal bleeding. It is possible that a mechanism similar to that postulated for aspirin operates in other forms of gastritis, for example that accompanying bile reflux.

The clinical presentation is similar to peptic ulcer disease, with epigastric pain which has some relation to food, flatulence and vomiting. Gastric bleeding may be prominent and may be the only manifestation of mucosal inflammation. Indeed, acute gastritis may account for up to 25% of the known causes of acute gastrointestinal haemorrhage. Radiology is of no help in diagnosis but gastroscopy is of much value in establishing the presence of the lesion.

The management includes withdrawal of all precipitating agents and the institution of a regimen used for peptic ulcer disease. Antacids are of most value and usually afford prompt relief. In the majority of patients the symptoms last for less than 3 weeks.

The management of haemorrhagic gastritis presents particular difficulty. Initially the approach is non-surgical with replacement of blood. Continual intragastric infusion of antacids may be used in an attempt to neutralize the hydrogen ions and thereby prevent backdiffusion. The aim should be to avoid surgical intervention if possible, particularly since no consistent or uniformly successful surgical procedure is available. The operative mortality is high. Partial gastrectomy has been recommended although it does not always control the bleeding. In recent years vagotomy and a drainage procedure have become popular and the results for both mortality and morbidity are encouraging. The operation may work by reducing acid output as well as gastric blood flow. The introduction of H_2-receptor antagonists may be of therapeutic benefit.

CHRONIC GASTRITIS

This term is used to describe a number of conditions including chronic superficial gastritis, chronic atrophic gastritis and chronic diffuse gastritis. The aetiology of chronic gastritis is varied and includes those factors responsible for acute gastritis. It has been argued that alcohol only causes acute gastritis and is not responsible for chronic gastritis. Bile reflux into the stomach may cause a chronic inflammatory reaction, probably by the same mechanism as has been proposed for salicylates. Cigarette smoking and hot tea have also been implicated. Gastritis occurs in association with gastric ulcer and gastric cancer.

Antibodies can be demonstrated to two antigenic components of the parietal cell: the microsomes and intrinsic factor. Parietal cell antibodies are directed against the microsomal component of the cell and are of the 7 S type. They can be demonstrated in the serum and gastric secretions. The pathogenic significance of parietal cell antibodies is uncertain but their presence indicates a reduction in gastric acid output. The antibody is found in less than 10% of symptomless normal subjects and the incidence increases with age, possibly because of the increased occurrence of chronic gastritis in the aged. About 50% of patients with chronic gastritis have the antibody. Its presence is an indication that there is inflammatory disease of the mucosa. Chronic gastritis is not associated with the presence of intrinsic factor antibodies which are restricted to patients with gastric atrophy.

Histologically chronic gastritis is recognized by infiltration of the mucosa with mononuclear and polymorpho-nuclear leucocytes, epithelial metaplasia and glandular atrophy. The changes may be superficial and either localized or diffuse.

The clinical status of chronic gastritis has been a subject of much dispute. A great number of minor gastrointestinal symptoms have been ascribed to the condition but it may produce a clinical picture very similar to chronic peptic ulcer disease. There is an association between chronic gastritis, gastric hyposecretion, parietal cell antibodies and various types of endocrinal dysfunction, including thyroid disease, adrenal insufficiency and diabetes mellitus. Patients with this group of disorders have an increased prevalence of anti-bodies directed against gastric, thyroid and adrenal tissue.

The diagnosis of chronic gastritis is difficult as the clinical picture is uncertain; radiological diagnosis is controversial. It is claimed that the condition should be suspected from a tubular stomach, the absence of folds along the greater curvature and a bald fundus. The skilled endoscopist may be able to recognize the thin mucous membrane with prominent vessels. Gastric biopsy may be helpful, although the lesion is characteristically patchy.

Management is unsatisfactory. Identifiable predisposing factors must be corrected and the most effective form of medical treatment is as for peptic ulcer disease.

GASTRIC ATROPHY

Gastric atrophy describes the mucosal alterations asso-ciated with Addisonian pernicious anaemia. The mucosal changes are those of extensive glandular atrophy in the absence of inflammatory cell infiltration. The pathogenesis of the atrophy is not understood. Antibodies to the gastric mucosa are present in the serum and in the gastric secre-tions. Parietal cell antibodies are detected in 90% of patients and intrinsic factor antibodies in about 60%. Two types of intrinsic factor antibody are recognized: one which blocks the combination of intrinsic factor with vitamin B_{12} ('blocking antibody') and the other which binds to the combination of intrinsic factor and B_{12} ('binding antibody'). Gastric cellular antibodies are not found in juvenile pernicious anaemia and the gastric mucosa is normal in these patients. As in chronic gastritis, Addisonian pernicious anaemia is associated with disorders of endocrine function and there is also an association with vitiligo and adult-onset hypogammaglobulinaemia.

Patients with pernicious anaemia may complain of flatulence, anorexia and vomiting. The atrophic process may extend into the small bowel and mild steatorrhoea may be present; the mucosa may be restored to normality by administration of vitamin B_{12}. The patients have reduced gastric secretion and achlorhydria which is non-responsive to histamine or other gastric acid stimulants ('histamine-fast achlorhydria'). Malabsorption of vitamin B_{12} can be demonstrated by the Schilling test and the reduced serum B_{12} values. The diagnosis is confirmed by finding intrinsic factor antibodies in either the serum or the gastric secretions. Because the atrophic process involves the parietal cells and not the pyloric gland area the output of gastrin is unaffected. Indeed, as a result of the lack of acid inhibition patients with pernicious anaemia have very high serum gastrin levels which may fall within the range of the Zollinger–Ellison syndrome.

The treatment of Addisonian pernicious anaemia is with 1 mg hydroxycobalamin intramuscularly daily for a week to be followed by intramuscular injections of 1 mg of hydroxycobalamin at 2-monthly intervals. The treatment must, of course, be continued for the rest of the patient's life. These patients have an increased incidence of gastric polyps and gastric cancer is three times commoner than in the general population. This presents considerable problems in the long-term management and regular endoscopy, barium meal studies and gastric cytology have been suggested to screen for the development of a cancer.

Menétrier's Disease (Giant Rugal Hypertrophy of the Gastric Mucosa)

Giant hypertrophy of the gastric mucous membrane is a rare disease in which there is degeneration of the glandular layer, overgrowth of the surface epithelium and moderate interstitial inflammation. The aetiology is unknown. The clinical features may simulate peptic ulcer disease. Characteristically there is leakage of protein from the gastric mucosa which results in hypoproteinaemia and generalized oedema. The plasma proteins find their way into the gut and are digested and the amino acids are reabsorbed. At the same time there is an increased rate of synthesis of plasma proteins by the liver. Gastric acid output is normal or subnormal. In longstanding cases gastric atrophy and achlorhydria supervene. The diagnosis is difficult to establish because full thickness biopsies of the mucosa are required in order to appreciate the hypertrophic folds. Endoscopy is helpful. The enlarged folds can be seen on barium meal but may be difficult to distinguish from polyps, lymphoma or even the Zollinger–Ellison syndrome. Management includes the use of high-protein diets and antacid preparations. Hypoproteinaemia is not necessarily an indication for surgery unless it is marked, when either a partial gastrectomy or a near total gastrectomy is recommended.

Non-Ulcer Dyspepsia

This term is used to include the syndromes of X-ray negative dyspepsia, duodenitis, hyperplasia of Brunner's glands and coarse mucosal folds in the duodenum. The symptoms are similar to those associated with duodenal ulcer disease. In some patients the maximal acid output falls within the range established for duodenal ulcers. Barium studies are either normal or else show enlarged duodenal folds which produce a nodular appearance on the X-ray. When radiological and endoscopic investigations are normal other causes for dyspepsia such as gall stones, aerophagy and dyspepsia due to smoking and alcohol should be sought. This effect may be given by either infiltration of the duodenal folds by inflammatory cells, 'duodenitis', or by hypertrophy of Brunner's glands. It is possible that in some patients there is a relationship between the increased acid output and the radiological changes. The diagnosis depends upon the most careful radiological and endoscopic investigations to exclude peptic ulcer disease particularly in the postbulbar region where ulcers are easily overlooked. Endoscopy is particularly helpful in revealing an oedematous congested or roughened duodenal mucosa. The lesion may be patchy. The diagnosis is established by finding inflammatory changes on biopsy. The management of the conditions is similar to that for peptic ulcer. Where flatulence is prominent metoclopramide, 10 mg orally three times a day, may be helpful. There is probably little benefit to be obtained from undertaking a vagotomy even if a high acid output is demonstrated.

Cancer of the Stomach

Cancer of the stomach was the commonest malignant tumour of the gastrointestinal tract but has been superseded by cancer of the colon and rectum. The aetiology is unknown. The disease is more common in patients of blood group A; in some families there appears to be an hereditary factor. The disease is particularly prevalent in Japan. Cancer of the stomach is three times more common in patients with Addisonian pernicious anaemia than in the general population. The tumour is twice as frequent in males as females and the incidence increases with age. The relationship between gastric ulcer and gastric cancer remains controversial but the evidence suggests that only rarely does a benign gastric ulcer undergo malignant change.

The growth is usually an adenocarcinoma with varying

degrees of anaplasia. Colloid change may occur. Macroscopically the tumours may be ulcerative, fungating or polypoid, nodular and infiltrative. In linitis plastica there is infiltration of the submucosa or muscle layers involving most of the stomach often without ulceration. The tumour is most frequently sited at the antrum or pylorus.

The early symptoms are vague and readily dismissed. Once symptoms have developed they may resemble many other gastrointestinal disorders and the diagnosis may be delayed longer. Epigastric discomfort, anorexia, loss of weight, nausea, vomiting, flatulence and constipation may all be complained of either singly or in combination. Epigastric pain may resemble peptic ulcer disease but in cancer the periodicity and the characteristic relationship of the pain to meals are typically absent. Vomiting may or may not be associated with gastric outflow obstruction. Physical examination can be unrevealing or obvious weight loss and cachexia are present. An abdominal mass suggests that the growth is unresectable. Evidence of extensive spread may be inferred from the finding of a palpable lymph node in the left supraclavicular fossa, enlargement of the liver and masses in the pelvis. Intracranial and osseous secondaries may occur. Gastrointestinal bleeding, usually occult but occasionally massive, is a feature in about one-third of patients. 'Coffee ground' vomiting, indicative of a slow ooze of blood into the stomach lumen, is not diagnostic of gastric cancer for it may be associated with any slowly bleeding lesion in the stomach. Acute perforation is rare. Whereas tumours in the pyloric region frequently present with vomiting, growths in the cardia may cause dysphagia and rarely a clinical picture very similar to achalasia of the cardia.

The diagnosis is confirmed by a combination of radiology, gastroscopy, biopsy and cytology. In capable hands the barium meal is an accurate means of diagnosing cancer, which is recognized as an ulcer or a space-filling lesion (Plate V) or as a small rigid stomach which cannot distend.

Ulcerative lesions may be confused with a benign gastric ulcer; features which suggest the lesion to be an ulcerating cancer include a crater which does not project beyond the outline of the gastric wall, infiltration, fixation of folds and diminished peristalsis. Fundal and cardiac cancers are difficult to detect and require careful positioning of the patient. Occasionally distortion of the gastric air bubble will be seen on plain radiography of the abdomen which should suggest a fundal cancer. The radiological differential diagnosis of tumours in the fundus is difficult because of the number of lesions in this region which may mimic cancer. These include lymphoma, leiomyoma, other benign tumours, eosinophilic granuloma, gastric varices, benign lymphoid hyperplasia, giant rugal hypertrophy and the many causes of extragastric compression. Additional radiological techniques may be required to resolve the problem and these include tomography, angiography and a barium enema.

Gastric secretory studies are usually of no help. The presence of acid does not exclude a cancer nor does achlorhydria establish the diagnosis of a malignant lesion. A variety of enzymes have been measured in gastric juice including lactic dehydrogenase, aspartate transaminase and β-glucuronidase but these have little discriminatory value.

Endoscopy with or without photography has greatly enhanced the diagnostic accuracy and the newer flexible instruments have the added advantage that the cardia and fundus can be visualized. Gastric endoscopy can be combined with biopsy but the dangers of missing malignant tissue because of an inadequate sample must be remembered and biopsies should be obtained from a number of sites in the lesion. Cytology is of considerable value, having an accuracy of 95% in able hands. The technique is of particular value in small ulcerative lesions on the greater and lesser curvature. The cellular sediment in the gastric aspirate from patients with cancer who have been given tetracycline shows fluorescent properties and this test has been used to distinguish benign from malignant lesions.

The major difficulty in diagnosis is to distinguish between benign and malignant gastric ulcers and between benign and malignant tumours. The presentation of gastric and colonic cancers may be surprisingly similar. The clinical picture of uraemia may cause confusion. Cancer of the cardia may be confused with a primary oesophageal growth.

The management of gastric cancer is by operation where possible and involves either a partial or a total gastrectomy. Subtotal (seven-eighths) gastrectomy is the standard resection undertaken. If the growth invades the high lesser curve region or the cardia a total gastrectomy is usually performed. Total gastrectomy is also the surgical procedure in patients with linitis plastica. Many patients have extensive local and distal spread at the lime of laparotomy. Under these circumstances no resection may be attempted, but removal of the primary growth often affords considerable symptomatic relief, particularly if the resection is undertaken for an obstructive or bleeding growth. Radiotherapy and cancer chemotherapy are of no value.

The overall postoperative mortality is around 25% and is greater for total than subtotal gastrectomy. The 5-year survival is around 20% and 10% at 10 years, but it is probable that survival can be improved considerably if the growth is removed when it is confined to the mucous membrane. Linitis plastica and cancer at the cardia have the worst prognosis. Lymph node involvement has the greatest influence on the prognosis, the 5-year survival rate being 40% in the absence of lymph node infiltration and 10% when the nodes are affected. Other favourable prognostic factors include the presence of symptoms for more than 3 years, the absence of a palpable mass and a lesion on the lesser curvature. The quality of life following total gastrectomy is surprisingly good if an adequate gastric reservoir has been fashioned and adequate replacement therapy prescribed.

Other Gastric Tumours

A variety of benign and malignant tumours may involve the stomach, the commonest of which are leiomyomas, adenomas and neuromas. Other forms of gastric neoplasms include carcinoid tumours, lymphoma, Hodgkin's disease and vascular tumours. Many of these lesions will appear as polypoid growths. The term 'polyp' is frequently used in a descriptive sense with regard to gastric tumours but has no histological implication. From the radiological point of view the majority of polyps less than 2 cm in diameter may be regarded as being benign adenomas.

Further Reading

Cantrell, E. G. (1971) The benefits of using cytology in addition to gastric radiology. *Q. Jl Med.*, **40**, 239–248.

Conn, H. O. and Blitzer, B. L. (1976) Non-association of adrenocorticosteroid therapy and peptic ulcer. *New Engl. J. Med.*, **294**, 473–479.

Davenport, H. W. (1967) Salicylate damage to the gastric mucosal barrier. *New Engl. J. Med.*, **276**, 1307–1312.

Edwards, F. C. and Coghill, N. R. (1968) Clinical manifestations in duodenal ulcer. *Q. Jl Med.*, **37**, 337–360.

Hartley, P. R. et al. (1970) Pathology and prognosis of carcinoma of the stomach. *Br. J. Surg.*, **57**, 877–883.

Irvine, W. J. (1965) Immunologic aspects of pernicious anaemia. *New Engl. J. Med.*, **273**, 432–438.

Ivey, K. J. (1971) Acute haemorrhagic gastritis. *Gut*, **12**, 750–757.

Levy, M. (1974) Aspirin use in patients with major upper gastrointestinal bleeding and peptic-ulcer disease. *New Engl. J. Med.*, **290**, 1158–1162.

Rhodes, J. et al. (1968) Coarse mucosal folds in the duodenum. *Q. Jl Med.*, **37**, 151–169.

Taylor, K. B. (1969) Gastritis. *New Engl. J. Med.*, **280**, 818–820.

5   Malabsorption Syndromes

The small intestine functions as the major site for the digestion and absorption of food. The absorption of fat, protein and carbohydrate is nearly 100% complete. The reserve capacity of the bowel is considerable and long portions may be resected without serious nutritional effects except for vitamin B_{12} and bile salts which have an absorptive mechanism which is localized in the distal half of the ileum. The intestine is unable to regulate absorption, which may be influenced by motility, intestinal blood flow, hormones and bacteria. The movement of fluid and electrolytes across the bowel wall is an important feature of normal intestinal function. Two types of fluid shift occur: fluid secreted by the alimentary glands and the simultaneous passage of water and electrolytes across the bowel wall. This flux of fluid into the lumen may amount to 30 litres/day. Thus a major manifestation of small intestinal disease is the faulty digestion and malabsorption of proteins, fats, carbohydrates, vitamins, electrolytes and water.

SMALL INTESTINAL HISTOLOGY

The normal histology of the small intestine has been defined clearly as a result of the regular use of the technique of peroral intestinal biopsy. A small bowel biopsy has become essential in the clinical assessment of small intestinal disease. The normal villus is long and slender, being three times longer than it is broad. It has a connective tissue core and is lined by a single layer of columnar epithelium which is comprised of absorptive, goblet and argentaffin cells. The epithelial cells originate in the crypts of Lieberkühn where there is intense mitotic activity; they migrate up the crypt on to the villus and are finally desquamated from the villus tip. During this migratory process the cell undergoes maturation. It is only the cells in the upper third of the crypt which have the adult configuration and only at the junction of the crypt and villus that the cell acquires the full complement of digestive enzymes. The absorptive capacity increases as the cell nears the villus tip. The crypts also contain argentaffin and Paneth cells.

The morphology of the small intestine mucosa varies according to the part of the bowel. Duodenal villi are broader (leaf-shaped) and more branched than the long slender finger-like villi seen in the jejunum (Fig. 3).

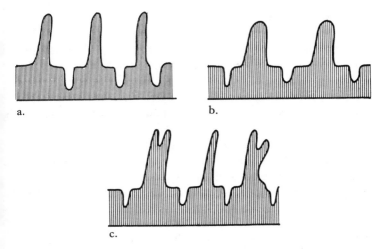

Fig. 3. Variations in the morphology of normal intestinal cell villi: *a*. Finger-shaped villi; *b*. Leaf-shaped villi; *c*. Branched villi.

Brunner's glands may be seen in the biopsy specimen. In the ileum the villi are shorter and broader, and relatively more goblet cells are present. There are also more collections of lymphoid tissue and in such regions the villi may be absent.

There is some variation in the shape of the normal jejunal villus from finger-like to leaf-like appearance (Fig. 3). Alternations in jejunal structure (blunted, shortened villi with hypercellularity of the lamina propria) and abnormalities of function (impaired absorption of fat, xylose and vitamin B_{12}) are demonstrable in a large number of healthy native residents in tropical areas who have no gastrointestinal symptoms. However, it is possible that this is not the 'normal' state of the mucosa, for when any hypoalbuminaemia or folate deficiency is corrected in these people the histological appearance reverts to that of healthy individuals living in temperate zones.

In order to interpret small bowel histology accurately it is essential that the specimen be correctly sectioned and properly orientated, thereby avoiding the artefact of blunted or widened villi. The dissecting microscope or hand lens is helpful in detecting abnormalities of villus morphology but it is no substitute for correctly sectioned and stained histological specimens.

The microvilli or brush border increase the surface area of the epithelial surface by a factor of 40. They are covered by a surface coat or glycocalyx made up of glycoprotein. The membrane of the microvillus is believed to be a lipid–protein mosaic comprising glycoproteins, glycolipids, phospholipids and cholesterol embedded in which is a variety of enzyme systems and carrier proteins (Table II).

Acid phosphatase, β-glucuronidase and glucosamidase are lysosomal enzymes in the mature columnar cell. Glucose-6-phosphatase and non-specific esterases are found in the microsomes. The immature cells in the crypts have low phosphatase and esterase activities which increase as the cell moves towards the villus tip. The amount of alkaline phosphatase in the cells may vary according to the ABO blood group or secretor status. Lactase activity develops during the last 3 months of intrauterine life. Experimental work suggests that elevated intestinal lactase activity can be induced by a high lactose diet, but this has not been demonstrated convincingly in man.

TABLE II. *Digestive and Transport Systems in the Intestinal Cell*

Digestive activities	Binding activities
Disaccharidases	Vitamin B_{12} (intrinsic factor binding)
Dipeptidases	Ca^{++} (binding protein)
Glycosyl transferases	
Glyceride synthetase	Transport activities
Alkaline phosphatase(s)	Hexose transport
Ca^{++} ATPase	Amino acid transport
	Bile acid transport

Primary malabsorption may occur following congenital or acquired absence of a component of the brush border. Examples include sucrose–isomaltose malabsorption, glucose–galactose malabsorption, Hartnup disease and cystinuria where the absorptive processes for certain amino acids are lacking.

The goblet cells are shaped like a brandy glass and are distended with mucus granules. Argentaffin cells are triangular in shape and contain large quantities of 5-hydroxytryptamine. Paneth cells are found at the base of the crypts and contain eosinophilic granules; their function is unknown.

The lamina propria forms the structural support for the villus and contains plasma cells, lymphocytes, macrophages, mast cells, fibroblasts and capillaries. The plasma cells, lymphocytes and macrophages in the connective tissue core are important for protection against invasion by organisms and foreign substances.

The migration of columnar cells up the villus takes about

4 days in man. Many factors influence the renewal process. There is an increased turnover in response to parasitic infection or partial intestinal resection; inhibition of renewal and migration occurs in the germfree state and during starvation. Paneth and argentaffin cells renew more slowly. Cell division occurs only in the crypts where mitoses are abundant. The shape of the villus is determined by cell turnover: finger-like villi reflect a turnover time of 4 days, leaflike villi turn over in 2 days and a flat mucosa turns over in less than 6 hours. The faster the turnover the more abnormal the villus shape. Cell exfoliation is one of the important routes by which metabolites can enter the gut lumen. Protein, vitamin B_{12} and lipids can enter the lumen in this manner, and whereas only 12% of the intestinal protein comes from shed cells, exfoliation accounts for nearly 80% of lipid in the gut lumen.

INTESTINAL HORMONES

A large number of peptide agents which are believed to have hormonal functions has been isolated from the gut but the physiological role of many of them is uncertain. The APUD system of intestinal cells, which can be recognized by immunofluorescent techniques, is probably the site of synthesis of many of these hormones. At least 11 types of endocrine cell are identified in the gastrointestinal tract. Among the many hormones produced are gastrin, cholecystokinin, secretin, vasoactive intestinal polypeptide (VIP), gastric inhibitory peptide (GIP), enteroglucagon, urogastrone, motilin and at least a dozen others which have not been clearly identified. These hormones have complex interactions affecting gastrointestinal and gall bladder motility, secretions and cell turnover. Gastrin and cholecystokinin exert an important trophic effect on the gut. Some hormones have been identified with particular disease states: gastrin with the Zollinger–Ellison syndrome (p. 5) and VIP with pancreatic cholera (p. 322).

INTESTINAL MOVEMENTS

Two basic types of intestinal movement are present: propulsive and non-propulsive (segmentation). The muscle cells of the longitudinal layer generate a 'basic electrical rhythm' or BER at a frequency of 12 cycles/minutes, and there is a decrease in activity from the duodenum to the ileum. Whether the slow waves originate from single or multiple pacemakers remains to be determined. Segmentation and propulsion probably differ in degree only; the mechanism is the same but the length of intestine activated differs. 'Peristaltic rushes' rarely occur in the small intestine and propulsive activity occurs over short segments only. Gastrointestinal hormones have an important influence on small intestinal motility. Motor activity is increased by cholecystokinin and to a lesser extent by gastrin and vasoactive intestinal peptide. Activity is inhibited by secretin.

Mechanism of Absorption

In the process of absorption molecules cross the plasma membrane to enter the intestinal cell. There are a number of mechanisms whereby the brush border may be traversed, including diffusion, non-ionic diffusion, active transport and carrier-mediated transport. Active transport refers to transport processes that require energy and the process is therefore coupled to cellular metabolism. Diffusion is movement determined by electrochemical potential differences. In non-ionic diffusion there is the association of an anion and cation which cross the membrane as a complex. The 'carrier' hypothesis has been developed to explain the passage of water-soluble molecules across the lipid plasma membrane. According to this hypothesis the transported substance binds to the carrier, the complex crosses the membrane and the substance is released on the opposite side of the membrane. No carrier has yet been identified with certainty.

The majority of nutrients tend to be absorbed in the upper small intestine where they are first exposed to the absorbing surface. This applies to fat, proteins, glucose, iron, folic acid, pyridoxine, riboflavine, ascorbic acid and water and electrolytes. Specific sites for absorption are present for vitamin B_{12} and bile salts and these are situated in the distal ileum. Unconjugated bile salts, and to a lesser extent the conjugated bile salts, can be absorbed in the jejunum by non-ionic diffusion but the major mechanism for conserving bile salts is by the active reabsorption process in the ileum. An awareness of the site of absorption of metabolites can be used for diagnosis of intestinal disease and also to predict the nature of the replacement therapy that may be required.

FAT ABSORPTION

Some gastric lipolytic activity is present in adults but it plays an insignificant role in the digestion of long-chain triglycerides. Normal fat digestion and absorption occur mainly in the upper small bowel. Pancreatic lipase preferentially hydrolyses the ester bonds in the α, α^1-positions with the production of long-chain fatty acids and β-monoglycerides. Some of the triglycerides are completely hydrolysed to fatty acids and glycerol. The rate of hydrolysis depends upon the degree of emulsification. Bile salts and lecithin aid emulsification of the fat, and the bile salts further favour lipolysis, removing lipolytic products from the fat/pancreatic lipase interface and thereby preventing reesterification of the glycerides. A co-lipase is present in intestinal secretions which serves to attach the lipase to the fat droplets thereby facilitating lipolysis.

In the aqueous medium of the small bowel the conjugated bile salts cluster together to form polymolecular aggregates known as micelles and the concentration at which this occurs is called the critical micellar concentration. The products of lipolysis—fatty acids and monoglycerides, which are essentially insoluble in water—enter these micelles to form a mixed micelle. The process whereby the insoluble end-products of the hydrolysis of triglycerides are brought into aqueous solution by the bile acids is known as micellar solubilization. Each micelle contains about 85 bile salt molecules. The concentration of bile salts in the upper jejunum is normally well above the critical micellar concentration. The exact mode of entry of the fatty acids and monoglycerides into the intestinal cell is not known but it is probably by a process of passive diffusion. Once inside the cell the monoglycerides and long-chain fatty acids are reesterified to triglycerides. This can take place either directly by esterification of the absorbed monoglyceride or via acylation of L-3-glycerophosphate. In either event fatty acids have to be activated to an acyl-CoA derivative. The newly reconstituted triglyceride is then associated with cholesterol ester, free cholesterol, phospholipids and protein to form a chylomicron; this process takes place on the smooth endoplasmic reticulum. The chylomicrons are released from the basal portion of the columnar epithelial cells and pass into the central lacteal of each intestinal villus from where they travel into the thoracic duct. In additional intestinal lymph contains lipoproteins of non-dietary origin representing *de novo* synthesis in the intestinal cell. These are smaller in size than chylomicrons and resemble plasma very low density lipoproteins (VLDL).

The presence of unconjugated bile salts is associated with ineffective fat digestion and absorption. This may come about for a number of reasons: the unconjugated bile salts are poor in forming micelles, they diffuse relatively rapidly from the upper small bowel and they may damage the intestinal mucosa. The end result is a lack of effective bile salts for micelle formation.

The digestion and absorption of the medium-chain triglycerides (containing fatty acids of chain length 6–12 carbon atoms) differs in a number of respects from the long-chain triglycerides. Medium-chain triglycerides can be effectively hydrolysed in the stomach while in the small intestine bile salts are not required for aqueous dispersion. Intraluminal enzymatic hydrolysis of the medium-chain triglycerides is more rapid and complete than for the long-chain triglycerides. Small quantities of medium-chain triglycerides enter the intestinal cells without prior hydrolysis. In the intestinal cell there is minimal reesterification to triglyceride and transport from the intestine is in the form of the medium-chain fatty acids which pass into the portal blood. They do not form chylomicrons.

Cholesterol esters, either endogenous or exogenous in origin, are hydrolysed by a pancreatic esterase to free cholesterol which is solubilized with the other lipid components of the mixed micelle. This absorbed cholesterol mixes with a pool of endogenously synthesized cholesterol, and cholesterol from these two sources is incorporated into the chylomicron. The cholesterol biosynthetic pathway is the same as in the liver; it undergoes a circadian rhythm and is probably regulated by both cholesterol and bile salts. Phospholipids also undergo hydrolysis in the intestinal lumen and the products are incorporated in the mixed micelle and resynthesized in the intestinal cell. The synthesis of cholesterol and phospholipids takes place on the smooth endoplasmic reticulum of the intestinal cells and is predominantly in the crypts. The precursor fatty acids are probably mainly derived from plasma or local synthesis because luminal lipid is less available to crypt cells. Phospholipids so synthesized may well be used for membranes in newly formed crypt cells.

The digestion and absorption of dietary fat is almost complete and the major portion of faecal fat derives from desquamation of colonic epithelial cells. On a fat-free diet there may be up to 3 g (11 mmol) of fat in the stool each day. The normal faecal fat measurement is less than 6 g/day (21 mmol/day) and does not alter appreciably with an intake of fat varying from 50 to 250 g/day. All forms of steatorrhoea will improve if the amount of dietary fat is reduced. Because of the differences in digestion and absorption between the medium- and long-chain triglycerides it is possible to feed medium-chain triglycerides to patients with fat malabsorption from a variety of causes without aggravating the diarrhoea. The medium-chain triglycerides are absorbed in these circumstances despite the malabsorption of the long-chain triglycerides and thus provide an essential supply of calories.

CALCIUM ABSORPTION

Calcium absorption occurs throughout the small intestine being maximal in the duodenum and upper jejunum. In this area, at least, there is an active carrier-mediated mechanism for the transport of ionized calcium. A two-step process is involved in which there is initially net uptake at the mucosal surface to be followed by active transport within the cell via a specific calcium-binding protein. It is probable that 1,25-dihydroxycholecalciferol stimulates both steps. Calcium absorption is reduced by phytic acid, oxalic acid and a high phosphate content in the diet. Bile salts are important for calcium absorption because they increase solubility as well as enhancing the absorption of exogenous cholecalciferol. It is unlikely that parathyroid hormone plays a direct role in calcium absorption.

CARBOHYDRATE ABSORPTION See p. 109.

IRON ABSORPTION See p. 254.

PROTEIN ABSORPTION See p. 113.

Mechanisms of Malabsorption

Intestinal malabsorption may be defined as 'any state in which there is a disturbance of the net absorption of any constituent across the intestinal mucosa'. The term may

TABLE III. *Causes of Malabsorption*

Abnormalities in the intestinal lumen
    Inadequate digestion
        Pancreatic insufficiency
        Acid hypersecretion (Zollinger–Ellison syndrome)
        Gastric resection; vagotomy
        Hyperthyroidism
    Altered bile salt metabolism
        Hepatobiliary disease
        Terminal ileal resection or disease
        Contaminated bowel syndrome associated with blind loops, fistulas, strictures, diverticula, scleroderma, diabetes mellitus

Abnormalities of mucosal cell transport
    Coeliac disease
    Tropical sprue
    Dysgammaglobulinaemia
    Intestinal lymphoma
    Protein–calorie malnutrition
    Pernicious anaemia
    Skin disease, e.g. dermatitis herpetiformis
    Parasitic disease, e.g. giardiasis
    Whipple's disease
    Amyloidosis
    Radiation damage
    Drug-induced malabsorption, e.g. neomycin
    Intestinal ischaemia
    Endocrine disease, e.g. Addison's disease, hypoparathyroidism, hyperthyroidism, carcinoid syndrome
    Abetalipoproteinaemia

Abnormalities of intestinal lymphatics
    Intestinal lymphangiectasia
    Tuberculosis
    Constrictive pericarditis

be used to describe the ineffective absorption of proteins, sugars, vitamins and fat. The common clinical use of the unqualified term 'malabsorption' is to describe fat malabsorption.

Regardless of the many causes of fat malabsorption there are certain common features. These include soft or loose stools, which are pale, frothy, bulky and malodorous at times. A floating stool is not a sign of steatorrhoea but reflects a high stool gas content unrelated to stool fat content. In some patients, such as those with coeliac disease, where lipolysis is adequate, bacterial action on the free fatty acids results in the production of hydroxystearic acid which may have a cathartic effect. Anorexia, weight loss, abdominal distension and flatulence are among the gastrointestinal symptoms which may occur. Nutritional deficiencies may develop in patients with longstanding malabsorption. Thus tetany, bone pain, fractures, abnormal bleeding, a painful tongue, muscle tenderness and skin changes are all encountered.

The many causes of malabsorption can be grouped on an anatomical basis or according to the mechanism for the altered physiology; the latter classification is preferred and is given in Table III. In some diseases more than one mechanism may operate, as in Crohn's disease, while in others the pathogenesis of the malabsorption has not yet been defined, e.g. dysgammaglobulinaemia, carcinoid syndrome, hyperthyroidism and hypoparathyroidism. All the conditions listed cause fat malabsorption and steatorrhoea. There are in addition specific defects of mucosal cell transport which cause malabsorption but not fat malabsorption: disaccharidase deficiency, monosaccharide malabsorption, specific disorders of amino acid absorption (e.g. cystinuria, Hartnup disease) and vitamin B_{12} malabsorption.

The diagnosis of the cause of fat malabsorption and steatorrhoea requires an adequate history and physical examination and the availability of a number of laboratory investigations. The most important investigation is the demonstration of steatorrhoea: stool fat in excess of 6 g/day (21 mmol/day). This is most reliably measured by a 3-day stool collection with the patient on a normal ward diet (about 80–100 g fat/day). ^{14}C-triglycerides have been used as a breath test for fat absorption. Abnormality of D-xylose absorption is better than glucose as a guide to carbohydrate malabsorption. A urinary output of less than 4 g (27 mmol) of a 25 g dose over 5 hours and a 2-hour blood level less than 30 mg/100 ml (2 mmol/litre) suggests damage to the upper small intestine. The test is normal in pancreatic malabsorption. Low urinary levels occur in renal disease and old age in the absence of gut abnormalities. Unfortunately bacteria in the upper small bowel may metabolize the xylose, and this causes a low urinary excretion which may be interpreted erroneously as indicating small bowel mucosal damage. A biopsy of the small intestinal mucosa using either a Crosby capsule or a Rubin suction biopsy tube is of great help because there are a number of causes of malabsorption with characteristic features on jejunal histology: coeliac disease, Whipple's disease, amyloidosis, dysgammaglobulinaemia, abetalipoproteinaemia and intestinal lymphangiectasia. Small bowel radiology has much to contribute to the diagnosis, complemented if necessary by arteriography and lymphangiography. Bacterial overgrowth may be assessed by duodenal intubation and culture of the small bowel contents, by measuring exhaled ^{14}CO$_2$ after the ingestion of a meal containing ^{14}C glycocholic acid, and by measuring the amount of indican in the urine although this may be misleading at times. The estimation of serum folic acid and vitamin B$_{12}$ levels is of help, as are the various isotopic methods for measuring vitamin B$_{12}$ absorption. In the absence of demonstrable gastrointestinal disease it will be necessary to assess liver and pancreatic function. A factor making diagnosis difficult may be the presence of pancreatic insufficiency in association with severe protein malnutrition. Tests of pancreatic function may be disturbed but will return to normal once the nutritional status has been corrected.

Coeliac Disease

Coeliac disease is the name favoured for the disease which has been variously called coeliac sprue, coeliac syndrome, adult coeliac disease, gluten-induced enteropathy, idiopathic steatorrhoea, idiopathic sprue and non-tropical sprue. The disease occurs in 0.1–0.2% of the population. It is generally agreed that the disease found in children is identical to that found in adults. Much of the confusion surrounding the disease, particularly in adults where the clinical syndrome tends to be less clearly defined, arises from an inability to define any aetiological factor or factors. The disease arises from the damaging effect which dietary gluten has on the small intestinal mucosa. Gluten is toxic only to patients with coeliac disease and instillation of a gluten solution on the normal mucosa of a treated patient will immediately cause damage to the epithelial cells. Gluten is a complex protein found mainly in cereal foods. Gliadin, a protein complex which can be separated from gluten, is also capable of inducing small intestinal cell damage. It is possible that the gluten alters the lysosomal membrane and autodigestion of the cell occurs. It remains to be determined whether the defect is an immunological reaction to gluten or an inborn error of metabolism in which there is a deficiency of a specific peptide hydrolase which is normally present in the intestinal mucosa. All the evidence indicates that any reduction in hydrolase activity is secondary to the mucosal damage. In about 20% of patients there is a family history and a polygenetic mode of inheritance is probable. Abnormal jejunal biopsies are found in 10% of parents of children with coeliac disease.

The essential defect in coeliac disease is a reduction in the number or even the absence of intestinal villi. The damage involves mainly the proximal small bowel, presumably because it is first to be confronted with dietary gluten. It is thought that there is damage to the mature intestinal cells ('enterocytes'), which are lost into the gut lumen, and that compensatory hyperplasia of the maturing cells ('enteroblasts') occurs in an attempt to repair the damage. In favour of this concept is the increased mitotic count seen in the intestinal crypts, the increased DNA found in the gut lumen and believed to have originated from the excessive desquamation of damaged mucosal cells, and an abnormally rapid rate of cell migration from the crypts to the luminal surface. The villi are leaf-shaped, bifid or short, thick and stunted, giving the mucosa a convoluted appearance (Fig. 4). When the damage is

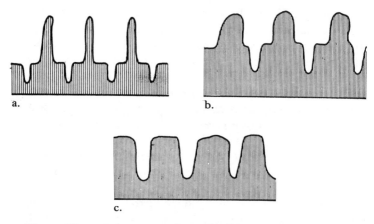

Fig. 4. Mucosal appearances in coeliac disease: *a.* Normal villi; *b.* Moderate villus damage; *c.* Severe villus damage.

severe no villi will be seen and the mucous membrane appears flat. The intestinal cells are abnormal, flattened, cuboidal, irregular in shape and size and with a disorganized brush border. There is increased plasma cell infiltration in the epithelium with a reduction in lamina propria lymphocytes and an increase in the goblet cells. The terms 'subtotal villous atrophy' and 'partial villous atrophy' have been used to describe the histological appearances. The mucosal changes do not represent atrophic changes and, indeed, the mucosal thickness may be normal or greater than normal. It is therefore better to describe the damage as mild, moderate or severe when assessing the histology.

Malabsorption is the result of the reduced surface area in the proximal gut. Digestion is impaired because of a reduction in the activity of the mucosal enzymes which is the consequence of the immaturity of the surface cells as well as the overall reduction in villi. A contributory factor is impaired secretion of cholecystokinin from the damaged mucosa. Thus there is, in response to a meal, a reduced output of bile and pancreatic enzymes.

The age of presentation varies from infants to middle age. Two-thirds of children present before 9 months and the majority of adults present between the ages of 30 and 50 years. The clinical syndrome is usually more severe in infants and children, who present with anorexia, nausea, vomiting, loss of weight, diarrhoea and failure to thrive. Rectal prolapse may occur, although it is more commonly associated with cytic fibrosis. The disorder is relatively mild in the majority of adults and clinical features are much more varied. In 30–50% of the adults it is possible to obtain a long history of ill health. Diarrhoea is frequent but not invariable. The character of the stool is not necessarily typical of steatorrhoea and patients may be unaware that their stools are abnormal. Abdominal distension, flatulence, weakness, anaemia, anorexia and vomiting are frequent complaints. Less commonly the patient may have muscle cramps, tetany, paraesthesia, bleeding, painful mouth and bone pain. Physical signs include loss of weight, abdominal distension which is particularly marked in children, pallor, increased pigmentation, hypotension, oedema, clubbing, glossitis and Chvostek and Trousseau signs. An interesting but unexplained association is loss of fingerprint markings.

The steatorrhoea is accompanied by a negative calcium

balance, vitamin D deficiency, osteomalacia or rickets, osteoporosis or a combination of these changes. Very low serum calcium values, normal serum alkaline phosphatase levels and normal bones suggest little compensatory parathyroid activity whereas normal or only slight hypocalcaemia, elevated serum alkaline phosphatase and osteomalacia indicate compensatory parathyroid activity ('secondary hyperparathyroidism'). Excess calcium in the stool may be due to malabsorption of dietary calcium or possibly an excessive endogenous faecal loss. The anaemia is usually due to iron deficiency from a combination of malabsorption and excessive exfoliation of cells. Folate deficiency is frequent and a low red cell folate level in children has some diagnostic value. Vitamin B_{12} lack is rare unless the mucosal lesion is sufficiently severe to extend to the ileum.

Loss of mucosal surface is associated with an impairment of the absorption of monosaccharides and disaccharides and this may increase the tendency to diarrhoea. In severe involvement the abnormal jejunal mucosa secretes water and electrolytes into the gut lumen. Protein malabsorption results in hypoproteinaemia, oedema, ascites and even secondary pancreatic insufficiency which may contribute to the fat malabsorption. There is an association between malignant disease in the gut and longstanding coeliac disease. The foregut and midgut are most likely to be affected and cancers of the oesophagus, stomach and small intestine and lymphomas of the intestine have all been reported. The relationship between the malignant disease and coeliac disease is complicated because, while it seems likely that the malignancy arises as a complication of the coeliac disease (and it is possible that the increased mitotic activity of the mucous membrane and the abnormal white cell population may predispose to the tumour formation), the suggestion has been made that the villus damage may be a non-specific response to a malignant growth elsewhere in the gut or indeed the body. Rare complications are intestinal ulceration, infertility, pulmonary fibrosis and a neuropathy which presents as ataxia involving the lower limbs.

Patients with coeliac disease have splenic atrophy and Howell–Jolly bodies can be demonstrated in the peripheral blood smear. There is an increase in the population of IgM secreting plasma cells in the jejunal mucosa and an increase in the quantity of IgM in the intestinal secretions, but in one-third of patients there is a reduction in IgM levels in the serum. The concentration of IgA may be increased in the serum although a small proportion of patients have a deficiency of IgA (p. 91). It has been demonstrated that in patients with coeliac disease the small intestinal mucous membrane responds to the presence of gluten with the increased production of IgA and IgM. This increased synthesis occurs soon after the introduction of gluten into the diet and before any disturbance of gastrointestinal function can be demonstrated. Reticulin antibodies (connective tissue antibodies), an IgG class antibody, are found in the serum of many adults or children with untreated coeliac disease. There may be an increase in HL-A1 and HL-A8 antigens.

There is no correlation between the absorptive function of the proximal small intestine and the severity of the mucosal lesion as judged by a single biopsy; nor is there a correlation between the mucosal abnormality and the degree of steatorrhoea, xylose absorption, oral glucose tolerance tests and haematological indices. Of more significance is the extent of the lesion and the reserve capacity of the bowel.

The diagnosis is established by demonstration of the characteristic mucosal changes in proximal small bowel biopsies and by the induction of a clinical and histological remission after the exclusion of gluten from the diet. The flat lesion seen on mucosal biopsies is highly characteristic of coeliac disease but not specific, for it may be seen in hypoglobulinaemia, Whipple's disease and intestinal lymphoma; however these conditions have other histological features which differentiate them from coeliac disease so that confusion should not arise. The mucosal morphology in dermatitis herpetiformis may be identical to coeliac disease. Similarities have also been reported in kwashiorkor and tropical sprue. The radiological appearance of the small bowel is helpful. The plain film of the abdomen, particularly in children, shows dilatation and fluid levels in the small intestine and there may be excess faecal material in the colon. Barium examination demonstrates dilatation of the small bowel, a smooth appearance to the mucosal outline and the barium will be segmented and scattered. Delayed transit time is not infrequent. The xylose tolerance test is abnormal but is of unreliable diagnostic value; the urinary excretion of 5-hydroxyindole acetic acid (5-HIAA) may be increased. The majority of the patients will have steatorrhoea and the faecal fat excretion may be greater than the measured fat intake. However, some patients do not have steatorrhoea despite the characteristic histological lesion.

TABLE IV. *The Differences Between Coeliac Disease and Crohn's Disease*

Feature	Coeliac Disease	Crohn's Disease
Abdominal pain	Uncommon	Frequent
Fever	Uncommon	Frequent
Anaemia	Iron deficiency Folate	Iron deficiency Vitamin B_{12}
ESR	Normal	Increased
Iron absorption	Abnormal	Normal
Vitamin B_{12} absorption	Normal	Abnormal
Barium studies	Dilatation, segmentation, clumping	Strictures, ulcers, fistulas

The differential diagnosis includes all the causes of steatorrhoea listed in Table III, the majority of which are readily excluded on clinical grounds. In children the main diseases to be considered are cystic fibrosis of the pancreas and giardiasis; in adults the differential diagnosis includes particularly Crohn's disease and chronic pancreatitis.

Some of the features distinguishing Crohn's disease from coeliac disease are shown in Table IV. In Arabs or Middle-Eastern Jews primary intestinal lymphoma may present with malabsorption and in some of these patients jejunal histology is indistinguishable from coeliac disease.

The basis for the treatment of coeliac disease in both adults and children is the introduction of a gluten-free diet. This implies the exclusion of wheat, rye, barley and malt from the diet and means that items such as canned meats, sausages, certain ice creams, gravies and beer and ale will have to be avoided. In Great Britain the Coeliac Society publishes a useful handbook of dietary advice. The great majority of patients will respond to such a diet by an immediate improvement in wellbeing, cessation of the diarrhoea and a return of the small intestinal mucous membrane to normal. There is a decrease in the number of plasma cells and lymphocytes to near-normal values. Occasionally it takes some months for the improvement to occur. The usual cause for failure to respond, or a relapse, is that the patient is not adhering strictly enough to the gluten-free diet. Relapses may occur during intercurrent infections. No matter how well a patient feels it is always necessary to maintain the gluten-free diet; this is of particular importance in women who may embark on pregnancy. Corticosteroid therapy is seldom required but its use can lead to clinical improvement in unresponsive patients. In severe involvement, and particularly in those patients who are not responding satisfactorily to gluten withdrawal, it is necessary to supplement the diet with iron, folic acid and vitamin B_{12}. Pancreatic enzyme supplements may be required if there is gross protein–calorie malnutrition. Some patients are symptomatically improved by the elimination of milk from the diet.

There is a small group of patients who have steatorrhoea and the characteristic flat mucosal lesion but who do not respond to gluten elimination. Such patients create considerable difficulty in classification: should this be called coeliac disease or not? Until the pathogenesis of coeliac disease has been defined it seems better to diagnose such patients as 'non-responsive coeliac disease' or 'unclassified sprue'. Some patients respond symptomatically to the gluten-free diet although the intestinal biopsy remains abnormal and this is in keeping with the concept that it is the extent and not the severity of the lesion which determines the clinical picture. These patients, too, present problems in classification. It must be pointed out that the majority of exceptions to the accepted clinical syndrome occurs in adults. Furthermore, the response to gluten withdrawal is not specific because many diarrhoeal states will improve on a diet free from gluten.

Tropical Sprue

This disease is characterized by diarrhoea, steatorrhoea, weight loss and malabsorption of folic acid and vitamin B_{12}. Oedema, neuropathy and glossitis are uncommon. The disorder is found exclusively in tropical and subtropical regions and may occur in endemic and epidemic forms. The aetiology is not known but there is good evidence to support the concept that there is bacterial overgrowth in the small bowel, although no specific bacterial or viral agent has been incriminated. It is possible that the bacterial proliferation produces excessive quantities of unconjugated bile acids which cause the steatorrhoea. Fat malabsorption correlates poorly with both the histological change and the xylose absorption test and relates best to vitamin B_{12}

malabsorption. Jejunal biopsies show changes similar to, but milder than, coeliac disease — leaf-shaped or convoluted villi and cuboidal changes in the surface epithelial cells. At times the histology may be indistinguishable from coeliac disease. Usually the epithelium is columnar and there is a dense inflammatory cell infiltration, although the lamina propria does not become as thickened as in coeliac disease. Such changes are quite non-specific: 'a normal biopsy may exclude the diagnosis of sprue but an abnormal biopsy does not necessarily confirm it'.

The significance of minor histological changes is made more confusing by the frequency with which they may be found in symptom-free individuals from tropical and subtropical regions. Minor degrees of xylose malabsorption may be found as well but faecal fat excretion is usually normal. Such changes are reported particularly from Puerto Rica, India, Pakistan and Thailand. The relationship of these histological and biochemical changes to tropical sprue remains uncertain; this may be a variant of normal in people living in subtropical regions or such persons may be considered as having subclinical tropical sprue (p. 76). At present the former explanation seems the more reasonable and it is believed that the mucosal changes are a non-specific reaction to dietary and infective insults on what would otherwise be normal mucous membrane by Western standards.

Patients with tropical sprue do not respond to a gluten-free diet but improve on pharmacological doses of folic acid and vitamin B_{12} as well as an oral antibiotic. Although haematological responses may follow antibiotic therapy alone the most effective form of treatment is a combination of drugs. A 3-week course of a broad-spectrum antibiotic, such as 250 mg oxytetracycline 4 times daily, and 5 mg folic acid 3 times daily, is usually sufficient to alleviate the intestinal symptoms and induce a gain in weight. Some patients, particularly when there has been a delay in initiating therapy, show a tardy response to treatment and it will be necessary to maintain the therapy for up to 6 months.

Whipple's Disease

Whipple's disease is a rare condition occurring mainly in males between the ages of 20 and 70 years. The patients present with weight loss, diarrhoea, arthralgia and abdominal pain. Clinical examination reveals hypotension, lymphadenopathy, skin pigmentation, pleural effusions, neurological abnormalities, fever and dependent oedema. Steatorrhoea is almost invariable and there is anaemia usually from iron deficiency, hypoalbuminaemia, hypokalaemia, and a prolonged prothrombin time. D-Xylose absorption may be abnormal and the barium studies of the small bowel show coarsening of the duodenal and jejunal folds. The diagnosis is established by a small bowel biopsy which shows the intestinal mucosa to be infiltrated by periodic acid Schiff positive macrophages. In severe involvement the villus structure may be totally obliterated but the distinction from coeliac disease is readily made. The periodic acid-Schiff positive macrophages may be found in virtually all the tissues of the patient so that a positive biopsy has been obtained from sites other than the bowel.

The aetiology is unknown but it is thought to be a response to infection by bacilli which can be demonstrated by electron microscopy of the intestinal mucosa and lymph nodes. The organisms have not been identified with certainty. The disease responds favourably to antibiotic therapy. Various regimens have been recommended. Satisfactory results may be achieved with 1200 000 units of procaine penicillin G plus 1 g streptomycin daily for 2 weeks, followed by oxytetracycline 1 g daily for a year. Clinical response is rapid, occurring within a month, but relapses are frequent if shorter courses of therapy are given.

Immunological Deficiencies and Steatorrhoea

IMMUNE SYSTEM OF THE INTESTINE

The small intestinal mucosa contains both thymus-dependent and thymus-independent lymphoid cells. The lamina propria normally has large numbers of plasma cells the majority of which produce IgA. The ratio of the IgA:IgM to IgE-producing cells is 20.3:1 and reflects the response of the bowel to antigenic stimulation from food, bacteria and drugs. The plasma cells are derived from large lymphocytes. The major immunoglobulin produced by the plasma cells in the small bowel is IgA and this plays an important role in the protective mechanism of the gut. It is normally absent in the neonate. IgA precursor cells are elaborated in Peyer's patches and other organized mucosal lymphoid tissue, are disseminated into the circulation and then return to the intestinal mucosa where they elaborate IgA.

IgA is a glycoprotein which appears in both the serum and the gastrointestinal secretions. In the serum the immunoglobulin exists as a 7S monomer (M.W. 170 000) whereas secretory IgA, the molecule present in intestinal secretions, is an 11S dimer (M.W. 390 000) comprising two monomeres of 7S IgA attached to the 'secretory piece' which is a glycopeptide of M.W. 58 000. The secretory piece is elaborated by mucosal cells (not lymphocytes) and has the functions of transporting IgA across the mucous membrane as well as protecting it from proteolysis. The intestinal plasma cells contribute the major fraction of circulating IgA. In contrast to IgA only small amounts of IgM and IgG can be detected in intestinal secretions.

The functions of the local T cell-mediated immune reactions in the small intestine mucosa are not identified but they probably play a role in immunity to parasitic infections. It has been suggested that they may also participate in the pathogenesis of coeliac disease, food allergy and intestinal infections.

TABLE V. *Immunoglobin Deficiency States Associated with Steatorrhoea*

Disease	Hypogamma-globulinaemia	Serum IgA	S.I. Biopsy	Response to Gluten-free Diet
Hypogamma-globulinaemia, hereditary or acquired	Yes	Low	Normal	No
Selective IgA deficiency	No	Absent	Flat, reduced plasma cells	Yes
Nodular lymphoid hyperplasia	Yes	Very low	Normal villi, lymphoid nodules	No
Intestinal lymphangiectasia	Yes	Low	Distorted villi, dilated lymphatics	No
Coeliac disease	Yes	Normal or raised	Flat	Yes

There is a high incidence of gastrointestinal symptoms in patients with immunodeficiency syndromes. Diarrhoea, intermittent vomiting and loss of weight are prominent; infection with *Giardia lamblia* is almost invariable and bacterial overgrowth frequent. Mucosal biopsies may show mild distortion of villous architecture (Table V).

In *severe hypogammaglobulinaemia*, either congenital or acquired, there is a general deficiency of IgA, IgG and IgM globulins. Steatorrhoea occurs in about 50% of these patients and can be reversed by infusions of γ-globulin. The small intestinal mucosa may be normal but in some patients moderate or severe villus damage is present and this is not responsive to gluten withdrawal.

A rare disease is *selective IgA deficiency associated with steatorrhoea*. Serum levels of the other immunoglobulins are normal. The villi are completely flat, plasma cells are absent and the patients respond to a gluten-free diet. The IgA deficiency is permanent and refractory to treatment. This rare syndrome may be difficult to distinguish from coeliac disease.

Another uncommon disorder is *nodular lymphoid hyperplasia* in which there is hyperplasia of the small intestinal lymphoid tissue. This is detected radiologically or by intestinal biopsy. Patients have diarrhoea or steatorrhoea and infection with *Giardia lamblia* is common. Serum IgA and IgM levels are very low while IgG are borderline normal; however, changes in the immunoglobulins vary quantitatively and qualitatively. There is no response to a gluten-free diet.

ALPHA-CHAIN DISEASE

Alpha-chain disease is a rare disorder which affects mainly young persons from the Mediterranean areas. The presenting features are abdominal pain, finger clubbing and steatorrhoea. Characteristically the small intestinal mucosa is heavily infiltrated with plasma cells and the villi are broad and distorted. The plasma cells synthesize an abnormal IgA molecule which is devoid of light chains and which may only be detected in the serum by special techniques. The prognosis is poor and many of the patients succumb to the development of a malignant intestinal lymphoma (p. 172).

In *intestinal lymphangiectasia* steatorrhoea is fairly common. It is disorder of development of lymphatics which are grossly dilated (p. 115).

Other rare syndromes include *infantile X-linked agammaglobulinaemia* and the *ataxia telangiectasia* syndrome.

The management of these various syndromes is usually complex and includes a low fat diet, antibiotics, metronidiazole for giardiasis, diuretic therapy if oedema is troublesome and infusions of plasma and γ-globulins.

Small Bowel Resection or Disease

Extensive resection of the small bowel or widespread disease such as Crohn's disease is associated with a syndrome of diarrhoea and malabsorption of fat, proteins and other nutrients. Eventually there is marked weight loss and inanition, and death may supervene. Experimental work suggests that the small bowel has the capacity to hypertrophy and this may explain the tendency to improve during the months following resection. Resection of the ileum is frequently more troublesome than the removal of large portions of jejunum because there is loss of bile acids, and the absence of the ileocaecal valve means that food is not held up in the remaining small intestine. The diarrhoea in these patients tends to be more marked. The amount of diarrhoea is also related to the length of colon removed.

Loss of the distal bowel function removes the specific absorbing sites for vitamin B_{12} and the conjugated bile salts, particularly the trihydroxy bile acids. Consequently there is an excessive loss of bile salts into the colon. Colonic reabsorption of bile salts is insufficient to compensate for this loss and although there may be a marked increase in the hepatic synthesis of bile salts such compensation is limited and may not make good the deficit. There is a reduction in the bile salt pool and bile acid secretion into the bile. Furthermore there is an alteration in the nature of the bile salts and the glycine conjugates increase relative to taurine. There is a marked fall in the cholate fraction but chenodeoxycholate is not as affected. Deoxycholic acid (the secondary bile acid produced by bacterial dehydroxylation of cholic acid) is absent from the bile in more than 50% of patients. However, alterations in bile salt metabolism in this syndrome are complex and they depend upon a number of variables such as the amount of reabsorption from the remaining small bowel and colon, and on the type and degree of bacterial activity.

Steatorrhoea results from a reduced concentration of conjugated bile salts in the duodenal lumen. Patients may have adequate duodenal bile salt levels at breakfast because of the overnight synthesis (in the liver) and storage (in the gall bladder) of bile salts, and this meal can be digested and absorbed normally. Meals taken later during the day cannot be digested as efficiently because the increased bile salt synthesis has not been able to compensate for the enormous loss of bile salts into the colon after each meal. This phenomenon of bile salt depletion over the course of the day is not restricted to ileal disease and has been recorded in coeliac disease and liver disease.

Bile acid synthesis increases from 0.4 g to 1.2 g daily. There is an increase in the amount of primary bile salts (cholic and chenodeoxycholic) and there is an excess of glycine conjugates. In the absence of the terminal ileum passive absorption becomes important favouring the absorption of the dihydroxy-bile salts (chenodeoxycholic and deoxycholic). Patients with intestinal resection are at greater risk to develop gall stones. Some patients develop hyperoxaluria and renal stones. This is believed to result from the increased absorption of dietary oxalate which takes place in the colons of patients with ileal resection.

The diarrhoea may be caused either by the cathartic effect of bile acid or unabsorbed fatty acids on the colonic mucous membrane, both of which cause water secretion by the colonic mucosa. The diarrhoeogenic effect of bile acids is usually more prominent if less than 100 cm of ileum have been removed; with larger resections steatorrhoea is marked and the effect of bacterial breakdown of the faecal triglycerides enhances the laxative effect. In a few patients gastric acid hypersecretion occurs and the lowered intestinal pH may contribute to the diarrhoea and steatorrhoea.

Management of these patients includes replacement of fluid and electrolytes and frequent small feedings of a low fat, low carbohydrate and high protein diet. Supplementation with vitamins, particularly B_{12}, is necessary. The patients will require careful psychological handling. Having the main meal of the day for breakfast is beneficial. Extra calories can be provided by feeding medium-chain triglycerides. In patients who have had less than 100 cm of ileum resected the diarrhoea may be controlled by feeding cholestyramine in doses approaching 16 g/day. The cholestyramine binds the bile salts, thereby preventing their irritating effect on the colonic mucosa. While there is some increase in the severity of the steatorrhoea it is not sufficient to be troublesome. Unfortunately cholestyramine does not appear to be effective if more than 100 cm of ileum has been resected. In these patients a fat-free diet and antibiotic therapy may be of help. The distinction between the response of patients with less or more than 100 cm of ileal resection to cholestyramine is not always clear. Evidence for gastric hypersecretion should be sought and if this is marked a vagotomy may be helpful. In severe malabsorption the intragastric infusion of 'space diets' may be tried. Such diets require little or no digestion for absorption and they are used when there is little remaining normal small bowel mucous membrane. The diets consist of simple sugars, L-amino acids and medium-chain triglycerides. They are administered slowly via a gastrostomy tube. With an improved understanding of the altered physiology of digestion and absorption which occurs in these patients it has become possible to offer more effective therapy and an increasing number are able to survive extensive intestinal resection. This applies particularly to infants, who now have the prospect of developing into normal healthy children.

Bacterial Overgrowth of the Small Bowel; 'Contaminated Bowel Syndrome'

The orderly peristalsis in the normal small bowel continuously clears the gut lumen of microorganisms, thereby preventing their proliferation. Thus the small intestine is sparsely populated with bacteria and the number of organisms rarely exceeds 10^4/ml of small bowel contents. Improvements in bacteriological culture techniques, particularly in the culture of anaerobic organisms, and intubation methods have led to a better documentation of the quantitative and qualitative aspects of small intestinal microflora.

The acid secretion in the stomach constitutes an important barrier to bacterial growth and the fasting jejunum is either sterile or harbours only moderate numbers of staphylococci (10^2–10^5 organisms/ml), streptococci and occasional low counts of enterobacteria, veillonella, anaerobic lactobacilli and other organisms. In the terminal ileum there are, in addition to the organisms mentioned above, types of bacteria typically found in the colon such as enterococci, enterobacteria and anaerobic bacteroides. It seems likely that the distribution of the bacteria varies during the day, with an increase in bacteria in the jejunum following the ingestion of food. Gastric acidity, bile and the normal peristalsis appear to limit bacterial growth and any disturbance in the balance of these factors enables micro-organisms to proliferate and spread along the small bowel.

The usual organisms implicated in the contaminated bowel syndrome are faecal in type : enterobacteria, clostridia and bacteroides, but the flora will vary according to the site and nature of the anatomical abnormality. Bacterial over-growth in the small bowel has considerable influence on intestinal absorptive mechanisms (Table VI). Deconjuga-tion of the bile salts is of paramount importance and occurs particularly when conditions favour the growth of anaerobic organisms, especially the bacteroides but also enterococci, clostridia and veillonella. Intestinal organisms may also dehydroxylate, oxidize or reduce the bile salts. Fat malabsorption results from the increase in unconjugated bile acids at the expense of the conjugated salts so that micelle formation becomes inadequate and fat digestion and absorption incomplete. The unconjugated bile acids probably also have a toxic effect on the intestinal mucosal cells. Intraluminal precipitation of the unconjugated bile acids is a further factor in reducing the micellar dispersion of lipolytic products. Carbohydrate absorption may be abnormal and impaired glucose, galactose and fructose absorption may occur. An impaired D-xylose tolerance is found in some patients with bacterial overgrowth. It is possible that the unconjugated bile salts have an inhibitory influence on sugar absorption. Protein deficiency and hypoproteinaemia can develop as a consequence of either the bacterial degradation of the intraluminal proteins or from the inhibitory effect of the unconjugated bile salts on amino acid transport in the intestinal cell. A variety of bacteria can compete with intrinsic factor for the binding of vitamin B_{12}. Because many bacteria can synthesize folic acid it is rare to have a deficiency of this vitamin. Over-growth of faecal type organisms in the small bowel is also responsible for the production of excess intestinal gas, particularly hydrogen. This is produced from bacterial fermentation of unabsorbed sugars.

Bacterial overgrowth is the common factor in a variety of gastrointestinal disorders associated with fat malabsorption. Any condition reducing or abolishing gastric acidity will enhance bacterial overgrowth. After partial gastrectomy or vagotomy and a drainage procedure there is rapid colonization of the upper small intestine. Long afferent

TABLE VI. *Effects of Bacterial Overgrowth in the Small Intestine*

Substrate	Effect	Result
Bile salts	Deconjugation	Free bile acids
	Dehydroxylation	Secondary bile acids
Tryptophan	Hydrolysis	Indoles
Amino acids	Deamination	Protein deficiency
	Deamidation	Free fatty acids
Vitamins	Binding of intrinsic factor to vitamin B_{12}	Vitamin B_{12} deficiency
	Synthesis of folic acid	Elevated serum levels
Carbohydrates	Utilization of D-xylose	Impaired D-xylose absorption
	Disaccharide malabsorption	Lactic acid and CO_2
Fatty acids	Addition of H_2O to double bond of unsaturated fatty acid	Hydroxy fatty acids in stool

loops are particularly prone to bacterial contamination. Patients with multiple duodenal and small intestinal diverticula frequently present with fat malabsorption and occasionally this may be a complication of the isolated diverticulum. Strictures, fistulas and partial obstruction of the small intestine also predispose to bacterial overgrowth by interfering with the flow of intestinal contents. About one-third of patients with Crohn's disease manifest the effects of excessive bacterial proliferation. Some patients with terminal ileal resection will have bacterial overgrowth in the rest of the small bowel. It is likely that the malabsorption associated with the primary motor disorders of the intestine, such as scleroderma and diabetes mellitus, is due to the effect of bacterial overgrowth. Abnormal bacterial colonization of the small bowel also occurs after irradiation of the abdomen, in patients with cholangitis, in cirrhotic patients with portasystemic encephalopathy and in patients with protein–calorie malnutrition.

The diagnosis is established by siphonage of the intestinal contents and demonstrating either the bacteria or their

TABLE VII. *Diagnostic Methods for the Contaminated Bowel Syndrome*

Test	Result
Intubation studies	Increased bacterial growth
	Increased unconjugated bile salts
	Increased secondary bile salts
	Increased free fatty acids
Stool	Increased fat
	Increased hydroxy fatty acids
Breath	$^{14}CO_2$
Urine	Increased indoles

metabolic effects (Table VII). Specimens must be cultured on selective and non-selective media.

Free bile salts may be demonstrated in the duodenal aspirate but a recent technique measures bile salt deconjugation by monitoring the quantity of exhaled $^{14}CO_2$ after the ingestion of a meal containing ^{14}C glycocholic acid. Increased $^{14}CO_2$ means either bacterial overgrowth or terminal ileal dysfunction so that more bile acids are in contact with colonic organisms, or both situations. But a negative breath test excludes stasis and bacterial colonization. The measurement of urinary indican, a metabolic breakdown product of tryptophan, is commonly taken to reflect bacterial activity in the small bowel, but an elevated excretion is unfortunately misleading and levels may be normal in the presence of bacterial overgrowth. Because the bacteria may metabolize xylose the D-xylose excretion test may be abnormally low when there is bacterial contamination and the patient may be erroneously thought to have a mucosal defect in the small intestine.

Malabsorption Associated with Skin Disease

Four associations are recognized between abnormalities of the skin and the gut:

1. A rash secondary to the malabsorption as in coeliac disease and tropical sprue.
2. The skin and the gut are both involved in the same pathological process as in the collagenoses.
3. The skin disease causes malabsorption (dermatogenic enteropathy).
4. The skin and gut lesions are indirectly related as in dermatitis herpetiformis.

Dermatogenic enteropathy is frequently encountered in patients with extensive eczema and psoriasis. Although bowel symptoms may be mild, steatorrhoea is frequent and other tests of malabsorption, such as D-xylose and vitamin B_{12} levels, are abnormal. The malabsorption disappears rapidly in those patients whose rash responds to treatment. Intestinal biopsies in these patients are normal.

Proximal intestinal abnormalities are almost invariable in dermatitis herpetiformis and histology of the mucous membrane of the small intestine is indistinguishable from coeliac disease. The lesion is patchy and less marked in the distal small bowel. The patients do not necessarily have the symptoms of malabsorption but the mucosal abnormality responds readily to gluten withdrawal, whereas the skin lesions respond slightly if at all.

Other Causes of Fat Malabsorption

IN NEWBORN INFANTS

Newborn and premature infants exhibit malabsorption of fat which is most marked with cow's milk. There is immature pancreatic function but more significantly the bile salt pool size is reduced and the intraduodenal bile salt concentrations are low.

VITAMIN B_{12} DEFICIENCY

Changes in intestinal mucosal structure and function occur in patients with B_{12} deficiency. These are accompanied by steatorrhoea of a mild degree, D-xylose malabsorption and impaired absorption of B_{12} intrinsic factor complex. It may take up to 2 months after instituting vitamin B_{12} therapy before intestinal function returns to normal.

DRUGS

Fat malabsorption has been reported following the use of a number of drugs, including neomycin, para-amino-salicylic acid, contraceptive pills, phenindione and large doses of calcium salts. Neomycin may interrupt normal fat digestion and absorption in a number of ways, including damaging the small bowel mucosa, inhibiting pancreatic lipase and combining with free fatty acids and thereby disrupting micelle formation. Cholestyramine causes fat malabsorption by binding bile acids. Malabsorption of fat-soluble vitamins occurs and hypoprothrombinaemia may ensue.

AMYLOIDOSIS

Amyloidosis may be associated with fat malabsorption. The infiltration of the submucosa by amyloid deposits can be diagnosed by a small bowel biopsy. The amyloid tissue may interfere with the absorptive processes but contributing mechanisms include abnormal intestinal motility and bacterial overgrowth.

ABETALIPOPROTEINAEMIA

Abetalipoproteinaemia (acanthocytosis) is a rare cause of fat malabsorption. The syndrome consists of steatorrhoea, atypical retinitis pigmentosa, 'spiny' or 'thorny' red blood cells (acanthocytes), an absence of β-lipoproteins in the blood, reduced serum cholesterol concentration and disturbances of neurological function involving particularly the cerebellum, posterior columns and the peripheral nerves. The small bowel morphology is characteristic, for the jejunal mucosa is engorged by fat-containing molecules. In the absence of the β-lipoproteins the protein coat of the chylomicrons cannot be formed and the absorbed long-chain triglycerides cannot leave the intestinal cells. There is no satisfactory therapy, but a diet in which medium-chain triglycerides are substituted for the long-chain fatty acids has proved beneficial.

SYSTEMIC MASTOCYTOSIS

Another rare cause for intestinal malabsorption is systemic mastocytosis. In this disease there is excessive proliferation of mast cells and the patient presents with urticaria pigmentosa, flushing, headache, tachycardia, nausea and diarrhoea. Some patients show malabsorption of fat, sugar and vitamin B_{12}. The small bowel biopsy shows an increase in the mast cells but normal villi. The mechanism of the malabsorption is uncertain but some patients respond to gluten withdrawal.

Sugar Intolerance

About half the calorie intake in man is from carbohydrate sources made up of 60% starch, 30% sucrose and 10%

lactose. The starch is mainly in the form of amylopectin and this is broken down by salivary and pancreatic α-amylases to α-dextrins, maltriose and maltose; this hydrolysis takes place in the intestinal lumen. Intraluminal hydrolysis of the oligosaccharides and dietary disaccharides does not occur to any extent. On the other hand it is also unlikely that the disaccharides enter the intestinal cell prior to hydrolysis and it is believed that the enzyme activity is confined to the membrane of the intestinal cell brush border. A simplified list of carbohydrate mucosal enzymes is given in Table VIII.

TABLE VIII. *Outline of Carbohydrate Digestion in Man*

Substrate	Enzyme	Product
Maltose	Maltase	Glucose
Maltriose	Maltase	Glucose
α-Dextrins	α-Dextrinase	Glucose
Lactose	Lactase	Glucose + galactose
Sucrose	Sucrase	Glucose + fructose

Disaccharidase activity is maximal in the upper jejunum and appreciably lower in the duodenum and ileum. The major end product of carbohydrate digestion is glucose, which accounts for 85% of the total monosaccharide load. Both glucose and galactose are absorbed by an active transport process which is sodium dependent. It is postulated that glucose and galactose are bound to a 'carrier' which transports these sugars across the lipid–protein membrane. Fructose is absorbed at a slower rate and independently of glucose. It probably has a separate carrier mechanism.

A number of disease states are characterized by the absence of disaccharidases. Primary deficiency of enzymes is uncommon, lactase deficiency being clinically the most important. Maltose deficiency is rare because of the presence of multiple maltases. Sugar malabsorption is often secondary to small intestinal disease, for example coeliac disease in which lactase deficiency is particularly prevalent. Maldigestion of starch due to pancreatic disease is rare in adults.

LACTASE DEFICIENCY (LACTOSE INTOLERANCE)

In man and virtually all other mammalian species lactase activity declines markedly after infancy to very low levels. The exceptions are those people of northern European descent and those of Hamitic origin who have consumed milk for several thousand years and in whom high intestinal lactase activity is believed to have had a selective evolutionary advantage. Lactose intolerance is therefore a state affecting those who ingest more milk than their enzyme system can manage. But the majority of lactase deficient subjects—90% of the population in many areas of the world—do not drink milk and therefore are untroubled by symptoms.

The bowel symptoms which follow milk ingestion in otherwise healthy subjects have been ascribed to milk protein allergy; but while such a disorder may exist the usual cause for the upset is a primary or isolated lactase deficiency. The frequency of the enzyme defect is uncertain but claims have been made that the disorder may be detected in 6–20% of white Americans and 60–75% of American Negroes. Racial differences in the incidence are suggested by the greater frequency of lactose intolerance in American Negroes, certain African tribes, Greek Cypriots, Australian Aborigines and South American Indians. The disorder affects males and females equally. It may present in a delayed or incomplete form.

The symptoms include abdominal discomfort, cramps, flatulence, abdominal distension and diarrhoea which typically occurs 1–2 hours after drinking milk. The amount of milk which may give rise to symptoms varies from $\frac{1}{2}$ to 3 glasses. The relationship of the symptoms to the ingestion of milk is not always apparent; thus a lack of history of milk intolerance does not exclude the diagnosis of lactase deficiency and conversely milk intolerance is not necessarily associated with lactase deficiency. The diarrhoea is the result of non-absorbed lactose passing into the colon where it is partly hydrolysed by bacterial lactase and undergoes bacterial fermentation; this produces excess gas and irritating metabolic products. The faeces contain intact lactose, glucose, galactose and lactic and acetic acids. The sugars exert an osmotic effect, while lactic and acetic acid have an irritating effect, and these factors in combination are responsible for the diarrhoea. Steatorrhoea is not a feature of lactase deficiency. The stool pH may fall from the normal neutral values to as low as 4.5; however, this does not always happen and stool pH measurements are not a reliable method for establishing the diagnosis.

The diagnosis is made from the history and a variety of laboratory tests. A lactose tolerance test can be performed in which 50–100 g of lactose are ingested and capillary blood glucose values determined. Patients with lactase deficiency do not have an increase in blood glucose values greater than 20 mg/100 ml (1.1 mmol) from baseline values. A glucose tolerance test is normal. Equally helpful is the development of symptoms during the test. A small bowel biopsy can be assayed for lactase activity which will be reduced, while the small bowel histology is normal in isolated, primary lactase deficiency. The diagnosis is suggested radiologically if barium mixed with 25 g of lactose is used. In lactase deficiency there is dilution of the contrast medium and active peristalsis in the distal small intestine. Lactose absorption can be assessed by measuring $^{14}CO_2$ output after the ingestion of ^{14}C-lactose.

The treatment is simply to avoid milk or milk products. Dietary items containing lactose which has already been fermented, such as yoghurt, may be taken without ill effect.

Lactase deficiency may complicate a number of gastro-intestinal disorders, such as coeliac disease, severe protein–

calorie malnutrition, ulcerative colitis, severe giardiasis, irritable colon syndrome, after severe gastroenteritis in children and after gastric surgery. In all these conditions lactase deficiency may contribute to the diarrhoea. If the underlying condition can be treated the intestinal lactase activity will return to normal.

SUCRASE–MALTASE DEFICIENCY

This is much less common than lactase deficiency. It is inherited as an autosomal recessive and occurs mainly in children. The symptoms are the same as in lactase deficiency and the management is to eliminate sucrose and amylopectin from the diet.

GLUCOSE–GALACTOSE MALABSORPTION

This is a rare condition inherited as an autosomal recessive. The monosaccharide sugars glucose and galactose cannot be transported by the intestinal cell and the treatment in such patients is to eliminate all dietary sugars except fructose.

Protein-Losing Gastroenteropathy

Some absorption of intact protein molecules can occur in the first few weeks of life but it is unlikely that significant protein absorption occurs in the adult. Normally albumin and other plasma proteins enter the lumen of the gastrointestinal tract and undergo digestion in common with all dietary proteins.

During the digestion of a protein-containing meal the small bowel contains a mixture of partially digested proteins, peptides and amino acids. It is probable that some peptide absorption occurs normally in man and this is hydrolysed in the cytoplasm of the intestinal absorptive cell by specific peptidases to form free amino acids. Naturally occurring L-amino acids which are released into the gut lumen during digestion are transported across the intestinal cell wall by an active transport process in which a carrier is thought to be involved. The amino acids can be classed into four groups, each of which has a specific transport mechanism: neutral amino acids, dibasic amino acids, dicarboxylic amino acids and the imino acid and glycine group. The rate of hydrolysis of protein is rapid and the amino acids are rapidly absorbed and transported via the portal blood. Defects in amino acid absorption are present in Hartnup disease (tryptophan malabsorption) and cystinuria (malabsorption of the dibasic amino acids).

Protein-losing gastroenteropathy should be regarded as an exaggeration of the normal process whereby protein leaks into the bowel to be digested and absorbed. If the loss is not too great and the absorptive mechanisms are unimpaired there will often be complete reabsorption of the amino acids and the plasma protein concentration will be unaltered. If the loss of proteins and peptides in the stool is sufficiently great the liver is unable to synthesize new protein sufficiently rapidly and the plasma concentration falls until a new steady state is reached between hepatic production and bowel loss. The proteins most affected are those with a slow turnover such as albumin and the γ-globulins. These proteins are markedly reduced in the blood, whereas fibrinogen and lipoprotein concentrations are virtually normal.

Patients with protein-losing gastroenteropathy present with oedema, ascites and hypoproteinaemia. Many will have complaints related to the underlying disease which is causing the protein leak into the gut. Frequently the conditions are also associated with fat malabsorption. The diagnostic tests are directed towards demonstrating the excessive loss of protein into the gut and determining the underlying pathology. Nitrogen balance techniques and immunochemical analysis of the gastrointestinal secretions give qualitative results. Quantitation of the protein loss can be achieved using a variety of radioactive-labelled agents including ^{131}I-polyvinylpyrrolidone, ^{51}Cr-albumin, [67]Cu-caeruloplasmin and [59]Fedextran. A small bowel biopsy is required to determine the nature of the gut lesion.

Protein-losing gastroenteropathy may occur as a non-specific manifestation of disease in many disorders (Table IX). In many of these the low serum protein levels and oedema form only a small part of the general clinical picture; in others oedema is the major and at times the only manifestation of disease. Once nutritional, liver and renal diseases have been excluded in patients with hypoproteinaemia it is mandatory to investigate whether there is an excessive loss of protein into the bowel.

It is of some diagnostic value to classify patients into lymphocytopenic and non-lymphocytopenic groups. Included in the non-lymphocytopenic group are those patients in whom the protein loss is secondary to gastrointestinal inflammation, malignant disease, allergy or coeliac disease. On the other hand lymphocytopenia may be a prominent feature when the protein-losing state is associated with disorders of the small intestinal lymphatics: intestinal lymphangiectasia, Whipple's disease, some patients with Crohn's disease and constrictive pericarditis. The depletion of immunoglobulins and lymphocytes via the lymphatics in these patients leads to skin anergy and impaired homograft rejection. This group also has low transferrin and caeruloplasmin concentrations in the serum.

Intestinal Lymphangiectasia

This disease is characterized by dilated intestinal lymphatics, loss of protein into the gut, hypogammaglobulinaemia, hypoalbuminaemia and oedema, which is marked and often asymmetrical. Ascites is frequently present and may be chylous in character. Gastrointestinal symptoms are usually mild and while fat malabsorption may occur it is usually not severe. The most frequent

TABLE IX. *Causes of Protein-Losing Gastroenteropathy*

Gastric
      Cancer of the oesophagus
      Cancer of the stomach
      Atrophic gastritis
      Giant rugal hypertrophy
      Allergic gastroenteropathy

Small intestine
      Coeliac disease
      Crohn's disease
      Tropical sprue
      Whipple's disease
      Acute infectious enteritis
      Contaminated bowel syndrome
      Parasitic infections
      Intestinal lymphangiectasia
      Fistula between small bowel and the thoracic duct

Colon
      Ulcerative colitis
      Infective dysenteries
      Megacolon

Others
      Constrictive pericarditis
      Agammaglobulinaemia

complaints are of vomiting, mild diarrhoea and occasional abdominal pain. The basic lesion is dilatation of the lymphatic channels in the small intestine and this can be demonstrated by small bowel biopsy. Dilated channels are also present in the submucosa, serosa and mesentery of the small intestine. The lymphangiectasia may be congenital and there are abnormalities of the peripheral lymphatic vessels. Such patients often present in childhood. On the other hand dilated lymph channels may be acquired, as in Whipple's disease, Crohn's disease and constrictive pericarditis. The loss of lymphocytes and immunoglobulins into the bowel lumen induces a state of severe anergy and impaired homograft rejection.

The protein loss is established by radioisotope techniques and a small bowel biopsy is required to demonstrate the dilated lymphatics. Features on the barium meal suggestive of lymphangiectasia are enlarged small intestinal folds, minimal dilation of the bowel and dilution of the barium in the distal bowel. Nodular abnormalities may be recognized. Lymphangiography is also helpful. The appearances vary depending upon the underlying pathology and include either hypoplasia of lymphatics or dilated and varicose vessels. Abnormalities may also be seen in the abdominal lymph nodes and peripheral lymphatics in patients with the congenital disorder. Retrograde flow of lymph may be recognized and the contrast medium may eventually be seen to appear in the small bowel lumen.

The management of these patients is difficult; diuretics, repeated abdominal paracentesis and albumin infusions may all be required. Restriction of dietary fat is helpful not only in reducing the steatorrhoea but also in lessening the intestinal lymph loss. Substitution of the usual dietary fat by the medium-chain triglycerides is of benefit. Intestinal resection is of help if it can be demonstrated that only a short segment of intestine is affected.

ALLERGIC GASTROENTEROPATHY

The concept of gastrointestinal allergy remains uncertain. There is a rare syndrome affecting young children in which extreme hypoproteinaemia, anaemia and eosinophilia are associated with oedema and growth retardation. Excessive loss of protein into the gut can be demonstrated. The disorder is alleviated by steroid therapy or by the elimination of certain foods, particularly milk.

Further Reading

Alpers, D. H. and Kinzie, J. L. (1973) Regulation of small intestinal protein metabolism. *Gastroenterology*, **64**, 471–496.

Ament, M. E. et al. (1973) Structure and function of the gastrointestinal tract in primary immunodeficiency syndromes. *Medicine, Baltimore*, **52**, 227–248.

Bayless, T. M. et al. (1975) Lactose and milk intolerance: clinical implications. *New Engl. J. Med.*, **292**, 1156–1159.

Dissanayake, A. S. et al. (1974) Jejunal mucosal recovery in coeliac disease in relation to the degree of adherence to a gluten-free diet. *Q. Jl Med.*, **43**, 161–185.

Doe, W. F. (1972) The secretory immune system of the intestine. *Gut*, **13**, 572–578.

Gang, I. A. and Ockner, R. K. (1975) Intestinal metabolism of lipids and lipoproteins. *Gastroenterology*, **68**, 167–186.

Gray, G. M. (1975) Carbohydrate digestion and absorption. *New Engl. J. Med.*, **292**, 1225–1230.

Grossman, M. I. et al. (1974) Candidate hormones of the gut. *Gastroenterology*, **67**, 730–755.

Duthie, H. L. (1974) Electrical activity of gastrointestinal smooth muscle. *Gut*, **15**, 669–681.

James, O. F. W. et al. (1973) Assessment of the ^{14}C-glycocholic acid breath test. *Br. med. J.*, **iii**, 191–195.

Laurence, D. J. R. et al. (1972) Role of plasma carcino-embryonic antigen in diagnosis of gastrointestinal, mammary, and bronchial carcinomal. *Br. med. J.*, **iii**, 605–609.

Lindebaum, J. et al. (1974) Small-intestinal function in vitamin B_{12} deficiency. *Ann. int. Med.*, **80**, 326–331.

Lipkin, M. (1973) Proliferation and differentiation of gastrointestinal cells. *Physiol. Rev.*, **53**, 891–915.

Newman, A. (1974) Breath-analysis tests in gastroenterology. *Gut*, **15**, 308–323.

Roberts, S. H. and Douglas, A. P. (1976) Intestinal lymphangiectasia: the variability of presentation. *Q. Jl. Med.*, **45**, 39–48.

Wharton, B. A. (1974) Coeliac disease in childhood. *Br. J. Hosp. Med.*, October, 452–466.

Wills, M. R. (1973) Intestinal absorption of calcium. *Lancet*, **i**, 820–823.

6   Appendicitis

Appendicitis is the commonest disease of the gastro-intestinal tract and accounts for the largest number of hospital admissions for bowel disorder. 112 000 patients were admitted to hospitals in England and Wales with this diagnosis during 1966; this was twice as many as the next most common diseases, peptic ulcer and malignant neoplasms. The disease is frequent in America and Europe but rare in Africa and Asia.

The aetiology of appendicitis remains uncertain. Factors which may play a role include obstruction to the lumen of the appendix by faecoliths, parasites and foreign bodies. Constipation has been implicated as have the 'faulty' diets of Western cultures which are low in undigestible fibre content. It has been claimed that there is a relationship between appendicitis and acute respiratory infections. A great variety of organisms have been isolated from the inflamed appendix including streptococci, staphylococci, coliform organisms and clostridia. The pathology is that of an acute inflammation which may extend to the surface of the organ and cause a local peritonitis. An abscess may form and this may be around the appendix or may occur in the pelvis or subdiaphragmatic space. If the appendix is obstructed it becomes distended with pus and gangrene and rupture will ensue. When the obstructed appendix ruptures there is less likelihood of a localized abscess and the development of a diffuse spreading peritonitis is more probable.

Appendicitis commonly occurs between the ages of 10 and 50 years. It is rare in infants and uncommon in children and the elderly, when the diagnosis is difficult and there is a rise in the morbidity and mortality. The typical clinical features include the sudden onset of cramping central abdominal pain, nausea, vomiting and anorexia. Constipation is present in about 60% of patients. After some hours the pain moves to the right lower quadrant, becoming persistent, and at this stage the patient will be febrile. On examination the patient is flushed and may have a slightly furred tongue. Tachycardia is a more consistent sign than fever. There is tenderness on deep palpation of the abdomen and rebound tenderness is a helpful sign. The classic site is at McBurney's point but the precise area of tenderness and guarding depends upon the position of the appendix. Guarding implies local visceral peritonitis whereas rigidity is a later sign and indicates that the peritonitis involves the lining of the anterior abdominal wall. A moderate polymorphonuclear leucocytosis is present.

The typical features of appendicitis are not always encountered and this makes the disease so dangerous. Physical signs may be minimal in the early stages of the illness, in obese subjects and particularly when the appendix is lying in a retrocolic or pelvic position. Irritation of the rectum causes diarrhoea, irritation of the bladder causes frequency of micturition and there may be haematuria if the inflamed appendix abuts on the right ureter. Tenderness on rectal examination is a valuable sign, particularly in the diagnosis of pelvic appendicitis. Spasm of the obturator or the psoas muscles may be demonstrated, depending upon the position of the appendix.

The diagnosis of an appendicular abscess may be difficult because of overlying guarding and rigidity, but the patient will be toxic and have a swinging temperature. When there is a pelvic abscess abdominal signs are minimal but diarrhoea is usually present and a tender boggy mass will be identified on rectal examination. If diffuse peritonitis develops there is a tendency for the pain to become reduced while at the same time the patient becomes gravely ill with vomiting, ileus, fever, tachycardia and hypotension. Rarely internal or external fistulas occur.

The differential diagnosis includes a number of acute intra-abdominal diseases. Acute non-specific mesenteric adenitis frequently presents with an identical clinical picture although central abdominal pain is often of longer duration, being present for some days; tenderness is located just to the right of the umbilicus. However the distinction between the two conditions is often difficult so that if there is any doubt a laparotomy should be performed. Acute ileitis due to Crohn's disease may cause confusion (p. 126). In acute pyelonephritis the pain is more persistent, fever is more marked and the urine is abnormal. Acute cholecystitis (p. 335) is usually accompanied by right upper quadrant pain, but the distinction between a high retro-colic appendix and an inflamed gall bladder may be impossible. A history of dysmenorrhoea, menorrhagia or vaginal discharge is suggestive of acute salpingitis and a tubovarian mass may be detected on rectal or vaginal examination. Other conditions which may mimic acute appendicitis include perforated duodenal ulcer with tracking of material down the right paracolic gutter, twisted right ovarian cyst and right basal pneumonia.

The diagnosis of appendicitis in infants and young children presents many difficulties. In infants suggestive diagnostic features include vomiting, fever, diarrhoea, crying fits and clutching at the abdomen with flexing of the thighs. The disease is readily confused with gastro-enteritis and the delay in hospital admission of children under 3 years with appendicitis is twice as long as for older children. Not surprisingly the appendix has perforated in about 80% of children under the age of 2 years by the time an operation is performed. Appendicitis in older children is a somewhat easier diagnosis as the classical clinical features are seen more frequently. Nonetheless the story may be atypical; diarrhoea and headache are not infrequent and the absence of fever may be misleading, but pain aggravated by movement is suggestive of appendicitis. The differential diagnosis in children includes acute non-specific mesenteric adenitis, which is commoner in children than in adults, acute urinary tract infection and acute tonsillitis. Children are prone to develop acute non-specific abdominal pain. Psychological disturbances in children frequently manifest with abdominal pain.

Once the diagnosis of acute appendicitis has been made the patient requires surgical treatment. The patient is prepared for operation by attention to the state of hydration, and analgesics are administered. It is argued whether antibiotic therapy is required for the uncomplicated patient and whether the use of antibiotics increases the chance of postoperative wound infection. Antibiotic therapy will always be necessary when there is generalized peritonitis. Peritoneal drainage is usually unnecessary if appendix is intact. The majority of surgeons recommend early operation for an appendix abscess and peritoneal drainage is undertaken with or without appendicectomy. The prognosis is excellent for the patient who undergoes early operation and the morbidity and mortality are very low. At present the mortality rate in the United Kingdom is 0.2% for uncomplicated appendicitis. The prognosis changes once peritonitis has ensued and the mortality rate rises to over 1% if peritonitis is localized and to around 3% when there is diffuse peritonitis. The outlook is less satisfactory in the very young or the aged and about 75% of all deaths occur in patients under 4 years or over 70 years of age.

The one factor that is particularly responsible for improving the prognosis is early operation which reduces the risk of peritonitis. Thus if there is any doubt about the diagnosis and there are no significant contraindications to surgery it is probably safest to submit the patient to a laparotomy. However, careful judgment must always be exercised in order to avoid unnecessary operations. An expectant approach may be adopted when the problem is that of abdominal pain in the absence of any features suggestive of peritoneal irritation; but implicit in this approach is the careful observation of the patient. If there are any signs of peritonitis then there will be no question that a laparotomy is indicated even if the origin of the underlying inflammation is uncertain.

Chronic Appendicitis

This is a controversial entity. Although pathological evidence for chronic appendicitis may be found it is doubtful whether there is an associated clinical syndrome. Recurrent abdominal pain located in the low right side of the abdomen and unaccompanied by local or systematic manifestations of inflammation must not be labelled chronic appendicitis. At operation these patients frequently have a normal appendix. The pain is likely to recur despite an appendicectomy and in many patients the cause of the pain is the irritable bowel syndrome or some emotional disorder.

7   Crohn's Disease

Crohn's disease is characterized by non-caseating granulomatous inflammation of the bowel which is distinguishable from tuberculosis. It is known by a variety of names including Crohn's disease, regional enteritis, terminal ileitis, granulomatous ileocolitis and granulomatous colitis. Since there may be difficulty differentiating Crohn's disease from ulcerative colitis both are often included in the term 'chronic inflammatory bowel disease'.

The aetiology is unknown. No bacterium or protozoon has been isolated from affected tissue but recent studies have implicated a viral agent. Patients with Crohn's disease show deficiencies in delayed-type hypersensitivity which presumably indicate impaired thymus-dependent cellular immunity. At present it seems possible that the disease is associated with an abnormal immune response in the gut wall. However, studies on the immune response in patients indicates that it is qualitatively normal when assessed by the response to skin test antigens, lymphocyte transformation and enumeration of circulating T and B lymphocytes.

The pathological features include thickening of the submucosa, ulceration, muscle hypertrophy, dilatation of the lymphatics and dense fibrosis. In contrast to ulcerative colitis which affects the mucosa and submucosa, Crohn's disease involves the full thickness of the bowel wall. The adjacent mesentery is hyperaemic and the lymph nodes are enlarged and oedematous. There is a marked tendency to fistula and abscess formation. The lesions may be single or there may be multiple affected areas separated by normal bowel—'skip lesions'. All parts of the gastrointestinal tract are affected. Microscopic examination of the Crohn's tissue reveals transmural inflammation, dilated lymphatics and oedema. Lymphoid granulomas are found deep in the submucosa, muscularis mucosa and on the serosal surface. The granulomas are formed by lymphocytes, epitheloid cells and the occasional giant cell. There is no caseation. Granulomas may also be demonstrated in the lymph nodes.

The disease affects males and females equally, the usual age of onset being 20–40 years. The incidence has been estimated to be between 0.8 and 1.5 per 100 000 for England and Scotland and the frequency of the disease is increasing. It is claimed that Crohn's disease is more common in the Jewish race and uncommon in non-white people. The disease may occur in families; Crohn's disease and ulcerative colitis tend to coexist in the same family and there is an association between Crohn's disease and ankylosing spondylitis.

Crohn's Disease Involving the Small Intestine

The disease may manifest as an acute illness or in a subacute form. Typically the inflammation involves the terminal ileum (Plate VI. Figs 1 and 2).

ACUTE ILEITIS

The clinical presentation is similar to acute appendicitis with sharp right lower quadrant pain, tenderness, guarding, fever and leucocytosis. This form of the disease accounts for about 10% of all patients.

SUBACUTE AND CHRONIC JEJUNOILEITIS

Diffuse involvement of the small intestine is the most serious form of the disease and has many clinical variants. About 87% of the patients complain of pain, 66% have diarrhoea, 55% have weight loss, 37% anorexia, 36% fever, 35% vomiting, 32% lassitude, 25% present as an acute abdomen, 24% have malnutrition and 15% have fistulas. The diarrhoea may be a manifestation of steatorrhoea which develops because of interruption of the enterohepatic circulation of the bile salts owing to destruction of the specific sites for bile salt absorption in the ileum; fat malabsorption also accompanies the excessive deconjugation of bile salts which follows bacterial overgrowth in the small intestine. In either situation there is an intraluminal deficiency of conjugated bile salts and if the hepatic synthesis cannot compensate sufficiently then fat maldigestion and malabsorption occurs. Secondary lactose intolerance occasionally contributes to the diarrhoea. Protein-losing gastroenteropathy occurs when there is secondary intestinal lymphangiectasia and loss of lymph. Thus hypoproteinaemia oedema and anaemia and hypocholesterolaemia may be present.

The malabsorption affects not only bile salts and fat but also vitamin B_{12}, electrolytes, water, iron and folic acid. Malnutrition is an important feature of the disease and follows a reduced dietary intake, an increased nutritional requirement and malabsorption.

The chronic inflammatory process may manifest as a palpable abdominal mass representing adherent loops of bowel which are often matted about an abscess. Intermittent abdominal pain can occur from inflammation or obstruction. Fistulas, either internal or external, may be a presenting manifestation of the illness or develop after some years. Vesicocolic and jejunocolic fistulas are not uncommon. The development of a faecal fistula contributes to the general debility and electrolyte imbalance. Occasional complications include perforation and massive haemor-rhage. There are indications that patients with Crohn's disease have an increased tendency to small intestinal and pancreatic cancers.

Anal lesions are frequent and are found in patients with the disease localized to the small bowel as well as those in which the disease is mainly in the large bowel. Involvement of the anal region presents as skin tags, perianal and peri-rectal abscesses or fistulas. Tenesmus, bleeding and diarrhoea are the usual complaints.

Crohn's Disease Involving the Colon

For every 100 patients with Crohn's disease of the bowel about 25 will have only small intestine involvement, 25 will have the disease limited to the colon, 45 will have both large and small gut affected and the remainder will have solely anorectal disease. Colonic disease is usually seg-mental, involving the transverse or ascending colon, but the whole of the colon may be diseased (Plate VI. Fig. 3).

Patients with Crohn's disease of the colon have many clinical features in common with ulcerative colitis. There is diarrhoea and the stools often contain pus, blood and mucus; other features include abdominal pain, fever, anaemia and weight loss. Stricture formation is character-istic and may lead to subacute obstruction. Acute fulmi-nating episodes and toxic dilatation of the colon are unusual. Patients with colonic Crohn's disease have an increased risk of developing cancer of the colon. Anal complications such as abscesses and fistulas are common although fresh rectal bleeding is unusual. Typically the rectum is nodular and rigid and the mucosa is thickened, oedematous and much pus is visible, but rectal examination and sigmoido-scopy may be normal in up to 50% of patients with colonic disease.

Extraintestinal Features

The clinical picture of Crohn's disease may be dominated by a number of systemic manifestations of the illness, including iritis, fever, aphthous stomatitis and erythema nodosum. In addition to an increased incidence of recurrent ophthous ulcers involvement of the oral mucous membrane by Crohn's disease manifests as hyperplasia of the mucosa with deep fissures and a cobblestone appearance. There are many similarities between the extraintestinal manifestations of Crohn's disease and those associated with ulcerative colitis. Arthritis may take the form of a subacute asymmetrical migratory polyarthritis of one or two weeks' duration. The knees and ankles are usually affected. There is an association between the activity of the bowel disease and the arthropathy. Another manifestation of arthritis is ankylosing spondylitis which may either precede or follow the bowel disorder. The spondylitis may be mild or, unlike the other form of joint involvement, it may be severe and crippling. Whereas the peripheral arthritis is specific to inflammatory bowel disease studies with the histocompatibility antigen (HL-A) W27 indicate that 75% of patients with inflammatory bowel disease and ankylosing spondylitis are W27 positive thus suggesting the occurrence of two associated diseases.

The liver is frequently abnormal and the disorder appears to be unrelated to the site and extent of the bowel involvement. Biochemical evidence of disturbed liver function occurs in 25% of patients. Bromsulphthalein retention is the test most frequently abnormal but elevated levels of serum aspartate transaminase, alkaline phosphatase and 5′ nucleotidase are encountered. Histological abnormalities are demonstrated in about 90% of patients who are examined and are not necessarily accompanied by biochemical evidence of liver dysfunction. The commonest changes are pericholangitis, focal necrosis, fatty change and minor degrees of portal fibrosis. Frank cirrhosis is rare. Other changes include sclerosing cholangitis, granulomas, amyloid deposition, microabscesses and pylephlebitis. There is no satisfactory explanation for the hepatic involvement which is very similar to that encountered in ulcerative colitis.

Renal complications include hydronephrosis and calculi. The stones are usually formed of uric acid crystals and are believed to result from a decreased urinary volume, decreased urinary pH, hypokalaemia and renal tract infection. There is also an increased tendency to form oxalate stones.

Recent evidence suggests that there is an increased incidence of gall stones, although the stones seldom produce symptoms.

Skin reactions in Crohn's disease may be altered. Many patients are negative to tuberculin 1:100 and show a depression of delayed type hypersensitivity reactions. Some authors report that up to 50% of patients have a positive reaction to the Kveim test.

Diagnosis

The diagnosis is based on histology and the radiological features. Unfortunately neither method is infallible and Crohn's disease is frequently suspected without conclusive proof being obtained. Material for histology may be obtained either at operation or from a rectal biopsy. The rectal biopsy is a useful technique, particularly since the naked-eye distinction between Crohn's disease and ulcerative colitis may be impossible. Biopsies characteristic of Crohn's disease may be taken from the rectum even when the disease is restricted clinically to the small bowel.

The most reliable indications of small bowel disease on a barium examination are contraction of the lumen and rigidity. Other signs include mucosal ulceration, 'spicules' extending into the bowel wall for a depth of not less than 2 mm, 'cobblestone' appearance, skip lesions, eccentric involvement, stenosis, obstruction, longitudinal and transverse ulcers, sinus tracts and fistulas. Oedema, irritability and spasm of the terminal ileum at an early stage produce narrowing and rigidity—the 'string' sign (Plate VI. Fig. 1). This sign indicates disease which is reversible and must not be confused with the fixed fibrosed and rigid intestine which is found in the chronic stage. Radiological signs of colonic involvement are similar to those in the small bowel: skip areas, ulceration, transverse fissures, asymmetrical involvement and pseudodiverticula.

In the acute phase the differential diagnosis includes appendicitis, mesenteric adenitis, yersiniosis, salpingitis and diverticular disease. Acute terminal ileitis may be due to *Yersinia* infection, but often there is no obvious cause. Only long-term follow-up can distinguish between this latter group and patients with Crohn's disease. The diagnosis is frequently made only at the time of surgery. Crohn's disease is an important consideration in a patient suffering from malabsorption. The condition must be differentiated from coeliac disease (Table IV, p. 92) but in the latter disorder pain and fever are absent, there is dilatation of the loops of barium-filled bowel and the small bowel biopsy will show the loss of villus structure. The distinction from ileocaecal tuberculosis is made with difficulty and is established with certainty only after surgical biopsy and culture. Cancer of the colon and malignant disease of the small bowel, particularly lymphoma, are usually distinguished on radiological grounds. There is much difficulty in differentiating between Crohn's disease of the colon and ulcerative colitis (Table XI, p. 144). A clinical, radiological and histological overlap exists between these two diseases and there are many patients who cannot be fitted neatly into one diagnosis. Ulcerative colitis is characterized clinically by frequent rectal bleeding, the tendency to have an acute or fulminating course, the development of cancer in a large number of patients and the frequency with which the rectum is involved. Radiologically ulcerative colitis is usually recognized on the left side of

TABLE X. *The Differential Diagnosis of Strictures in the Colon*

Disease	Features of Stricture
Annular cancer	Usually 3–4 cm in length; destruction of mucosa; shouldered ends
Diverticular disease	Usually more than 6 cm in length; preservation of mucosal folds; tapered ends
Ischaemic colitis	Usually at splenic flexure; variable length; tapered ends; 'thumb printing'; asymmetrical; may be transient
Ulcerative colitis	Rare; concentric; asymmetrical; tapered ends
Crohn's disease	Common; variable length; concentric; tapered ends; distinguish from ulcerative colitis by other radiological features suggestive of ulcerative colitis v. Crohn's disease
Irradiation	Usually in sigmoid; long segment; tapered ends; mucosal ulceration; 'thumb printing'
Tuberculosis	Long segment; tapered ends; symmetrical; shortening of ascending colon; loss of ileo-caecal angle
Cathartic colon	'Pseudostrictures'; variable appearance during examination; atonic colon; dilated in parts; devoid of haustration
Lymphogranuloma venereum	Rectum and sigmoid involved; long tubular stricture; tapered upper limit
Extrinsic pressure	Long segment; palpable mass
Colonic infiltration (metastases)	Displacement and stretching; later narrowing; nodularity
Endometriosis	As for metastases, but the mucosa is intact

the colon, the bowel contour is symmetrical, fistulas and strictures are rare and established ileal inflammation does not occur. In ulcerative colitis a short segment of terminal ileum abutting on the ileocaecal valve may be dilated, whereas in Crohn's disease there is narrowing of the ileal lumen with destruction of the mucosa. The differential diagnosis of colonic strictures is given in Table X.

Treatment

The treatment of Crohn's disease is difficult and unsatisfactory because of the very variable clinical course and the marked tendency for the disease to recur. Common to all therapeutic approaches is prompt attention to the state of nutrition with replacement of blood, restoration of the fluid and electrolyte balance and correction of vitamin deficiencies. Diarrhoea can be treated with codeine phosphate but anticholinergic preparations must be used with care as they may predispose to intestinal obstruction. A low-fat diet, supplemented with medium-chain triglycerides if necessary, is of benefit when steatorrhoea is present. A milk-free diet is required if lactose intolerance is demonstrated. Antibiotic therapy is of little value unless intestinal bacterial overgrowth is present. At present specific drug therapy for Crohn's disease comprises either corticosteroids alone or in combination with the immunosuppressive agent, azathioprine. There is no agreed therapeutic regimen and it is disputed whether either drug alone or in combination is beneficial. Indeed some authorities do not use either agent in the management of Crohn's disease. The few clinical trials have given conflicting results but demonstrate at least that azathioprine has a steroid-sparing effect. A suggested therapeutic programme is the combination of 40 mg prednisolone and 2 mg/kg azathioprine orally daily for one month. Thereafter the dose of prednisolone is reduced gradually to 15 mg daily and maintained for a further 3 months. Azathioprine is continued for one year and then withdrawn.

Patients require careful surveillance because of the many potential side-effects, but the above regimen has proved easy to manage and has few attendant haematological problems. It may be necessary to alter the dose schedule if an exacerbation of the disease occurs. It is doubtful whether sulphasalazine (Salazopyrin, Azulfidine) has any useful role.

The majority of patients will require an operation at some stage of their illness. The usual indication is intestinal obstruction but surgery may be necessary for haemorrhage or perforation. The usual procedure is to resect the diseased segment of bowel. Considerable problems arise in patients who have many operations, for this will inexorably lead to a situation in which there is insufficient small bowel left for normal digestion and absorption. Thus conservative surgery is advocated at all times. Since it may not be possible to distinguish acute Crohn's ileitis from the idiopathic group of acute ileitis, and since patients with acute Crohn's ileitis do not appear to progress frequently into the chronic disease, if acute ileal inflammation is found at laparotomy, no resection is necessary. The appendix may be removed with safety because there is no increased chance of developing a fistula.

Extensive colonic involvement necessitates a total colectomy but if the rectum is free of disease an ileorectal anastomosis may be satisfactory. However, the long-term prognosis is often unfavourable because the disease tends to recur in the anal stump. Segmental colonic disease is treated by local resection if possible but again there is the risk of a recurrence.

Postoperative recurrences usually occur at the site of anastomosis. Recurrence is commoner in the small intestine and the risk is greater in patients who have developed the disease in their youth. About 80% of recurrences will occur within 5 years of the initial operation and 24% of patients with ileal involvement will go on to develop disease in the colon. Fifteen years after the initial operation the recurrence rate is over 90%. The need for reoperation does not diminish with each operation; thus Crohn's disease becomes more dangerous with time and the overall mortality rate is around 10%.

Further Reading

Dyer, N. H. and Dawson, A. M. (1970) Diagnosis of Crohn's disease. A continuing source of error. *Br. med. J.*, **i**, 735–737.

Farmer, R. G. et al. (1975) Clinical patterns in Crohn's disease: a statistical study of 615 cases. *Gastroenterology*, **68**, 627–635.

Marshak, R. H. (1975) Granulomatous disease of the intestinal tract (Crohn's Disease). *Radiology*, **114**, 3–22.

Perrett, A. D. et al. (1971) The liver in Crohn's disease. *Q. Jl Med.*, **40**, 187–209.

Truelove, S. C. and Peña, A. S. (1976) Course and prognosis of Crohn's disease. *Gut*, **17**, 192–201.

Williams, J. A. (1971) The place of surgery in Crohn's disease. *Gut*, **12**, 739–749.

Ulcerative colitis is a non-specific inflammatory disease of the colon. Despite intensive study the aetiology remains obscure. There is no evidence that infection plays a primary role although bacterial invasion of a damaged mucosa may precipitate a relapse. It has been suggested that ulcerative colitis is the consequence of an allergic or hypersensitivity reaction by the colon but conclusive supporting evidence for this concept is lacking. Circulating antigens to milk may be demonstrated in some patients but their significance is debated. Psychological factors are probably only of secondary importance, leading to a relapse rather than initiating the disease. There is much dispute whether ulcerative colitis should be regarded as an auto-immune disease. Antibodies to fetal colonic mucosa can be demonstrated in some patients and the leucocytes from colitic subjects have a cytotoxic effect on fetal colonic cells. It has been argued that ulcerative colitis only develops in those individuals who have a polygenetic predisposition to the disease. There is a familial tendency to ulcerative colitis; furthermore there is a high incidence of eczema, hay fever, polyarthritis and ankylosing spondylitis in patients with ulcerative colitis and their relatives.

The whole or part of the colon may be involved by the inflammatory process. The commonest site is the rectosigmoid and descending colon. Inflammation may be limited to the distal 8–10 cm of colon (ulcerative proctitis) or there may be total colonic involvement. Right-sided colitis is rare. The lesion is essentially of the mucous membrane with loss of goblet cells, marked acute inflammatory cell infiltrate and crypt abscesses. In severe inflammation there is loss of the surface epithelium of the colon and this produces extensive shallow ulcers. The epithelial remnants appear as tags called pseudopolyps. Another mechanism for pseudopolyp formation is granulation tissue which projects into the bowel lumen. If the inflammation extends below the muscularis mucosa there will be loss of muscle tone and toxic dilatation of the colon may ensue. The disease is confined to the colon and the small intestine is not affected. When the ileocaecal valve is incompetent some retrograde spread of 'backwash' of colonic contents occurs and this causes dilatation of the terminal ileum but there is no permanent damage.

Ulcerative colitis affects all age groups but is most commonly encountered between 20 and 40 years. There is a slight female preponderance. It is claimed that prevalence rates are higher in Jews and in white compared to black people. Patients with ulcerative colitis are usually intelligent or highly educated.

The illness is not uncommon in pregnancy. Ulcerative colitis is frequently quiescent during the antenatal period but may be exacerbated in the puerperium. The pregnancy is generally unaffected by the colitis.

The disease may present in a number of ways and acute, subacute and chronic forms are recognized, the latter being subdivided into chronic intermittent and chronic continuous varieties. Characteristically there is diarrhoea with blood and mucus in the stool. The diarrhoea is often worse in the morning, the patient passing between 2 and 4 stools within an hour of rising and then having only 1 or 2 bowel actions during the rest of the day. On the other hand the patient may pass formed stools and some patients complain of constipation. Rectal bleeding is frequent. The abdomen is usually not tender but in severe colitis the bowel is tender to palpation, with guarding, and the colon may be slightly dilated.

The degree of systemic upset varies and is not necessarily related to the extent of the colonic inflammation. In general the very young and the aged tend to be more severely ill. The patient may appear well; on the other hand there may be nausea, vomiting, weight loss and fever. Patients who are severely affected will be toxic, febrile, anaemic, dehydrated and hypotensive. Attempts have been made to use various serum proteins such as orosomucoid and lysozyme as an index of activity but results have been conflicting and no better than the haemoglobin, white blood count and erythrocyte sedimentation rate.

A sigmoidoscopy is essential for the diagnosis. In severe involvement there is marked denudation of the mucous membrane. Although it is not possible to recognize actual ulceration, bleeding will be marked and a mucopurulent discharge evident. In milder forms of the disease there are mucosal oedema (recognized from the thickening of the rectal valves) and diffuse hyperaemia so that the normal mucosal vascular pattern is no longer recognizable. The mucous membrane is extremely friable and submucosal haemorrhages and bleeding readily occur when the mucosa is stroked by the end of the instrument or with a swab. When the disease is in an inactive phase the mucous membrane remains abnormal with a dry, dull and granular appearance; it is readily traumatized and polyps may be seen.

Complications

Local rectal complications are frequent and rectal examination reveals skin tags, fissures, fistulas or abscesses.

Colonic Complications

In addition to the rectal complications there are a number of serious complications involving the colon—toxic dilatation, perforation, haemorrhage and the development of cancer. Toxic dilatation is an ominous event indicative of extensive colonic disease with wide superficial ulceration. The essential feature is severe transmural destruction of circular and longitudinal muscle. The precipitating causes include anticholinergic drugs, narcotics, hypokalaemia and a barium enema. The patients are all critically ill with abdominal distension and diffuse tenderness, diminished peristaltic activity, fever, toxaemia and severe diarrhoea. The high mortality rate makes it essential that the diagnosis of toxic dilatation is made early. Regular gentle abdominal examinations are necessary and the abdominal girth should be measured. Daily plain radiographs of the abdomen will facilitate the early recognition of distension. Sigmoidoscopy is contraindicated.

Perforation of the colon usually occurs as a complication of toxic dilatation but occasionally perforation ensues in a bowel not obviously distended. The classical features of peritoneal soiling may be absent, particularly in critically ill patients or those receiving large doses of corticosteroids. The diagnosis may be suspected from unexplained fever or tachycardia and confirmed by a plain radiograph of the abdomen to demonstrate air under the diaphragm. A perforation which seals off locally may develop into a paracolic abscess. Occasionally a patient with apparently mild ulcerative colitis will develop a life-threatening rectal haemorrhage. Strictures, in contrast to Crohn's disease, are rare and are recorded in only 1% of patients. There is thickening and hypertrophy of the muscle rather than fibrosis and the appearance can be reversible. However, the demonstration of a stricture should always raise the possibility that a cancer has developed in the colitic bowel.

Patients with ulcerative colitis are at risk of developing

cancer of the colon. The risk is greatest when there is total colonic involvement and when the disease is longstanding and has followed a chronic continuous course. Thus the cancer risk is particularly marked when the illness has developed in childhood. The probability of malignant change becomes greater after 10 years of the disease and cancer occurs in 3% of colitics after 10 years, in 20% of those patients who have had the disease for 20 years and in 43% after 35 years. The cancers occur throughout the colon whereas cancer developing in an otherwise normal colon is more frequent in the rectosigmoid region. The growth is often multicentric in origin and there is a tendency to metastasize early. The prognosis is poor.

EXTRACOLONIC COMPLICATIONS

Between 0.5 and 1.3 g of iron (nearly a quarter of the total iron content of an adult) may be lost during an attack of ulcerative colitis, and iron deficiency anaemia is not uncommon. Loss of protein from the damaged mucosa is associated with hypoalbuminaemia.

A variety of skin lesions may be recognized. These include clubbing of the fingers and toes, erythema nodosum, papulonecrotic lesions and ulcerating erythematous plaques on the shins. Pyoderma gangrenosum is an uncommon but characteristic lesion and typically develops in severely ill patients although it is rarely present in the absence of obvious diarrhoea. There are ulcers on the lower limbs although sometimes other parts of the body are affected and these are typically undermined, irregular and have a bluish margin.

An arthropathy very similar to that observed in Crohn's disease occurs: either associated ankylosing spondylitis in patients who are positive for HL-A-W27, or a specific recurrent, asymmetrical acute peripheral arthropathy most commonly involving the knee or ankle. There are many similarities between the liver dysfunction which may be demonstrated in ulcerative colitis and that occurring in Crohn's disease. Liver disorder may be demonstrated in 15–95% of patients depending upon how the liver function is assessed. The usual histological changes are fatty infiltration, cellular infiltration, fibrosis and pericholangitis. Chronic liver disease, including active chronic hepatitis and cirrhosis, is unusual. Other hepatic complications include serum hepatitis, granulomas, sclerosing cholangitis, bile duct cancer, amyloidosis and hepatic abscesses. The abnormal histology is not always accompanied by disturbances of biochemical function and the most consistent alteration is an increased concentration of the serum alkaline phosphatase, which correlates with bile ductular proliferation; other changes include increased serum globulin levels and abnormal bromsulphthalein retention.

ULCERATIVE PROCTITIS

It is clinically useful to distinguish patients with ulcerative proctitis. This is a milder form of ulcerative colitis in which the inflammatory process is limited to the distal 13 cm of the colon. Sigmoidoscopic and barium studies provide evidence that the remainder of the large bowel is normal. Rectal bleeding is often the only complaint but there may be diarrhoea and tenesmus. Constitutional upset is slight and the patient rarely develops colonic and extracolonic complications. The clinical course is mild in over 90% of patients and complications occur in less than 10%. Spread of the inflammatory process to the rest of the colon occurs in under one-third of the patients.

Diagnosis

The diagnosis of ulcerative colitis is made by exclusion. Stool cultures are negative for known pathogens and all other causes for dysentery are excluded, such as cancer, diverticular disease, ischaemia and toxic and metabolic causes. Sigmoidoscopy is always necessary and at this time a biopsy is taken. There is not always a correlation between the sigmoidoscopic, radiological and histological features and the diagnosis is based upon a consideration of all three examinations. Once the disease has developed the mucous membrane remains permanently abnormal histologically despite the appearances to the contrary on sigmoidoscopy and radiology. The suggestion has been made that rectal biopsies may be of value in making a diagnosis of malignant change which has occurred at any site in the colon. Suspicious features are precancerous polyps and abnormal proliferation and distortion and dysplasia of the epithelium. It remains to be determined if all or only some of the patients with dysplastic features progress to cancer. Since the epithelial dysplasia is patchy, and may spare the rectum, multiple biopsies are necessary.

The radiological examination is of help in the diagnosis and assessment of patients. The plain film of the abdomen is particularly useful in the acute stage for it may be possible to see thickening of the colonic wall, loss of haustrations and a nodularity which indicates pseudopolyps. Colonic dilatation can be detected early and serial radiographs are essential in following the course of toxic dilatation. In chronic ulcerative colitis the colonic gas shadow may suggest the shortened bowel devoid of any haustral pattern.

A barium enema will indicate the presence of the inflammation. It is not very accurate in predicting the extent of the lesion. But it must be appreciated that this investigation is not essential for the diagnosis; it is not without hazard and therefore it is contraindicated in patients with acute ulcerative colitis. The preparation of the bowel must always be gentle. Typically there is symmetrical narrowing and shortening of the affected portion of the colon, haustrations are absent and pseudopolyps will be recognized (Plate VII). Skip lesions are not seen. The presence of fine spike-like projections of barium beyond the lumen indicates ulcer craters and this is an indication that the disease is active. Another sign of activity is confluent submucosal pools of barium—'confluent lacunar sepsis'. The radiological examination of the rectum is frequently helpful since it is rarely spared; the retrorectal (presacral) space is greater than 15 mm, indicating contraction of the rectum, the rectal valves are thickened and the rectal folds are irregular, distorted and thickened. The radiological recognition of a cancer superimposed upon colitic mucous membrane is extraordinarily difficult and the diagnosis is seldom made until the growth is fairly advanced.

Colonoscopy may be used in the diagnosis of ulcerative colitis. The two main advantages of the technique are to demonstrate the extent of the disease and in the early detection of cancer. Colonoscopy is also of help in distinguishing Crohn's disease and ulcerative colitis. The differential diagnosis is mainly from Crohn's disease of the colon. The distinguishing features are discussed on p. 131 and summarized in Table XI. Occasionally it is not possible to tell with certainty which form of colitis a patient has and these patients are best diagnosed as having 'inflammatory bowel disease'. Thus pseudopolyps may occur in both diseases and have similar appearances, collar-button ulceration is common to both, and while toxic dilatation is more frequent in ulcerative colitis it does occur in Crohn's colitis. Other disorders to consider include cancer, ischaemic colitis, tuberculosis, amoebiasis and rhistosomiasis.

Treatment

The successful treatment of patients with ulcerative colitis demands a high standard of medical and nursing care. Great attention is required to the physical and psychological needs of the patient. Difficult decisions may have to be taken regarding the timing of surgical intervention

TABLE XI. *The Differences Between Chronic Ulcerative Colitis and Crohn's Disease of the Colon*

Features	Ulcerative Colitis	Crohn's Disease
Clinical	Bloody stool frequent	Bloody stool uncommon
Anal lesions	Common	Commoner than ulcerative colitis
Rectal examination	Oedema	Rigid, nodular
Sigmoidoscopy	Bleeding; friable; oedema; no vascular pattern	Purulent, nodular
Barium enema	Continuity of lesions; shortening of the entire colon; left-sided mainly; irritable, spasm; serrations; pseudo-polps; strictures rare; terminal ileum dilated	Skip lesions; often right-sided; rigid; oedema; intramural fissures; pseudodiverticula; strictures frequent; terminal ileum narrowed
Cancer	Frequent	Very slight increase
Pathology	Superficial crypt abscesses	Oedema; granulomas; lymphoid hyperplasia; transverse fissures

and the disease is best managed by a team of physicians and surgeons.

Prompt attention to fluid and electrolyte balance can be life-saving; replacement of blood and protein is necessary. Abdominal pain and diarrhoea can be relieved with codeine phosphate. A warm pad on the abdomen frequently provides considerable relief from discomfort. No specific diet is required and the patient is encouraged to eat as much as possible. A few patients are lactose intolerant and therefore a trial of milk-free diet is of value. If there is no improvement within a few days the patient returns to the normal ward diet. Nasogastric suction and intravenous supplementation is required for the patient who vomits and presents signs of colonic ileus and dilatation.

Specific therapy consists of salicylazosulphapyridine (sulphasalazine) and corticosteroids. In general the steroids are administered orally or parenterally together with sulphasalazine when the patient has severe illness; in the milder forms of the disease, including ulcerative proctitis, the corticosteroids are often administered rectally. A daily oral dose of 40 mg prednisolone is an effective starting dose in acute ulcerative colitis although larger doses administered parenterally have been used, particularly in the fulminating forms of the disease. The dose is reduced once a response has been achieved and the patient is maintained on the smallest dose capable of holding the condition quiescent. A regimen of 48-hour prednisolone administration has been advocated in children as a method of reducing adrenal suppression while at the same time retaining the therapeutic effects of the steroids. Prednisolone for local rectal installation is given as a retention rectal enema. Disposable packs are available of 20 mg prednisolone in 100 ml and may be used once or twice a day. This form of medication is particularly effective in ulcerative proctitis.

The dose of sulphasalazine varies from 2 to 4 g daily. As the drug can cause gastrointestinal upset it is advisable to begin with a small dose (0.5 g thrice daily) and build up to the maximum dose that is tolerated. Sulphasalazine can be used alone in the milder forms of the illness or given together with steroids. It is given in maintenance doses of 1–2 g daily to prevent recurrence of attacks. Side-effects include dyspepsia, skin rashes, haemolytic anaemia and rarely, agranulocytosis.

In recent years the antimetabolite drugs have been introduced for the treatment of severely ill patients. The agent most favoured is azathioprine. Striking successes have been claimed but enough experience with this form of therapy has not been accumulated so it is premature to assess its place in the management of ulcerative colitis.

Surgical intervention is required in the acute illness if the patient fails to respond to medical therapy; chronic disease may also be an indication for an operation. Thus an operation may be performed either as an urgent procedure or electively. A high mortality and morbidity accompanies the emergency operation and the decision to operate should be made early. An urgent operation is indicated in the patient who remains toxic despite 3–6 days of adequate medical therapy, in the patient who is developing toxic dilatation of the colon, or when there is severe haemorrhage. Surgery is also undertaken earlier in the elderly patient. A fine judgment of timing is required; if the operation is performed too soon an unnecessary ileostomy is created, if too late there is a high operative mortality rate. A fever of 38.3 °C, more than 12 stools daily, abdominal pain and profuse bleeding which persist for 4 days after admission to hospital is generally taken as an indication for surgery.

The aim of surgical treatment is to remove the diseased bowel and the majority of surgeons favour proctocolectomy and ileostomy as either a 1- or a 2-stage procedure. Colectomy and ileostomy with preservation of the rectal stump is less popular because the rectal stump will continue to discharge mucus, blood and pus. Operations attempting to conserve apparently normal portions of the colon are unsuccessful for they are invariably followed by the development of the disease in the retained segment of colon. An ileorectal anastomosis has been introduced as an alternative to proctocolectomy. This operation has the advantage of preserving the rectum but the risk remains of continuing or subsequent disease in the rectal stump. In unskilled hands the operation has a high failure rate. Most patients find that diarrhoea persists after anastomosis; but since the bowel motions may be less frequent than before the operation many patients feel that an ileorectal anastomosis is preferable to an ileostomy. The risk remains that cancer will develop in the rectal stump.

An elective proctocolectomy is recommended for those patients in whom chronic diarrhoea interferes with life. The greatest difficulty remains the place of surgery in the prevention of cancer. Because of the high cancer risk in colitic patients a plea has been made for the removal of the colon in all patients who have had ulcerative colitis for more than 10 years. This whole topic remains much debated and there is no agreement among surgeons and gastroenterologists as to how patients should be selected for prophylactic proctocolectomy.

Ulcerative colitis is associated with a high morbidity and in increased mortality rate. Despite the absence of symptoms the colonic mucosa rarely returns to normal. The majority of patients responding to medical therapy will relapse within a year. There is no way of preventing such relapses; long-term steroid therapy is ineffective but it has been suggested that continuous administration of sulphasalazine in a dose of 2 g daily is of value. Although corticosteroids and sulphasalazine have undoubtedly proved beneficial for the milder and moderately ill patient these drugs do not appear to have improved the outlook for severely ill patients in whom the mortality rate remains as high as 28%. Toxic dilatation carries a mortality rate of around 20%. The mortality rate is higher in the first attack of the disease as well as in the very young and the aged. The mortality rate for emergency surgery is 25%; it is lower for urgent operation and falls to less than 3% when an elective procedure is performed. The development of cancer carries a high mortality and the results of surgery are disappointing. There is evidence that many of the liver lesions may regress after colectomy and it is possible that hepatic fibrosis and cirrhosis may be arrested. Significant liver disease rarely develops after colectomy.

Comparison between the clinical course of ulcerative colitis and Crohn's disease shows that patients with ulcerative colitis tend to have a more acute initial illness and more often require urgent surgery during this episode. The matter of surgical intervention is often settled within 2 to 4 years of the initial illness whereas in Crohn's disease the operation rate continues to rise. Thus ulcerative colitis becomes less dangerous with time while Crohn's disease is more chronic, progressive and has a greater tendency to anal complications. On the other hand should ulcerative colitis involve the whole colon the 20-year survival is reduced to 50%.

The outlook for a patient with ulcerative proctitis is considerably better and the overall mortality rate is under 2%. The life expectancy of a patient with a proctocolectomy is not much different from the population in general.

Further Reading

Cook, M. G. and Goligher, J. C. (1975) Carcinoma and epithelial dysplasia complicating ulcerative colitis. *Gastroenterology*, **68**, 1127–1136.

Devroede, G. J. et al. (1971) Cancer risk and life expectancy in children with ulcerative colitis. *New Engl. J. Med.*, **285**, 17–21.

Lennard-Jones, J. E. and Ritchie, J. K. (1974) The diagnosis and management of colitis. *Br. J. Hosp. Med.*, February, 180–186.

Norlan, C. C. and Kirsner, J. B. (1969) Toxic dilatation of the colon (toxic megacolon): etiology treatment and prognosis in 42 patients. *Medicine, Baltimore*, **48**, 229–250.

Schachter, H. et al. (1970) Ulcerative and 'granulomatous' colitis—validity of differential diagnostic criteria. *Ann. int. Med.*, **72**, 841–851.

Sparberg, M. et al. (1966) Ulcerative proctitis and mild ulcerative colitis: a study of 220 patients. *Medicine, Baltimore*, **45**, 391–412.

There are a variety of syndromes associated with reduced blood supply to the gut. The clinical distinctions between the different pathological conditions are far from certain and the clinical presentations are not always clear. There is often overlap and no classification is satisfactory. The following scheme attempts to provide diagnostic groups which have clinical significance: ischaemic colitis, intestinal ischaemia, haemorrhagic enterocolitis and a further category comprising miscellaneous disorders.

Ischaemic Colitis

The main blood supply to the colon is via the marginal artery which is fed by branches of the right and left colic vessels. There are two sites where the marginal artery is poorly developed so that ischaemic episodes may produce bowel damage: the splenic flexure and the caecal region. Damage to the left colic artery causes ischaemia in the region of the splenic flexure.

The pathological changes vary according to the degree and extent of the vascular occlusion. The most severe outcome is gangrene of the colon. The usual event is the development of an ischaemic stricture in the region of the splenic flexure; histologically the affected segment shows inflammatory cell infiltration, macrophages laden with haemosiderin and fibrosis. The mildest outcome is the development of transient ischaemic colitis with complete resolution. About one-third of the patients with ischaemic colitis have arterial occlusion but venous obstruction or intramural vessel occlusions may cause an identical clinical syndrome. Factors responsible for the reduced blood supply include splanchnic vessel occlusion, vasoconstriction and low flow states and these may operate singly or in combination. Predisposing factors include diabetes mellitus, connective tissue disorders, arteriosclerosis and possibly the contraceptive pill.

The majority of patients are in the sixth or seventh decades and usually have other features of cardiovascular disease. There is sudden onset of severe lower abdominal pain, vomiting, fever and diarrhoea. The stool is mixed with blood although pure bright red blood may be passed. Abdominal examination reveals tenderness which is present locally over the descending colon but more generalized when peritonitis develops. Mild abdominal distension is present and varying degrees of shock, fever and leucocytosis occur.

The clinical course may take one of three directions: the development of gangrene occurs in a few patients and is accompanied by a high mortality; half of the patients develop an ischaemic stricture, usually in the region of the splenic flexure, and the remainder undergo complete recovery.

Radiological support for the diagnosis comes from the plain film of the abdomen which, in addition to showing the features of intestinal obstruction, may demonstrate the presence of gas in the bowel wall and a fixed dilated splenic flexure. A barium enema performed when the patient has improved is usually abnormal. The most consistent feature is a stricture of varying length involving the splenic flexure, but the descending colon and sigmoid may also be narrowed. Other abnormalities include a ragged 'sawtooth' appearance of the mucosa and sacculation of the bowel

(Plate VIII. Fig. 1). Two weeks after the initial episode the colon has a tubular appearance with some sacculation and after 6 weeks the barium enema will be normal. In mild cases the barium enema will be normal. The role of angiography in the diagnosis of ischaemic colitis remains to be defined. Since it is usual to find good filling of the vessels up to the marginal artery sophisticated techniques are required to demonstrate the intramural circulation.

The differential diagnosis is chiefly from ulcerative colitis, Crohn's disease and cancer (Plate VIII. Fig. 2). Rectal involvement occurs in ulcerative colitis and Crohn's disease but is rare in ischaemic colitis. The barium enema appearances are distinctive: sacculation is a feature confined to ischaemic colitis, stricture is rare in ulcerative colitis in which shortening of the whole colon and loss of haustrations are more characteristic; colonic involvement is more patchy in Crohn's disease.

The management depends upon the severity of the bowel damage. All patients will require urgent resuscitation, remembering that many have some cardiovascular dysfunction. Attention to shock, infection, heart failure and anaemia is required. Gangrene of the colon is an indication for immediate resection of the bowel with exteriorization. The mortality rate is high. Ischaemic colitis may be treated expectantly in the initial stages by careful use of antispasmodic agents and a mild laxative. An initial period of gastric suction and intravenous feeding may be required. Corticosteroids should not be administered. If the patient is acutely ill exteriorization of the bowel will be needed. A stricture is treated by resection and anastomosis, usually as a 1-stage procedure. The operative mortality for such elective operations is low and it is unusual for a recurrence to occur.

Intestinal Ischaemia

Ischaemic episodes involving the small bowel may be sudden and complete, causing acute infarction, or they may be more gradual so that a state of chronic intestinal ischaemia ensues.

The aetiological factors responsible for mesenteric infarction include arterial and venous thrombosis and embolism. However, at times no obstruction to the vessels can be demonstrated. The more peripheral the block the greater the damage. The usual vessel involved is the superior mesenteric artery but obstruction in the region of the coeliac axis is also encountered. Precipitating factors include atheroma, aneurysm of the aorta, embolism, arteritis, hypotensive states and severe cardiac disease. Venous thrombosis causes a similar clinical picture although the evolution is slower. Patients are elderly and many with the acute syndrome give a history of preceding chronic intestinal ischaemia.

The symptoms include severe central abdominal pain followed by anorexia, nausea and vomiting. Diarrhoea and rectal bleeding are often present but occasionally haematemesis occurs. Physical findings include hypo-tension, hypothermia, low cardiac output and a mottled cyanosis of the abdominal wall. The initial abdominal examination may not suggest extensive bowel necrosis but later distension, tenderness and ileus will become apparent. Elevated serum amylase levels may be misleading. Radio-graphs of the abdomen show nonspecific features including excess gas in the small intestine, dilatation and air–fluid levels. More specifically thickening and oedema of the mucosa and wall may be seen and these observations are more prominent when there is venous obstruction. Such changes may be recognized on plain radiographs of the abdomen as well as barium studies. Rarely air is seen in the portal vein.

The initial treatment is resuscitation of the patient before surgical intervention. At operation it may be difficult to decide if an area of bowel is viable. The appropriate area of necrotic bowel is resected. When extensive portions of bowel have been removed the patient presents a problem in postoperative management both in the immediate phase and in the long term when malnutrition is common. When an embolus has occurred embolectomy with or without resection of gut will prove effective. Vascular surgery may be attempted when the vessels are clearly diseased but unfortunately the small bowel is frequently quite necrotic at the time of operation.

At least 2 of the 3 main arteries to the gut must be occluded for chronic intestinal ischaemia to occur, or there must be a reduction of no less than two-thirds of the normal cross-sectional area of the large vessels supplying the bowel. The symptomatology is variable and undoubtedly many patients have a considerably reduced blood supply without symptoms. Clinical features include nausea, vomiting, anorexia, weight loss, diarrhoea and abdominal pain of a non-specific character. The term *intestinal angina* has been used to describe a syndrome affecting the elderly in which severe cramping upper abdominal pain follows a meal; there may be nausea, vomiting and diarrhoea. Over a period of time the interval between the ingestion of food and the onset of pain becomes shorter until complete arterial obstruction occurs and the patient presents with acute intestinal ischaemia. The syndrome of intestinal angina is not universally accepted and is certainly rare. Gross intestinal ischaemia may present with malabsorption. The finding of a bruit over the vessels is seldom a helpful sign. The treatment is unsatisfactory but reconstructive vascular surgery has been attempted.

Haemorrhagic Enterocolitis

This is an uncommon manifestation of vascular insufficiency. There is mucosal haemorrhage and necrosis which may involve the colon, small bowel or stomach and the damage may be patchy or in continuity. The mucosal surface is haemorrhagic, necrotic and dark brown in colour.

Histologically there is superficial mucosal necrosis with little evidence of any inflammatory reaction. It is not possible to demonstrate occlusion of the large vessels but microscopic examination of the capillaries and arterioles reveals vasodilatation. It is rare to find any evidence of thrombosis. The cause of the mucosal damage is not apparent. Almost certainly it is multifactorial. Most patients are elderly and it is thought that a combination of chronic congestive cardiac failure, digitalis therapy, vasoactive endotoxins and other unrecognized factors causes a profound alteration in mesenteric blood flow.

The clinical features include the sudden onset of abdominal pain, nausea, vomiting, haematemesis, bloody diarrhoea and ileus. The patient becomes severely shocked and the mortality rate is high. Treatment is unsatisfactory and is directed at restoring fluid and electrolyte balance. Attempts to improve splanchnic blood flow are seldom effective.

Miscellaneous Disorders

INTRAMURAL HAEMATOMAS

Intramural haematomas may complicate a number of diseases including Henoch–Schönlein purpura and idiopathic thrombocytopenic purpura. They may occur in patients on anticoagulant therapy and following trauma. The main complaint is abdominal pain. The radiological features suggestive of a haematoma include crowding of the valvulae conniventes into a 'coiled spring' appearance, a narrow rigid segment of bowel with a spiculed 'picket fence' appearance and 'thumbprinting'. The appearances are transitory and therapy is directed towards the underlying haematological condition. Nasogastric suction and intravenous replacement therapy will be necessary if there is intermittent or incomplete obstruction.

ANTICOAGULANT THERAPY

About 10% of patients on anticoagulant therapy develop gastrointestinal complications. These include haemorrhage into the bowel lumen which may be spontaneous or secondary to underlying disease, intramural haemorrhage, retroperitoneal haemorrhage, haemorrhage into the abdominal organs, including the ovary, adrenal gland, pancreas, rectus abdominus and urinary tract, and reactions to anticoagulant drugs including hepatitis and diarrhoea.

COELIAC AXIS COMPRESSION

This is a syndrome about which there is much uncertainty. The patients complain of epigastric discomfort which is related to both meals and posture. On examination there is a bruit in the epigastrium which alters with position and respiration. Lateral aortography shows anterior compression of the coeliac axis. The mechanism is believed to be due to compression of the coeliac axis by the median arcuate ligament of the diaphragm. The treatment recommended is division of the constricting band. It has been claimed that stenosis may persist after relief of the compression and that reconstructive surgery to the coeliac artery is necessary in order to achieve a satisfactory result. Unfortunately the angiographic appearances may be identical in patients with and without complaints. Furthermore the results of surgery are variable and unpredictable. At present it seems unlikely that compression of the coeliac artery causes any identifiable syndrome.

ANEURYSM OF THE ABDOMINAL AORTA

Aneurysm of the abdominal aorta is a complication of generalized arterial disease and arteriosclerosis of the aorta. The aneurysm may be symptomless and found on routine examination, when it must be distinguished from simple ectasia of the aorta. On the other hand the patient may present with abdominal pain, weight loss and a pulsatile abdominal mass. The pain may be worse after meals and may radiate to the back. There may be evidence of vascular occlusion to the kidneys, bowel and lower limbs. Because of the potential hazard presented by the aneurysm some authorities advise elective resection of an aneurysm which is found by chance in symptom-free patients. Preoperative angiography is useful in such patients as it defines the anatomical extent of the aneurysm which influences the decision to operate and the operative approach.

Leakage or rupture of the aneurysm occurs in the absence of any previous history suggesting its presence. There is sudden severe mid-abdominal or low back pain radiating to one or both groins and accompanied by varying degrees of shock. Haematemesis or rectal bleeding occurs if the aneurysm ruptures into the lumen of the bowel. The patient is shocked and a tender abdominal mass is found which is usually pulsatile. The tenderness may be localized to one flank and one or more of the leg pulses may be absent.

The diagnosis is confirmed by a plain radiograph of the abdomen which shows loss of the psoas shadow and disruption of the calcification in the aortic wall. Abdominal paracentesis may reveal blood in the peritoneal cavity. Usually the diagnosis is clinically obvious and as little time as possible should be wasted on diagnostic techniques. The patient must be resuscitated rapidly in preparation for early surgery. Occasionally the diagnosis is uncertain and conditions likely to cause confusion are myocardial infarction, dissecting aneurysm and intestinal infarction.

Unless recognized and treated early a ruptured aneurysm of the abdominal aorta carries a high mortality rate. The patient's survival depends upon placing a clamp upon the aorta as early as possible and then replacing the vessel with a graft. If surgery is prompt the mortality rate may be reduced to less than 50%. Because of the potential hazard presented by the aneurysm some authorities advise elective resection of an aneurysm which is found by chance in patients who are symptomfree.

Further Reading

Brewster, D. C. et al. (1975) Angiography in the management of aneurysms of the abdominal aorta. *New Engl. J. Med.*, **292**, 822–825.

Edwards, J. A. et al. (1970) Experience with coeliac axis compression syndrome. *Br. med. J.*, **i**, 342–345.

Khilnani, M. T. et al. (1964) Intramural intestinal haemorrhage. *Am. J. Roentg.*, **92**, 1061–1071.

Mannick, J. A. (1967) Diagnosis of ruptured aneurysm of the abdominal aorta. *New Engl. J. Med.*, **276**, 1305–1307.

Marcuson, R. W. (1974) Ischaemia of the colon. *Br. J. Hosp. Med.*, May, 203–209.

Pierce, G. E. and Brockenbrough, E. C. (1970) The spectrum of mesenteric infarction. *Am. J. Surg.*, **119**, 233–239.

Williams, L. F. (1971) Vascular insufficiency of the intestines. *Gastroenterology*, **61**, 757–777.

Malignant tumours of the gastrointestinal tract account for 20% of all neoplasms. With few exceptions such as the relationship of pernicious anaemia to gastric cancer and ulcerative colitis with cancer of the colon the aetiology is quite obscure. Tests of both cell-mediated and humoral immunity are depressed in patients with gastrointestinal tumours but this observation has not helped resolve the enigma of carcinogenesis.

Gastrointestinal tumours can produce a variety of antigens which can be detected in the peripheral blood and are consequently of diagnostic value. Carcinoembryonic antigen (CEA) is a glycoprotein which is found in the blood of patients with mainly colonic but also gastric, pancreatic and breast cancers. It may also be present in the blood of some patients with chronic inflammatory bowel disease. The main diagnostic value of CEA is in the detection of secondary malignant recurrences following removal of the primary colonic cancer. Alpha-fetoprotein is another antigen associated mainly with primary malignant disease of the liver but also on occasions with gastric neoplasms. It is of much diagnostic help in the diagnosis of primary hepatocellular cancer.

Cancer of the Colon and Rectum

Cancer of the colon is one of the commonest of malignant tumours. It is much more frequent in northwest Europe and in North America than in East Africa, Asia and South America. In the United Kingdom cancer of the colon and rectum is the second commonest killing cancer, accounting for some 14 000 deaths annually. In the United States of America colorectal cancer accounts for more new cases annually than any other type of cancer. The reason for this geographical variation is uncertain and it cannot be due solely to racial factors. The differences may be related in part to the adoption of a sophisticated high-standard pattern of living. There is much dispute whether diet plays a role. Diets high in protein, or high in fat or low in bulk-fibre have all been implicated. There is evidence to implicate meat, particularly beef, as a food associated with the development of large bowel cancer. It has also been suggested that dietary differences might determine the composition of the gut bacterial flora and that certain anaerobic bacteria produce carcinogenic derivatives from bile acids. Faecal stasis might occur on a low bulk-fibre diet. Thus a high fat, low bulk-fibre diet might produce the right conditions for the bacterial production of carcinogens while faecal stasis would favour carcinogenesis.

Both ulcerative colitis and familial polyposis coli are recognized to be premalignant conditions, and there are a number of less common hereditary disorders associated with colonic polyps which may predispose to cancer (p.164). Nearly two-thirds of all cancers of the colon and rectum arise from previously benign adenomatous polyps or villous adenomas. The potential for malignant change is greater with a villous adenoma. Adenocarcinoma of the colon, in the absence of colonic polyps, has been shown to occur more frequently in certain families.

The majority of patients are aged 40–70 years with a maximum of patients being in the sixth decade. The disease occurs more frequently in females. Almost half the cancers are in the sigmoid colon and two-thirds are found distal to the splenic flexure. About 20% of patients have more than one tumour, either benign or malignant, in the colon or rectum.

More than 80% of the tumours are adenocarcinomas, the remainder being colloid cancers. Growths on the left side tend to be infiltrating and obstructive whereas in the ascending colon the tumour is proliferative. Peristaltic activity may cause the growth to be polypoidal. The spread is by local infiltration or via the lymphatics and blood. Cancer of the colon has been classified and staged according to the histology or the extent of spread and there is a correlation between histology, tumour spread and prognosis. In Broder's histological classification the number of anaplastic cells are assessed and 4 grades are recognized, from Grade 1 in which less than 25% of the cells are anaplastic to Grade 4 in which the tumours have more than 75% anaplastic cells. The Duke staging method recognizes 4 categories: Grade A in which the growth is limited to the bowel wall; Grade B where spread is beyond the wall; Grade C1 is limited lymphatic spread; and Grade C2 is extensive lymphatic spread.

The commonest presenting symptom is pain; this is often difficult to define or localize. It may be colicky in character, a dull and persistent ache or very severe if intestinal obstruction is present. Pain tends to be a feature of right-sided lesions. An alteration in bowel habit is the predominant feature of left-sided cancer with constipation being a marked complaint. Diarrhoea can occur with either right- or left-sided lesions. The passage of bright red blood rectally is more frequent in left-sided cancers; those on the right cause occult bleeding and the patient presents with the features of an unexplained anaemia. Other symptoms include vomiting and weight loss. When there is a growth in the rectum the complaints include local pain, tenesmus and bleeding. The duration of symptoms cannot be used to predict the extent of the growth. Acute intestinal obstruction occurs in 10–15% of growths on the left side and transverse colon, but is rare in right-sided lesions. The acute development of a hernia or appendicitis in an elderly patient should arouse the suspicion of a colonic cancer. The patient may present with features of metastatic spread.

Physical signs will be absent in about one-third of patients. A tumour may be palpable and is more often felt in the ascending colon. Signs of intestinal obstruction, anaemia or distant spread may be elicited. Rare modes of presentation are torrential rectal bleeding and perforation.

The diagnosis is established by a combination of digital examination, sigmoidoscopy and biopsy whenever possible and barium enema. The importance of the digital and sigmoidoscopic examination in patients with rectal bleeding, anaemia, or symptoms suggestive of large bowel disease cannot be overstated. It has been estimated that nearly half of colonic cancers can be felt on a rectal examination and two-thirds can be seen with the sigmoidoscope. Colonoscopy enables visualization of the whole colon and has made a significant diagnostic impact particularly to determine the presence of tumours in the rest of the colon. A biopsy must always be obtained from a suspicious lesion. The barium examination will frequently reveal a localized constricting or ulcerative lesion on the left side while on the right the tumours tend to be larger (Plate VIII. Fig. 2). Careful and adequate bowel preparation is essential and an adequate examination requires much radiological expertise. This is of particular importance in the examination of the sigmoid loops, the hepatic and splenic flexures and the caecum. Colonic cytology is unpopular necessitating colonic lavage, but in expert hands has a diagnostic yield of 85%. The presence of CEA has been reported in patients with colonic and rectal cancers. The antigen has not proved to be a useful screening test.

Regrettably there is a significant delay in making a

diagnosis of colonic cancer. First, there is the patient delay and the average patient has symptoms for about 7 months before seeking medical advice; this may be almost a year in the case of patients with rectal growths in whom rectal bleeding is often ascribed to haemorrhoids. Secondly there is the medical delay and nearly 20% of patients undergo a further 8 months of medical surveillance before a correct diagnosis is achieved. This is usually because of failure to perform adequate rectal and sigmoidoscopic examinations.

A large number of diseases enter into the differential diagnosis and the clinician must constantly bear in mind the possibility of a colonic neoplasm in patients with gastrointestinal complaints. Upper gastrointestinal disorders which may be suggested include peptic ulcer and gall bladder disease. Diverticular disease of the colon is an important consideration but the presence of colonic diverticula should not divert attention from the possibility of a tumour in another area of the colon. The infectious dysenteries can be readily excluded by stool culture. All rectal masses must be submitted to biopsy prior to extensive surgery to avoid mistaking an amoeboma for a rectal cancer. Crohn's disease occasionally causes confusion.

The treatment of cancer of the colon and rectum is by either a curative or a palliative operation. A right hemicolectomy is undertaken for growths on the right side; segmental resection is performed for growths arising from the transverse colon; involvement of the distal part of the transverse colon or the splenic flexure or descending colon requires a left hemicolectomy. Sigmoidectomy and end-to-end anastomosis is adequate for sigmoid tumours. Generous removal of mesentery is a major determinant of a curative operation. Cancer of the rectum usually requires an abdominoperineal resection and the creation of a permanent colostomy. If the growth lies above the peritoneal reflection it may be possible to undertake an anterior resection and anastomosis leaving the rectum intact. Intestinal obstruction invariably results from a left-sided growth and is an indication for a defunctioning colostomy followed by a second operation. Patients with extensive local or generalized spread pose problems in management, particularly for the surgeon who has to decide whether to undertake an extensive operation or perform a palliative short-circuit procedure. Single liver metastases have been resected with favourable results. There is little place for chemotherapy and radiotherapy in the management of these tumours.

The prognosis is improved by careful preoperative assessment. Anaemia and electrolyte imbalance must be corrected and most surgeons recommend preoperative bowel preparation. Assessment of liver function including a liver scan is helpful to detect hepatic secondaries. During the operation great care must be exercised not to spread tumour cells around the peritoneal cavity. The length of the colon must be examined for the possibility of a second tumour. The prognosis following surgery is variable. The overall 5-year survival rate is around 30% and it is claimed that there has been little improvement in this figure over the past 30 years. The survival rate in patients submitted to a curative operation is as high as 50% in some centres. There is a clear relationship to staging; patients with Grade A growths have 5-year survival rates around 80% with much lower figures for Grades B and C. However, it seems probable that 'early' lesions have a better prognosis, not because of short duration of symptoms and an early diagnosis but rather because there is a strong host resistance or an inherently low malignant potential of the cancer.

The measurement of the CEA levels after removal of the primary growth is a useful method of detecting recurrence because elevated serum concentrations occur months before the clinical symptoms. Careful long-term surveillance is also required as one in ten patients will develop a second tumour. Colonoscopy is of potential value for this purpose.

Intestinal Polyps

The term 'polyp' is used to describe any tumour which projects from the intestinal mucous membrane. It is a clinical expression and it is essential that its use be qualified by a histological description.

ADENOMATOUS POLYP

This tumour arises as a consequence of focal hyperplasia of the mucosal glands of the intestine. It is found particularly in the large bowel. A fibromuscular stalk develops because of peristaltic activity. It is a benign lesion and must be distinguished from polypoidal cancers. The usual presenting features are rectal bleeding and altered bowel habits. Polyps may be diagnosed at the time of sigmoidoscopic or barium enema examinations undertaken for the investigation of vague abdominal pain and discomfort. It is necessary to distinguish the radiological appearances of a polyp from faeces and air. Air contrast barium studies are of much help.

The management of the adenomatous polyp in the colon is made difficult because of the controversy over whether it should be regarded as a premalignant lesion. The origin of a cancer can seldom be identified clearly from what was originally an adenomatous polyp. About 25% of colons or rectums removed for cancer contain adenomatous polyps. Some polyps do undergo malignant change and since it is not possible to tell with certainty which these are it has been suggested that all adenomatous polyps in the colon must be regarded as premalignant. The larger the polyp the greater the risk of malignancy. The size can be assessed sigmoidoscopically or by a barium enema. If the polyp is less than 1 cm in diameter the risk that it is a malignant growth is under 1%; when the polyp is greater than 2.5 cm in diameter the chance of malignancy increases to nearly 50%. The greater the degree of epithelial dysplasia the greater the cancer risk.

Careful histology of the polyp and stalk is essential in order to exclude a malignant growth. If malignancy is demonstrated a decision is required regarding further surgery. Polyps in the rectum and distal colon can be removed via a rigid sigmoidoscope using a diathermy snare. The majority of polyps in the remainder of the colon can be excised endoscopically with the help of a flexible fibreoptic colonoscope. Polyps as large as 5 cm may be removed in this way. Larger tumours require colotomy and polypectomy. Careful histological examination of the polyp and its stalk is essential to exclude that it is a malignant growth.

Villous Adenoma (Papillary Adenoma)

These are broad-based flat tumours with fronds which vary in length. Histologically the tumours show long papillary projections springing almost directly from the basement membrane. Villous adenomas are found almost exclusively in the rectum and lower sigmoid colon. They are recognized to have a high malignant potential. They are larger than adenomatous polyps, severe epithelial dysplasia is common and they should be managed in the same way as a cancer. The presentation is similar to an adenomatous polyp but in addition the patient may have profuse watery diarrhoea which is rich in mucus. Hypokalaemia may be a prominent feature. The mechanism for the potassium depletion is thought to be by loss of fluid and mucus from the surface of the tumour. The mucosa in this area of the bowel is normally rich in goblet cells and the large surface area possessed by the tumour permits of massive volumes of mucus to be secreted.

Inherited Gastrointestinal-Polypsis Syndromes

There is a variety of polypoid conditions which are familial and which affect the gastrointestinal tract. The most important features determining into which syndrome a patient is grouped are the distribution of the polyps within the gut, their pathological characteristics and the distribution of extraintestinal manifestations (Table XII). All the syndromes are rare, the most commonly encountered being familial polyposis coli which has an occurrence of 1 in 8300 births.

Familial Polyposis Coli

In this condition the colon contains multiple adenomatous polyps varying from 50 to a few thousand. The disease is inherited as an autosomal dominant but new mutations occur and explain the occasional patient who does not have a positive family history. Affected members are not born with polyps; these usually appear after the age of 10 years. There is a strong tendency for the adenomas to become malignant and 33–50% of patients who present with symptoms will have a superimposed cancer. Malignant change is inevitable if the patient lives long enough. The number of polyps varies from 50 to many thousands and they extend throughout the colon and rectum. The stomach and small intestine are unaffected and there are no extra-intestinal lesions.

The average age at presentation is 27 years. There is a further 12 years between the diagnosis of polyposis and the development of cancer, the average age of diagnosis of this complication being 39 years. The usual symptoms are rectal bleeding, mucus discharge, diarrhoea, abdominal pain, weight loss and other complications associated with a colonic cancer. Diagnosis is by sigmoidoscopy, biopsy and barium enema.

The standard treatment is colectomy and ileorectal anastomosis because the observed rate of neoplasm in untreated patients is 80%. Thereafter careful follow-up is necessary to remove any remaining polyps and to detect any which develop in the retained rectum. This is done by

TABLE XII. *Inherited Gastrointestinal–Polyposis Syndromes*

Syndrome	Nature of Polyps	Location of Polyps	Extra-Abdominal Manifestations	Malignant Potential	Inheritance
Familia polyposis coli	Adenomatous	Colon and rectum	None	Great	Autosomal dominant
Gardner syndrome	Adenomatous	Colon and rectum, rarely small bowel	Multiple bony and soft tissue tumours	Marked often in duodenum	Autosomal dominant
Turcot syndrome	Adenomatous	Colon	Brain tumours	Only in brain	Autosomal recessive
Peutz-Jeghers	Hamartoma	Generalized	Melanin pigmentation	2–3% often in duodenum	Autosomal dominant
Juveline polyposis generalized	Hamartoma	Colon and rest of gut	None	Slight	Autosomal dominant
Juvenile polyposis coli	Hamartoma	Colon	None	Slight	Autosomal dominant

168 GASTROENTEROLOGY

means of fulguration at the time of sigmoidoscopy. The examination is made initially every 3 months but later can be undertaken at 6-monthly intervals. Regular examinations of the rectal mucosa are required for the rest of the patient's life. An operation is advised on any patient who has symptoms; in symptomless patients known to have colonic polyps the colectomy and ileorectal anastomosis is best undertaken in the late teens before there is an appreciable likelihood of malignant change.

Once a new patient has been diagnosed it is essential to investigate the rest of the family. A family tree is carefully constructed and the parents and siblings are examined sigmoidoscopically. Good relationships between the doctor and family are necessary for this. In persons with polyposis coli the polyps are always in the rectum, so that a barium enema is of little further value in making the diagnosis. Once it is established which members of the family do and which do not have polyposis coli it is possible to offer advice regarding cancer prevention. Those members with colonic polyps will require colectomy and ileorectal anastomosis. Those without will need surveillance and it is probable that if a patient reaches the age of 30 years without having developed polyps it is unlikely that these will develop. Children do not require to be examined until they are in their late teens unless there are symptoms.

Gardner Syndrome

This includes adenomatous polyposis of the large bowel, osteomas of the skull and mandible, multiple epidermoid cysts, soft tissue tumours of the skin and abnormal dentition. Small intestinal and gastric polyps are also present. There is a very slight tendency for all the extracolonic polyps to undergo malignant change and duodenal cancer in the periampullary region is being recognized with increasing frequency.

CRONKHITE–CANADA SYNDROME

In this inherited condition there is the association of gastrointestinal polyps, alopecia, nail dystrophy and skin pigmentation.

TURCOT SYNDROME

In this rare disorder there are colonic polyps and an association with brain tumours. The syndrome is probably inherited as an autosomal recessive.

Familial polyposis coli has also been associated with cancer of the thyroid, extra-alimentary sarcomas and mesenteric fibromatosis.

PEUTZ–JEGHERS SYNDROME

This syndrome is inherited as a simple Mendelian dominant and 40–55% of the offspring are affected. The disease is usually recognized in early life. The polyps are harmartomas which are formed by normal epithelium arranged on a branching stroma composed of smooth muscle fibres derived from the muscularis mucosa. Polyps are usually in the jejunum and ileum and less frequently in the stomach and colon. Malignant change is rare but does occur and cancers have been reported from the stomach, duodenum and small bowel. There is also an association between this syndrome and cancer of the ovary which is reported to occur in 5–14% of patients.

There is abnormal melanin pigmentation of the lips and buccal mucous membrane which resembles freckles and is present in over 80% of patients. Other areas which may be pigmented include the periorbital regions, the palms and the soles. The major clinical features include episodes of gastrointestinal bleeding, abdominal pain and intussusception.

Because malignant change affects only a very small percentage of the patients the management comprises surgical treatment for episodes of bleeding or obstruction. An intussusception should be reduced surgically without resection if possible. The long-term outlook for these patients is guarded, as they run the risk of eventually having much of their small bowel resected with the development of severe malabsorption and malnutrition. Female patients must be carefully assessed for the presence of coexisting ovarian tumours.

Juvenile Polyps

In this uncommon disease the polyps appear to be hamartomas and have a familial predisposition. The mode of inheritance is uncertain. The polyps have an epithelial component surrounded by abundant connective tissue stroma which often has a primitive mesenchymal appearance. The surface is covered by a single layer of columnar epithelial cells. The tumours frequently appear cystic because of retained mucus. The polyps may be found anywhere in the gastrointestinal tract (generalized juvenile gastrointestinal polyposis) or localized to the colon (juvenile polyposis coli), when the polyps are less numerous than in familial polyposis coli. Symptoms usually start by the age of 6 years and include rectal bleeding, prolapse and obstruction. Marked cachexia may occur in infants. There may be associated congenital abnormalities involving particularly the heart and the nervous system but extra-intestinal manifestations are rare. There is a slightly increased risk of malignancy.

Carcinoid Tumours

Carcinoid tumours are found throughout the gastrointestinal tract; it is the commonest tumour of the appendix and one of the commonest tumours in the small intestine. They comprise about 1.5% of all gastrointestinal neoplasms. Carcinoid tumours may be found in the bronchus, pancreas, gall bladder, ovary and teratomas but 90% originate in the gastrointestinal tract and of these 90% are found in the appendix. The tumours are usually benign or only locally invasive. The ileal carcinoid tumour arises from the embryonic midgut; the tumour is formed of cells which contain silver-staining granules and which have spherical nuclei. This type of tumour spreads to the liver and both primary and secondary growths contain high concentrations of 5-hydroxytryptamine. Carcinoid tumours of the rectum arise from the hindgut; they have a negative argentaffin reaction and are not accompanied by disturbances of 5-hydroxytryptamine metabolism.

The tumours may present with local intestinal manifestations including pain, obstruction and bleeding; their presence may become apparent because of the systemic effects of excess circulating kinins, including 5-hydroxytryptamine, bradykinin and histamine, and these are believed to be responsible for the carcinoid syndrome. Characteristically this syndrome comprises flushing, intestinal hypermotility and bronchospasm. The flushing is commonly either a short-lived episodic diffuse erythema affecting the face and neck, or a longer-lasting violaceous flush associated with facial telangiectasis and suffused conjunctiva. The intestinal hypermotility manifests as severe watery diarrhoea and hypokalaemia. Patients may develop right-sided cardiac lesions such as pulmonary stenosis and tricuspid incompetence. Tryptophan is required for the formation of 5-hydroxytryptamine and in the presence of large tumour masses all the body supplies of tryptophan are utilized. Protein and nicotinic acid synthesis becomes inadequate under these circumstances and hypoproteinaemia and pellagra may ensue.

Carcinoid tumours are found more frequently than the carcinoid syndrome. Only when the primary gastrointestinal growth has metastasized to the liver do the humoral effects become apparent. This is because the metabolites from the tumour which reach the liver via the portal circulation are inactivated in this organ whereas hepatic metastases secrete the metabolic products directly into the systemic circulation.

The diagnosis is usually made only after the tumour has been removed. If the tumour is recognized at the time of surgery a wide local resection, including a generous wedge of mesentery, is usually adequate. When the carcinoid syndrome is suspected the urine is tested for 5-hydroxy-indole acetic acid which is the metabolic breakdown product of 5-hydroxytryptamine. The treatment of the carcinoid syndrome is unsatisfactory. Large single metastatic hepatic tumours can be removed surgically but the operative risk is great because these patients are very sensitive to anaesthetic agents and may become hypotensive. Pharmacological therapy has been introduced to counteract the metabolic effects of the syndrome and some of the agents used include codeine phosphate, methysergide and perphenazine for diarrhoea and phenoxybenzamine, phenothiazines, α-methyldopa and corticosteroids for the flushing.

Lymphoma of the Gastrointestinal Tract

Malignant lymphoid tumours may involve the gastro-intestinal tract either as a primary growth or as a mani-festation of generalized disease. The usual site is the stomach and the usual pathology is either a lymphosarcoma or a reticulum cell sarcoma.

Lymphoma is a rare tumour of the intestine and occurs as an isolated disorder, as a complication of coeliac disease in adults or in association with immunoglobulin disorders, particularly those involving the heavy chain subclasses of IgA (α-chain disease, Mediterranean lymphoma). This last association is found primarily in the Middle East, affecting Sephardic Jews and Arabs, and possibly in South Africa. The disease is three times more common in males, but in α-chain disease the sex incidence is equal and the age of onset is frequently below 30 years.

The patients present with abdominal pain, nausea, vomiting and weight loss. Malabsorption is usually present, as are clubbing of the fingers and hepatomegaly. Histologically there is prominent plasma cell infiltration and the villi show moderate to severe damage and flattening. The affected segment of bowel is recognized radiologically to be thickened and rigid with a coarse nodular mucosal pattern and segmental narrowing or dilatation. Treatment includes surgical excision and the use of corticosteroids, abdominal irradiation and cytoxic agents. The prognosis is poor and the 5-year survival rate is 10–30%.

Other Intestinal Tumours

There are a variety of benign neoplasms of the bowel, including neurofibromas, leiomyomas, adenomas, haemangiomas and lipomas. Malignant tumours include adenocarcinomas, melanomas and secondary growths. The signs and symptoms are common to all histological types and include nausea, vomiting, abdominal pain and tenderness, loss of weight, altered bowel habits and an abdominal mass. Tumours in the colon present with rectal bleeding. Intestinal obstruction occurs from intussusception but malignant tumours may obstruct by circumferential growth. Surgical resection is usually necessary.

Further Reading

Calman, K. C. (1975) Tumour immunology and the gut. *Gut*, **16**, 490–499.

Erbe, R. W. (1976) Inherited gastrointestinal-polyposis sydromes. *New Engl. J. Med.*, **294**, 1101–1104.

Grahame-Smith, D. G. (1968) The carcinoid syndrome. *Hospital Medicine*, **2**, 5, 558–566.

Morgan, J. G. et al. (1974) Carcinoid tumors of the gastrointestinal tract. *Ann. Surg.*, **180**, 720–727.

Morson, B. (1974) The polyp-cancer sequence in the large bowel. *Proc. Roy. Soc. Med.*, **67**, 451–457.

Wilson, J. M. et al. (1974) Primary malignancies of the small bowel. *Ann. Surg.*, **180**, 175–179.

Winawer, S. J. et al. (1976) Screening for colon cancer. *Gastroenterology*, **70**, 783–789.

Wolff, W. I. and Shinya, H. (1974) Earlier diagnosis of cancer of the colon through colonic endoscopy (colonoscopy). *Cancer*, **34**, 912–931.

Two major patterns of motility are recognized in the colon: segmentation and propulsion. *Segmentation* is the predominant type of motor activity and is the consequence of narrow stationary contraction rings. The effect of this is to cause turbulence and slowing of the faecal stream and may explain the observation of reduced motor activity in diarrhoea and much motor activity in constipation. *Propulsion* is effected by mass movement which shifts large quantities of faecal material from one region of the colon to another. The neurohumoral control of colonic movements is poorly understood. After eating there is an increase in motor activity and at this time the mass movements tend to be more frequent. This effect has been ascribed to the vagus (the gastrocolic reflex) but there is also evidence to suggest that this phenomenon may be a response to a hormone, possibly gastrin. Cholecystokinin has also been shown to influence colonic motor activity.

The stool varies in weight with a daily mean of 120 ± 40 g. In general the normal stool is firm and formed. As the passage of the faecal stream is delayed in the colon more water is absorbed and the stool becomes lighter and firmer. Potassium absorption takes place in the colon. It is usual to pass one stool daily but there is much variation both within and between individuals and some normal people have 2–3 stools daily whereas others pass one stool every 2 or 3 days. It is possible that this is related to diet, for in many underdeveloped areas where there is a high roughage diet it is normal to pass more stools daily than in those parts of the world where a more sophisticated diet of highly refined foodstuffs is consumed. The rectal mucosa is rich in goblet cells and normally some mucus is present around the stool, particularly if it has been in the rectum for a while. Normally the rectum is empty and the stimulus to defaecation comes from a mass movement of stool into the rectum. It is the distension of the rectum together with the pressure on the perineum which gives rise to the desire to empty the bowel.

The gastrointestinal tract contains about 100 ml gas. Gastric air has a composition similar to the atmosphere and is clearly derived from swallowed air. The composition of flatus varies widely: hydrogen 0.06–47%, methane 0–26%, carbon dioxide 5.1–29%, oxygen 0.1–2.3% and nitrogen 23–80%. The mixture depends upon the varying proportions of swallowed air and microbial gas production. Exactly how much is contributed from each source remains to be determined but it appears that the major proportion may come from bacteria. Hydrogen and methane and probably carbon dioxide are derived only from bacterial metabolic processes which occur normally in the colon. Carbon dioxide may be produced by acid neutralization of bicarbonate; the other source is diffusion from the blood into the bowel lumen. Virtually all the nitrogen is from swallowed air. It is probable that certain foods such as onions, cabbages and beans are associated with the production of excess flatus and this may be a reflection of bacterial action on suitable substrates.

Irritable Bowel Syndrome

The irritable bowel syndrome is a disorder in which there is colonic pain and disordered bowel habit for which there is no recognizable cause. The condition has been given a variety of names including the irritable colon syndrome, spastic colon, mucous colitis and mucomembranous colitis. The use of the latter two terms is deplored because there is no inflammation of the colon; hence 'colitis' is a grossly misleading description inevitably causing confusion with ulcerative colitis.

The aetiology is unknown but it is generally held that psychological factors are important and some studies have indicated that patients are significantly more neurotic and anxious than control subjects. Nearly half the patients associate stress with an exacerbation or recurrence of symptoms. Inflammation, infection and hypolactasia are not involved and although laxative abuse may exacerbate the symptoms it is not an aetiological factor.

The syndrome is usually encountered in patients between 20 and 60 years of age and women are afflicted twice as frequently as men. It is probably encountered frequently in practice, although not always recognized. The site of pain is variable but is always over one or other part of the colon; it may occur in bouts or continuously, and is usually cramping but may be described as a dull ache or stabbing in character. The pain may be postprandial. Defaecation is usually followed by relief of pain but some patients complain that after the passage of a stool the desire to defaecate remains. Some disorder of bowel motility is common; diarrhoea or constipation occur alone or in combination. Thus it is possible to distinguish two groups of patients within the syndrome: a spastic colon group in which there is a tendency to pain and constipation, and a group with painless diarrhoea in which frequency of bowel action is the sole complaint. There may be excess of mucus in the stools but never any blood unless there are associated haemorrhoids. A few patients believe that exacerbations are precipitated by food, particularly 'acid fruits'.

There is little abnormality on physical examination other than localized or generalized tenderness along the colon. The caecum may be palpable and tender; another feature is a tender cord-like descending colon which can be rolled within the abdomen. It is not infrequent to find an appendicectomy scar. Sigmoidoscopy and mucosal biopsy are normal. The barium enema is normal except for areas of spasm. Postevacuation films may show poor emptying, with barium held in saccules formed by the excessive segmentation. Motility studies indicate increased intraluminal pressures with some disturbance of colonic motor activity. The complaints of bloating and pain are not due to an increased volume of intestinal gas.

A clinical variant is the splenic flexure syndrome in which there is left upper quadrant pain, flatulence and distension. These symptoms are often worse after a meal. Plain radiographs of the abdomen show a persistent gas bubble in the splenic flexure.

The management of patients with the irritable bowel syndrome includes the judicial use of psychotherapy and drug therapy. The patient's stress situation must be discussed, the nature of the illness explained and modest psychotherapy is frequently beneficial. A confident but patient approach is necessary. At the same time symptomatic relief can be obtained by the use of drugs such as bulk laxatives, diphenoxylate, propantheline, dicyclomine and codeine phosphate. Anticholinergic agents are of value in those patients who complain predominantly of pain; codeine phosphate is beneficial when diarrhoea is prominent. It is frequently necessary to alter therapy in an attempt to find the one drug or combination of drugs which will suit a particular patient. Therapy may need to be continued for many months and the patient will need reassurance and support.

The prognosis is variable, with the painless diarrhoea group having the better outcome. The majority of patients can be helped temporarily at least. All will have a tendency to relapse under conditions of emotional stress. However, if the patients are given insight and understanding into their complaint they can frequently tolerate the relapse and by introducing and manipulating their own drug therapy the symptoms can be controlled.

Diverticular Disease of the Colon

Diverticular disease of the colon is a common cause of morbidity in Western communities. It affects females slightly more frequently than males and the incidence increases with age so that nearly 50% of people over the age of 50 years can be shown to have some colonic diverticula.

In recent years there has been a reappraisal of the pathology and pathogenesis of diverticular disease and in particular a better understanding of the clinical and radiological distinctions between 'diverticulosis' and 'diverticulitis'. It is believed that the basic disorder is one of muscle dysfunction involving mainly the sigmoid colon. There is an increase in the tone of the longitudinal muscle which causes a shortening of the bowel. The muscle is thicker than normal but there is no hypertrophy or hyperplasia. The mucous membrane is thrown into redundant folds and the lumen of the bowel is narrowed, thus enabling complete obstruction to occur. In such circumstances the normal segmentation of the colon promotes the formation of abnormally high intraluminal pressures. Because of the shortened longitudinal muscle small closed pockets are produced by the rings of segmentation (Fig. 5). The abnormally high pressures inside the pockets force the mucosa through the bowel wall at the point where it is weakest: the site of penetration by the blood vessels. Thus the colonic diverticula are mucosal herniations occurring in 2 rows on either side of the colon. Diverticulitis (or more correctly peridiverticulitis) is a complication of diverticular disease and is usually the consequence of faecal material obstructing the narrow neck of the diverticulum at the point where it passes through the circular muscle. The wall of the diverticulum consists of mucous membrane only and therefore when acute inflammation occurs it extends readily into the peridiverticular tissue.

The reason for the muscle thickening is not understood. It may represent a disorder of muscle function and tone; it is possible that the colon lumen is narrowed in people taking a diet inadequate in bulk-fibre. On a low-residue diet the stool bulk is reduced and this permits of excessive segmentation and increased intraluminal pressure.

Diverticular disease is frequently asymptomatic and found incidentally at post mortem or on barium enema examination. Mild disturbance of bowel habit may be a

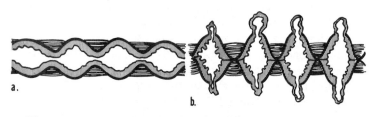

Fig. 5. The pathogenesis of diverticular disease: a. Thickening of the colonic muscle and shortening of the bowel; b. Segmentation of the colon causes closed pockets with high intraluminal pressures which force the mucous membrane through the colonic wall.

feature but it is less certain whether diverticular disease can be blamed for anorexia, flatulence, distension and food intolerance. Some patients have severe pain in the left iliac fossa or lower abdomen which is recurrent and cramping in character. Abdominal palpation may reveal a tender contracted sigmoid colon. Signs of inflammation are absent and there is no fever, tachycardia or leucocytosis.

Sigmoidoscopy is normal as is the rectal biopsy. It is not possible to see the orifices of the diverticula using the standard rigid 25 cm long sigmoidoscope. The air-containing diverticula may be seen on the plain film of the abdomen but the diagnosis is established by a barium enema. This shows the barium-filled sacs scattered along the course of the colon. The sigmoid and descending colon are most affected. The muscle abnormality may be recognized by the barium-filled colon having a sharp, serrated 'sawtooth' appearance. More marked muscle thickening causes a rather bizarre appearance and the barium column is broken up, the bowel lumen is narrowed and the diverticula are seen arising from the apex of the mucosal projections. Such an apparently disorganized appearance must not be regarded as mucosal distortion from inflammation and these radiographic features must not be interpreted as evidence in favour of diverticulitis.

The clinical features of diverticulitis are similar to those of uncomplicated diverticular disease and include lower abdominal pain, nausea, vomiting and an alteration in bowel habit—either constipation or diarrhoea. The colon will be palpable and tender with guarding of the anterior abdominal muscles. Important additional features which indicate the presence of inflammation are fever, tachycardia, toxaemia, elevated erythrocyte sedimentation rate and leucocytosis. The condition may present as a recurrent or chronic problem. The acute presentation resembles left-sided appendicitis. Acute diverticulitis is associated with a number of complications including local perforation and the development of a pericolic abscess, free perforation and peritonitis, fistula formation, portal pyaemia, large bowel obstruction and haemorrhage.

Rectal bleeding is rarely severe although at times it may be torrential and life-threatening. Minor episodes of bleeding are common, possibly the commonest complication of diverticulitis, but it is frequently impossible to be certain that the bleeding arises from a colon in which diverticula happen to be present and not from some other undisclosed site in the gut. An abscess presents as a tender mass in the left iliac fossa with the characteristic constitutional features associated with infection and pus. It may burst into the bowel but a more serious outcome is free rupture into the peritoneal cavity or the formation of a faecal fistula. Peritonitis may be faecal or purulent. Internal fistulas may develop: a vesicocolic fistula is uncommon in females because the uterus keeps the bladder and the colon apart. Dysuria, frequency and pneumaturia are suggestive features. When there is a colovaginal fistula air, faeces or pus are passed per vaginam. Large bowel obstruction may occur from oedema in acute diverticulitis or from fibrosis when there is chronic inflammation. There may be bouts of colic, distension and constipation, or complete obstruction may supervene.

The recognition of diverticulitis on barium enema examination is uncertain and unreliable. Features indicative of inflammation include fistula formation and marked and persistent luminal narrowing with loss of the normal mucosal folds.

The main differential diagnosis is from cancer of the colon, but other diseases to be considered include Crohn's disease, ischaemic colitis and ulcerative colitis. The diagnosis is established after sigmoidoscopy and a barium enema but it must be appreciated that diverticula must never be blamed for symptoms until the presence of other colonic or extracolonic diseases has been excluded.

Patients with diverticular disease require no treatment if they have no symptoms. In the event of pain attempts must be made to ensure regular bowel actions and to relieve muscle spasm. A normal diet is advised with sufficient bulk and fibre to ensure adequate stool volume. Bulk laxatives are helpful. Antispasmodic agents such as belladonna or propantheline provide relief of pain, as does external warmth applied to the abdomen. In the intervals between the attacks of pain a high-residue diet is recommended.

Acute diverticulitis is treated with bed rest, oral fluids and antispasmodic agents. Pethidine can be used for severe pain; morphine is contraindicated because it raises intraluminal sigmoid pressures and in this way increases the

PLATE I

Fig. 1. Benign stricture of the oesophagus (arrow)
secondary to oesophageal reflux.

Fig. 2. Cancer of the mid-oesophagus with a malignant stricture
(arrow) and a fistula between the oesophagus and left main
bronchus (arrow).

PLATE II

Fig. 1. Sliding hiatus hernia and tertiary contractions of the oesophagus.

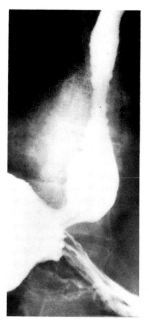

Fig. 2. Para-oesophageal hiatus hernia.

PLATE III

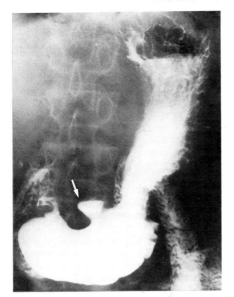

Fig. 1. Benign gastric ulcer.

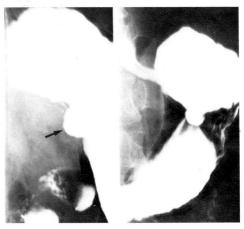

Fig. 2. Two views of a benign gastric ulcer (arrow).

PLATE IV

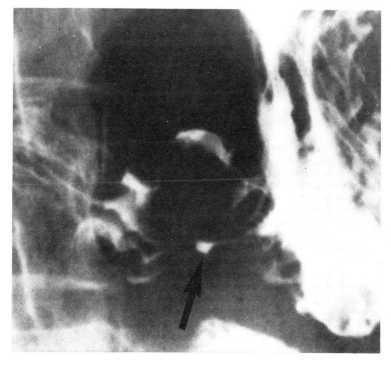

Fig. 1. Duodenal ulcer. The arrow indicates the fleck of barium
occupying the ulcer crater.

PLATE V

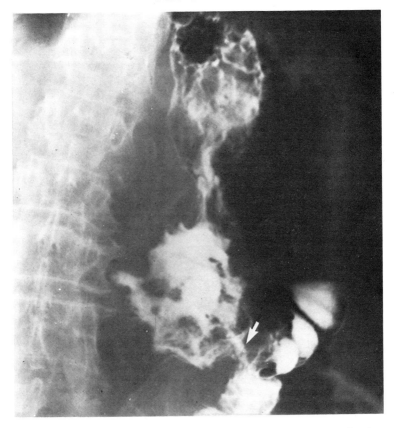

Fig. 1. Cancer of the stomach. The arrow indicates a gastrocolic fistula.

PLATE VI

Fig. 1.

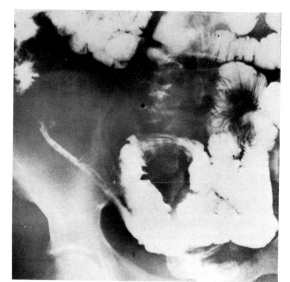

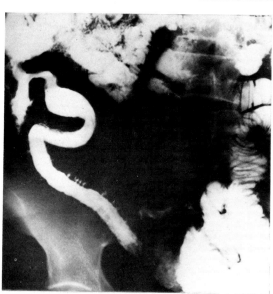

Fig. 2.

PLATE VI (*continued*)

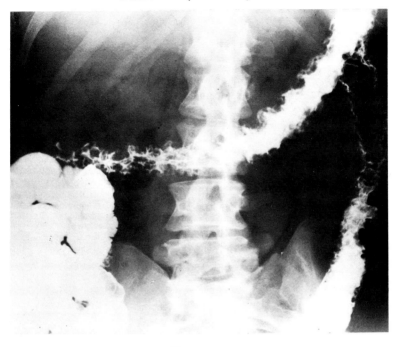

Fig. 3.

Crohn's disease of the terminal ileum.
Fig. 1. 'String sign.'
Fig. 2. Terminal ileal involvement with deep fissures and ulcers. In both examples there is disease affecting the caecum.
Fig. 3. Crohn's disease of the colon.

PLATE VII

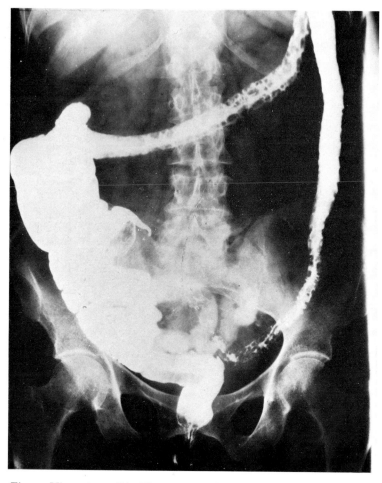

Fig. 1. Ulcerative colitis. Transverse and descending colon involvement with pseudopolyps.

PLATE VII (*continued*)

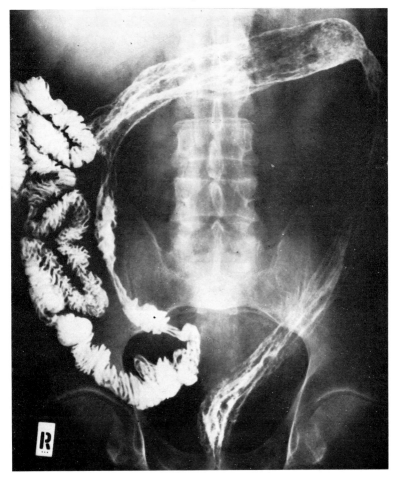

Fig. 2. Chronic total ulcerative colitis showing the shortened, narrowed featureless bowel.

PLATE VIII

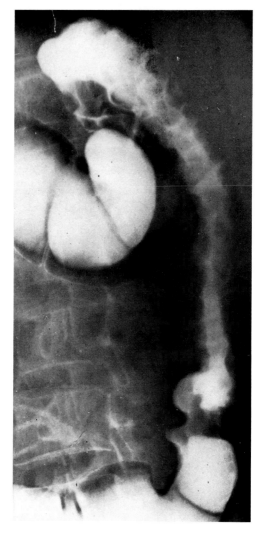

Fig. 1. Ischaemic colitis.

PLATE VIII (*continued*)

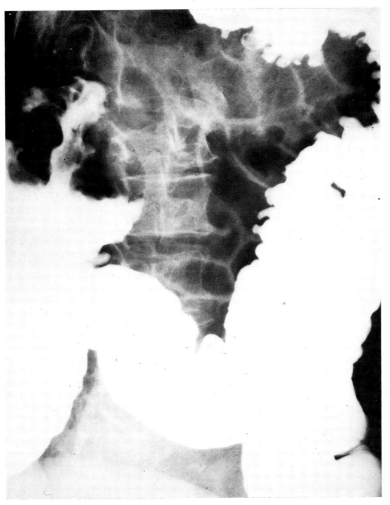

Fig. 2. Cancer of the caecum.

PLATE IX

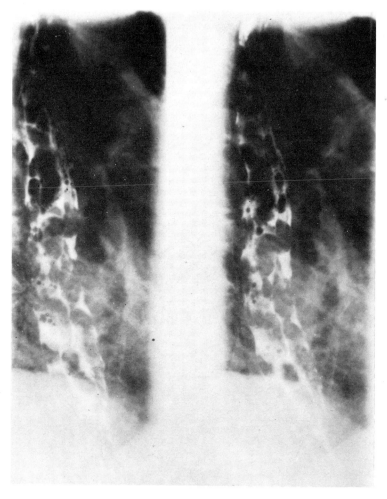

Fig. 1. Oesophageal varices.

PLATE IX (*continued*)

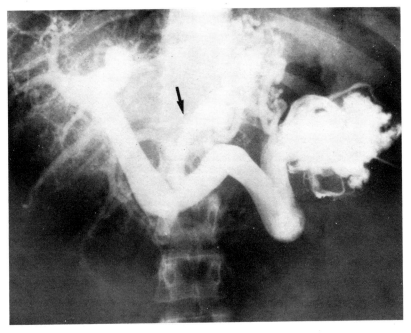

Fig. 2. Splenic venogram. The arrow indicates the anastomosis around the gastric veins which feed the oesophageal varices.

PLATE X

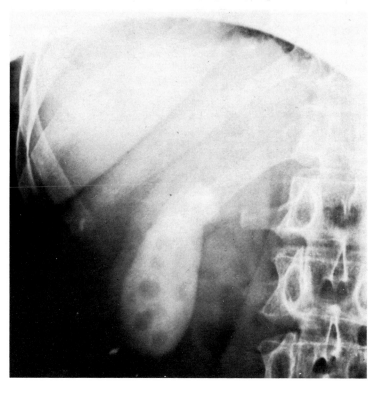

Fig. 1. Oral cholecystogram showing radiolucent gall stones.

PLATE X (*continued*)

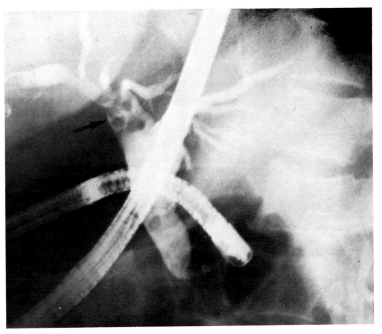

Fig. 2. Endoscopic retrograde cholangiopancreatogram. The arrow indicates translucent gall stones in the common bile duct.

PLATE XI

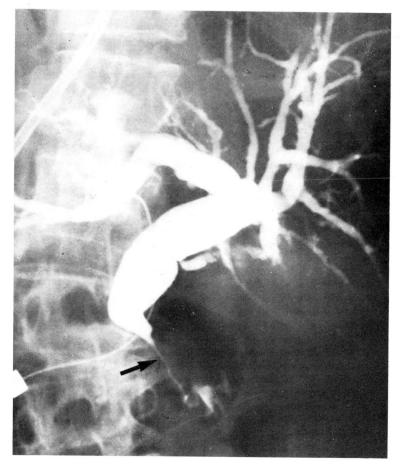

Fig. 1. Percutaneous transhepatic cholangiography. The arrow indicates a stricture of the intrapancreatic portion of the common bile duct and this is due to cancer of the head of the pancreas.

possibility of perforation. Systemic antibiotic therapy is usually necessary and oxytetracycline or ampicillin given either orally or parenterally is generally adequate. A single episode of diverticulitis requires no further treatment but recurrent attacks, particularly if associated with obstruction, are an indication for resection. Large bowel obstruction may be relieved by a one-stage operation but if the operation is technically difficult a relieving colostomy or staged procedure must be used. Abscess formation, peritonitis and fistulas generally require an initial period of stabilization on antibiotic therapy followed by bowel resection. The choice of the surgical procedure depends upon the experience and facilities of the surgeon. A primary end-to-end anastomosis is practised by experienced operators but for many the safest procedure is a defunctioning colostomy followed subsequently by the removal of the sigmoid colon and closure of the colostomy. Sigmoid myotomy has been recommended.

The prognosis is variable. The diverticula tend to increase in number with age, as do the morbidity and mortality. About 20% of patients with diverticular disease require surgery for the complications of the disease. Two-thirds of patients can expect to be rendered free of symptoms following surgery. Most patients who die do so from inflammatory complications and the overall mortality is about 5% of all patients admitted to hospital.

Pseudomembranous Enterocolitis

This disorder is characterized by the formation of a membrane comprising necrotic cells, fibrin and white blood cells over the mucosal surface of the bowel. Both small and large intestines may be involved but not uncommonly the membrane is confined to the colon and the term 'pseudomembranous colitis' is used. Pseudomembranous colitis may develop in severe systemic disorders, colonic obstruction and in the postoperative state, but recently it has been described as a complication of lincomycin and its derivative, clindomycin, therapy. Colitis begins within 2 weeks of starting the antibiotic. The illness varies from being mild to very severe and is characterized by fever, watery diarrhoea with moderate bleeding, abdominal pain and collapse. At procotoscopy the mucosa is seen to be oedematous and friable with yellow/white plaque-like membranes. The differential diagnosis is from other forms of acute colitis particularly ulcerative colitis. The clinical course is prolonged, usually 4–6 weeks, and the prognosis is generally favourable requiring only supportive management such as intravenous fluid and electrolyte replacement and codeine phosphate.

Gastrointestinal Effects of Irradiation

The gastrointestinal tract together with the haematopoietic system is markedly radiosensitive. Irradiation affects DNA synthesis and in the immediate post-radiation period there is a dose-dependent depression of DNA synthesis. After 2 or 3 days compensatory proliferation of cells ensues, particularly in the jejunum and colon.

The effects of irradiation will depend upon the dose and extent of the irradiated field. Mucosal changes include a reduction in the crypt mitoses, reduction in villus height and infiltration of the lamina propria with plasma cells and polymorphonuclear leucocytes. After cessation of therapy recovery occurs within 3 weeks. The gut is liable to be affected by ionizing radiation during the treatment of cervical and uterine cancer, ovarian cancer, abdominal Hodgkin's disease and other abdominal lymphomas.

Symptoms may be minimal or absent, despite morphological changes. More severe acute changes include proctitis, sigmoiditis or enteritis. The patient may complain of diarrhoea, rectal bleeding and pain. Rarely chronic irreversible bowel damage occurs: it is thought that about 2% of patients with gynaecological cancers treated with pelvic irradiation develop permanent sequelae. These include strictures and intestinal obstruction, fistulas, perforations, chronic diarrhoea and fat malabsorption. The malabsorption may follow the mucosal damage, intestinal lymphatic obstruction or bacterial overgrowth. There may also be malabsorption of vitamin B_{12}. Therapy will depend upon the underlying mechanism and includes fat restriction if there is lymphatic obstruction, antibiotics for the contaminated bowel and cholestyramine for damaged ileum.

The Digestive Tract in Connective Tissue Disorders

All the disorders of connective tissue may involve the gastrointestinal tract. *Scleroderma (systemic sclerosis)* in particular may present as a primary disorder of bowel function and intestinal dysfunction occurs in two-thirds of patients. The gut involvement may precede the cutaneous manifestations of the disease. Fibrosis of the smooth muscle in the oesophagus causes disordered oesophageal motility (p. 9). Usually this manifests as dysphagia but patients may not complain of difficulty with swallowing and the oesophageal involvement is detected only when barium studies or manometry indicate weakened or absent peristalsis. Oesophageal emptying is delayed. The disorder is worse in the lower oesophagus. Another cause for dysphagia is oesophageal reflux with stricture formation. This is believed to be the consequence of sclerodermatous involvement of the oesophagogastric junction which affects the competence of the sphincter mechanism. The oesophageal mucosa is usually normal but it may show hyperkeratosis, chronic inflammation or ulceration in the distal third.

There is interference with normal peristalsis in the small intestine and characteristically the duodenum is most affected. Localized dilatation of the bowel is recognized on barium examination, which also shows clumping and segmentation of the barium and a delayed transit time.

Malabsorption of fat occurs, although the mechanism is not fully understood. Bacterial infection, impaired blood supply and poor lacteal drainage all play a role. Antibiotic therapy may be of some help. Severe sclerodermatous involvement gives rise to ileus which may simulate intestinal obstruction. Colonic involvement causes chronic constipation. The liver is rarely affected but hepatic fibrosis and even primary biliary cirrhosis have been recorded.

Involvement of the intestinal vessels in *polyarteritis nodosa* occasionally produces severe consequences which dominate the clinical picture. The presentation is varied and includes severe abdominal pain which may simulate acute appendicitis, single, multiple or recurrent perforations, ulcerative lesions in the large or small bowel, peritonitis, intraperitoneal haemorrhage and malabsorption. Hepatic lesions include multiple infarcts and fibrosis.

Abdominal involvement in *systemic lupus erythematosus* includes intestinal ulceration and perforation, peritonitis, ileus, pancreatitis and hepatic fibrosis and cirrhosis. The syndrome of systemic lupus erythematosus, positive LE cells and liver involvement may be difficult to distinguish from chronic active hepatitis with positive LE cells and 'vasculitis' (p. 251). However, in chronic active hepatitis the histology of the liver shows plasma cell infiltration and rosette formation, the serum aspartate transaminase and γ-globulin levels are markedly elevated and the smooth muscle antibody is usually present; in systemic lupus erythematosus the histology of the liver lesion is more non-specific and the biochemical changes are less marked.

Dermatomyositis may be associated with dysphagia because of damage to the cricopharyngeus muscle.

It is claimed that gastric ulcers are more frequent in patients with *rheumatoid arthritis* and these patients are at risk to bleed from the gastrointestinal tract possibly as a complication of therapy with steroids and other anti-inflammatory agents. An associated vasculitis may cause bowel complications; fat malabsorption and gastrointestinal protein loss also occur.

In *familial Mediterranean fever* the patient experiences recurrent episodes of peritonitis. About one-third of patients develop systemic amyloidosis and this may be associated with malabsorption, constipation, bleeding and intestinal ulceration and perforation.

Pseudoxanthoma elasticum is an inherited dystrophy of elastic fibres. Patients present with gastrointestinal bleeding or occasionally abdominal pain. The diagnosis is established by the characteristic skin appearance particularly at the elbows and neck, and the angiod streaks in the retina.

In the *Ehlers–Danlos syndrome* there is fragility of the skin and friability of tissues with loose-jointedness. The commonest gastrointestinal manifestation is a hernia, but bleeding and perforations also occur.

Gastrointestinal Manifestations of Diabetes Mellitus

The gastrointestinal tract often features prominently in the symptomatology of diabetes mellitus. About 75% of patients developing diabetic ketosis have anorexia, nausea and vomiting. Gastric dilatation is frequent in ketotic coma. Abdominal pain may be difficult to interpret. It may herald the onset of diabetic acidosis; but acute appendicitis or pancreatitis in a diabetic may precipitate ketosis. Rarely the diabetic may have sharp shooting abdominal pains similar to those experienced in tabes dorsalis.

Nearly one-third of diabetic patients have gastric mucosal atrophy with circulating parietal cell antibodies and a reduction in gastric acid output. Constipation is a frequent symptom and the mechanism is not always clear. Gastric emptying is delayed, there are dilated loops of bowel and marked lengthening of transit time. The diabetic occasionally has troublesome diarrhoea; this is believed to be a manifestation of autonomic neuropathy which has caused altered bowel motility. Characteristically the diarrhoea occurs in patients between 20 and 40 years of age who have severe diabetes complicated by retinopathy, peripheral neuropathy and kidney disease. The bowel actions are profuse, watery and urgent and may occur only at night—diabetic nocturnal diarrhoea. Faecal incontinence is commonly encountered and may reflect in the afferent impulses arising from the anal sphincter. The diarrhoea may be a manifestation of steatorrhoea. In the majority of patients the intestinal mucosa is normal or near normal and the mechanism of the malabsorption is believed to be related to the disordered gut motility and the associated bacterial overgrowth. Thus antibiotic therapy is helpful at times. A second, less common, cause of fat malabsorption is a flat intestinal mucous membrane which is similar in appearance to that in coeliac disease. These two causes for fat malabsorption may coexist; therefore a small bowel biopsy must always be performed when a diabetic patient is shown to have steatorrhoea. Other gastrointestinal disorders associated with the diabetic state include pancreatitis, gall stones and disorders of oesophageal motility (p. 9).

Gastrointestinal Complications of Leukaemia

It is not always appreciated that the gut is involved in leukaemia and that serious intestinal complications occur before and during therapy. Leukaemic infiltrates may affect the oesophagus, stomach and small and large bowel. Haemorrhagic lesions are common and severe gastrointestinal bleeding occurs in nearly 20% of patients and has a high mortality rate. Ulceration may occur in any part of the bowel, particularly the anorectal region. Treatment of the leukaemia may induce the development of intestinal moniliasis, and resolution of a leukaemic plaque may be associated with free perforation. Agranulocytic abscesses and acute gangrenous appendicitis are other hazards.

Gastrointestinal Complications of Chronic Renal Disease

Anorexia, nausea and vomiting are frequent in chronic renal failure. Gastrointestinal bleeding has been related to the high incidence of duodenal ulcers. Results of gastric acid output measurements have been conflicting. It has been suggested that there is impairment of gastric acid secretion but that following institution of regular haemodialysis there is an increase in basal and stimulated acid output. The reason for this is not clear. Gastric acid hypersecretion is probably related to an increase in circulating gastrin which is the consequence of the diseased kidney being unable to metabolize this hormone. Uraemic diarrhoea might be a manifestation of the hypergastinaemia but another factor is possibly an alteration in intestinal bile salt profile. Renal transplantation may be complicated by a variety of gastrointestinal upsets particularly bleeding from peptic ulceration or oesophagitis or gastritis.

Retroperitoneal Fibrosis

In retroperitoneal fibrosis a mat of fibrous tissue covers the posterior abdominal wall, extending from the pelvic brim to the pelvis of the kidney and may even spread into the mediastinum. The aetiology is unknown; inflammatory causes, trauma and drugs (including methysergide maleate and the β-blocking agent, practolol) have all been implicated. The condition has been associated with sclerosing cholangitis, pseudotumour of the orbit, portal hypertension, thyroiditis and Gardner's syndrome. Although anorexia, nausea and vomiting may occur the brunt of the disease falls on the renal system. Backache and loin pain are frequent and uraemia occurs in about 50% of patients with bilateral ureteral involvement. Intravenous pyelography shows medial displacement of the ureters, which are narrowed and kinked, and distortion of the bladder. Severe and extensive ureteric narrowing causes hydronephrosis. There may be obstruction of the inferior vena cava. The diagnosis is difficult to establish and although it may be suspected from the pyelogram or caval venography it is usually made at the time of a laparotomy. The treatment is unsatisfactory and includes steroid therapy and ureterolysis combined with extraperitoneal lateral displacement of the ureter.

Adult Hypertrophic Pyloric Stenosis

Hypertrophic pyloric stenosis in the adult accounts for about 3% of patients who present with gastric outflow obstruction. The condition may be grouped into 3 types:

1. The late stage of infantile hypertrophic pyloric stenosis.
2. Hypertrophic pyloric stenosis commencing in adult life but secondary to gastrointestinal disease.
3. Primary adult hypertrophic pyloric stenosis.

The patients complain of vomiting after meals and abdominal discomfort. On examination a distended stomach may be found and a fluid splash can be heard. Gastric ulcers may form secondary to the gastric stasis. Delay in gastric emptying is seen on barium studies and the pyloric canal is narrowed and elongated with an upward curvature. treatment is surgical and involves either a partial gastrectomy or a pyloroplasty.

Diarrhoea, Constipation and Vomiting

Together with abdominal pain the symptoms most commonly encountered in gastrointestinal disorders are diarrhoea, constipation and vomiting. It is the task of the clinician to determine the cause for the symptom and then treat the underlying condition so far as is possible; but it will often be necessary to treat the major symptom in its own right whether or not the causative factors have been identified.

Diarrhoea

Diarrhoea may be defined as the frequent passage of loose stools, and it is useful to distinguish diarrhoea from dysentery, which is diarrhoea accompanied by blood and mucus. Using this definition of dysentery it is a general rule that dysentery results from organic large bowel disease. Diarrhoea, too, can originate from the colon but it also occurs in gastric and small intestinal diseases.

If a patient presents with dysentery then investigations are directed towards the colon. Stool culture, rectal examination, sigmoidoscopy and colonoscopy, and a barium enema are undertaken to exclude diseases such as bacterial and protozoal infections, ulcerative and granulomatous colitis and tumours.

The diagnostic assessment for diarrhoea includes determining whether there is infection (simple food poisoning or some other infective agent), whether there is colonic disease and whether the diarrhoea is a manifestation of fat malabsorption. On the other hand no specific cause may be found for the loose stools.

A number of drugs are of empirical value in the management of diarrhoea:

Opium Derivatives

Codeine phosphate, 15–60 mg orally per dose, may be repeated at varying intervals depending on the severity of the diarrhoea. Tinct. opii may also be used.

Anticholinergic Drugs

These are often of value but it is difficult to achieve a therapeutic result in the absence of troublesome side effects. Atropine and belladonna are less frequently used today and

commonly prescribed agents are 15 mg tablets of propantheline 4 times daily or 10 mg tablets of dicyclomine 4 times
daily.

Kaolin

The absorbent kaolin may be used either as a powder
(2–10 g) or as a mixture (15–30 ml dose) and the patient is
advised to take a dose after each bowel action. In this way
the dose is reduced as the diarrhoea comes under control.
Kaolin is often prescribed with morphine as kaolin and
morphine mixture, BPC, 15–30 ml 4 times a day. Another
useful combination is Lomotil, which combines a codeine
derivative, diphenoxylate, with atropine; the usual dose is
1 tablet 4 times a day but because of side effects the patient
often finds that 2 tablets taken at night just before going to
bed is an effective method of deriving a therapeutic effect
without troublesome side effects.

Antibiotics

Antibiotic therapy is not recommended for diarrhoea.
Bowel infections persist longer and there is the hazard of
significant side effects if antibiotics are given. An obvious
exception to this statement is typhoid fever.

Attention to fluid and electrolyte balance, particularly
potassium, is mandatory at all times and if there is any
doubt about the state of hydration the patient must be
managed in hospital. This applies particularly to the aged
and to young children.

CONSTIPATION

Constipation may be defined as the difficult passage of
hard stools. The frequency of bowel actions is not important: a patient passing a hard stool with difficulty once or
twice a day is constipated whereas a patient emptying the
bowel of a soft stool twice a week should not be regarded
as having constipation. There are very many causes of

constipation and these may be grouped in the following categories:

1. Large bowel disorders including tumours and diverticular disease.
2. Obstructive lesions in the small bowel.
3. Local rectal complaints, particularly fissures.
4. Faulty bowel habits.
5. Miscellaneous causes including depression and hypothyroidism.

A rectal examination is always necessary, not only to exclude tumours, but also to determine whether a fissure is present, because the patient does not necessarily complain of rectal pain. Sigmoidoscopy and barium enema examination are essential before significant colonic pathology can be regarded as having been excluded.

There are a number of laxative agents which may be used in the symptomatic management:

TABLE XIII. *Classification of Laxatives*

Anthracene derivatives	Senna, aloes, rhubarb, cascara
Salts	$MgSO_4$, $Mg(OH)_2$, Na_2SO_4
Phenylmethanes	Phenolphthalein, bisacodyl
Polysaccharides	Cellulose and its derivatives Gums Mucilages Algal-agar, alginates Bran
Detergents	Dioctyl sodium sulphosuccinate, bile salts
Miscellaneous	Lactulose, liquid paraffin, castor oil

Laxatives can be classified broadly according to their chemical structure and properties (Table XIII).

Bacterial derivatives of the anthracene laxatives stimulate the myenteric plexus in the colon. The effect occurs within 8–12 hours of ingestion and the drugs are best given at night. Senna, usually in the form of tablets (Senokot) is widely used, as is cascara elixir in a dose of 2–5 ml.

Many of the phenylmethanes are absorbed and excreted in the bile in the conjugated form. After undergoing bacterial deconjugation they stimulate colonic peristalsis. Phenolphthalein is included in a variety of laxative preparations. Bisacodyl may be given as 5 mg tablets or as a suppository. The agent is inclined to be irritating: the tablets may cause severe cramps and the suppositories can induce proctitis.

The polysaccharide substances comprise many of the colloid or bulk laxatives. These indigestible plant substances swell in water, increase faecal bulk and stimulate peristalsis. Methylcellulose, 1–1.5 g and agar, 4–16 g are widely used. Other popular agents are derivatives from methyl cellulose. They may be given as a single dose in the evening or more frequently.

Saline laxatives have a rapid osmotic effect taking 2–3 hours to work. They are usually given in the morning. The most widely used is magnesium sulphate, 4–8 g.

Dioctyl sodium sulphosuccinate is a popular and useful laxative administered as 20 or 100 mg tablets thrice daily. Lactulose is a synthetic disaccharide which is not hydrolysed in the small intestine and passes into the colon where it undergoes degradation to short chain fatty acids and lactic acid which have an osmotic and irritative effect. The dose is 30 ml daily.

In managing a patient with constipation it is important to diagnose and deal with local rectal disease. Where the cause is faulty bowel habit the patient should be instructed to obey the urge to defaecate and attempt to establish the gastrocolic reflex. The urge to go to stool in the mornings should be encouraged. High residue diets are helpful and plenty of vegetables and high bulk-fibre cereals are recommended.

When faecal impaction is severe it may be necessary to

administer an enema. The most widely used enema is a solution of green soap and water made up in a dilution of 1:10. Between 500 and 1000 ml of the solution are administered rectally via a rubber catheter and a funnel. The enema is retained for 10–15 minutes and then evacuated. Other enemas include olive oil (100–200 ml) and glycerine and olive oil. A number of disposable enemas are available. Enemas are not without danger, causing rupture of the bowel and water intoxication if an excessive volume of fluid is administered. These complications are particularly liable to occur in infants and young children. The danger of administering an enema in ulcerative colitis must be appreciated, for this procedure may induce a severe exacerbation of the illness including perforation.

Constipation in neonates, infants and young children presents a particular problem. Organic causes such as imperforate anus, meconium ileus and Hirschsprung's disease present in the neonatal period and require surgical treatment. Malnutrition and dehydration may cause hard stools. Psychological disturbances are a frequent cause of constipation in older children and the management includes the use of psychotherapy as well as laxatives. Any severely constipated child will show a variety of behaviour disorders, and there will be abdominal pain, distension and failure to thrive. The faeces which accumulate in the rectum will leak and there will be continuous soiling; there may be disturbance of bladder function too so that the child is 'wet' as well.

Laxative abuse is a syndrome affecting mainly women aged 20–70 years. There is persistent, excessive and often surreptitious ingestion of laxatives. The patients complain of either constipation or diarrhoea, abdominal pain, weakness, nausea, vomiting and weight-loss. Most of them have a psychiatric illness which underlies their laxative abuse. Hypokalaemia occurs in most patients and renal damage may ensue. In about 10% of patients characteristic changes are found on barium enema including absent haustra, colonic distension and pseudostrictures, the findings being more prominent on the right side: cathartic colon.

Liquid paraffin may induce paraffinomas and phenolphthalein is prone to cause rashes. It is particularly dangerous to administer a laxative to a child with abdominal pain.

VOMITING

Vomiting is a symptom common to a great number of gastrointestinal disorders and while frequently associated with gastric and duodenal disease vomiting may occur as a reflex phenomenon in intestinal, colonic and hepatic disturbances. It is also a feature of organic obstruction in the gastrointestinal tract. Vomiting also occurs in systemic illnesses which do not directly affect the gut, and it is an important symptom of central nervous system disorders. There are pathways between the vestibular system and the medullary vomiting centres and excessive stimulation of these pathways is the explanation for the vomiting of motion sickness. Vomiting occurs in pregnancy, particularly during the fourth to eighth weeks, and is related to high oestrogen levels. Emotional factors may be the sole cause of vomiting. It is useful to distinguish peripheral causes of vomiting (responses to afferent stimuli in the gastrointestinal tract) from central causes (responses to mechanisms in the brain stem and higher centres). There are two centres in the brain stem responsible for vomiting: the emetic centre in the lateral reticular formation which mediates all vomiting and a chemoreceptor trigger zone (CTZ) in the medulla which is stimulated by digitalis, morphine and in uraemia and diabetic ketosis. Atropine and its derivatives and antihistamines inhibit the emetic centre and thus prevent all vomiting; phenothiazines inhibit only the CTZ.

Useful agents for the treatment of vomiting include hyoscine, 0.6–1.2 mg every 6 hours, and cyclizine, 50 mg every 6 hours, which are particularly valuable for motion sickness and other vestibular causes of vomiting. Longer-acting antihistamines include promethazine, 25 mg twice a day, and meclazine, 25 mg twice daily. Other anticholinergic agents are propantheline, 15 mg thrice daily, and dicyclomine, 10 mg three times a day; they are of value in vomiting of pregnancy and may be taken at night to prevent morning sickness. Chlorpromazine, 25–50 mg thrice daily, is active against CTZ stimulation and is widely used as an antiemetic. Metoclopramide, 10 mg three times a day, increases the strength of the gastric antral contractions and speeds gastric emptying. It has been used successfully to treat the nausea and vomiting accompanying a variety of gastrointestinal disorders.

The side effects of all these drugs must be remembered. Atropine-like antiemetics cause tachycardia, blurring of vision, dry mouth and reduced gut motility. Antihistamines not only have mild atropine-like effects but also cause drowsiness and in a few patients induce disorder of the extrapyramidal system.

ABDOMINAL PAIN

Pain in the abdomen is a major symptom of gastro-enterological disease. The mechanism varies depending upon the underlying disorder: irritation of the parietal and/or visceral peritoneum and excessive intestinal contractions or distension are important factors. Visceral pain is diffuse and poorly localized whereas parietal peritoneal inflammation is well localized, constant and has associated muscular rigidity.

It is convenient to consider the very many causes of abdominal pain in two categories: those in which the presentation is acute, and in which the underlying disease frequently necessitates prompt surgical intervention, the 'acute abdomen'; and those diseases that are non-surgical, in other words 'medical'. In this latter group the presentation of pain may be either acute or more gradual.

The Acute Abdomen

Important causes all of which are indications for laparotomy are acute appendicitis, perforated peptic ulcer, small and large bowel obstruction, acute cholecystitis and a ruptured viscus. Acute pancreatitis does not require exploratory laparotomy but the diagnosis may be sufficiently uncertain to warrant operation.

Medical Causes of Abdominal Pain

In some situations the pain is excruciating and readily confused with the acute abdomen while in others it is less severe and more chronic. The pain may arise from abdominal organs or be referred from the heart, mediastinum, pleura or spine, or may arise from a metabolic disorder. Among the very many conditions to be considered are myocardial infarction, pericarditis, dissection of the aorta, mediastinitis, pleurisy, Coxsackie B virus infection (Bornhom disease), pneumothorax, hepatic congestion, pyelonephritis and renal calculus, pain referred from the spine, tabes dorsalis, herpes zoster, sickle cell anaemia, familial Mediterranean fever, acute intermittent porphyria, lead poisoning, hypercalcaemia, hyperlipidaemia (particularly Type I, chylomicronaemia), Addison's disease, haemochromatosis, diabetic ketoacidosis and uraemia.

Chronic abdominal pain may be a feature of psychiatric disorders particularly depression. Recurrent abdominal pain is frequently encountered in children. Very few of them have a demonstrable organic cause. Many of such children grow up in families in which abdominal pain is common; in other children anxiety and, less frequently, depression is a cause. Treatment is based on informal supportive psychotherapy for the patient and his family including explanation, reassurance and discussion.

A variety of investigations will be required depending upon the disease under consideration. Ultimately, and in the face of persistent pain, the clinician will consider diagnostic laparotomy. In general a laparotomy to seek the cause of abdominal pain is to be avoided; however, when all possibilities have been exhausted a laparotomy is justifiable and, indeed, essential for occasionally a remediable cause is found. More frequently the operation serves to reassure both the clinician and the patient that no recognizable intra-abdominal disorder is present thereby paving the way for appropriate supportive medical and psychotherapy.

Ileostomy Care

The greater use of surgery in the management of ulcerative colitis has been accompanied by a steady increase in the number of patients with permanent ileostomies. The successful management of an ileostomy depends upon its site and construction. It is also essential that the patient is adequately prepared psychologically before operation. The purpose and nature of the operation must be explained, as well as the kind of life that the patient can expect with an ileostomy. The patient should be introduced to a member of the Ileostomy Association because it is always reassuring for the prospective ileostomist to discuss the future with a healthy individual who has adapted well to the ileostomy. In managing these patients it must be remembered that the perineal wound may normally take up to a year to heal.

The site for the ileostomy is important and whenever possible it should be selected preoperatively. Stomas should not be in the mid-line, in a scar, in a crease or fold, or be constructed too near the iliac crest. The easiest ileostomy to care for is one that protrudes for several centimetres, thereby avoiding leakage of ileostomy contents. A temporary appliance is fitted in the operating room. It is transparent and allows for ready inspection of the stoma. Once the wounds are healed and the sutures removed a permanent appliance is fitted.

There are a great variety of appliances and all are basically similar, having an adhesive facepiece and a bag. Temporary appliances may take the form of a single adhesive model, or two-piece models which consist of an adherent facepiece and a bag which can be removed. Temporary bags are generally constructed of clear plastic and have sealed ends or the ends may be open but secured with a clip. Modifications include flaps so that belts can be used and a karaya gum ring for stomal protection. Permanent ileostomy appliances may be either one-piece or two-piece. The one-piece fits directly to the skin, whereas the two-piece appliance consists of an adhesive flange and a removable bag. The orifice of the faceplate is made so that it fits snugly around the stoma. The ileostomy stoma is insensitive to pain and great care must be exercised in centring the appliance over the stoma. The bag may be of plastic or rubber and either type of appliance may be worn with or without a belt; most patients find a belt unnecessary. Permanent bags are supplied with a screw or spout outlet and some have a valve to allow for the escape of gas.

The comfort and success of the ileostomy depends on the health of the skin around the stoma. Some form of adhesive is necessary to hold the appliance in place and to prevent leakage of ileostomy effluent. The ileostomy effluent contains digestive enzymes which rapidly damage and excoriate the skin, causing pain and preventing the correct fixing of the ileostomy bag. Karaya gum is a natural resin which can be used to protect the skin; it is applied directly to the skin either as a powder or as a disc. The powder is applied to the moist inflamed skin and a tenacious film of karaya gum is formed to which the adhesive may be applied. It is essential to protect the small area of skin between the stoma and the appliance. Adhesives that are in use include silicone and rubber cement and the patient should always be patch tested before their application. Correct skin hygiene is essential and the area around the stoma must be cleansed carefully when the bag is removed; old gum and adhesive are removed and any minor skin irritation is attended to. Bacterial or fungal infection will require treatment with an antibiotic or mycostatin powder.

It is inevitable that there will be some odour from the ileostomy bag but there are many methods which are in use to reduce objectionable odours. Attention to the diet is helpful; a variety of commercial preparations is of benefit: bismuth subcarbonate, 0.6 g 3 times a day with meals, is probably better than chlorophyll or activated charcoal. Another method is to place crushed aspirin (0.6 g) or 20 drops of sodium benzoate in the bag. Careful washing and drying of the bags reduces unwanted odours.

There is an increased hazard of dehydration and sodium depletion and ileostomists run the risk of renal stones. The stones are usually of uric acid. They are thought to follow diminished renal output and the excretion of a permanently acid urine which is the result of loss of fixed base from the gastrointestinal tract. Patients with an ileostomy must be warned about the danger of fluid and electrolyte loss and they are advised to take sufficient fluid. Salt tablets may be needed. The stoma may become prolapsed with consequent oedema and pressure necrosis. Recession of the stoma causes it to lie flush with the skin and this leads to problems of bag attachment, leakage of effluent and finally skin erosion. Patients may develop partial mechanical obstruction—'ileostomy dysfunction'. There is cramping abdominal pain, distension, vomiting and an excessive watery discharge which may exceed 1.5 litres daily. The obstruction is usually due to foods which leave a gummy residue. The majority of patients respond to gentle irrigation and aspiration with a catheter. This form of ileostomy dysfunction can be prevented by avoiding eating large quantities of indigestible cellulose. Organic obstruction necessitating surgical intervention may be secondary to adhesions, recurrent ileitis or gross stomal oedema.

No patient should be discharged from hospital without full knowledge of ileostomy care and without advice to join the Ileotomy Association. Patients can look forward to a near-normal life. Those who retain the rectum have no difficulties with sexual function. Rectal excision is associated with ejaculatory or erectile impotence in up to 30% of males. Women can achieve an orgasm but have an increased frequency of dysparunia. About 50% of patients have psychological problems relating to their sexual life.

Colostomy

There are more than 100 000 patients with a permanent colostomy in the United Kingdom, the great majority of whom have undergone surgery for anorectal cancer. Right-sided colonic contents are fluid and irritating, whereas faeces from the left colon tend to be solid and non-irritating. Colostomy stomas should, where possible, be fashioned from the sigmoid or descending colon; the right transverse colostomy is difficult to manage. In the absence of a sphincter mechanism it is not possible to exercise any control over the colostomy but with training a regular emptying habit may be achieved. Nonetheless more than one-third of colostomy patients are never able to manage continence and some form of appliance is necessary. An appliance will be required in all patients during the immediate postoperative period. All colostomy subjects should know how to use a colostomy bag. The colostomy appliances are basically similar to those used for an ileostomy except that the aperture is larger. A popular model is the two-piece non-adhesive belted appliance. Leakage and skin irritation is not a problem because the stool is firmer and non-irritant. If continence has been achieved it is possible to dispense with the bag: the peristomal skin is protected by silicone cream and the stoma covered by cellulose wadding supported by tape or a girdle. In contrast to an ileostomy the colostomy stoma is constructed flush with the skin.

The usual method for colostomy control in the United

Kingdom is by natural evacuation and the use of colostomy irrigation is not advocated as a method to stimulate colonic contractions. This is achieved by controlled fluid intake and dietary restrictions. Patients with a colostomy are liable to complications such as stricture, prolapse, recession, haemorrhage and obstruction. The commonest problem is minor degrees of stomal stricture which can be managed by gentle finger dilatation. This should be undertaken with caution and only by the medical attendant. If frequent dilatation is necessary the stoma should be refashioned. Other difficulties include wearing suitable clothes, odour, irregular colostomy function and sensitivity to various foods.

Ileostomy and colostomy subjects require careful psychological preparation and follow-up. Anorectal surgery in males is accompanied by a high incidence of postoperative impotence. Much social adjustment may be necessary and at least 25% of stoma patients become overtly depressed. There is a great danger of social isolation. Thus although the patient with a stoma may remain in good physical health regrettably the quality of life is often below what might be anticipated.

Further Reading

Cummings, J. H. (1974) Laxative abuse. *Gut*, **15**, 758–766.

Ivey, K. J. (1975) Are anticholinergics of use in the irritable colon syndrome? *Gastroenterology*, **68**, 1300–1307.

McConnell, J. B. et al. (1975) Gastric function in chronic renal failure. *Lancet*, **ii**, 1121–1123.

Young, S. J. et al. (1976) Psychiatric illness and the irritable bowel syndrome. *Gastroenterology*, **70**, 162–166.

Viteri, A. L. et al. (1974) The spectrum of lincomycin-clindamycin colitis. *Gastroenterology*, **66**, 1137–1144.

Whelton, M. J. et al. (1971) Ileostomy and colostomy care. *Br. J. Hosp. Med.*, September, 315–322.

The anal canal is 5 cm long and is surrounded in the upper two-thirds by an inner ring of the internal anal sphincter outside which lies the puborectalis muscle and a portion of the external anal sphincter. The lower one-third of the anus is surrounded solely by the striated external anal sphincter. The tone of the anal sphincters keep the canal closed, the major contribution coming from the internal sphincter. The angle between the axis of the rectum and anus, which is produced by the puborectalis sling, is important for controlling the passage of solid faeces. The upper part of the canal relaxes in response to distension and by a conscious 'sampling' response gas is passed but solid and fluid material retained. Defaecation is a balance between environmental factors and cortical inhibition of basic reflexes from the anus and rectum. In assuming the squatting position the angle between the rectum and anus is straightened, intrarectal pressure is increased by the Valsalva manoeuvre, the internal and external anal sphincters relax possibly by reflex inhibition induced by straining. The external anal relaxation is maintained by a reflex arising from stimulation of the anal canal by passage of the stool.

Haemorrhoids

INTERNAL HAEMORRHOIDS

Internal haemorrhoids are a mass of varicose veins which arise from the haemorrhoidal plexus of veins. In contrast to external haemorrhoids the veins are covered by mucous membrane. The cause of this extremely common condition is not known but constipation and straining may play a role.

Internal haemorrhoids are classified as *first degree* (haemorrhoids which bleed but do not prolapse), *second degree* (haemorrhoids which prolapse on defaecation but return spontaneously) and *third degree* (haemorrhoids which prolapse and which have to be replaced manually).

The symptoms may be minimal and initially there is only slight rectal bleeding. Characteristically bleeding occurs after defaecation but bleeding may also occur during and occasionally before the passage of a stool. The blood is usually on the outside of the faeces and not intimately mixed with the motion. The bleeding may be of a large volume. At a later stage there is a sense of rectal fullness and the patient becomes aware of a mass prolapsing from the anus. There may be a mucous discharge and pruritus ani. Haemorrhoids are seldom painful unless they become complicated. The patient may also present with the systemic effects of a severe iron deficiency anaemia. The complications of internal haemorrhoids include strangulation which occurs when the anal sphincter grips a prolapsed haemorrhoid, thereby causing marked oedema, and eventually thrombosis. This is an extremely painful condition and it is difficult to replace the haemorrhoid. Other complications are ulceration, fissure and spreading infection. All patients complaining of rectal bleeding or haemorrhoids require a thorough rectal examination which must include digital palpation and endoscopy. It is always necessary to consider the presence of associated large bowel disease such as cancer, colitis and diverticular disease and the associated clinical features may suggest the need for a barium enema. Haemorrhoids may develop acutely if they are secondary to a colonic cancer.

Patients with haemorrhoids should be treated with attention to the diet and a suitable laxative is introduced in an attempt to obtain regular soft bowel actions. When the haemorrhoids alone are responsible for rectal bleeding injection therapy is effective, and all first and second degree haemorrhoids can be treated by this method. The patient is re-examined 6 weeks after the injection of the sclerosant and the injections repeated if a satisfactory result has not been achieved. Many surgeons favour treating haemorrhoids by the rubberband ligation technique which can be undertaken on outpatients under local anaesthesia. In the Lord technique digital dilatation of the anal canal and lower rectum, followed by the insertion of a foam plastic pack to prevent a haematoma, is undertaken under general anaesthesia, but on an outpatient basis. Haemorrhoidectomy is less commonly performed and is reserved for third-degree haemorrhoids and large external skin tags. Prolapsed thrombosed haemorrhoids are usually treated by bed rest; the foot of the bed is elevated and lead lotion is applied to the perianal region. However, some surgeons recommend immediate operation for these patients.

The results of surgery for haemorrhoids are generally satisfactory although some patients are troubled by minor complaints such as redundant folds of perianal skin, mild anal narrowing and occasional leakage of faeces and flatus.

EXTERNAL HAEMORRHOIDS

These form at the anal margin and are covered with skin. They manifest either as an acute anal haematoma or as anal skin tags.

External anal haematomas usually follow straining at stool or coughing. The patient experiences swelling and acute pain in the skin around the anus. Rectal examination reveals a dark blue, firm, easily palpable swelling covered by skin. The haematoma must not be confused with a melanoma. Either the lesion subsides or pressure necrosis of the overlying skin occurs with extrusion of the blood clot. A secondary abscess may develop. Treatment is by application of local anal anaesthetic ointments. If the lesion is seen at an early stage and is very painful it will be necessary to evacuate the haematoma under an anaesthetic.

Anal skin tags must be distinguished from anal warts, condylomas, leukoplakia and cancer. The tags may be unrelated to anal pathology or secondary to an anal fissure. They may also be associated with internal haemorrhoids. If the skin tags are large they can be removed. Any underlying anorectal lesion must be treated.

Anal Fissure

This is an ulceration of the skin in the anal canal. The fissure is usually sited posteriorly in the anus and may be acute or chronic. Predisposing factors include prolapsing internal haemorrhoids, ulcerative colitis, Crohn's disease and other large bowel disorders.

The main symptom is sharp, 'tearing', localized rectal pain which is experienced during and immediately after defaecation. A small amount of bleeding may occur and blood is recognized on the surface of the stool or on the toilet paper. In chronic anal fissures there is oedema of the skin and fibrosis which result in the development of a 'sentinel pile' which is usually seen in the midline posteriorly.

The treatment of the established fissure is by stretching of the anal sphincter or by surgical excision. When the fissure is small and acute a combination of stool softeners and local anaesthetic ointments containing corticosteroids may be effective and these are applied just before and after defaecation.

Anal Fistula

Infection in the anal glands produces the primary lesion. In 95% of patients the fistulous tract is short, taking a path below the external anal sphincter. Treatment is simple; the tract is laid open and healing is rapid. Uncommonly the tract is long and tortuous and may almost encircle the anus. Surgery is difficult, sometimes extensive and as more of the sphincter muscle is divided there is increasing risk of anal incontinence.

Cryptitis and Papillitis

The anal crypts and papillae which lie at the junction of the anus and rectum are particularly vulnerable to trauma and infection. Mild infection produces local rectal discomfort and burning which is frequently experienced only at the time of defaecation. More extensive inflammation causes oedema and the sense of incomplete defaecation. Slight bleeding and a mucous discharge are other features. The inflammation may occur in association with other rectal disorders such as fissures and haemorrhoids. Proctoscopic examination shows the area around the crypts to be reddened and oedematous and a small bead of pus may be seen in the crypt. Prompt treatment is required otherwise cryptitis may be complicated by anal fistula and an ischiorectal abscess. Local anaesthetic ointments and a local or systemic antibiotic may be tried but if the inflammation persists a minor surgical operation is required.

Descending Perineum Syndrome

This condition is probably more common than is generally appreciated. There is a reduction of the reflex contraction of the pelvic floor muscles which normally occurs following defaecation. Gentle straining will produce bulging of the perineum and eventually there is permanent lengthening of the muscle fibres with sagging of the pelvic floor and a decreased angulation at the anorectal junction. The effect of this is to reduce the efficiency of the anal sphincter mechanism and some degree of faecal soiling occurs.

Typically the patient complains of a sensation of a lump or obstruction in the anal canal, particularly during defaecation, which gradually subsides when the straining stops. Other symptoms include slight rectal bleeding which accompanies the mucosal prolapse, anal discharge, rectal pain and pruritus ani. There is frequently a long history of constipation and straining at stool. On examination during straining the perineum will be seen to sag as much as 4–8 cm below the lower limits of the bony pelvis. The anal sphincter is lax. On proctoscopy the anterior rectal wall is seen to bulge into the rectum when the patient strains.

The treatment is to achieve normal bowel motions. The rectal prolapse can be treated by injection, but if it is large surgical excision is necessary. Surgical intervention is also required if there is marked weakness and some degree of anal incontinence and a postanal perineorrhaphy is performed.

Solitary Ulcer of the Rectum

This condition affects young adults and is characterized by bleeding at the time of defaecation, the passage of mucus, anal pain and mild diarrhoea. In a few patients the pain is experienced in the lower abdomen. Rectal examination is often normal although some oedema and induration may be detected. On sigmoidoscopy the mucosa is essentially normal with the exception of one or two circular ulcers which are seen 7–10 cm from the anal margin. The ulcers are 2 cm in diameter and usually situated anteriorly astride a rectal valve. Characteristically the base of the ulcer is shallow and covered with a yellow grey slough.

The treatment is unsatisfactory. Many agents have been used locally with limited success and attempts at surgical excision have been followed by recurrence of the ulcer. The ulcers may persist unchanged for many years.

Pruritus Ani

This is a common condition and may account for up to 10% of patients seen in any large rectal clinic. The patient complains of irritation in and around the anus. The causes are many and complex and are listed in Table XIV. There are

TABLE XIV. *Causes of Secondary Pruritus Ani*

Local rectal causes
    Haemorrhoids
    Fissure
    Cryptitis
    Descending perineum syndrome

Parasitic infection
    Enterobius vermicularis (threadworm)

Fungus infection
    After long-term antibiotic therapy

Systemic disease
    Diabetes mellitus, particularly if uncontrolled

Allergic states

Vaginitis
    Menopause
    Trichomonas or *Monilia* infection
    Leukorrhoea

Psychological causes
    Particularly in stress and anxiety states

some patients with apparently primary pruritus ani in whom no underlying cause can be identified. It is possible that for some patients their own faeces have an irritant effect on the perianal skin and these are helped by careful swabbing of the perianal area after a bowel action and to sleep with a tissue between the buttocks to absorb moisture.

1% hydrocortisone cream may be helpful. All patients with pruritus ani require careful history taking and physical and rectal examinations. The management will depend upon the underlying condition.

Further Reading

Hardcastle, J. D. (1969) The descending perineum syndrome. *Practitioner*, **203**, 612–619.

Madigan, M. R. and Morson, B. C. (1969) Solitary ulcer of the rectum. *Gut*, **10**, 871–881.

Tagart, R. E. B. (1974) Haemorrhoids and palpable anorectal lesions. *Practitioner*, **212**, 221–238.

The Liver Cell

Although it is customary to refer to the liver lobule as having an efferent vein placed centrally it is more correct to regard the liver as being made up of functional groups of acini in which the efferent vein is peripherally placed, with the portal tracts occupying a more central position. Each portal tract includes connective tissue, lymphatics, an arteriole, a hepatic venule and a bile duct or ductule. The liver parenchyma comprises plates of liver cells which are one cell thick, separated by sinusoids which are lined by epithelium. Between the liver cells and the sinusoids is the space of Disse, which is the site for the formation of the hepatic lymph. Küpffer cells lie in the walls of the sinusoids and have an important role in phagocytosis.

The morphological and functional features of the normal liver cell have been widely studied. Of particular relevance to the changes in liver cell dysfunction are the endoplasmic reticulum and the Golgi apparatus. The endoplasmic reticulum is the site of many specific metabolic and secretory functions of the cell, such as protein synthesis and secretion. The Golgi apparatus consists of lamellae and vesicles. It is related to the canaliculus of the hepatocyte which is the site for bile secretion. The bile canaliculus represents the space between liver cells; at this point the plasma membrane is thrown into microvilli. It is therefore part of the liver cell and nor morphologically related to the bile ductules and ducts; these are lined by the biliary epithelium.

There is probably functional heterogeneity within the hepatic lobule. Thus alkaline phosphatase activity is more marked at the sinusoidal surface and periportal cells have less smooth endoplasmic reticulum than do the centrilobular cells. The significance of this compartmentalization of activity remains uncertain but it may explain the different patterns of histolotical damage which are found in the various forms of liver disease.

The Functions of the Liver

The liver plays a major role in the diverse metabolic processes of the body and is responsible for the synthesis, storage and secretion of a great variety of metabolites. Many are excreted into the bile, reabsorbed by the intestine and pass via the portal blood back to the liver to appear again in the bile. Such substances are said to undergo an enterohepatic circulation and include the bile salts, bilirubin, cholesterol, vitamin B_{12}, folic acid and many oestrogens and a variety of drugs such as digitalis glycosides. Disturbances in the function of the liver cells are reflected in alterations in carbohydrate and lipid metabolism; but it is the changes in the bile pigments, bile salts and the proteins which are of particular interest to the clinician because of their relevance to the diagnosis of the presence and nature of chronic liver disease.

BILIRUBIN METABOLISM

Normally between 250 and 300 mg of bilirubin are produced daily in the normal male; about 85% of this is derived from the breakdown of haemoglobin haem which has originated from mature circulating erythrocytes. About

5.6–7.2 g haemoglobin are degraded each day. In the reticuloendothelial cells particularly of the spleen, and also in the parenchymal cells of the liver, the haem ring is open at the α-methane bridge, a carbon atom is lost and a linear tetrapyrrole is formed. This process is catalysed by haem oxygenase. Iron and globin are removed and re-utilized. Biliverdin is formed and this pigment is reduced to bilirubin either spontaneously or under the effect of bilirubin reductase. Sources of bilirubin other than mature red cells include the breakdown of newly formed erythrocytes in the bone marrow, the synthesis of excessive haem during red cell formation and the direct synthesis of bilirubin in the liver from two other haem fractions, one associated with cytochrome P-450 and the other being a rapidly turning over haem fraction. The breakdown of the red cells in the bone marrow may contribute to the jaundice in pernicious anaemia and thalassaemia. The bile pigment from non-haemoglobin sources does not make a significant contribution to the total bile pigment content of the body.

Bilirubin which has been produced in the reticuloendothelial cells is unconjugated and relatively insoluble in

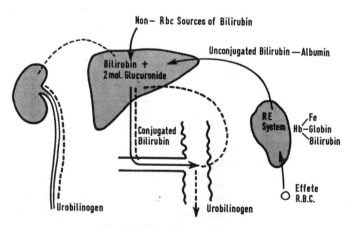

Fig. 6. Bilirubin metabolism.

water; it is transported in the serum attached to albumin, 2 molecules of unconjugated bilirubin being bound to 1 molecule of albumin (Fig. 6). The concentration of unbound bilirubin is increased in hypoalbuminaemia and by drugs such as salicylates and sulphonamides which compete for protein binding sites in the plasma. Unconjugated bilirubin is rapidly and selectively taken up by the liver cells and bound to two hepatic cytoplasmic protein fractions called the Y and the Z protein. Y (also known as ligandin) is the major organic anion binding protein, and its concentration in the liver cell can be increased by the administration of phenobarbitone. Bilirubin is transferred from the cytoplasmic proteins to the endoplasmic reticulum, where it is conjugated with 2 molecules of glucuronic acid to form bilirubin diglucuronide. The responsible enzyme is uridine diphosphoglucuronyl transferase which is sited mainly on the microsomes. Increased activity of this enzyme can be induced by a number of drugs including phenobarbitone. Bilirubin diglucuronide is excreted into the bile at the bile canaliculus, probably by an active transport mechanism. The bilirubin of normal bile is 95–99% conjugated, mainly as the diglucuronide but conjugation with acidic disaccharides also occurs. Glucuronyl transferase activity is rate-limiting for excretion. Another major determinant is micelle formation at the canalicular membrane and bilirubin conjugates are associated in bile with the mixed micelles of bile salts, phospholipids and cholesterol.

Conjugated bilirubin is water soluble and is of a large molecular size and therefore not absorbed from the small intestine. In the terminal ileum and the large bowel bacterial β-glucuronidases hydrolyse the molecule and at the same time the bilirubin is reduced to urobilinogen.

Some of the urobilinogen is absorbed by the terminal ileum and the colon and enters into an enterohepatic circulation, by passing to the liver, where it is excreted into the bile intact and unaltered. Urobilinogen bound to albumin

TABLE XV. *The Classification and Causes of Jaundice*

Hyperbilirubinaemia			
Conjugated		Simple conjugated	Unconjugated
Cholestatic			
Intrahepatic	Extrahepatic		
Viral hepatitis	Cancer of the head of the pancreas	Viral hepatitis	Haemolysis
Drugs		Cirrhosis	Drugs
Alcoholic hepatitis	Cancer of the ampulla of Vater	Dubin Johnson syndrome	Gilbert's syndrome
Secondary cancer	Gall stones		Crigler–Najjar syndrome
Cirrhosis, particularly primary biliary cirrhosis	Biliary atresia		Transient non-haemolytic unconjugated hyperbilirubinaemia
Pregnancy	Sclerosing cholangitis		
Ulcerative colitis			
Malignant lymphoma			

also finds its way into the systemic circulation and is excreted by the kidney by processes of both glomerular filtration and tubular secretion. The amount of urinary urobilinogen depends on a large number of variables, including the quantity of bile pigment formed, intestinal bacteria (the ingestion of a broad spectrum antibiotic will eliminate urobilinogen from the urine), liver disease and renal factors, for urobilinogen excretion is increased by good hydration and an alkaline urine.

An elevation of the serum bilirubin level over 2.5–3.0 mg/100 ml (50 μmol/l) blood appears clinically as *jaundice* and this is a cardinal indication of disturbed liver cell function. Jaundice may result from an increased bilirubin load following haemolysis, from disturbances of the bilirubin transport from the serum across the liver cell membrane, from disturbances of conjugation and from interference with excretion. It is convenient to distinguish two major forms of hyperbilirubinaemia—conjugated and unconjugated (Table XV). Unconjugated hyperbilirubinaemia classically occurs in haemolytic disease but there are a number of syndromes of unconjugated non-haemolytic hyperbilirubinaemia such as in the newborn, following certain drugs, Gilbert's syndrome and occasionally following viral hepatitis. Conjugated hyperbilirubinaemia is found in a great number of liver disorders. Elevated conjugated bilirubin levels may be accompanied by other evidence of hepatic excretory failure, such as elevated serum levels of alkaline phosphatase, cholesterol and bile salts. This is called cholestatic jaundice and is another way of implying obstructive jaundice. Cholestasis may be either extrahepatic or intrahepatic, similar biochemical disturbances being present in both. Conjugated hyperbilirubinaemia as the sole evidence of liver dysfunction is found after viral hepatitis, in cirrhosis and in the rare disorder the Dubin Johnson syndrome.

Bile Salt Metabolism

Bile salts are the end product of the hepatic metabolism of cholesterol and they represent a major pathway for the excretion of sterols. The initial, and rate-limiting, step in the conversion of cholesterol to bile salts is 7α-hydroxylation. The primary bile salts formed in the human liver are cholic acid (a trihydroxy bile acid) and chenodeoxycholic acid (a dihydroxy bile acid) (Fig. 7). These are excreted

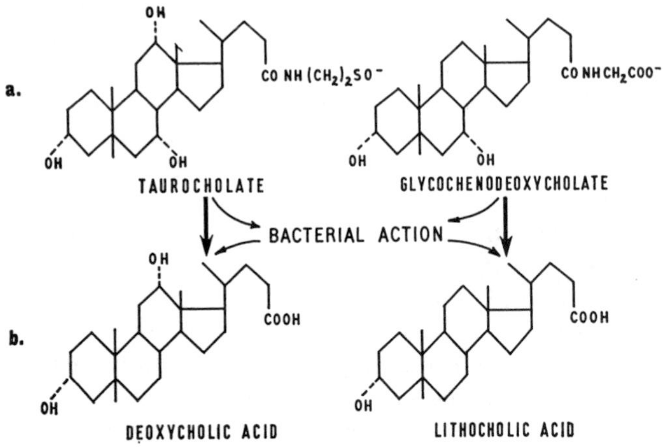

Fig. 7. Bile salts in man: *a*. Primary bile salts; *b*. Secondary bile salts.

into the bile conjugated to the amino acids glycine or taurine and the ratio of glycine to taurine conjugates is 3:1 in man. In the terminal ileum and colon the bile salts undergo both deconjugation to the free bile salts and 7α-dehydroxylation, so that deoxycholic acid (a dihydroxy bile acid) is formed from cholic acid and lithocholic acid (a monohydroxy bile acid) is derived from chenodeoxycholic acid. These bile acids are absorbed and re-excreted in the bile in the conjugated form and are known as the secondary bile acids. The human liver does not alter the secondary bile acids (Fig. 8). In addition to conjugation the bile salts undergo sulphation which increases their polarity and aids renal excretion. Sulphation is important when there is cholestasis. Sulphation assumes particular

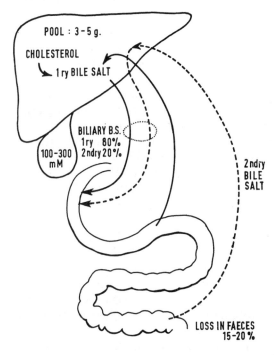

Fig. 8. The enterohepatic circulation of bile salts (B.S.). The gall bladder normally contains 100–300 mmol/litre of bile salts.

significance in lithocholic acid metabolism because it militates against retention of this potentially toxic bile salt.

Bile normally contains a slight excess of dihydroxy bile salts over trihydroxy salts and there are only trace amounts of lithocholate. The bile salt pool in man is approximately 3–5 g. The bile salts undergo an enterohepatic circulation and between 10 and 40 g are excreted daily into the bile. This implies many recyclings of a molecule during the day and it is likely that the total bile salt pool turns over about twice during a meal. Because there are highly efficient means of preventing the loss of bile salts only about 0.8 g is lost daily into the faeces and this amount is readily replaced by hepatic synthesis. This synthesis in turn is controlled by the homeostatic feedback regulation of bile salts returning to the liver via the portal circulation. There is probably a specific bile acid receptor protein in liver surface membranes.

The gastrointestinal tract has considerable capacity for the reabsorption of bile salts and in so doing maintains the integrity of the enterohepatic circulation. Bile salt absorption takes place in both the proximal and the distal small intestine, but it is the ileal reabsorption which is quantitatively the more important. In this latter site there exists an active transport mechanism for the reabsorption of the conjugated bile salts, the maximum transport velocity being greater for the trihydroxy than the dihydroxy salts. Other mechanisms which play a role include passive ionic diffusion of the conjugated bile salts, which occurs in both jejunum and ileum, and passive non-ionic diffusion of unconjugated bile salts, which occurs rapidly in the ileum. Both passive ionic and non-ionic diffusion occur in the colon but the mucosa contains no active transport mechanisms for bile salts.

Apart from serving as a means of sterol excretion the bile salts are involved in a number of physiological functions of importance. Because the molecules contain both hydrophilic and hydrophobic end groups they form micelles and function as physiological 'detergents', thereby helping to solubilize biliary cholesterol and intestinal lipids. Bile salts emulsify ingested lipids and acid in the formation of the mixed micelles of monoglyceride, free fatty acids and bile salts; these mixed micelles also contain cholesterol and the fat-soluble vitamins. The bile salts enhance the reesterification of triglycerides in the intestinal cell, inhibit cholesterogenesis in the intestinal mucous membrane and influence a number of other transport systems in the intestinal cell. In the liver cell the bile salts exert feedback inhibition on bile salt synthesis but it is held that they do not participate directly in the hepatic regulation of cholesterol formation.

Normally there is a slight rise in peripheral serum bile salt concentrations which relates to gall bladder emptying. Patients who have had a cholecystectomy do not demonstrate the postprandial fluctuations but have persistent, moderate elevation of serum values. There is reduced postprandial rise in patients with the bile acid malabsorption that accompanies ileal disease or resection.

Any form of liver disease in which there is obstruction to or reduction in the flow of bile will cause retention of bile salts, elevation of serum values and a fall in the intraluminal concentration of the bile salts. This obstruction may be either extra- or intrahepatic and the major effect is to cause faulty digestion and absorption of fat so that the patient has steatorrhoea. Steatorrhoea occurs in about 50–80% of patients with chronic liver disease and is found in all forms of cirrhosis regardless of the aetiology. It also occurs in patients with acute liver disturbance, such as viral hepatitis. In patients who are clinically icteric the associated fat malabsorption will be anticipated but it is not generally appreciated that malabsorption may also be found in patients who do not have elevated serum bilirubin levels.

The mechanism for steatorrhoea in liver disease is complex and it is probable that in some patients more than one factor operates. In cirrhosis there is a reduction of up to 50% in the total bile salt pool. In icteric patients the intestinal bile salt deficiency is related to the failure of the liver cell secretion, but the finding of reduced concentrations in nonicteric patients suggests that synthesis is also reduced in some cirrhotics. Other factors which may also contribute to the fat malabsorption include alterations in intestinal bacterial flora, portal hypertension with accompanying oedema and malfunction of the small bowel, drugs such as neomycin and pancreatic insufficiency. In many cirrhotic patients pancreatic function is normal; however, alcoholic cirrhosis is frequently complicated by pancreatic fibrosis and inflammation and in these patients reduced pancreatic function contributes to the steatorrhoea.

BILE FORMATION

Hepatic bile is formed by the admixture of at least 3 solutions which differ in origin and composition. The major component is formed by the active secretion of bile salts into the bile canaliculus with the associated osmotic flow of water and inorganic electrolytes. Another important component produced at canalicular level is a bile salt independent fraction which is associated with the active transport of sodium ions. In addition an electrolyte, bicarbonate-rich alkaline solution is produced by the bile ductules (Fig. 9). The total volume of hepatic bile produced each day is about 1 litre.

Hepatic bile is concentrated in the gall bladder by the active transport of sodium, chloride and bicarbonate ions with accompanying movement of water. Potassium is absorbed solely by a passive mechanism. In the process of absorption there is a 90% reduction in the volume of hepatic bile. The principal cation becomes sodium and the major anion is bile salt. Substances to which the gall bladder mucosa is impermeable, such as cholesterol, bile salts and bilirubin diglucuronide, are concentrated 8–10 times. The total daily output of gall bladder bile is 100–150 ml. The differences between hepatic and gall bladder bile composition are shown in Table XVI.

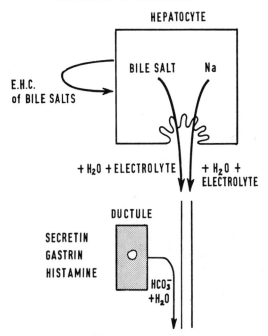

Fig. 9. The formation of bile. Secretin, gastrin and histamine stimulate the ductular component of bile.

TABLE XVI. *The Major Constituents of Hepatic and Gall Bladder Bile*

Constituent	Hepatic Bile	Gall Bladder Bile
Sodium (mmol/litre)	145	210
Potassium (mmol/litre)	4	12
Chloride (mmol/litre)	90	20
Bile salts (mmol/litre)	40	300
Cholesterol (mmol/litre)	3	15
Phospholipids (mmol/litre)	700	3500
Dry weight (mg/ml)	20	130
Osmolality (mosm/litre)	280	280
pH	7.5–8.0	7.0–7.5

Protein Metabolism

The parenchymal liver cell is the principal site of synthesis for the plasma enzymes, lipoproteins, coagulation factors, glycoproteins and lipoproteins. Plasma contains 60–80 g/litre of protein which may be grouped as albumin, globulin and fibrinogen. In adults the total pool of albumin amounts to 4.5–5.0 g/kg. Blood levels are 1.2–2.1 g/kg which amounts to about one-third of the total exchangeable albumin pool. Albumin has a fundamental role in the exchange of water between tissues and blood and it also serves as an important vehicle for the transport of a great variety of substances in the blood. Albumin synthesis occurs in the liver and any situation leading to a diminution in the body amino acid pool is associated with a reduced synthetic rate. The site of albumin degradation has not been elucidated satisfactorily but the intestine may be important. Hypoalbuminaemia is a constant feature of chronic liver disease and is the result of reduced hepatic synthesis; there is a rough correlation between the rate of albumin synthesis and serum values.

The normal liver does not form immunoglobulins but in chronic liver disease hepatic production of immuno-globulins accompanies the infiltration of the portal areas and parenchyma by lymphoid and plasma cells. It remains to be established whether the globulins are synthesized by these cells. Current opinion holds that exogenous antigens, probably of gut origin, are not sequestered by the liver either because of portasystemic shunting or damage to Küpffer cells. The antigen is redistributed to other immunizing sites, particularly the spleen. The plasma electrophoretic β and γ regions contain the immuno-globulins A, G, D, E and M. IgG predominates in the serum of patients with chronic active hepatitis and serum IgM levels are raised in primary biliary cirrhosis. In cirrhosis there is a fusion of the β–γ peaks because of an increase in the faster moving globulins; there is an increased amount of β-globulin in cholestasis; in active chronic hepatitis there is a narrower and more distinct γ peak. In general the diagnostic value of serum electrophoresis is limited.

Alterations in the serum immunoglobulin levels are associated with changes in certain circulating antibodies and these do have some diagnostic significance. A great number of non-specific antibodies are known to occur in patients with chronic liver disease but no organ-specific liver antibody has been demonstrated. Antinuclear factor is present in 30–50% of patients with chronic active hepatitis and in half the patients with idiopathic cirrhosis or primary biliary cirrhosis. The antimitochondrial antibody appears to be a response to a lipoprotein that may be a membrane transport protein. The antibody is found in nearly 90% of patients with primary biliary cirrhosis and 25% of patients with idiopathic cirrhosis and chronic active hepatitis; it is rarely found in patients with mechanical obstruction to the main bile ducts. The smooth muscle antibody is found in 75% of patients with chronic active hepatitis, 50% of patients with primary biliary cirrhosis and 25% of patients with idiopathic cirrhosis.

Primary liver cancer is associated with the appearance in the serum of α-fetoprotein. This protein is a normal component of fetal serum and disappears from the circulation a few weeks after birth. The fetoprotein may be detected in nearly 75% of non-Caucasian persons who have primary liver cancer but in only 33% of Caucasians with this disease. It also appears in some patients recovering from acute viral hepatitis. In patients with obstructive jaundice a unique lipoprotein (lipoprotein X) appears, comprising mainly a 1:1 molar mixture of cholesterol and phospholipids and less than 5% protein. Its presence is a sensitive test of obstructive jaundice but since it appears in both intra- and extrahepatic cholestasis the protein cannot be used in the differential diagnosis of jaundice.

Haptoglobin, an α_2-globulin undergoes variable changes in liver disease and it too, is of little diagnostic value.

The liver manufactures most of the clotting factors and in liver disease profound disturbances of blood coagulation may occur. The factors most affected are II (prothrombin), V, VII and X. Antihaemophilic globulin and fibrinogen levels are rarely affected. Increased fibrinolysis is observed in liver disease. There is an increase in plasminogen activator due to failure of hepatic clearance and the damaged liver may fail to produce the normal inhibitor of fibrinolysis. Under these circumstances low plasma levels of fibrinogen occur. Other factors contributing to the abnormal and excessive bleeding in liver disease are thrombocytopenia, impaired platelet aggregation and occasionally an excess of circulating antithrombin. Severe liver disease is accompanied by the appearance of spur-shaped red cells and mild to moderate haemolysis. The spur erythrocytes have an excess of free cholesterol in their plasma membranes.

Assessment of Liver Function

The biochemical evaluation of liver cell function in routine clinical practice attempts to answer two questions: is there liver cell death?; and is there cholestasis? Evidence for liver cell death is given by an increase in serum amino-transferase values, a prolongation of the prothrombin time and drop in serum albumin concentrations. Cholestasis is indicated by a rise in serum conjugated bilirubin, cholesterol, alkaline phosphatase, bile salts and 5'nucleotidase. Elevation of the serum alkaline phosphatase without concomitant elevation of bilirubin values may occur in space-occupying lesions of the liver, hepatic granulomas, occlusion of one main hepatic duct and partial obstruction to the common bile duct. Gamma-glutamyltranspeptidase is elevated in cholestasis; however it is also a valuable indicator of alcoholic liver disease. The abnormal retention of bromsulphthalein is another index of liver cell excretory failure.

Renal Changes in Liver Disease

There are a number of associations between liver and kidney disease; toxic, infectious, infiltrative or inflammatory disorders can affect both organs. However, two forms of renal dysfunction are particularly associated with primary liver disease: renal tubular necrosis and renal circulatory failure associated with uraemia. The distinction between these two forms of renal disorder is not always clear.

Renal tubular necrosis may complicate toxic liver injury and may also occur as a complication in patients who have marked hypotension after severe gastrointestinal bleeding. Bilirubinaemia increases the risk of tubular damage and the deeper the jaundice the greater this risk. This applies particularly to jaundiced patients who undergo surgery. The mechanism is believed to be due to a marked drop in renal bloodflow and also because the renal parenchyma is more susceptible to ischaemic damage in the icteric patient who undergoes surgery. A mannitol diuresis prevents renal damage by maintaining renal blood flow. Mannitol is given prophylactically to patients undergoing surgery who have serum bilirubin values greater than 15 mg/100 ml (250 mmol/litre). During the hour preceding the operation 500 ml of a 10% mannitol solution are infused and the infusion may be repeated postoperatively if the urine output falls. Patients with tubular necrosis may benefit from renal dialysis.

Some patients with cirrhosis develop *renal tubular acidosis* for reasons which are not apparent. This has important clinical consequences because these patients are liable to alterations in renal ammonia metabolism which may predispose to episodes of hepatic coma; the defect in acidification may also be associated with impairment of renal potassium conservation.

Spontaneous renal failure is an increasingly recognized complication of terminal cirrhosis and is apparently becoming more frequent because of the use of powerful diuretic agents. The renal disorder is usually found in ascitic patients, many of whom have portal hypertension and liver coma. The patients have hyponatraemia, hypokalaemia and uraemia. The features of liver failure predominate and oliguria is a late manifestation. The exact mechanism of the renal failure is unknown but there may be a disturbance of renal haemodynamic function. There is little alteration in renal morphology. The spontaneous development of azotaemia in hepatic decompensation has a bad prognosis and few patients recover. The management is unsatisfactory. Standard procedures are used to treat the liver failure and careful attention is paid to fluid and electrolyte balance. Dialysis gives disappointing results.

Portal Hypertension

Cirrhosis of the liver is associated with death of liver cells, fibrosis and regeneration. The regenerating liver cells form nodules with the total disorganization of the liver architecture. This is the essential feature of hepatic cirrhosis and is responsible for the production of portal hypertension. The mechanism for the raised portal venous pressure is complex and is related to both nodule formation and fibrosis. There is distortion of the portal vascular bed, obstruction to the flow of blood through the liver and increased portal pressure. Vascular anastomoses open up both inside and outside the liver in an attempt to bypass the impedance to portal blood flow. Outside the liver there is opening up of connections between the portal and systemic venous systems and the site which has acquired particular clinical significance is the lower end of the oesophagus; but anastomoses around the umbilicus and the renal vein are also clinically important. Internal anastomoses develop between hepatic arterioles and portal venules and between hepatic and portal venules.

An elevated portal pressure may be suspected from the presence of oesophageal varices which can be seen on a barium swallow or at oesophagoscopy. An estimation of the portal pressure is usually obtained by measuring the intrasplenic pressure which is an accurate reflection of the pressure in the portal bed. Normally the intrasplenic pressure varies from 3 to 14 mmHg and levels greater than 16 mmHg are indicative of portal hypertension. Two other techniques which are used to demonstrate the increased portal pressure are umbilical vein catheterization and direct measurement of the intrahepatic pressure. The presence of a portal collateral circulation may be demonstrated by a number of techniques, other than barium meal and splenic venography, which depend upon the bypassing of the liver by portal blood. Portal hypertension is associated with the development of many of the complications of cirrhosis including gastrointestinal bleeding, coma and ascites. The existence of a portasystemic collateral circulation implies portal hypertension but occasionally the anastomoses are sufficiently large to permit a reduction of portal pressure to normal values.

Measurement of the pressure in the large hepatic veins, the wedged hepatic pressure, helps to determine the cause of an elevated portal vein pressure. The upper limit of the normal wedged hepatic vein pressure is 5–6 mmHg. In cirrhosis of the liver there are similar elevations of both portal and wedged hepatic vein pressures and these average about 20 mmHg. In the past the causes of portal hypertension have been classified as presinusoidal, sinusoidal and postsinusoidal, but this is probably incorrect. It is preferable to regard portal hypertension as being due to presinusoidal or parenchymatous causes and these can be distinguished on the basis of the intrasplenic and wedged hepatic vein pressures (Table XVII).

TABLE XVII. *Classification of Portal Hypertension*

Portal Hypertension	Intrasplenic Pressure	Wedged Hepatic Vein Pressure	Cause
Presinusoidal	Elevated	Normal	Blocked portal or splenic vein Schistosomiasis Portal tract infiltration
Parenchymal	Elevated	Elevated	Cirrhosis

Uncommon causes of portal hypertension in which both portal and wedged hepatic vein pressures are elevated, but in which liver parenchymatous structure is essentially normal, include veno-occlusive disease and a blocked hepatic vein (Budd–Chiari syndrome).

Cirrhosis of the Liver

The clinical features and complications of cirrhosis are common to all forms of the disease regardless of the cause, although individual types of cirrhosis may have additional distinctive clinical and biochemical features. The patient with uncomplicated hepatic cirrhosis has few symptoms. There may be undue fatigue, slight weight loss and a reduction of libido but well-compensated cirrhosis is often discovered accidentally on physical examination or at the time of laparotomy for an unrelated condition.

Examination of the hands and skin of the cirrhotic patient is frequently rewarding and provides important clues to the diagnosis. Signs include palmar erythema, clubbing of the fingers and white nails. Palmar erythema is found in conditions other than cirrhosis, such as pregnancy, rheumatoid arthritis and thyrotoxicosis. Vascular spiders are seen on the skin, particularly around the neck, shoulders and chest and rarely below the umbilicus. Jaundice is present, although not invariably, and there may be slight excess of skin pigmentation and loss of hair. Gynaecomastia is occasionally present. Cirrhotic patients have a hyperdynamic circulation and flow murmurs in the heart are frequently heard. It may be possible to see abdominal wall collateral veins and a hum may be noted. The spread of the veins around the umbilicus has been called the 'caput medusa' and the term Cruveilhier–Baumgarten syndrome is used to describe the association of a venous hum, caput medusa and dilated umbilical veins. The significance of this syndrome is that it indicates the presence of a patent portal vein and for practical purposes it occurs only in intrahepatic causes of portal hypertension, usually cirrhosis. Some cirrhotic patients show lid lag and lid retraction and give the impression of having thyrotoxicosis.

Abdominal examination reveals splenomegaly which is usually taken as an indication of portal hypertension. The liver may be enlarged or reduced in size depending on the cause of the cirrhosis. Diagnostically an enlarged liver is not as helpful as a small liver because, while there are many causes of hepatomegaly, reduction in liver size occurs mainly in acute liver failure or in cirrhosis; and these two conditions are usually readily distinguished clinically.

Cirrhotics are susceptible to infection, of which tuberculosis, both pulmonary and peritoneal, is the most important. Spontaneous bacterial peritonitis is an occasional complication, the most common organisms being *Escherichia coli* and *D. pneumococcus*. Septicaemia and urinary tract infections are other hazards. There is an increased frequency of gall stones. Cirrhosis is associated with reduced fertility in females and pregnancy is uncommon. Some patients have arterial unsaturation and may be markedly cyanosed. Hyperglycaemia and rarely hypoglycaemia may complicate cirrhosis. Target red cells have an increase in membrane lipid. Selective increases in red cell cholesterol occur and are associated with low serum lecithin–

cholesterol acyltransferase activity. Changes in the red cell lipids are associated with an alteration in the cell shape forming spur cells and there is an accompanying haemolytic anaemia. Impaired activity of this serum enzyme in liver disease may explain in part the low concentration of serum cholesterol esters found in cirrhosis. Thrombocytopenia and leucopenia may develop and may reflect hypersplenism but the haematological defects are seldom of sufficient magnitude to warrant splenectomy. There is a lower incidence of myocardial infarction and extrahepatic malignant disease. Although the suggestion has been made that there is a reduced incidence of hepatic metastases in cirrhotic livers this is probably erroneous.

The patient with cirrhosis usually presents only when the disease has become complicated by liver cell failure or portal hypertension. These two factors, singly or in combination, are responsible for the development of jaundice, gastrointestinal bleeding, coma and fluid retention, which are the main reasons for a cirrhotic patient seeking medical advice. A fifth complicating factor is the development of primary liver cell cancer.

The assessment of the patient with cirrhosis must include an evaluation of liver cell function, an attempt to demonstrate a portasystemic collateral circulation and portal hypertension, the histological documentation of cirrhosis if possible and a decision as to the probable cause of the cirrhosis. Liver cell failure is associated with a low serum albumin concentration and disorders of the clotting mechanisms. Elevated serum transaminase levels indicate that there has been damage or death of liver cells. The presence of portal hypertension and a portasystemic collateral circulation is suspected clinically by the presence of foetor hepaticus, a liver flap, splenomegaly and a caput medusa. Oesophageal varices are seen radiologically as polypoid filling defects in a dilated oesophagus (Plate IX). The abnormality in portal haemodynamics is confirmed by splenic venography at which time the intrasplenic pressure should be measured. Supportive evidence for cirrhosis is provided by an isotopic scan of the liver and by coeliac axis arteriography. Liver histology is normally obtained by percutaneous needle biopsy and it provides considerable support for the diagnosis. The biopsy indicates the activity of the cirrhosis as judged by the extent of liver cell necrosis and the inflammatory response. It also indicates the stage of the cirrhosis: whether there is young or old fibrous tissue. The biopsy will show the presence of an associated hepatoma and may provide an indication of the probable aetiology.

Treatment of cirrhosis is unsatisfactory. There are no pharmacological agents which either arrest or reverse the fibrotic process. Therapy is aimed first at dealing with any underlying cause such as alcohol, iron overload or bile duct obstruction, and secondly at treating the various complications including gastrointestinal bleeding, neuropsychiatric changes and fluid retention. A prolonged prothrombin time is managed with intramuscular injections of vitamin K_1, 10 mg daily for 3 days. Fresh blood or platelet transfusions are of value. Excessive fibrinolysis may be treated with ε-aminocaproic acid. Patients with uncomplicated cirrhosis require no specific therapy or diet although dietary manipulations are important when dealing with fluid retention and coma. Because of the known hepatotoxic effects of alcohol it is advisable to forbid alcohol to all patients regardless of the cause of the cirrhosis. The patient is encouraged to lead as normal a life as possible with adequate physical exercise. Medical supervision is necessary so that the development of complications can be recognized and treated early. Liver transplantation is currently being explored as a surgical approach to the treatment of cirrhosis but many technical problems require to be overcome before it can be offered as a worthwhile alternative.

The death rate for cirrhosis is lower in England and Wales than in France or the United States of America. In

England the rates are higher among the upper social classes, whereas the reverse holds for the United States of America. Evidence is mounting that alcohol is becoming an increasingly important cause of cirrhosis in the United Kingdom. The cause of death is usually liver cell failure, with gastrointestinal bleeding and infection being important contributory factors. Hepatoma is becoming an increasingly important cause of death. The prognosis depends on a number of variables, including the aetiology of the cirrhosis, and the method of presentation (whether by gastrointestinal haemorrhage or fluid retention). Thus the published figures are not always comparable. It might be anticipated that with improvements in the management of the complications of cirrhosis the survival rates of patients would have proved, but this is apparently not so. Comparison of data obtained between 1916 and 1938 with death rates for the 1960s suggests that there has been little improvement in overall survival during the last two decades. The 5-year survival is around 10%. Patients presenting with bleeding varices probably have a slightly worse outlook than patients with ascites. One factor which greatly improves the prognosis is abstinence from alcohol, but this only applies to the alcoholic. The 5-year survival of such patients is over 50%.

Complications of Cirrhosis

GASTROINTESTINAL BLEEDING

Bleeding from the gut is an important and potentially lethal complication of cirrhosis. It can be the first indication of liver disease. The most important cause of gastrointestinal haemorrhage is bleeding from oesophageal varices but other causes include gastric and duodenal ulcers (it is claimed that there is a great frequency of duodenal ulcers in patients with portal hypertension), acute gastric erosions and a generalized bleeding tendency. The factors responsible for causing oesophageal varices to bleed remain completely unexplained but an elevated portal pressure is believed to be important. Varices appear to rupture rather than erode.

The patient presents with either haematemesis or melaena. Occasionally the first sign of bleeding is the development of hepatic coma. If the bleeding is torrential the patient may pass fresh or barely altered blood per rectum. Depending on the amount and speed of the blood loss there is hypovolaemia and hypotension. The patient is at great risk of developing liver cell failure because in the cirrhotic liver the arterial blood contributes proportionally more than the portal blood to the total liver blood flow, this being the reverse of normal. The hypotension and associated reduction in liver blood flow may cause severe liver cell dysfunction which gives rise to coma, jaundice and ascites. A further cause of liver coma is the increased load of protein present in the gut after the haemorrhage. Another hazard is the precipitation of renal failure.

The cause of the bleeding is established by a combination of a barium swallow and meal, endoscopy and splenic venography. Endoscopy is a most useful technique the main hazard of which is the necessary sedation which increases the risk of hepatic encephalopathy. Where multiple disorders are demonstrated the precise site of bleeding may be difficult or impossible to determine. Experience in the United Kingdom suggests that the usual cause for bleeding is oesophageal varices but the dilemma is greater in the United States where alcoholic cirrhosis is common. These patients may at any one time have oesophageal varices, acute gastric erosions and a generalized clotting effect.

The initial management is to restore the blood volume. Blood transfusion is given through a central venous cannula and the venous pressure is carefully monitored. If large amounts of blood are necessary it is advisable to use freshly donated blood. Steps are taken to avoid neuro-psychiatric complications by gently washing out any blood from the stomach and administering an enema. Oral neomycin, 1 g 6-hourly is given to suppress bacterial breakdown of protein. It is unwise to prescribe sedatives or morphine. Intramuscular vitamin K (10 mg daily) is given for 3 days. A nasogastric tube can be passed with safety; it is used for two reasons: to wash out blood from the stomach and to monitor the onset of further bleeding. If there is no bleeding during a period of 24 hours the tube is removed. The pulse and blood pressure are also recorded and serve as a guide to progress and further haemorrhage.

Variceal bleeding may be reduced by the intravenous administration of vasopressin (Pitressin) which is given in a dose of 20 units in 100 ml of 5% glucose over 10 minutes. Vasopressin increases splanchnic arterial resistance and reduces portal pressure. It also causes contraction of oesophageal muscle. The drug may be repeated after 4–6 hours but with subsequent infusions there is a reduction in its effectiveness. It controls bleeding in about 50% of patients. Vasopressin also stimulates intestinal contractions and may have additional benefits in ridding the bowel of blood. Great care must be exercised in the occasional patient with ischaemic heart disease. Success has also been reported using an infusion of vasopressin or adrenaline selectively into the abdominal arteries.

If the patient continues to bleed despite vasopressin the use of balloon tamponade or surgical intervention is con-sidered. A third therapeutic measure, the direct injection of sclerosants into the varices via an oesophagoscope, is in use in some centres. Compression of the varices may be achieved by the Sengstaken–Blakemore three-lumen oeso-phageal compression tube. The tube has many dis-advantages, including a tendency to cause laryngeal and oesophageal ulceration and aspiration pneumonia. For this reason tamponade is infrequently used and the best use for the Sengstaken–Blakemore tube is probably as a temporary measure in the patient who is about to undergo emergency surgery.

The nature of the emergency surgical procedure for the patient with actively bleeding varices is controversial. The two procedures favoured are either an oesophageal transection or a portacaval anastomosis, and there is no agreement as to which is the better. What is certain is that any form of emergency surgery carries a high mortality of around 60%. It is likely that emergency transoesophageal suture of the varices carries the lowest risk and it can be followed by an elective portacaval anastomosis at a later date.

Once the patient has recovered from the bleeding on the standard medical regimen, a decision has to be taken on whether to operate to reduce the portal pressure. Although the immediate mortality for elective surgery is less than 10% there is a significant morbidity and the long-term results are uncertain; thus patients must be chosen with care. The frequency and severity of the haemorrhage, the patient's occupation and the availability of adequate medical and transfusion services must all be considered. Factors believed to indicate a favourable outcome include a bilirubin below 3 mg/100 ml (50 mmol/litre), a serum albumin level greater than 25 g/litre and the absence of

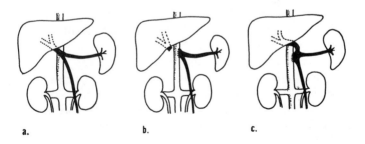

a. b. c.

Fig. 10. Operations to reduce portal hypertension: *a*. Normal anatomy of the portal vein; *b*. End-to-side portacaval anastomosis; *c*. Side-to-side portacaval anastomosis.

ascites or mental changes during the bleeding episode. Surgery is usually undertaken on patients who are below the age of 50 years. Many operations have been described and the most efficient is a portacaval anastomosis performed either as an end-to-side or a side-to-side procedure (Fig. 10). A splenorenal anastomosis produces a smaller portasystemic shunt and is less effective in reducing the portal pressure. A mesocaval shunt between the superior mesenteric vein and inferior vena cava has been advocated.

A large number of complications may follow the creation of a surgical shunt, of which the most important is the development of neuropsychiatric sequelae. The overall incidence of significant encephalopathy is 20% and the incidence is greater after portacaval than splenorenal anastomoses. Other complications include hepatocellular failure, diabetes mellitus, iron overload, oedema and ascites.

The creation of a surgical portasystemic shunt is an effective method of preventing further variceal bleeding and only 7% of patients have recurrent bleeding. However, the survival of cirrhotic patients with surgical shunts is probably no longer than that of non-shunted patients, the only difference is that the mode of death is altered. The shunted patients tend to die from hepatocellular failure or peptic ulcer disease. The 5-year survival is around 40%. There is no evidence that a prophylactic shunt (that is a shunt undertaken in a cirrhotic patient who has varices that have not bled) prolongs the life expectancy.

Occasionally it is necessary to perform a portasystemic shunt for bleeding varices on patients in whom the cause of the portal hypertension is not cirrhosis. In such patients the cause of the raised portal pressure is frequently not established with certainty but many have hepatic fibrosis with portal vein sclerosis in the absence of true cirrhosis. The outlook after surgery in these patients is good and they have a 5-year survival as high as 80%.

NEUROPSYCHIATRIC COMPLICATIONS (HEPATIC ENCEPHA-
LOPATHY)

Patients with cirrhosis of the liver show a chronic
fluctuating neuropsychiatric disorder which is associated
with an extensive portal collateral circulation. The shunts
may have developed spontaneously or have been created
surgically. The metabolites responsible for the cerebral
disturbance have yet to be identified. The basic mechanism
appears to be the bypassing of the liver by absorbed products of protein digestion and ammonia is frequently
implicated. The cerebral accumulation of false neuro-
transmitters such as octopamine, has been proposed as
well as short-chain fatty acids. Other factors which predispose to the encephalopathic state include electrolyte
imbalance, particularly potassium deficiency, drugs such
as morphine and sedatives, and infections.

The syndrome consists of a reversible disorder of mood,
personality and intellect which is subject to wide fluctuations. The patients have a disorder of sleep and experience
nightmares and inversion of the sleep rhythm. Irritability,
childishness, untidiness, apathy, hypothermia and hyper-
ventilation are early features. Constructional apraxia is a
prominent feature and the patient cannot write clearly or
draw figures such as stars or houses. The speech becomes
slow and slurred and a flapping tremor is elicited. Hepatic
foetor is present.

As the encephalopathy becomes more marked the patient
passes into a phase of noisy restless precoma with abnormal
facial grimaces and smacking of the lips. Reflex activity is
increased and ankle clonus may be apparent but the plantar
response remains flexor, only becoming extensor in deep
coma. In the terminal phase the patient is deeply unconscious and hyperventilating and there is often a high fever.
The electroencephalogram is abnormal. There is slowing
of the frequency and, once coma supervenes, large bilater-
ally synchronous waves are recorded from the frontal and

central regions. The condition is essentially reversible and the only pathological change is diffuse enlargement of the astrocytes. The encephalopathic state is not specific and a similar tremor and electroencephalogram are found in other toxic confusional states.

The initial stage in therapy is to recognize the precipitating cause so that steps can be taken to counteract this. Important factors include injudicious diuretic therapy and abdominal paracentesis which can induce a state of electrolyte imbalance and potassium depletion. Excessive protein in the gut is another factor and this may follow a large protein meal or an upper gastrointestinal haemorrhage. Other contributory factors include infections and constipation. Every cirrhotic patient should be assessed with regard to protein tolerance and cerebral function and this becomes of particular importance if diuretic therapy or surgery is contemplated. Electroencephalographic monitoring is very helpful.

The treatment is based upon protein restriction and sterilization of the bowel. Protein intake is reduced to 20 g daily or less. When the patient is unconscious feeding is undertaken with a nasogastric tube and the patient is given 1500–2000 calories daily in the form of 20% glucose. The osmotic effect of the sugar may cause diarrhoea but this is not necessarily unwelcome as the laxative effect serves to rid the bowel of unwanted protein. Oral neomycin (6 g daily) sterilizes the gut and is very effective in hepatic coma. The antibiotic may be continued on a long-term basis to prevent encephalopathy in doses of 2–4 g daily but there are hazards including ototoxicity, steatorrhoea and staphylococcal enteritis. A laxative is given and if the patient is unconscious magnesium sulphate is administered via the nasogastric tube. Great care must be exercised in the use of sedatives and the patient can usually be managed without them. Occasionally their use is unavoidable and small doses of chlorpromazine or diazepam are effective and do not necessarily increase the degree of encephalopathy. The course of the encephalopathy is monitored by electroencephalography.

Certain patients are particularly prone to develop recurrent hepatic encephalopathy and some form of long-term management is necessary. Protein restriction and neomycin form the basis of the prophylaxis but a variety of other means is available. Lactulose is a synthetic disaccharide comprising glucose and fructose and is given in oral doses of 30 ml 4 times daily. It passes into the colon where it undergoes bacterial degradation. The stool pH is lowered and an osmotic and fermentative diarrhoea is produced. The reduction in the stool pH causes a movement of ammonia from the blood to the colonic lumen where it is converted to the non-absorbable ammonium ion. Attempts have been made to colonize the colon with non-ammonia producing bacteria such as *Lactobacillus acidophilus*. A freeze-dried preparation of the organism is available (Enpac) but has not proved reliable in maintaining the normal mental state. Since the colon is the site where the bacteria are presumed to produce those factors responsible for encephalopathy attempts have been made to exclude the large bowel surgically. Procedures used include total colectomy and ileorectal anastomosis, ileostomy, and ileosigmoidostomy with colonic exclusion. These operations have had variable success and are not widely used.

The chronic fluctuant reversible encephalopathy of cirrhosis must be distinguished from an uncommon permanent disorder of nervous function encountered in some cirrhotic patients. This syndrome is associated with both spontaneous and surgical portasystemic shunts and is characterized by dementia, dysarthria, ataxia, choreoathetosis and spasticity. The cerebrum, cerebellum, midbrain and medulla are affected and show a diffuse cortical laminar necrosis, microcavitation which involves particularly the midbrain and an increase in the size of the astrocytes. Occasionally a Parkinsonian-like state develops. This state of chronic hepatocerebral degeneration is irreversible. It is readily confused with Wilson's disease.

Hepatic encephalopathy must be distinguished from the coma which accompanies acute liver cell failure. In this condition shunting of portal blood does not play a role and the response to the treatment outlined above is rarely favourable. Other causes of neurological deterioration in a cirrhotic patient include infections, acute alcoholic intoxication and withdrawal syndromes and cerebral metastases from a hepatoma. These all need to be considered when assessing a cirrhotic patient who has developed mental changes.

FLUID RETENTION

Fluid retention in cirrhotic patients presents as ascites and/or peripheral oedema. The appearance of ascites implies a combination of hepatocellular failure and portal hypertension. Portal hypertension in the presence of normal liver function (as in extrahepatic portal vein obstruction) and marked liver cell damage without portal hypertension (as in acute liver cell necrosis) are seldom accompanied by significant ascites. Ascites usually occurs in the cirrhotic patient who has a reduced serum albumin concentration. Thus the necessary factors are a low serum colloid osmotic pressure together with an elevated portal venous pressure. The presence of ascites and the associated reduction in renal blood flow initiates certain hormonal mechanisms. Excessive aldosterone secretion is the most important and this causes increased tubular reabsorption of sodium so that urinary sodium levels are very low. There is evidence of another as yet unknown hormone which may be elaborated in response to changes in the volume of the extracellular fluid. This hormone may be implicated in the alterations in the renal handling of sodium which are found in cirrhosis.

The ascitic fluid is in the nature of a transudate and has

a protein level usually less than 15 g/litre. Occasionally much higher protein concentrations (up to 30–40 g/litre) are encountered in uncomplicated ascites and it is believed that in these patients yet another factor operates—overproduction of hepatic lymph because of hepatic outflow block. The exact route whereby lymph reaches the peritoneal cavity is not known.

Ascites and oedema may develop gradually or rapidly. An important precipitating factor is excessive sodium intake from food or from sodium-containing drugs, particularly antacid preparations. Ascites may follow a surgical portacaval anastomosis when it is believed to be due to outpouring of lymph. The patient has few complaints other than the cosmetic effect but excessive ascitic fluid is uncomfortable and may contribute to the development of bleeding varices or renal failure. Some patients with ascites also develop large pleural effusions, particularly in the right hemithorax. The fluid is thought to enter the chest through tears which develop in the tendinous portion of the diaphragm because of the increased intra-abdominal pressure. A large abdominal paracentesis is not performed because of the danger of inducing hypovolaemia, hyponatraemia, hypokalaemia, liver coma and renal failure, but it is safe, and indeed essential, to remove a small quantity of fluid for diagnostic purposes. The protein content is measured, cultures are undertaken and a cytological examination is made. It is always necessary to ensure that the ascites is an indication of shifts of body fluids and not a manifestation of peritonitis secondary to tuberculosis or other bacterial infections or to a hepatoma. If the ascites is very tense and causing much discomfort and respiratory difficulty it is necessary to withdraw a larger volume but this must be done very cautiously. The combination of spontaneous hyponatraemia and ascites presents a formidable therapeutic problem.

Cirrhotic patients who have fluid retention should be admitted to hospital. During the first 5–7 days the patient is maintained on a restricted sodium diet (22 mmol of sodium daily) and 1.5 litres of fluid daily. The patient is weighed regularly and the metabolic status assessed, particularly the serum levels of sodium, potassium, chloride and urea. The renal function and neurological status are also monitored. Measurement of the urinary sodium output is frequently helpful. Marked shifts of fluid and electrolytes from the various body compartments occur during this period of stabilization. Factors determining the response to bed rest and sodium restriction include the degree of sodium overload and the nature of the liver disease; when the process can be halted or reversed as in the alcoholic then relatively simple measures are effective.

If after the first week the daily loss of weight is less than 1 kg oral diuretics are introduced. There is a variety of diuretics and diuretic programmes but the essential feature is to introduce the diuretics gradually to avoid too brisk a diuresis. Weight loss of 1 kg/day is adequate for patients with ascites and oedema. When there is only ascites the daily loss of weight should not be greater than 0.5 kg. Peripheral oedema is more readily mobilized than ascitic fluid and if more than 0.5 kg is lost it is an indication that there has been depletion of the extracellular fluid volume including the plasma. Thiazides, frusemide (up to 80 mg daily) or ethacrynic acid (up to 100 mg daily) are used, beginning with small doses and increasing according to the diuretic response. If the weight loss is not maintained spironolactone (up to 150 mg daily) is added and this agent is also useful when the serum potassium levels drop. Oral potassium is usually necessary and the usual dose is 60–80 mmol daily, preferably in the form of the chloride salt. Other agents which are used include amiloride (up to 20 mg daily) and triamterene (up to 250 mg daily). When there is hyponatraemia associated with resistant ascites fluid intake may be restricted to 1 litre/day although many patients find this unpleasant.

By careful and patient manipulation of the diet and

diuretics it is possible to obtain a satisfactory diuresis in the majority of cirrhotic patients and there are few who can be regarded as having refractory ascites. Steroid therapy and mannitol infusions have been recommended for these patients but are seldom effective. A number of surgical procedures have been advocated but none has stood the test of time. Surgery is hazardous and the mortality and morbidity are appreciable. Recently a pump which withdraws ascitic fluid, filters fluid and crystalloids and reinforces a protein concentrate has been used in the management of patients with resistant ascites. The aim of treatment is not to 'dry out' the patient completely. The patient should be made as free of ascites as possible without running the risk of complications. A small volume of residual ascites is of no consequence and should not serve as a challenge to the physician.

Diuretic agents must be given with considerable caution to patients who are uraemic, bleeding or likely to develop encephalopathy. There are many complications which can be induced by the diuretics and their number and severity will depend upon the clinical state of the patient and the vigour with which the treatment has been pursued. Complications include hypotension, hyponatraemia, hypokalaemia, hypochloraemic alkalosis, uraemia and hepatic encephalopathy. Less serious but nonetheless troublesome are nausea, vomiting, weakness and cramps. Male patients on spironolactone have a tendency to develop gynaecomastia.

JAUNDICE

Jaundice may occur early in the course of cirrhosis and persist at a mild level. The patient may become icteric during a phase of decompensation with reversible deterioration of liver cell function. The patient dying in liver failure is usually icteric. The serum bilirubin comprises both the conjugated and unconjugated forms and represents a combination of haemolysis, failure of conjugation and failure of excretion. About 70% of cirrhotic patients are icteric at some state of their illness, the majority having values of less than 10 mg/100 ml (170 μmol/litre). Occasionally marked intrahepatic cholestasis occurs with serum bilirubin concentrations greater than 25 mg/100 ml (425 μmol/litre).

When there is marked cholestasis pruritus is troublesome. It is treated with antihistamines, methyltestosterone or cholestyramine. The latter is a bile salt binding resin which is administered in doses of up to 16 g daily and increases the loss of bile salts in the faeces.

PRIMARY LIVER CANCER

This is discussed on p. 287. Patients with cirrhosis, particularly alcoholic cirrhosis, run an increased risk of developing primary liver cancer. In some patients the clinical features of the hepatoma are the first indication of the liver disease. The patient presents with right upper quadrant pain, fever, haemoperitoneum, jaundice and occasionally cerebral deposits. The diagnosis is established by liver scan, biopsy, arteriography and the demonstration of serum α-fetoprotein.

Aetiology of Cirrhosis

There is no satisfactory classification for the different morphological types of cirrhosis or for the various causes for the liver damage. Older terminology such as 'portal', 'postnecrotic' and 'biliary' cirrhosis have misleading implications and are best discarded. An anatomical classification which is currently in use employs the terms 'micronodular', 'macronodular' and 'mixed' to describe the nature of the cirrhotic process according to the size of the regenerating nodules.

It is not always easy to identify the precise cause of the

cirrhotic process and aetiological factors differ from one country to another. Accepted and identifiable causes for cirrhosis include alcohol, iron (haemochromatosis), copper (Wilson's disease), α_1-antitrypsin deficiency, galactosaemia, following viral hepatitis, fibrocystic disease of the pancreas and rarely cardiac failure. Cirrhosis is the end result of two syndromes of unknown aetiology—chronic active hepatitis and primary biliary cirrhosis (note the confusion of terminology: cirrhosis is usually present when the diagnosis of chronic active hepatitis is made, and the patient with primary biliary cirrhosis may die of liver failure before the hepatic lesion has evolved to cirrhosis). In many patients no cause can be found for the cirrhosis and the patient does not fit into any specific clinical syndrome. The terms 'idiopathic' or 'cryptogenic' cirrhosis are used for such patients. Prolonged extrahepatic obstruction and schistosomiasis cause marked portal fibrosis but not cirrhosis as customarily defined.

ALCOHOLIC LIVER DISEASE

Alcohol is a widely consumed beverage and alcoholism has many medical and social consequences. The liver metabolizes about 95% of the ingested alcohol and this occurs at a fixed rate. The initial step in metabolism is the oxidation to acetaldehyde under the influence of alcohol dehydrogenase. Recent observations suggest that there is also a microsomal system capable of oxidizing the alcohol and that this may undergo an adaptive increase in activity. The final step in the metabolism of alcohol is oxidation to carbon dioxide via the citric acid cycle. The metabolism of alcohol is associated with an increase in reduced nicotinamide adenine dinucleotide (NADH) and an increase in the ratio NADH/NAD which in turn has profound influence on lipid, carbohydrate and uric acid metabolism.

There is evidence that alcohol has a direct toxic effect on the liver cells. In alcoholic cirrhosis it is undoubtedly the alcohol which causes the cirrhosis and other factors play a lesser but contributory role. These factors included the pattern of alcohol consumption (the steady daily consumer is more at risk), diet and hereditary factors. It is difficult to be certain just how much alcohol is necessary to cause cirrhosis but it seems that more than 160 g daily (about two-thirds of a bottle of whisky) exceeds the metabolic capacity of the liver and that after 10 years the risk of cirrhosis becomes considerable.

A number of syndromes of alcoholic liver disease are recognized: alcoholic fatty liver, acute alcoholic hepatitis, sclerosing hyaline necrosis of the liver and alcoholic cirrhosis. Although cirrhosis is the end result of the toxic effect of alcohol on the liver it does not necessarily develop via any of the other syndromes of alcoholic injury.

Alcoholic Hepatomegaly

The earliest feature of alcoholic liver disease is modest hepatomegaly. This is a reflection of the inductive increase in the smooth endoplasmic reticulum and irregularity and swelling of the mitochondria of the liver cells. The changes are reversible.

Alcoholic Fatty Liver

There are many metabolic reasons why triglycerides might accumulate in the liver of the alcoholic and the fat may be derived from hepatic and extrahepatic sources. The process may be acute or chronic. In the acute stage the liver is enlarged and tender. The patient may be febrile and icteric. Oesophageal varices can be demonstrated and these subside when the fat disappears. The liver biopsy shows the liver to be laden with fat and intracellular clumps of eosinophilic hyaline material (Mallory's bodies) may also be found. Some patients show hyperlipaemia and a haemolytic anaemia and the name Zieve's syndrome has been given to this association. If the patient stops taking alcohol the morphological abnormalities disappear and the liver reverts to normal.

Alcoholic Hepatitis

Alcoholic hepatitis manifests as either an acute or a chronic syndrome. In the acute phase the patient has fever, jaundice and right upper quadrant pain. The liver is enlarged and tender. Biochemical features include an elevation of the serum transaminase and λ-glutamyltrans-peptidase levels and marked leucocytosis. The liver histology is that of considerable cellular necrosis and inflammatory cell infiltration, a variable amount of fat and alcoholic hyaline material and a fibrous reaction which merges into cirrhosis. Hyaline occurs in 10–20% of alcoholic subjects and indicates the presence of hepatic necrosis and hence a poor prognosis. Thus alcoholic hepatitis is a more serious condition than fatty liver and is potentially cirrhotic. The patient may develop liver failure and the mortality is around 10%. The condition must be distinguished from viral hepatitis.

Alcoholic Sclerosing Hyaline Necrosis

This presents in a similar manner to acute alcoholic hepatitis, with fever, abdominal pain and an enlarged liver. Jaundice and leucocytosis may be marked and the condition is readily mistaken for cholangitis. Ascites and portal hypertension may develop in the absence of cirrhosis. The liver histology shows hyaline necrosis of liver cells, polymorphonuclear neutrophil infiltration and an intense sclerosis of the centrilobular sinusoids and veins. The prognosis is poor, with a mortality rate exceeding 50%; the outlook is improved in the absence of marked fatty change.

Alcoholic Cirrhosis

In many countries alcohol is the most frequently recognized cause of cirrhosis. It has not been established what percentage of those who drink alcohol to excess develop cirrhosis and the figures vary from 1% to 30%. Patients with alcoholic cirrhosis present the clinical picture of florid liver disease with marked vascular spiders, gynaecomastia, jaundice and ascites. They may be often well nourished but show limb muscle wasting and parotid enlargement. Dupuytren's contracture may occur more frequently in cirrhotic subjects although its presence in no way establishes the diagnosis of alcoholism or alcoholic cirrhosis. There will be other features of alcoholic poisoning: gastritis (as evidenced by anorexia and early morning vomiting), pancreatic disease and mental deterioration. Liver histology shows a micronodular cirrhosis in which fat and inflammatory cells occur together with a residual of alcoholic hyaline material. In the patient who continues to take alcohol the outlook is poor and death occurs from liver failure. This usually appears as a combination of bleeding varices, ascites, a bleeding tendency and jaundice. The 5-year survival can be doubled if total abstinence is achieved. In the patient who has stopped drinking the cirrhosis tends to transform into the macronodular variety. The development of a hepatoma in patients who have given up drinking is a significant risk and this complication occurs in 15% of alcoholic cirrhotics.

Treatment

The treatment of alcoholic liver disease consists of complete withdrawal of alcohol, replacement of vitamins and other nutrients, a high protein diet and antibiotics for any secondary infection. Syndromes of alcohol withdrawal require careful management. The complications of cirrhosis, such as variceal bleeding, fluid retention and hepatic coma, are managed in the routine manner. There is no evidence that steroid treatment is of value in any of the syndromes of acute alcoholic liver disease.

The key factor in the development of chronic progressive liver disease in the alcoholic is cellular immunoreactivity. Immunological studies of patients with alcoholic hepatitis indicate that it is the alcoholic hyaline which acts as the stimulus for lymphocytes to become hyperactive thereby enhancing collagen synthesis.

CHRONIC ACTIVE HEPATITIS

Chronic active hepatitis is a disorder of liver function of undetermined cause. It is also known by the names active chronic hepatitis, 'lupoid' hepatitis and plasma cell hepatitis. The disease starts as acute liver cell inflammation but the inflammation persists in a chronic manner and eventually a macronodular cirrhosis develops. The end stage of the disease process is an 'inactive' cirrhosis as judged chemically and histologically. The incidence of the disease and the frequency with which chronic active hepatitis contributes to hepatic cirrhosis varies in different parts of the world. The reason for this is not known but it may partly represent differences in the use of the term active chronic hepatitis.

It has been suggested that chronic active hepatitis follows an attack of viral hepatitis. Chronic active hepatitis could be either a manifestation of persisting hepatitis or an immunological reaction to liver cells which have been damaged by a virus. HB_s Ag has been found in a high percentage of the patients but there are marked and unaccountable geographic variations in the number of patients having the antigen. The fact that the disease involves many systems and there are immunoglobulin disturbances has led to suggestions that this disease is a manifestation of disordered immunity and that it should be classed as an autoimmune disease. Genetic factors are important and there is a high prevalence of immunological abnormalities in the relatives of patients with chronic active hepatitis. Hepatitis is not a manifestation of systemic lupus erythematosus.

Chronic active hepatitis is commoner in females and in the young, although all ages are affected. The onset may be relatively acute, resembling viral hepatitis, or more insidious with general ill health. The presentation at a more advanced stage of liver disease includes jaundice, ascites, bleeding varices and coma. In many of these patients the liver is cirrhotic. A characteristic feature is involvement of extrahepatic tissues—arthritis and arthralgia, iritis, nephritis, ulcerative colitis and a variety of skin conditions including allergic capilleritis, erythema nodosum and acne. The lungs may be involved. Nearly half the patients show some features of Sjögren's syndrome including keratoconjunctivitis sicca, xerostomia, enlarged parotid glands and occasionally rheumatoid arthritis. Characteristic biochemical features include a moderate elevation of the serum bilirubin concentration, slight reduction of the serum albumin but marked elevation of serum transaminase and γ-globulin values. IgG is particularly raised. The LE test is positive in 15%, antinuclear factor is positive in 30–50%, antimitochondrial antibody is positive in 25% and smooth muscle antibody is positive in 70% of patients.

There are clinical and immunological differences between HB_s Ag positive and HB_s Ag negative patients. Patients positive for the antigen are mainly males with little evidence of multisystem disease and autoantibodies. Chronic active hepatitis patients who are negative for the antigen tend to be females with high autoantibody titres, biochemical evidence of active liver disease, multisystem involvement and a relatively poor prognosis.

The liver biopsy shows a fairly typical appearance, labelled 'chronic aggressive hepatitis'. There is liver cell necrosis and disruption of the normal lobular pattern with groups of liver cells forming rosette-like complexes. Septa of connective tissue are laid down between the islands of liver cells and there is an inflammatory cell infiltrate composed primarily of plasma cells although lymphocytes are also prominent. It is believed that these plasma cells are responsible for the excessive production of immunoglobulins. The aggressive fibrosis commences at the portal zones and eventually the damage evolves into a macronodular cirrhosis with little evidence of cellular infiltration.

The differential diagnosis includes viral hepatitis, Wilson's disease, $\alpha-_1$ antitrypsin deficiency and certain drugs including isonicotinic acid hydrazide, methyldopa and oxyphenisatin which may all cause similar clinical and morphological features. Primary biliary cirrhosis may also need consideration for there is clinical and serological overlap between the two diseases.

Prednisolone is recommended for patients who have evidence of clinical, biochemical or histological activity. An initial oral dose of 20–30 mg daily is reduced to maintenance therapy of 10–15 mg daily, and continued for at least 6 months. At this time the steroids can be stopped in many patients. A relapse is an indication for a further course of prednisolone. Immunosuppressive therapy alone appears to be ineffective but for those patients who develop marked side-effects on prednisolone the introduction of 50 to 100 mg azathioprine orally daily may have a steroid-sparing effect. Cirrhosis and its ensuing complications are treated according to standard methods.

The prognosis is variable and unpredictable and the course tends to be relapsing. The greatest mortality is within the first 2 years of making the diagnosis and may be up to 50% after 5 years. There is evidence that a very few patients make a complete recovery but the outlook for most patients is the inexorable progress to cirrhosis of the liver. However, the impact of effective steroid therapy on this process remains to be evaluated.

HAEMOCHROMATOSIS

Dietary iron is ingested in the form of the ferrous or ferric salt or as haemoglobin iron. About 20–40% of the iron in food is released by peptic activity in the stomach and acid is also necessary to hold the ferric iron in solution; thus achlorhydria reduces the amount of iron which is available to the body. On the other hand the availability of haem iron is unaffected by gastric acid. The ferrous iron and the haem remain in solution in the alkaline pH of the duodenum but the ferric iron will precipitate unless it is chelated to other substances such as ascorbic acid, fructose, mucopolysaccharides and amino acids.

Iron entering the mucosal cells of the upper small intestine is either linked to the cell protein apo-ferritin and stored as ferritin, from which small amounts of iron are released into the plasma, or is rapidly transported across the cell into the plasma. Radioimmunoassay techniques have identified ferritin in the serum. Most of the ferritin in the mucosal cell is lost to the body when the villus cells are exfoliated. Absorbed iron is transported in the blood attached to the plasma protein transferrin. The mechanism controlling iron absorption is not understood but it may be the ability of the cell to synthesize ferritin. There is increased iron absorption in iron deficiency states because of a reduction in the amount of ferritin in the mucosal cells; however, a humoral factor has also been postulated. There are three factors which are known to influence iron absorption: body iron stores, erythropoiesis and hypoxia. None of these factors explain the iron overloading which occurs in idiopathic haemochromatosis.

Haemochromatosis is the disease resulting from the excessive storage of iron in the body. The normal body iron stores amount to 3–4 g, whereas in haemochromatosis the stores are of the order of 20–60 g. It is an uncommon inborn error of metabolism in which there is excessive intestinal absorption of iron. The condition is probably inherited as a recessive characteristic but it is likely that spontaneous mutants occur fairly frequently. The disease is much commoner in males and usually presents in middle age. It has been argued that idiopathic haemochromatosis is related to alcoholism (many alcoholic beverages have a high iron content) and nutritional deficiencies, but there is not much support for this pathogenesis. Iron overload may develop in chronic haemolytic states, after the multiple blood transfusions which are required in chronic refractory anaemias, and in the South African Bantu who has a very high intake of dietary iron. In all these conditions, if the body iron stores become sufficiently large, the clinical and pathological features of haemochromatosis develop. Iron overload may also occur in alcoholic cirrhosis and at times the distinction from idiopathic haemochromatosis may be very difficult. After portacaval anastomosis there is a tendency for the body iron stores to increase.

One of the commonest signs of haemochromatosis is skin pigmentation particularly on the exposed areas: the colour is usually dusky brown, less commonly it is the well known (but difficult to recognize) slate-grey colour. Pigmentation is seen on the gums, buccal mucosa and conjunctiva. Iron deposition in the pituitary and gonads is associated with diminished endocrine function and causes loss of body hair, testicular atrophy and impotence. About 75% of patients have diabetes mellitus and this may be an early feature of the disease. The mechanism for diabetes is multifactoral and includes the insulin insensitivity characteristic of cirrhosis, pancreatic islet cell damage and inheritance of the gene for idiopathic diabetes mellitus. Many diabetics will show the neuropathy, nephropathy and angiopathy usually associated with genetic diabetes mellitus. Exocrine pancreatic dysfunction is uncommon despite the heavy deposition of iron in the gland. Over 50% of the patients have evidence of arthropathy—a progressive polyarthritis commencing in the small joints of the hands. At a later stage the large joints are involved and radiographs show characteristic loss of joint space, articular cartilage erosion and sclerosis of subchondral bone. Widespread chondrocalcinosis associated with the deposition of calcium pyrophosphate crystals occurs and is encountered particularly in the knee joint. Hepatomegaly is invariably present. About 15% of the patients have myocardial disease and subendocardial fibrosis associated with the iron deposition. Right-sided heart failure occurs and the ECG shows a low voltage tracing, flattened T waves and occasionally a dysrhythmia. Rarely patients develop an unexplained syndrome of acute abdominal pain, circulatory collapse and sudden death.

The typical biochemical features of the disease are shown in Table XVIII.

TABLE XVIII. *Biochemical Changes in Haemochromatosis*

	Haemochromatosis	Normal
Serum iron (μmol/litre)	40	13–30
Total iron-binding capacity (μmol/litre)	55	60
Saturation (%)	90	35

The iron-binding capacity is a measure of the iron-carrying globin in the serum and the level is reduced in haemochromatosis because of the liver damage. Iron absorption may be measured by a double isotope method and it is possible to measure iron stores using either of two iron chelating agents—desferrioxamine or diethylenetriamine penta-acetic acid (DTPA). Serum ferritin levels correlate with iron stores and are elevated in haemochromatosis.

Iron stains on the liver biopsy show excess iron in the liver cells and to a lesser extent in the Küpffer cells; pigment deposition is particularly prominent at the periphery of the nodules. At an early stage mild portal fibrosis occurs, but with increasing iron overload a frank macronodular cirrhosis supervenes.

The treatment of idiopathic haemochromatosis is venesection and it may be necessary to remove 50 or more litres of blood. Each 500 ml venesection removes 250 mg iron and a venesection should be performed monthly. Progress is followed by estimating the haemoglobin, monitoring the liver size (which reduces when the iron stores return to normal), observing the improvement in the diabetic state and measuring the iron stores. Desferrioxamine in the therapeutic doses removes only 10–20 mg iron daily and is less effective than venesection; it is used mainly for patients with secondary haemochromatosis complicating refractory anaemia or haemolysis when venesection is not possible. Complications such as heart failure, gonadal atrophy and liver failure are treated in the standard manner. Members of the family should have their serum iron values measured in order to assess whether there is any increase in iron levels.

The prognosis for the untreated patient is poor and two-thirds of the patients die within 5 years of diagnosis being made. Venesection treatment, on the other hand, improves the outlook and 89% of patients survive 5 years. Liver function improves although it is unlikely that the fibrosis is affected. Unfortunately it appears that the treated patient runs a risk of developing primary liver cancer.

WILSON'S DISEASE

Wilson's disease or hepatolenticular degeneration is a rare inborn error of copper metabolism. The disease is transmitted as a recessive and there is usually a history of parental consanguinity.

The feature of the disease is an excess of copper in tissues, particularly the liver and basal ganglia of the brain. The primary defect is a decreased biliary excretion of copper.

The age of onset varies from 5 to 39 years but the disease is most frequently encountered in children; the sexes are equally affected. The presenting features are either hepatic or neurological. In young patients Wilson's disease usually presents as a disorder of liver function with general ill health, failure to thrive and jaundice. The onset may be sufficiently acute to suggest viral hepatitis, or the patient may present with the features of liver failure: variceal bleeding and ascites. In the older patient it is often the neurological features which are prominent. These include a coarse flapping tremor and dysarthria which are more marked in adults, and dystonia and athetoid movements which are a feature of the illness in children. Inattentiveness at school and even schizophrenia are other forms of presentation, and the patient may first come to the attention of the psychiatrist. Adults tend to have a slower progress of the neurological disturbances than do children.

The pathognomonic sign of Wilson's disease is the Kayser–Fleischer ring. This is seen as a greenish-brown layer of pigment on the deep surface of the cornea. The ring commences at the limbus and extends inwards towards the pupil. It is the result of copper deposition in the Descemet's membrane. Rarely copper deposition in the lens causes a cataract. Another uncommon feature which is characteristic of this disease is blue lunulae. An unusual mode of presentation is with haemolytic anaemia.

Copper deposition in the proximal tubules causes aminoaciduria, glycosuria, uricosuria and phosphaturia. The liver biopsy shows ballooning of the liver cells with mild fatty infiltration and nuclear vacuolation. At times there is severe liver cell inflammation and varying degrees of necrosis. Portal fibrosis evolves into macronodular cirrhosis and the cirrhosis is often histologically active with much cellular damage and newly formed fibrous tissue. Copper may be demonstrated using the rubeanic stain but a more reliable method is to measure the liver copper content. There is nothing diagnostic in the liver biopsy and the increased liver copper may also be found in longstanding cholestasis; but as a rule the clinical picture is sufficiently different from obstructive jaundice that confusion does not arise. The three most useful tests are the serum caeruloplasmin level which is measured by determining copper oxidase activity, serum copper levels and urinary copper levels (Table XIX).

The differential diagnosis includes viral hepatitis and chronic active hepatitis. Copper studies should always be undertaken on any young person who has subacute or chronic liver disease and a careful examination must be made for the Kayser–Fleischer rings using a slit-lamp. Patients with chronic active liver disease present particular difficulties because they may also have increased hepatic and urinary copper, however, serum caeruloplasmin concentration is not as low as in Wilson's disease. In the older patient there may be some confusion between chronic hepatic encephalopathy complicating portasytemic shunts in a patient with non-Wilsonian hepatic cirrhosis.

TABLE XIX. *Screening Tests for Wilson's Disease*

	Wilson's Disease	Normal
Plasma copper (μmol/litre)	1.5–12	13–24
Serum caeruloplasmin (mg/litre)	<200	200–400
Urinary copper (μmol/24 hour)	>3.2	<0.8

Treatment is aimed at reducing the body stores of copper and this is achieved by using the copper chelating agent D-penicillamine which increases urinary copper excretion. The dose of penicillamine hydrochloride is 1.2–1.8 g daily administered orally. It must be continued indefinitely and a useful index of progress is the disappearance of the Kayser–Fleischer rings. Penicillamine therapy may be associated with a number of toxic side effects. It has a weak antipyridoxine effect and therefore pyridoxine is given with the penicillamine. Dietary restrictions are of little value. It is essential to assess the state of the copper stores in the relatives of patients with Wilson's disease in order to detect presymptomatic patients. Serum transaminase levels and copper studies are necessary and if any biochemical abnormality is detected a liver biopsy is performed. Liver copper analysis is a useful method for detecting asymptomatic homozygotes who have increased copper levels, whereas in heterozygotes the liver copper level is normal. The subjects with the increased liver copper content are given penicillamine even if they are symptomfree. Biochemically normal young children from Wilson's disease families require copper studies to be repeated when they are older.

The prognosis of the untreated patient is poor, with death resulting from liver failure or the consequences of the neurological disorder. The outlook is much improved for the treated patient and regression of the liver damage and the portal hypertension may be expected together with improvement in the neurological function.

PRIMARY BILIARY CIRRHOSIS (CHRONIC NON-SUPPURATIVE DESTRUCTIVE CHOLANGITIS)

Primary biliary cirrhosis is an uncommon cause of cirrhosis affecting mainly middle-aged females. The cause is unknown; the disease presents as chronic persistent intrahepatic cholestasis. The hepatitis-associated antigen has been found in the serum of some patients but its role in the pathogenesis of the disease remains to be established. There are genetic and immunological features in common with chronic active hepatitis.

The patient presents with mild, slowly progressive jaundice; occasionally itching precedes the onset of jaundice by a year or more. Once cholestasis has become established the patient has the features of chronic fat malabsorption such as pale stools and diarrhoea. Vitamin D and calcium deficiencies are associated with osteomalacia and osteoporosis, bone pain occurs and other features are crush fractures of the vertebrae and a proximal myopathy. Vitamin K deficiency manifests with a reduction in the prothrombin level. The two major effects of the cholestasis are pruritus and cholesterol deposition in the tissues. There may be marked palmar xanthomas, xanthelasma and deposits of cholesterol in the nervous system may cause a peripheral neuropathy. Cholesterol deposition also occurs in bone.

The biochemical features of cholestasis are prominent: the serum bilirubin reaches levels of 30–40 mg/100 ml (500–650 μmol/litre), serum cholesterol values are frequently greater than 10 mmol/litre and serum alkaline phosphatase may be greater than 100 KA units. On the other hand the serum transaminase concentration may be only minimally elevated. Serum protein changes are primarily an elevation of β-lipoproteins but terminally the serum albumin level falls. There are characteristic and diagnostically helpful alterations in the serum immunoglobulins and circulating antibodies. IgM levels are elevated, the antimitochondrial antibody is positive in 98% of patients and the smooth muscle antibody is present in 50%. Patients with primary biliary cirrhosis also show disturbances of delayed-type hypersensitivity (cell based immunity). There is depression of the Mantoux response, a tendency to granuloma formation and impaired lymphocyte transformation.

The diagnosis of primary biliary cirrhosis by liver biopsy can be extremely difficult both at an early stage of the disease before cirrhosis has actually developed and at the end stage when the cirrhotic process is advanced. The most characteristic lesion is the reduction in the number of small intrahepatic bile ducts. Another feature is pericholangitis of the medium size intrahepatic bile ducts. There is infiltration of the portal tracts by lymphocytes and plasma cells and sarcoid-like granulomas are seen in 30–50% of the biopsies.

At an early stage of primary biliary cirrhosis the differential diagnosis includes the other causes of cholestasis such as drugs, viral hepatitis in a cholestatic phase, chronic active hepatitis and extrahepatic biliary obstruction. The antimitochondrial antibody test is particularly helpful because it is rarely positive in extrahepatic and drug causes of cholestasis. Once cirrhosis is established it becomes difficult to differentiate primary biliary cirrhosis from cholestatic idiopathic cirrhosis but at this stage of the disease the distinction is of little practical value. There is considerable overlap immunologically and histologically between primary biliary cirrhosis, chronic active hepatitis and some cases of idiopathic cirrhosis and this has aroused much speculation about the relationship between these three diseases. The suggestion has been made that they may arise from a single process but this is unproven.

Treatment is aimed mainly at reversing the nutritional deficiencies. Monthly intramuscular injections of 10 mg vitamin K, 100 000 I.U. vitamin A and 100 000 I.U. of vitamin D are recommended. Calcium supplements are given in the form of 32 g of calcium gluconate daily or the equivalent of effervescent calcium tablets. Intravenous infusions of calcium have been used to treat severe bone pain. Steatorrhoea is managed by a low fat diet with medium-chain triglyceride supplements to increase the calories. Mild pruritus is helped by methyl testosterone (25 mg thrice daily orally) or norethandrolone (10 mg thrice daily orally); both drugs cause a mild increase in the jaundice. Cholestyramine (6–10 g orally daily) is of much value in treating severe pruritus and has the further effect of reducing serum cholesterol levels and so diminishing the tissue cholesterol deposits. Corticosteroids are contraindicated as they may enhance the bone disease. Patients who develop the complications of cirrhosis and liver cell failure are treated according to standard regimens. Bleeding oesophageal varices may be managed with a portacaval shunt because patients tolerate the operation well and have a low incidence of hepatic encephalopathy.

The life expectancy of a patient with primary biliary cirrhosis is about 5 years from the time of diagnosis although some patients may live as long as 10 years.

ALPHA$_1$--ANTITRYPSIN DEFICIENCY

Deficiency of this glycoprotein is an important cause of cirrhosis in children and occasionally in adults. The protease inhibitor (Pi) system has a number of variants under the control of a single autosomal gene locus. About 80% of the population are Pi^{MM}. The genotype Pi^{ZZ} (homozygous α_1-antitrypsin deficiency) and the heterozygote Pi^{Z-} are associated with liver disease in some 20% of patients. About 50–60% of patients with severe deficiency may develop emphysema in early adult life and 10–20% of deficient individuals will have no clinical disease. The reason for these differences is not clear.

The liver cells of patients with antitrypsin deficiency demonstrate an accumulation of periodic acid-Schiff positive inclusion bodies. This material is an α_1-antitrypsin which is deficient in sialic acid and other carbohydrate residues; but the precise mechanism for the liver damage remains unexplained.

The disease usually presents as an acute hepatitis within the first 4 months of life. The clinical picture varies with vomiting, lethargy, hypotension and varying degrees of jaundice. There is elevation of the serum bilirubin, aminotransferases, and alkaline phosphatase. The child may succumb at this stage. In those that survive the jaundice slowly subsides but the serum aminotransferases and alkaline phosphatase remain elevated. Cirrhosis of the liver eventually ensues and becomes clinically apparent in late childhood or occasionally only in early adult life. There is hepatomegaly and portal hypertension. A few patients also develop emphysema. There may be an association between α_1-antitrypsin deficiency and primary liver cell cancer. The liver biopsy shows necrosis, cholestasis, inflammatory cell infiltration and a periportal fibrous reaction. The periodic acid-Schiff positive inclusion bodies are characteristic. Cirrhosis is either micronodular or macronodular.

The differential diagnosis includes the various causes of neonatal jaundice particularly biliary atresia. In older children viral hepatitis and Wilson's disease need consideration. There is no specific treatment and no way of preventing progression to cirrhosis.

Further Reading

Bissell, D. M. (1975) Formation and elimination of bilirubin. *Gastroenterology*, **69**, 519–538.

Blendis, L. M. (1975) Fluid retention in liver disease. *Br. J. Hosp. Med.*, January, 47–54.

Brunt, P. W. (1974) Antitrypsin and the liver. *Gut*, **15**, 573–580.

Cooper, R. A. et al. (1974) Role of the spleen in membrane conditioning and hemolysis of spur cells in liver disease. *New Engl. J. Med.*, **280**, 1279–1284.

Doniach, D. and Walker, G. (1974) Mitrochondrial antibodies (AMA). *Gut*, **15**, 664–668.

Grace, N. D. and Powell, L. W. (1974) Iron storage disorders of the liver. *Gastroenterology*, **64**, 1257–1283.

La Russo, N. F. et al. (1974) Dynamics of the enterohepatic circulation of bile acids. *New Engl. J. Med.*, **291**, 689–692.

Malt, R. A. (1976) Portasystemic shunts. *New Engl. J. Med.*, **295**, 24–29 and 80–86.

Mosbach, E. H. and Salen, G. (1974) Bile acid biosynthesis. *Am. J. dig. Dis.*, **19**, 920–929.

Parbhoo, S. (1975) The management of bleeding in liver disease. *Br. J. Hosp. Med.*, January, 17–28.

Schenker, S. et al. (1974) Hepatic encephalopathy: current status. *Gastroenterology*, **66**, 121–151.

Sherlock, S. (1974) Chronic hepatitis. *Gut*, **15**, 581–597.

Sherlock, S. and Scheuer, P. J. (1973) The presentation and diagnosis of 100 patients with primary biliary cirrhosis. *New Engl. J. Med.*, **289**, 674–678.

Starzl, T. E. et al. (1976) Orthotopic liver transplantation in ninety-three patients. *Surgery Gynec. Obstet.*, **142**, 487–505.

Triger, D. R. and Wright, R. (1973) Hyperglobulinaemia in liver disease. *Lancet*, **i**, 1494–1496.

Zetterman, R. K. et al. (1976) Alcoholic hepatitis. *Gastroenterology*, **70**, 382–384.

Hepatitis can be caused by a number of viruses including hepatitis A virus, hepatitis B virus, Epstein–Barr virus, cytomegalic inclusion virus, herpes virus and yellow fever virus. The term 'viral hepatitis' includes both hepatitis A and B infection. Clear distinction between these two forms of liver infection has been hindered by the continued failure to culture either virus and differentiation until recently has been on clinical grounds. The identification of antigenic material as a marker of the virus infection in the blood of many patients with type B infection has led to improved documentation of the epidemiology, occurrence and natural history of hepatitis B infections. No such information exists for type A infection. Viral hepatitis is probably very common but overt liver involvement occurs in only one of every three or four patients with the infection.

Type A viral hepatitis, or infective hepatitis, or short incubation hepatitis is responsible for the epidemic form of the disease although sporadic infections also occur. Epidemics arise from the ingestion of contaminated food or water. Other sources of infection include oysters, clams and other shellfish. Non-human primates may be carriers of the virus. Parenteral transmission may occur from contaminated needles. The disease occurs mainly in the autumn and affects children more often than adults. The incubation period is from 15–50 days.

Type B virus infection is also known as serum hepatitis, syringe jaundice, homologous serum hepatitis or long incubation hepatitis. The incubation period is 50–180 days. The route of infection is mainly parenteral and it is the disease which typically occurs in hospitals, among medical personnel and in units where blood transfusions are frequent. Faecal–oral transmission also occurs. Many of the isolated cases of viral hepatitis in the community are due to type B infection.

HEPATITIS B ANTIGEN (HB AG)

Infection with the hepatitis B virus is associated with the appearance in the serum of one or more antigens: 1. Hepatitis B surface antigen, HB_s Ag; 2. Hepatitis B core antigen, HB_c Ag; 3. The Dane particle which is probably the complete virus composed of the core and surface particles. Various subtypes of HB Ag exist and four main phenotypes are described. A further antigen associated with HB Ag is the 'e' antigen. This is of importance because its presence is related to the occurrence of liver damage. Thus the 'e' antigen is found more frequently in patients with HB antigenaemia who have chronic hepatitis and cirrhosis than in patients with acute viral hepatitis. On the other hand those patients with acute viral hepatitis who have 'e' antigen are more likely to progress to chronic liver disease than those who are negative for the antigen or who harbour anti-e antibodies. The 'e' antigen may be a marker of infectivity and patients with anti-e antibodies are unlikely to transmit the virus. Because of the failure to propagate the hepatitis B virus in tissue cultures the precise relationship of the HB Ag and the virus remains uncertain.

Hepatitis B virus may be transmitted by parenteral inoculation and by ingestion of HB Ag positive blood or material. Drug addicts are particularly at risk as are medical personnel. Hepatitis B infection is a hazard in renal dialysis units, oncology wards, operating theatres, medical laboratories and hospital wards. Whole blood, single donor plasma, pooled plasma, fibrinogen and antihaemophilic globulin can all transmit the disease; however, since the screening of blood donors for HB Ag the incidence of hepatitis transmitted in this way has been reduced. Non-parenteral transmission of the HB virus can occur via the faeces, urine and saliva. Saliva is probably the main vehicle for such infections. Transmission is by droplet infection through sneezing, coughing, kissing or chewing toys. HB virus infections can be hetero- and homosexually transmitted. It is this virus which is probably responsible for many isolated cases of adult viral hepatitis. Infants of women who acquire hepatitis B infection late in pregnancy or soon after delivery have high rates of infection.

Post-transfusion hepatitis continues to occur despite careful screening for viruses such as hepatitis A, hepatitis B, Epstein–Barr and cytomegalic inclusion viruses. This suggests that further hepatitis-producing agents remain to be identified.

Exposure to HB Ag results in a variety of clinical patterns. The antigen can be detected in the blood at an early stage of the disease often before the development of symptoms. Eighty-five per cent of patients clear the antigen from the serum within 4–6 weeks of symptoms. Some 10–15% experience chronic antigenaemia in which there is persistent hepatitis, while 1–3% progress to chronic aggressive hepatitis and cirrhosis of the liver and these patients may be those in whom positive antigenaemia is associated with the 'e' antigen. One per cent of patients die of fulminant hepatitis. Hepatocellular cancer may also be a consequence of HB infection. In general the more severe the clinical illness the less likely are chronic sequelae to develop; in the majority of patients with chronic hepatitis there is no preceding recognition of acute hepatitis. The observation that the titre of HB_s Ag is inversely proportional to the degree of liver damage has led to the suggestion that unusually rapid and effective clearance of HB_s Ag (by immune complexing with HB$_s$ antibodies) may be involved in the pathogenesis of fulminant hepatitis.

There is a wide difference in the carrier rate of HB Ag in different parts of the world: 0.2% in the UK and 0.15% in Canada whereas the rate is much greater in the Mediterranean and Far Eastern countries. Other situations in which the carrier rate is increased include patients with polyarteritis nodosa, Down's syndrome, patients who have been transfused recently, those who receive regular renal dialysis, patients who have undergone cardiac bypass, organ transplantation and who are on immunosuppressive therapy. The carrier rate is greater in drug addicts, homosexuals and prostitutes. There is no evidence that medical and paramedical personnel who are chronic carriers are a risk to their patients.

A variety of tests for HB Ag is available. Gel diffusion, electrophoresis and complement fixation are relatively insensitive. More commonly used are haemagglutination or radioimmunoassay which differ slightly in sensitivity and specificity.

Hepatitis A infection is more important as a worldwide cause of hepatitis. Clear identification of the agent has not been achieved and it cannot be grown on tissue culture. Virus-like particles have been observed in the stools of patients with type A hepatitis. Because they disappear at the height of the infection it appears that patients with clinically manifest hepatitis A infection are not infective.

Clinical Features

The clinical features of the illness are the same for both infectious and serum hepatitis. There is a pre-icteric phase lasting up to a week, during which time the patient feels unwell and complains of severe nausea, vomiting, anorexia, malaise and headache. There is intolerance of fatty foods. The patient loses the desire for cigarettes. Fever is usually mild. During this prodromal phase urticaria and a maculopapular rash appear, and polyarthritis occurs in up to 25% of patients. The arthropathy may be either an arthralgia or an arthritis which may be confused with the early stage of acute rheumatoid arthritis. The arthritis is associated with high titres of HB_s Ag and abnormalities of the complement system. Rarely glomerulonephritis occurs. These extrahepatic manifestations of viral hepatitis may represent a syndrome similar to serum sickness and caused by circulating immune complexes.

After a week the patient becomes icteric and at this stage there is an improvement in wellbeing. Appetite returns and the fever subsides as the urine becomes darker and the stool somewhat paler. The liver is moderately enlarged and tender and the spleen is palpable in 25% of patients. A tender lymphadenopathy may be detected. A few transient spider naevi are seen and small oesophageal varices are occasionally detected, only to disappear as the patient recovers.

The earliest biochemical abnormality is an elevation of serum transaminase levels and this precedes the onset of jaundice by 2 weeks. During the anicteric phase there is bilirubinuria and an excess of urinary urobilinogen. At this stage, too, HB_s Ag may be detected in the serum. The icteric phase is associated with raised bilirubin levels which are usually less than 170 μmol/litre. The increase is in both the conjugated and the unconjugated fractions. Serum alkaline phosphatase and γ-glutamyltranspeptidase levels are elevated. The serum protein concentrations are initially normal but as the illness becomes protracted the albumin level falls and the globulin rises. IgG and IgM levels are usually elevated. Smooth muscle antibody is positive in over 80% of the patients. Other changes observed are an elevated erythrocyte sedimentation rate and a mild prolongation of the prothrombin time. A slight rise in serum α-fetoprotein values (normally associated with hepatocellular cancer) probably indicates liver cell regeneration.

Diagnosis

A liver biopsy is unnecessary in the diagnosis of the typical illness but will be required when the clinical diagnosis is uncertain. Histological features suggesting viral hepatitis include liver cell damage and single liver cell necrosis. There is cellular infiltration and proliferation of sinusoid-lining cells; lymphocytes and plasma cells accumulate in the portal and periportal zones. Varying degrees of cholestasis are present. Another variable is the amount of fibroblast activity and the degree of bile duct damage and proliferation.

The differential diagnosis includes a large number of conditions which cause jaundice: haemolytic disease and Gilbert's syndrome (both characterized by unconjugated hyperbilirubinaemia), chronic active hepatitis, Wilson's disease, drug jaundice, Weil's disease, infectious mononucleosis and the various causes of extrahepatic biliary obstruction including cholangitis. It is very necessary to make the diagnosis of viral hepatitis without resort to a laparotomy; patients submitted to a diagnostic operation have a significant mortality rate and a high morbidity.

Prophylaxis

Prophylaxis against viral hepatitis includes attention to general hygiene and the safe disposal of urine and faeces of infected patients, but the virus is usually widespread in the community by the time patients are being diagnosed. The virus is usually present in all the members of a household where there is a patient with viral hepatitis.

Failure to propagate the virus has hampered the development of a safe and effective vaccine. Screening of patients for HB_s Ag is one way of containing the disease; another is the use of passive immunization. Normal human immunoglobulin (750–1000 mg i.m.) can prevent clinical hepatitis A infection but is of no value against hepatitis B. Immunoglobulins containing a high titre of HB_s antibodies can be obtained by plasmaphoresis and may be offered to those who have had an acute intensive exposure to the HB virus. If hepatitis B immunoglubulin is unavailable such patients might be offered standard immune serum globulin. The HB immune globulin is not indicated in patients having multiple transfusions or for the carrier state. Persons going into those parts of the world where hepatitis is endemic may be offered standard immune globulin. Great care must be exercised in the handling of blood, needles, syringes, tubing and other apparatus in renal, haemophilia and other units which work with large volumes of blood. Careful attention to technique is essential and spilt blood must be thoroughly cleansed. All staff and patients in such units must be screened for HB antigen and patients who carry the antigen must be treated in a separate area. All blood donors should be screened for the presence of HB antigen before being accepted on the donor panel.

Treatment

There is no specific treatment for the illness. The patient is put to bed during the acute phase of the infection but once the serum bilirubin levels fall the patient is allowed out of bed to spend most of the day in a chair. It is probable that early mobilization causes relapses and cholestasis; nonetheless the traditional management tends to be over-cautious. Patients may be moderately active once the serum bilirubin is below 50 μmol/litre. They can return to work although the bilirubin has not returned to normal. The same attitude applies to the serum transaminase values and it may take from 3 to 6 months before the liver function tests return to normal. Full physical activity is permitted after 3 or 4 months. A special dietary regimen is unnecessary although most patients do not tolerate much fat in their food; there is no indication for a high protein diet. Alcohol should be avoided for 6 months. No drug is effective in the disease and there is no indication for vitamin supplements, amino acids, lipotropic agents or antibiotics. Corticosteroids are to be avoided as they may predispose to chronicity. Most patients can be managed at home.

The average patient is icteric for 2–6 weeks and can return to work about 3 weeks after the jaundice has faded. The disease is more severe during pregnancy and at the menopause. Occasional epidemics are characterized by severe manifestations of the disease. The patient who recovers has a perfectly normal liver both functionally and histologically and the occasional portal scar is of no significance. Death is rare, the mortality being less than 2 per 1000. Death occurs in the first few days from acute liver failure or after 3 weeks' duration of illness from subacute hepatic necrosis.

Prediction of Chronicity

The potential for an acute infection with type B virus to become chronic is increased when the patient is a male, the attack has been relatively mild and when there is depression of immunological responses such as in chronic renal disease and cancer. The use of steroids during the acute illness may predispose to chronicity. Factors which suggest the development of a chronic illness include the continued elevation of the serum γ-globulin, HB_s Ag, 'e' antigen and the persistence of antibodies to the core antigen. The liver biopsy shows hepatic necrosis with accompanying intralobular and interlobular bridging of the portal triads. At present there is no way of halting or reversing the progression to chronic liver disease such as chronic active hepatitis and cirrhosis.

Clinical Variants of Viral Hepatitis

There are a number of clinical variants in the typical course of viral hepatitis.

ANICTERIC HEPATITIS

This condition is diagnosed by an increase in the serum transaminase level or by finding the presence of HB_s Ag in the blood. An increasing number of patients are recognized to have anicteric hepatitis and this is particularly likely to occur during an epidemic of hepatitis when many persons undergo blood tests. In general the illness is accompanied by few symptoms and signs: malaise, nausea and mild abdominal pain. The liver may be slightly tender. The development of cirrhosis is rare. It has been suggested that the patient who has had anicteric hepatitis is at particular risk of developing progressive and permanent liver damage but this concept is not widely accepted.

'POSTHEPATITIS SYNDROME'

This is probably a common sequel of viral hepatitis and manifests as malaise, easy fatiguability, mild anorexia, abdominal discomfort, fat intolerance and some depression. Physical examination, liver function tests and liver biopsy are normal. The cause for the syndrome is uncertain. It may be related to the other 'postviral infection' syndromes that are seen after influenza and infectious mononucleosis; undoubtedly psychological factors are important. No special treatment is required and the patient should be firmly reassured that the liver is normal.

POSTHEPATITIS HYPERBILIRUBINAEMIA

A few patients who recover from viral hepatitis continue to have a mild hyperbilirubinaemia. The bilirubin is usually of the unconjugated form. It is probable that some of the patients have Gilbert's syndrome (p. 293) and the viral hepatitis is incidental. Other tests of liver function will be normal. This is a rare consequence of viral hepatitis and requires no special treatment.

Cholestatic Hepatitis

In some patients the disease runs a more prolonged course and the jaundice persists for 7–20 weeks. Serum bilirubin levels are 350 μmol/litre or higher and remain steady. The patients show other features of cholestasis, such as pruritus, diarrhoea, prolonged prothrombin time and elevation of the serum alkaline phosphatase and cholesterol concentrations. The liver shows mild liver cell damage in the presence of marked cholestasis. The differential diagnosis is from extrahepatic cholestasis particularly and a liver biopsy is usually necessary. The ultimate outlook is good and the bilirubin levels gradually fall. Cirrhosis of the liver is not a consequence. A diet high in protein and low in fat is usually acceptable; vitamin K and possibly other fat-soluble vitamins are required; drugs for pruritus may be necessary (p. 262). Prednisolone (30 mg daily) has the effect of reducing the bilirubin levels and the patient looks and feels better but there is no accompanying improvement of the liver histology. Because corticosteroids do not have a similar effect on serum bilirubin levels in extrahepatic cholestasis their administration has been recommended as a diagnostic test in difficult problems of cholestatic liver disease.

Relapsing Hepatitis

Occasionally a patient has a recurrence of jaundice a few weeks or months after making an apparently satisfactory recovery from viral hepatitis. It is possible that this occurs in 2–15% of patients. The causes for a relapse are not always clear and it remains uncertain whether premature activity is responsible. The management is the same as for the initial episode and the patient can be given reassurance that the liver will recover completely. However, it is essential to be certain that the diagnosis is that of relapsing hepatitis and not chronic active hepatitis, Wilson's disease or extrahepatic obstruction. It is therefore necessary to undertake a liver biopsy.

CHRONIC HEPATITIS

Chronic hepatitis is an uncommon outcome of viral hepatitis in the UK and USA but is seen more frequently in parts of the Mediterranean, Africa and the Far East. Progression to the chronic form of the disease is related to the genetic background and immunological status of the individual and to the nature of the hepatitis B virus infection, particularly the continued replication of the virus in the liver cells. This is suggested by the presence of hepatocytes with a 'ground glass' appearance to the cytoplasm.

When the hepatitis has persisted for more than 6 months it is said to be chronic. Two forms of chronic hepatitis are distinguished. In *chronic persistent hepatitis* the lobular structure is preserved, inflammation is mainly portal and there is little necrosis or fibrosis. Serum transaminase levels may fluctuate over the years; but there is little deterioration in liver function and the course is non-progressive and benign. The second, more sinister, outcome is that of *chronic active hepatitis* (p. 251) which is characterized pathologically by a chronic aggressive hepatitis in which proliferation of Küpffer cells, spotty liver cell necrosis, collapse of tissue and fibrosis bridging areas of collapse and necrosis are characteristic. Erosion of the limiting plates may occur and if the inflammation of fibrosis persists cirrhosis ensures in about one-third of patients.

POSTHEPATITIS CIRRHOSIS

Posthepatitis cirrhosis is an uncommon outcome of viral hepatitis. Massive necrosis is followed by healing and insignificant scar formation. Cirrhosis, when it does arise is more likely to follow a chronic aggressive hepatitis. The cirrhosis is usually of the macronodular variety.

ACUTE LIVER FAILURE

Other names for this syndrome include acute fulminant hepatitis, acute hepatic necrosis, massive liver necrosis and the older one of acute yellow atrophy. It is rare for viral hepatitis to progress to acute liver failure and the complication usually occurs within 10 days of the onset of the illness. The severity and speed of the necrosis vary and at times it is so rapid that the patient dies before jaundice has developed. The patient is drowsy and confused, with a liver flap. The liver shrinks rapidly and is percussed out with difficulty; a generalized bleeding tendency develops and fluid retention occurs. Complications include bleeding peptic ulcers, renal failure, pancreatitis, acidosis, severe hypoglycaemia and infections, particularly septicaemia and pneumonia. Serum bilirubin levels are often only moderately elevated, while the transaminase concentration may rise to greater than 1000 I.U. On the other hand some patients die with values which are barely abnormal. Many of the clotting factors are depressed. There are few reliable prognostic signs. The prothrombin time is the most helpful of the biochemical indices and a markedly prolonged time indicates a bad prognosis. Electroencephalographic changes are also of value and marked flattening and slowing of the waves is an ominous sign. Prognosis is worse in the elderly. The outcome appears improved in those patients showing a rise in serum and α-fetoprotein values. The development of deep coma is usually fatal.

The mortality rate is difficult to assess because of differing definitions of acute liver failure but once deep coma has supervened the mortality is in the region of 85%. Uncontrollable cerebral oedema is an important cause of death.

The diagnosis is usually obvious although the cause of the hepatic necrosis may not be apparent. Other causes of acute liver failure must be considered (Table XX). It is also necessary to differentiate the coma associated with the syndrome of chronic portasystemic encephalopathy

TABLE XX. *The Causes of Acute Liver Failure*

Infections
   Viral hepatitis
   Disseminated herpes simplex
   Coxsackie virus
   Yellow fever virus
   Epstein–Barr virus

Metabolic disorders
   Acute fatty liver of pregnancy
   Reye's syndrome

Ischaemia
   Acute Budd–Chiari syndrome
   Ligation of hepatic artery
   Heat stroke

Poisons
   Amanita phalloides
   Paracetamol
   Halothane
   Monoamine oxidase inhibitors
   Tetracycline
   Halogenated hydrocarbons
   Yellow phosphorus

---

from the coma of acute liver failure. In portasystemic encephalopathy there is a previous history of liver disease and the physical examination indicates chronic liver failure. The outcome of the coma is more favourable in portasystemic encephalopathy.

The treatment of acute liver failure is uncertain and unrewarding. Conventional therapy includes a protein-free diet of 1000–1500 calories which is usually administered as 10 or 20% glucose either via a nasogastric tube or intravenously. A central venous catheter is inserted and a careful fluid balance chart is kept to avoid overloading the circulation. Salt-poor albumin infusions are used if albumin levels fall very low. The control of abnormal bleeding is difficult and requires the measurement of various clotting factors. Vitamin K (10 mg daily of the water-soluble form) is administered intramuscularly but it rarely improves the prothrombin level in severe hepatocellular failure and there is little benefit from continuing its use for longer than a week if there is no response. Fresh frozen plasma may be used in an attempt to correct factors V, VII, IX and X, and fresh whole blood corrects an additional platelet deficiency. The haemorrhagic state may be accompanied by intravascular coagulation; this is suspected when there is thrombocytopenia and an increase in serum fibrin/fibrinogen degradation products. The use of large doses of heparin and fresh frozen plasma can be beneficial if introduced at an early stage of the liver cell failure.

Drugs are used with extreme care. Oral neomycin (up to 4 g daily) is used to sterilize the bowel and a systemic antibiotic is added if infection develops. Diuretics are indicated in exceptional circumstances only and sedatives are avoided. If the patient is very restless 5 mg i.v. diazepam or 25 mg i.m. chlorpromazine are given. Progress is judged by following the electroencephalogram, liver function tests, blood sugar, blood clotting mechanisms and blood urea. It is debatable whether cortiscosteroids, either in conventional doses (prednisolone 30–60 mg daily) or in massive doses (prednisolone 150–200 mg daily), are of any benefit but most patients usually receive steroids more in hope than from conviction.

Because of the poor outlook for a patient in liver failure treated with the conventional therapy a number of other methods and techniques have been introduced. These include peritoneal dialysis, haemodialysis, human cross circulation, exchange transfusion, plasma exchange, heterologous liver perfusion, auxiliary hepatic transplantation and artificial liver support systems. Most of the methods are only available in specialized units and none has been shown to be effective in reducing the mortality rate.

Further Reading

Knodell, R. G. et al. (1975) Etiological spectrum of post-transfusion hepatitis. *Gastroenterology*, **69**, 1278–1285.

McAuliffe, V. J. (1976) e: A third hepatitis B antigen? *New Engl. J. Med.*, **294**, 779–780.

Rueff, B. and Benhamou, J.-P. (1973) Acute hepatic necrosis and fulminant liver failure. *Gut*, **14**, 805–815.

Sherlock, S. (1976) Predicting progression of acute type-B hepatitis to chronicity. *Lancet*, **ii**, 354–356.

Villarejos, V. M. et al. (1974) Role of saliva, urine and feces in the transmission of type B hepatitis. *New Engl. J. Med.*, **291**, 1375–1378.

Drug Jaundice

One of the major functions of the liver is to protect the body against intoxication from both endogenous and exogenous sources. Conjugation to a diglucuronide is necessary for bilirubin excretion and the bile salts are excreted as the glycine and taurine conjugates. Esterases also play a role. The smooth endoplasmic reticulum of the liver cells contains a number of enzymes which catalyse the metabolism of drugs to water-soluble compounds which are more readily excreted by the body. The excretion of foreign compounds can be thought of as occurring in two phases. In phase I the compound is rendered slightly water soluble by a variety of processes of which hydroxylation is the most important. The hydroxylating enzyme system is cytochrome P450. It belongs to the group of mixed-function oxidases and is situated on the smooth endoplasmic reticulum. In phase II of the process the hydroxylated compound is rendered highly water soluble, and therefore readily excretable in urine or bile, by conjugation to glucuronide, or glutathione, or sulphate or amino acids. There are marked individual variations in drug hydroxylations and it is probable that drug metabolism is governed by genetic factors. Hepatic drug metabolism appears to decrease with ageing thereby reducing the metabolic clearance of drugs.

The hydroxylating system can be induced by drugs and this is accompanied by an increase in the size of the smooth endoplasmic membranes which can be seen on electron microscopy. The majority of lipid-soluble compounds metabolized by the microsomal hydroxylase have some inducing properties. Drugs metabolized by cytochrome P450 include barbiturates, diazepoxides, phenothiazines, antihistamines, oral contraceptives and anabolic androgens. Important inducing agents which are widely used are phenobarbitone and alcohol. Uridine diphosphoglucuronyl transferase, which is responsible for bilirubin conjugation, is a microsomal enzyme and it can also be induced; this has led to the therapeutic use of phenobarbital in the treatment of unconjugated hyperbilirubinaemia.

There are a great number of drugs which affect liver function, some more than others. A list is given below in this attempt to classify the nature of the hepatic disturbance and the drugs responsible. In general the major effect on the liver is to cause either jaundice alone or more widespread alteration in liver cell structure and function.

INTERFERENCE WITH BILIRUBIN METABOLISM

Haemolysis
    Para-aminosalicylic acid, quinine, phenacetin
Serum binding of bilirubin to albumin
    Salicylates, sulphonamides which compete with bilirubin for albumin
Interference with bilirubin uptake by the liver cell
    Flavaspidic acid
Interference with bilirubin conjugation
    Novobiocin
Interference with bilirubin excretion
    C-17 alkyl substituted steroids as in methyltestosterone and norethandrolone; abnormalities of the canaliculi are present. Jaundice is mild and reversible; all patients are liable to develop jaundice. All the icterogenic steroids are active by mouth.

DIRECT HEPATOTOXICITY

Carbon tetrachloride, chlorophenothane (DDT), benzene derivatives, tetracyclines, paracetamol and various metallic compounds. The clinical picture is one of varying degrees of hepatocellular damage and histology shows a combination of necrosis, fatty change and slight cellular infiltration.

HEPATITIS-LIKE REACTION

Hydrazine-amine oxidase inhibitors such as iproniazid and phenelzine, halothane, methoxyflurane, ethionamide, cycloserine, trichloroethylene (can cause hepatic necrosis in 'solvent sniffers'), oxyphenisatin acetate (a component of some laxative preparations), isoniazid (isonicotinic acid hydrazine) and methyldopa.

CHOLESTATIC REACTION

Phenothiazine groups such as chlorpromazine. This is an individual sensitivity reaction and cannot be related to dose.

'MIXED' REACTION

Para-aminosalicylic acid and rarely sulphonamides and erythromycin estolate. The liver reaction is intermediate between the hepatitic and the cholestatic reactions and is characterized by fever, lymphadenopathy, rashes and an eosinophilia which appear within 4 weeks of taking the drug.

CHLORPROMAZINE JAUNDICE

This is a rare complication of phenothiazine therapy which occurs in sensitive subjects. The onset is usually within the first 1–3 weeks of commencing therapy. The clinical picture is one of marked cholestasis which lasts for

1–4 weeks but rarely for as long as 3–30 months. In such patients pruritus, steatorrhoea and xanthomas become troublesome complaints and the clinical picture may be confused with either primary biliary cirrhosis or extra-hepatic biliary obstruction. The liver histology is that of cholestasis and portal infiltration with mononuclear cells and eosinophils. Prognosis is good and the patient usually recovers completely.

HALOTHANE HEPATITIS

It is generally accepted that halothane causes a hepatitis-like reaction. The incidence is very low. Jaundice is uncommon after the first exposure when the sequence of events is fever developing about 8–14 days after the anaesthetic followed one week later by jaundice. Liver damage is more likely to occur after the second or subsequent exposure to halothane and in these patients the onset of jaundice is more closely related in time to the anaesthetic administration. Fever and jaundice appear on the fourth post-anaesthetic day and an eosinophilia develops. The liver is only slightly enlarged and splenomegaly is rare. The pathological picture suggests viral hepatitis but careful light and electron microscopic studies show several differences between the two conditions. There is a high mortality in patients with well-developed hepatitis and the mortality is increased in patients subjected to multiple exposures. The prognosis is worse in obese patients who manifest the early onset of jaundice after anaesthesia and who have a prolonged prothrombin time. However, many grades of severity occur and the overall mortality is about 20%. The patient is treated on the regimen for acute liver failure. Because about two-thirds of patients with halothane hepatitis have had more than one exposure to the anaesthetic it is advised that no patient should receive a second anaesthetic with halothane; its use in a single exposure is not discouraged. It is not clear how soon after the first exposure it is safe to have a second halothane anaesthetic but at least 4 weeks and possibly as long as 3 months is probably a reasonable interval.

METHOTREXATE LIVER DAMAGE

Methotrexate has proved to be excellent therapy for severe psoriasis. Unfortunately about 50% of patients on the drug develop hepatic fibrosis which is irreversible and may progress to cirrhosis. Other histological changes which are observed include severe fatty change, nuclear vacuolation and inflammation. An elevated serum alkaline phosphatase is usually associated with considerable liver damage although the converse is not true. It appears that the hepatotoxicity of methotrexate is greater when administered as a 'continuous low dose' than when given on an 'intermittent' regimen.

ORAL CONTRACEPTIVES

Mild disturbance of liver function is probably frequent in women taking oral contraceptive tablets. This is not unexpected because both the oestrogen and the progesterone components in most of the oral contraceptive tablets are 17 α-alkyl-substituted steroids. Bromsulphthalein retention is increased in 40% of women on the contraceptive pill; less frequently elevations of the serum transaminase and alkaline phosphatase occur. Postmenopausal women are more frequently and severely affected. There is no evidence that the incidence of abnormal liver function tests increases with the duration of the therapy and the finding of abnormal liver function tests is not an indication for discontinuing the tablets. In a few women oral contraceptives cause overt jaundice and this usually occurs within 4 weeks of taking the tablets. The patient develops dark urine, arthralgia, fever, rashes and systemic symptoms. The serum bilirubin concentration is seldom elevated above 170 μmol/litre and the transaminase levels are equally only moderately raised.

Liver histology reveals stasis of the bile in the canaliculi and little inflammatory reaction. If this type of reaction is detected the drug must be discontinued, whereupon the liver will return to normal both functionally and histologically. Although direct evidence is lacking it is possible that there is a causal relationship between hepatic vein occlusion (the Budd–Chiari syndrome, p. 295) and oral contraceptive tablets. It is also claimed that neonatal jaundice related to breast feeding may be more frequent in women who have had oral contraceptive drugs. Oral contraceptives are contraindicated in women with a history of recurrent jaundice of pregnancy (p. 299) and with evidence of acute or chronic disturbance of liver cell function. A previous history of viral hepatitis is not a contraindication to their use.

The long-term use of oral contraceptives may be associated with the development of focal nodular hyperplasia of the liver. There are histological features of an hamartoma; the lesion is neither an adenoma or a hepatocellular cancer. The extent of the nodular transformation varies but large space-occupying lesions may occur which are liable to intrahepatic bleeding.

PARACETAMOL HEPATOTOXICITY

Overdose with paracetamol, usually self-induced, can cause acute centrilobular hepatic necrosis. Plasma concentrations of paracetamol greater than 300 μg/ml at 4 hours and 50 μg/ml at 12 hours following ingestion are likely to be associated with liver damage. There is elevation of aminotransferases, a metabolic acidosis and prolonged prothrombin time. Hepatic failure may develop after 4 days and has a poor prognosis. The management is that of acute liver failure (p. 277). Cysteamine appears to have a protective effect against liver damage but it must be administered within 10 hours of paracetamol ingestion. An initial loading dose of 2 g is given as an intravenous infusion in 5% dextrose followed by an infusion of 0.4 g over 8 hours. Cysteamine has a number of unpleasant side-effects and its precise role in the management of paracetamol overdose remains to be determined.

Tumours of the Liver

Tumours of the liver are mainly metastatic in origin and primary liver tumours are relatively uncommon.

Primary Cancer of the Liver (Hepatoma)

There is a marked geographical variation in the incidence of primary liver cancer. Whereas the tumour accounts for less than 1% of deaths from cancer in Europe and the United States of America it is 50 times more frequent in Africa south of the Sahara and in South-East Asia. The aetiology is unknown. Over 60% of patients have associated cirrhosis, particularly of the macronodular variety. Primary liver cancers develop in about 30% of alcoholic cirrhotics who have ceased to take alcohol. Other factors which have been implicated include malnutrition, iron overload, parasitic infections and ingestion of carcinogenic myco-toxins such as aflatoxin which is a frequent contaminant of food in parts of Central Africa. Exposure to vinyl chloride, used in the production of polyvinyl chloride (PVC), may be followed after 5–25 years by the develop-ment of hepatic angiosarcomas.

The majority of tumours are hepatocellular in origin but invasive tumours do arise from bile duct epithelium and mixed cell types are encountered. There is little purpose in distinguishing the various histological types and all gradations between benign and malignant primary liver tumours are seen. The typical malignant hepatoma contains cells which resemble normal liver cells but are smaller and contain hyperchromatic nuclei. There may be attempts at lobule formation. The liver frequently contains many small tumours and it has been suggested that such tumours are of multicentric origin rather than a unicentric growth which has given rise to widespread intrahepatic secondary deposits. The tumours are usually confined to the liver. Distant metastases occur in one-third of patients and are mainly in the lungs and brain. Peritoneal seeding occurs as does involvement of the regional lymph nodes. All ages are affected and males 4 times more frequently than females.

The usual clinical presentation is that of a cirrhotic patient who suddenly declines in health with loss of weight, anorexia, fever and a dull aching continuous right upper quadrant pain. The liver is felt as being large, irregular in outline, hard and tender. Auscultation may disclose either a bruit or a friction rub. The rapid onset of ascites is fairly characteristic and the fluid is often blood-stained or has a high protein content. The ascites may follow acute portal vein thrombosis, hepatic vein occlusion or peritoneal seeding. Signs of liver cell failure are frequent, particularly variceal bleeding and hepatic coma. The clinical picture in Africans is different from that in patients in the Western Hemisphere; the African often presents at a relatively late stage when the tumour is large and there is considerable hepatomegaly but despite this there are few, if any, signs of liver cell failure.

The biochemical tests of liver function show varying degrees of abnormality. The serum bilirubin levels may be surprisingly low and the patient is often not clinically jaundiced. The most constant and helpful biochemical feature is an elevation of the serum alkaline phosphatase and 5′ nucleotidase. α-Fetoprotein can be detected in the serum of 30% of Caucasian patients and 75% of patients from Africa and Asia (p. 225). There is an association between hepatoma and HB Ag but the rate is variable between different countries. Hepatomas are occasionally associated with a variety of metabolic, endocrine, haemato-logical and neurological syndromes: hypoglycaemia, hyperlipidaemia, hypercalcaemia, macroglobulinaemia, erythremia, thrombocytopenia, disturbances of coagulation, acanthosis nigricans and cerebellar atrophy.

The diagnosis may be established by a liver biopsy. The site for insertion of the needle can be determined by hepatic scintiscanning using ^{198}Au colloid gold or ^{99m}technetium. The liver scan will show filling defects which indicate the presence of tumour and the needle can be directed in their direction. Liver biopsy in hepatoma is potentially hazardous because it has occasionally been followed by fatal bleeding. The tumour may also be demonstrated by arteriography, splenic venography and peritoneoscopy.

The treatment is unsatisfactory and is mainly directed towards the relief of symptoms. If the growth is believed to be localized as a single mass in a lobe a partial hepatectomy may be attempted. Unfortunately at the time of laparotomy the tumour will all too frequently be found to have extended into both lobes. Radiotherapy and systemic chemotherapy are unrewarding and the infusion of chemotherapeutic agents via a catheter placed in the hepatic artery has also given disappointing results. Ligation of the hepatic artery has not proved successful. Orthotopic liver transplantation has been attempted in a few patients.

The prognosis of a primary liver cancer is dismal and the average length of life once the diagnosis has been established is about 8 months. A positive test for serum α-fetoprotein worsens the prognosis and patients have a survival time of only 4 months.

SECONDARY TUMOURS OF THE LIVER

Malignant tumours frequently spread to the liver. Common sites for the primary growth are the stomach, breast, colon and bronchus. The cirrhotic liver is not less prone than a normal liver to metatic involvement from extrahepatic neoplasms. The patient may be relatively symptom-free or complain of anorexia, nausea, vomiting, weight loss and right upper quadrant and epigastric pain.

Jaundice is usual but not invariable. Examination of the patient reveals varying degrees of ill health and the liver is characteristically enlarged although one-third of infiltrated livers are of normal size. The liver is very hard and irregularly nodular. The nodules can be felt to be umbilicated only if they are very large. A bruit or a friction rub may be heard over the liver. Occasionally portal hypertension ensues and the spleen may be palpable.

The most sensitive screening test is a radioactive liver scan which detects deposits greater than 3.0 cm in diameter. A liver biopsy provides histological confirmation of the diagnosis in 75% of patients in whom the diagnosis is suspect but in only 25% of livers where there is no clinical or biochemical grounds for suspecting metastatic disease. Peritoneoscopy is a useful technique and has the advantage that a biopsy from a suspicious area can be obtained under direct vision. Biochemical tests are less reliable and the most helpful are the serum alkaline phosphatase and 5′nucleotidase; less reliable are the serum bilirubin, the serum transaminases and the bromsulphthalein retention test. Radiological techniques such as coeliac arteriography, splenic venography and air insufflation have a role in the diagnosis.

Treatment is unsatisfactory. Hepatic lobectomy may be attempted for a single metastasis. Regional perfusion with antimetabolites via an indwelling catheter in the hepatic artery has been used. On the whole any form of therapy is unrewarding and the management is mainly palliative. Any form of treatment makes very little difference to the survival and only 10% of patients live longer than a year once the diagnosis of secondary growths in the liver has been established.

BENIGN TUMOURS OF THE LIVER

There are a variety of simple tumours which occur in the liver. Haemangiomas are the most common; they are usually small, asymptomatic and of no clinical significance. Occasionally giant haemangiomas are encountered and their presence is suspected when a venous hum is heard over the liver. The main significance of haemangiomas is that their presence, or suspected presence, is a contra-indication to liver biopsy. Treatment is unsatisfactory and both surgical excision and radiation therapy have been used.

Extrahepatic Cholestatic Jaundice

The major diagnostic problem in a patient with obstructive jaundice is to decide whether the cause is intrahepatic or extrahepatic (Table XV). Extrahepatic cholestatic jaundice follows bile duct obstruction which is usually due to gall stones, pancreatic cancer or bile duct stricture. Less common causes are hydatid disease, round worms and a choledochal cyst. The clinical features vary according to the underlying disease. Right upper quadrant pain, jaundice, pruritus and fever are usually present either singly or in combination. Steatorrhoea may occur and the urine contains bilirubin but no urobilinogen. Typical biochemical features include elevated serum conjugated bilirubin, alkaline phosphatase, 5'nucleotidase, γ-glutamyl-transpeptidase and cholesterol levels. The antimitochon-drial antibody test is negative. There is prolongation of the prothombin time, which is readily reversed by vitamin K therapy. The serum transaminase is usually only slightly elevated. The characteristic clinical and biochemical features may become blurred by varying degrees of liver cell dysfunction and at times the serum transaminase concentration may be greater than 100 I.U. A major diagnostic advance has been the introduction of endoscopic retrograde cholangiopancreatography (ERCP) whereby the biliary duct system is cannulated endoscopically via the ampulla of Vater. Aspiration needle biopsy of the liver can be performed with safety if the bleeding tendency is corrected and the patient is watched carefully. Histology of the liver shows accumulation of bile in the centrizonal areas, mild mononuclear cell infiltration in the portal zones, bile thrombi and bile infarcts. Eventually portal fibrosis ensues but it is doubtful whether true cirrhosis ever develops because of extrahepatic biliary obstruction.

The treatment is to relieve the obstruction and this invariably means either a curative or a palliative surgical procedure.

Extrahepatic Portal Vein Obstruction

Extrahepatic portal vein thrombosis in adults is usually associated with a hepatoma which complicates cirrhosis of the liver. Occasionally it reflects a clotting disturbance. In children the cause is seldom apparent although umbilical sepsis has been implicated. Cavernous malformation of the portal vein is probably a sequel to portal vein thrombosis and it is rarely, if ever, found as a primary venous anomaly. Portal vein obstruction causes portal hypertension and a marked portasystemic collateral circulation develops. Liver cell function is little affected.

Extrahepatic portal vein obstruction usually presents with haematemesis from bleeding oesophageal varices. In children the age of onset is from 3–8 years and the bleeding may be precipitated by an upper respiratory tract infection. Despite frequent gastrointestinal bleeding liver cell function remains adequate and jaundice, ascites and coma are rare. The presentation in adults is similar, although the acute onset of ascites, which may be blood-stained, may be the first indication of disease.

The diagnosis is established by a barium swallow which shows the varices, and a splenic venogram which demonstrates that the portal vein is blocked and a collateral circulation has developed. The usual site for the occlusion is at the hilum of the liver. A very large spleen may be associated with features of hypersplenism (anaemia, leucopenia and thrombocytopenia) but this seldom has clinical significance. Treatment is essentially conservative, particularly in children. Blood is replaced as required and intravenous pitressin (20 units in 100 ml 5% dextrose and water given over 10 minutes) is administered in order to reduce the splanchnic blood flow. The usual sequence of events is that the bleeding stops and surgical intervention is not necessary. A special diet is not required but iron supplements are usually indicated. It is vital that the veins should be preserved; good technique is required and surgical 'cut-downs' must be avoided. There is no satisfactory operation; the portal vein cannot be used for reconstructive surgery and various procedures such as splenectomy, gastric and oesophageal transection and total gastrectomy and oesophagectomy have not found favour. A mesocaval shunt is advocated should surgical intervention become essential. Usually the episodes of bleeding become less frequent as the child grows older.

Idiopathic Unconjugated Hyperbilirubinaemia (Gilbert's Syndrome)

This syndrome is characterized by chronic mild unconjugated hyperbilirubinaemia in otherwise healthy persons. There is no evidence of overt haemolysis and the cause for the failure to clear unconjugated bilirubin from the plasma is not always apparent. Some patients may have a deficiency of the microsmal enzyme bilirubin uridine diphosphoglucuronyl transferase, while in others the uptake and transport of unconjugated bilirubin by the liver cell may be at fault. Although by definition overt haemolysis is not a feature of the syndrome many patients have a slightly reduced red cell survival. The syndrome is probably more frequent than currently appreciated. It is an inherited disorder, the genetics of which are uncertain; males are more frequently affected.

The patient has vague and variable symptoms such as

abdominal pain and discomfort, nausea, vomiting and malaise. These often follow physical exertion or an excess of alcohol, when the patient may become slightly icteric. Physical examination reveals a healthy person who may be slightly jaundiced and may have a minimally tender liver. The serum bilirubin is elevated, usually between 25 and 40 μmol/litre and it is rarely greater than 70 μmol/litre. The levels fluctuate and at times fall to normal values. Bilirubin levels increase when the patient fasts and this relationship between serum bilirubin values and calorie intake may explain some of the fluctuations in bilirubin levels. The hyperbilirubinaemia is of the unconjugated variety and the conjugated levels are normal as are cholecystography and liver histology. The demonstration that a 72-hour fast induces a two- to three-fold increase in unconjugated bilirubin values can be used diagnostically.

Gilbert's disease must be distinguished from other causes of unconjugated hyperbilirubinaemia (Table XV), including posthepatitis hyperbilirubinaemia, drug jaundice and cirrhosis. Radiology of the gall bladder, a red cell survival test and a liver biopsy are usually necessary before a diagnosis can be made with confidence.

There is no specific therapy. The patient should have the nature of the illness explained and be reassured that there is no chronic liver damage. The patient is warned against excess fatigue and over-indulgence in alcohol. The recent observation that phenobarbitone increases the activities of the enzymes on the smooth endoplasmic reticulum of the liver cell suggested that this drug might be used to induce glucuronyl transferase activity. On balance it is better if these patients receive no supportive drug therapy.

A rare, more severe form of unconjugated non-haemolytic hyperbilirubinaemia is the *Crigler–Najjar syndrome*. This is usually obvious shortly after birth when the infant becomes deeply jaundiced, the serum bilirubin concentrations varying between 250 and 420 μmol/litre. Kernicterus occurs in 85% of the affected infants. It is likely that glucuronyl transferase deficiency is in part or wholly responsible for the jaundice and phenobarbitone therapy has been used with variable success.

Another familial disorder affecting bilirubin metabolism is the *Dubin Johnson syndrome*, in which there is conjugated hyperbilirubinaemia and dark pigment in the liver cells. The patients complain of right upper quadrant pain and discomfort and are mildly icteric. There is an excretory defect of the liver cells and serum bilirubin levels rise to 30 to 100 μmol/litre. Bromsulphthalein retention is abnormal and the gall bladder is not outlined on cholecystography. The syndrome is familial and the mode of inheritance is that of an autosomal recessive trait. Some patients also demonstrate abnormal excretion of the isomers of urinary coproporphyrin and deficiency of factor VII. Liver biopsy is characteristic and shows normal cells containing dark pigment.

The *Rotor syndrome* is a variant of conjugated hyperbilirubinaemia in which the excretory defect is present but the liver cells do not contain any abnormal pigment.

It is probable that there is some interrelation between the various types of familial conjugated and unconjugated hyperbilirubinaemia and that the features of the different syndromes may exist in the same patient or alternatively that different families may contain more than one clinical variant.

Budd–Chiari Syndrome

In this rare condition there is occlusion of the hepatic veins. The aetiology varies. There may be thrombosis associated with a disorder of blood coagulation such as polycythaemia rubra vera and leukaemia. The oral contraceptive agents have been implicated in the thrombotic process and thrombosis may complicate hepatoma and trauma. Rarely a congenital membranous diaphragm causes partial or complete occlusion of the veins. The obstruction causes intense hepatic venous congestion, pain, hepatomegaly, ascites and eventually liver cell necrosis and coma. The obstruction is diagnosed by hepatic venography which indicates narrow or occluded veins and a distinctive pattern in the small venous channels. Inferior vena cavography shows the IVC to be narrowed and distorted in its intra-hepatic course. The liver scan shows generalized failure of uptake of the isotope except in the caudate lobe which has a separate venous drainage. The liver biopsy demonstrates intense central vein congestion and eventually portal fibrosis. The management is symptomatic and aimed at controlling the ascites which can be severe and very disabling. Any underlying haematological disease is treated. Rarely it is possible to operate upon and relieve a membranous obstruction. The prognosis is poor and few patients survive longer than one year.

A syndrome which presents in a similar manner to the Budd–Chiari syndrome is *hepatic veno-occlusive disease.* This has been described mainly from the West Indies but occurs in other parts of the world. There is fibrosis and obliteration of the central and sublobular hepatic veins. The aetiology is thought to be a toxic endophlebitis caused by pyrrolizidine alkaloids in plants of the genera *Senecio, Heliotropium* and *Crotolaria.* The poisons are usually ingested as an infusion of 'bush tea' which is made from the toxic plants.

Neonatal Jaundice

Jaundice during the neonatal period is a normal event and develops after the second day of life, reaching a peak during the first week and then fading rapidly. This 'physiological' unconjugated hyperbilirubinaemia reflects a combination of delayed maturation of the hepatic glucuronyl transferase system and an increase in haemolysis. Jaundice occurring within 36 hours of birth is indicative of severe haemolysis and must be taken seriously. There are a great many other causes of neonatal jaundice and these are listed in Table XXI.

TABLE XXI. *The Causes of Neonatal Jaundice*

Unconjugated Hyperbilirubinaemia	*Conjugated Hyperbilirubinaemia*
Physiological jaundice	*Infection*
Rh, ABO blood group incompatibility	Syphilis
Glucuronyl transferase deficiency	Rubella
Inherited haemolytic syndromes	Cytomegalovirus
Breast-milk jaundice	Herpes simplex
High intestinal obstruction	Coxsackie virus
Hypothyroidism	Hepatitis B virus
Novobiocin therapy	Bacterial infections
	Neonatal hepatitis
	Extrahepatic obstruction
	Biliary atresia
	Choledochal cyst
	Hereditary
	Galactosaemia
	Tyrosinaemia
	Cystic fibrosis
	Antitrypsin deficiency

Genetic disorders are an uncommon cause of neonatal jaundice but recognition of galactosaemia and cretinism is of particular importance because institution of the appropriate treatment reduces the risk of mental retardation. 'Breast milk jaundice' is a rare and harmless cause of neonatal jaundice and is believed to be due to the presence in the milk of an inhibitor of glucuronide formation, but it may also be related to a reduction in fluid intake. Its presence is not an indication to discontinue breast feeding. A relationship has been claimed between the use of oral contraceptive tablets prior to the pregnancy and the development of neonatal jaundice.

Reye's Syndrome (Encephalopathy and Fatty Liver)

This is a newly recognized syndrome affecting children up to the age of 16 years. The aetiology is unknown but there are indications that it may be a viral infection. Typically the brain and the liver are affected and are injured early in the course of the disease with damage to all the cortical neurones and hepatocytes. There is intense cerebral oedema with swelling of the astrocytes and damage to the neuronal mitochondria. The liver is enlarged with a yellow or white colour reflecting the massive fatty change. This colour may be recognized at the time of liver biopsy which characteristically shows numerous small fat droplets in all hepatocytes in the absence of inflammation, necrosis or cholestasis. The mitochondria show swelling and distortion and histochemical studies indicate severe mitochondrial dysfunction which is believed to be the major reason for the steatosis.

Following a prodromal, virus-like illness of 3–7 days the child begins vomiting and rapidly develops an encephalopathy. Lethargy, agitation and delirium are followed within a few hours by coma and a decerebrate posture. At the same time the liver becomes moderately enlarged with a smooth round edge, the aminotransferases, blood ammonia and free fatty acid levels rise and the blood sugar falls. There is no jaundice. Death is due to cerebral oedema and not from hepatic failure. The liver lesion is rapidly reversible even in severely affected patients.

There is no specific therapy and management is supportive being directed mainly towards reversing the cerebral oedema. Mildly affected children require attention to fluid and electrolyte balance. The severely ill need intensive care, endotracheal intubation and the administration of 1.5–2.0 g mannitol over 15 minutes repeated at 6-hourly intervals. Acidosis is corrected, and fluid and electrolytes carefully monitored. Exchange transfusion has been suggested. Because the illness progresses so rapidly it is difficult to recognize at an early stage; but the only method for reducing the mortality from the present rate of over 50% is the prompt and timely institution of appropriate therapy.

Jaundice in Pregnancy

Jaundice is a rare event in pregnancy and it is convenient to group the causes into two categories.

INTERCURRENT JAUNDICE

This is the occurrence of jaundice in a woman who also happens to be pregnant. Viral hepatitis is the commonest cause and accounts for 41% of all cases of pregnancy jaundice. Gall stones may become symptomatic during the pregnancy. Rarely a patient with significant underlying liver disease, such as chronic active hepatitis, Wilson's disease or cirrhosis, becomes pregnant.

JAUNDICE PECULIAR TO PREGNANCY

Acute Fatty Liver of Pregnancy

This occurs during the last trimester and appears as jaundice, nausea, vomiting, haematemesis, abdominal pain and coma. The prognosis is poor and few patients survive. The cause is unknown but there may be a relationship to protein malnutrition. Liver histology shows fine droplets of fat in the liver cells with little necrosis, and this is similar to the appearance which develops when tetracycline is administered either orally or intravenously in doses greater than 2.0 g daily. Treatment is for liver cell failure.

Recurrent Intrahepatic Cholestatic Jaundice of Pregnancy

This is a mild form of cholestatic jaundice occurring during the last trimester. The urine is dark, the stools pale and the patient may have pruritus. There are no abnormal physical signs other than the icterus. The maternal and the fetal health are unaffected and the jaundice fades within 2 weeks of delivery. In addition to the slight elevation of serum bilirubin the levels of alkaline phosphatase and 5'nucleotidase are also raised. The prognosis is excellent, although the jaundice will recur with subsequent pregnancies and may also develop if the patient takes the contraceptive pill. The aetiology is unknown but the disorder may represent a cholestatic response to a steroid produced during pregnancy.

Jaundice rarely occurs in *eclampsia* and *hyperemesis gravidarum*.

Jaundice in the Postoperative Period

Mild transient jaundice may follow a variety of major surgical procedures and has been reported particularly after open-heart surgery. Causative factors include multiple blood transfusions, infection, hypotension, drugs including the anaesthetic, postoperative pancreatitis, cholangitis, damage to the extrahepatic duct system and portal phlebitis. Serum bilirubin levels are usually less than 170 μmol/litre and the patient is icteric for only a few days. Jaundice may follow multiple halothane anaesthetics (p. 284). A benign form of postoperative intrahepatic cholestasis is occasionally encountered after major surgery. It is associated with the biochemical and histological features of cholestasis and carries a good prognosis. A more severe form of cholestasis may occur, in which the serum bilirubin rises to levels of 600 μmol/litre or greater. This is usually encountered in patients who undergo surgery for massive haemorrhage into the body tissues such as a bleeding abdominal aneurysm. The jaundice may reflect an increased pigment load on a liver which has impaired excretory function because of severe hypotension.

Further Reading

Felsher, B. F. and Carpio, N. M. (1975) Caloric intake and unconjugated hyperbilirubinemia. *Gastroenterology*, **69**, 42–47.

Ihde, D. C. et al. (1974) Clinical manifestations of hepatoma. *Am. J. Med.*, **56**, 83–91.

Johnson, J. D. (1975) Neonatal nonhemolytic jaundice. *New Engl. J. Med.*, **292**, 194–197.

Makk, L. et al. (1976) Clinical and morphologic features of hepatic angiosarcoma in vinyl chloride workers. *Cancer*, **37**, 149–163.

Moult, P. J. A. and Sherlock, S. (1975) Halothane-related hepatitis. *Q. Jl. Med.*, **44**, 99–114.

Patin, J. C. (1975) Reye's syndrome (encephalopathy and fatty liver). *Gastroenterology*, **69**, 511–518.

Prescott, L. F. et al. (1976) Cysteamine, methionine, and penicillamine in the treatment of paracetamol poisoning. *Lancet*, **ii**, 109–113.

Scheuer, P. J. and Bianchi, L. (1974) Guidelines for diagnosis of therapeutic drug-induced liver injury in liver biopsies. *Lancet*, **i**, 854–857.

Stauffer, J. Q. et al. (1975) Focal nodular hyperplasia of the liver and intrahepatic hemorrhage in young women on oral contraceptives. *Ann. int. Med.*, **83**, 301–306.

Tavill, A. S. et al. (1975) The Budd–Chiari syndrome. *Gastroenterology*, **68**, 509–518.

The pancreas is responsible for the secretion of most of the important digestive enzymes. In addition to this exocrine function the gland serves as an endocrine organ since the islets of Langerhans produce insulin from the β cells, glucagon from the α cells and gastrin from the δ cells. The protein content of the digestive enzymes amounts to 100 g daily and contributes appreciably to the turnover of protein in the bowel. Important enzymes produced by the pancreas include trypsinogen, chymotrypsinogen, lipase, amylase, phospholipase, cholesterol esterase and collagenase. The enzymes are contained in the zymogen granules which are such a prominent feature of the micro-anatomy of the normal secreting gland. Pancreatic secretions also contain water and electrolytes including sodium, calcium, bicarbonate and chloride. There is a close relationship between chloride and bicarbonate in pancreatic juice and there are two main hypotheses to explain the electrolyte composition of the secretion. The 'admixture' hypothesis postulates that bicarbonate and chloride are secreted by the acinar cells, although it is not clear whether the chloride is derived from the same cells as the bicarbonate or whether the two anions originate from different acinar cells. This concept is more favoured than that of 'ductal modification' which proposes that bicarbonate is secreted by the pancreatic cells and is exchanged for chloride across the pancreatic duct epithelium.

The exocrine secretions of the pancreas are under hormonal and neurological control. Secretin and cholecystokinin/pancreozymin are secreted by the intestinal mucosa in response to acid and amino acids. Because cholecystokinin and pancreozymin are identical hormones the older name, cholestokinin, is used. The secretin-releasing mechanism appears to be deep within the mucosa of the upper small bowel and is pH sensitive. The rate of secretin release depends on a combination of the length of bowel stimulated and the hydrogen ion concentration at the receptor site. Thus when the small intestinal mucosa is abnormal, as in coeliac disease, there is pancreatic dysfunction because of insufficient stimulation of the gland by the usual hormonal mechanism.

Secretin stimulates fluid and bicarbonate output and is greatly potentiated by cholecystokinin, which is also responsible for stimulating enzyme output. Cholecystokinin stimulation depletes the acinar cells of zymogen granules. The action of cholecystokinin is to increase both the synthesis and also the secretion of the enzymes. Secretin is a low molecular weight polypeptide composed of 27 amino acid residues and is similar in structure to glucagon. Cholecystokinin is composed of 33 amino acid units. The C-terminal end of cholecystokinin is similar to that of gastrin, which explains why these two hormones share similar actions. Vagal action stimulates enzyme rather than fluid output and in patients with a vagotomy a reduced output of pancreatic enzymes has been recorded. It is possible that the trypsin inhibitors which are normally present in the pancreatic secretions have not only an inhibitory effect on the proteolytic enzymes, and therefore a protective role, but also a positive feedback effect to stimulate further proteolytic enzyme output.

The adult pancreas requires an adequate supply of protein to ensure normal synthesis of the pancreatic export proteins. Thus in protein–calorie malnutrition there is a relative pancreatic insufficiency which can be restored to normal by an adequate diet. The pancreas has the capacity to regenerate its parenchyma and recover its exocrine secretory capacity. There is experimental evidence in animals to show that the pancreas possesses a great power of adaptation to individual nutrients and that diet can influence the nature of the enzyme output by the gland.

A close and important relationship exists between gastric and pancreatic secretions. Hypersecretion of gastric acid follows pancreatic duct ligation, a pancreatic fistula or total pancreatectomy. Pancreatic hormones influence a wide range of gastrointestinal functions. Insulin depresses gastric secretion and motility; secretin has an important stimulant effect on bile flow causing an increase in the fluid and bicarbonate secretion by the ductular cells and possibly fluid and electrolyte transport in the intestine. The interplay between the various hormones and the products of stimulation is complex and disease of either the pancreas or the upper small bowel may influence gastrointestinal function in a variable and at times unpredictable manner.

Pancreatitis

The classification of the different forms of pancreatitis has always presented difficulties. A classification which is widely used and which has clinical significance divides inflammatory pancreatic disease into acute pancreatitis, relapsing acute pancreatitis and chronic pancreatitis. The first two conditions are acute forms of inflammation and the essential feature is that the pancreas reverts to a normal functional state once the causative factors for the inflammation have been removed. Chronic pancreatitis includes calcific pancreatic disease and chronic pancreatitis with acute exacerbations. In this form of the disease anatomical and functional changes persist in the pancreas even after the precipitating cause (if it can be identified) has been eliminated.

The frequency of pancreatic disease varies widely in different parts of the world. Acute and chronic pancreatitis are relatively common in the United States of America, France and South Africa but inflammatory pancreatic disease, particularly the chronic variety, is uncommon in the United Kingdom. The reason for this is not immediately apparent although alcohol intake is usually blamed.

Acute Pancreatitis

This condition is essentially an autodigestion of the pancreas. Whereas lipase, amylase and phospholipase are normally present in the pancreatic juice in the active form trypsin is found as the inactive precursor trypsinogen. The means whereby this enzyme is activated is unknown but it must be noted that it is not possible to detect trypsin in the acutely inflamed gland so that the exact role of trypsin remains in doubt. The gland undergoes varying degrees of oedema and haemorrhage as well as coagulative necrosis and the distinction between oedematous and haemorrhagic forms of the disease is arbitrary. The latter variety is said to have a worse prognosis. The pancreas contains large stores of trypsinogen and kallikreinogen, both of which, in the active form, release bradykinin from bradykininogen. Bradykinin may well be responsible for many of the haemodynamic changes found in acute pancreatitis.

The main aetiological factors in acute pancreatitis are biliary tract disease and alcohol, the latter being commoner in the United States of America, France and South Africa although there is evidence that alcohol is of increasing importance in the United Kingdom. No cause can be identified in up to 35% of patients. Uncommon causes include trauma, hereditary factors, hyperparathyroidism, hypercalcaemia, vitamin D intoxication, hyperlipidaemia, following renal transplantation, infection with bacteria, viruses or parasites, diabetic ketosis, uraemia, haemochromastosis, pregnancy, vasculitis and drugs such as corticosteroids and chlorothiazide. Acute pancreatitis may complicate a penetrating duodenal ulcer and may be the first presentation of cancer of the pancreas. There is no single hypothesis to account for the inflammation following these various factors. Indeed there is no adequate explanation for the pathogenesis of pancreatitis following the two commonest causes—biliary tract disease and alcohol. Reflux of bile up the pancreatic duct with activation of the enzymes is not an acceptable explanation. It may be that obstruction of the duct or ampulla is associated with raised pressure following pancreatic stimulation and this permits back diffusion of enzymes into acinar tissue thereby causing necrosis and inflammation. Vascular damage may be another reason for the initiation of tissue autolysis. Occlusion of the duct or ampulla could be from a gall stone, a tumour, 'spasm' following alcohol ingestion or protein plugs which precipitate and cause stones as may occur in the pancreas of chronic alcoholic patients. In the United Kingdom women are affected more frequently than men and this may reflect the frequency of biliary tract disease in females. The disease occurs over a wide age range.

The clinical picture is well recognized, with upper abdominal pain being the most important component. This may follow excessive alcohol intake and the usual interval between the alcohol and the onset of pain is 12–48 hours. The pain is usually so severe that the patient is admitted as an 'acute abdomen'; it is felt widely over the abdomen but it may be localized in the epigastrium or to the right and left upper quadrants. Radiation of the pain through to the back in the lower thoracic region is common and occasionally the patient obtains relief by sitting forward. The pain is usually severe for 24 hours and then passes off over a period of days. Anorexia, nausea and vomiting are prominent and uncommonly the patient presents with a haematemesis. On examination there is a varying degree of shock, collapse, tachycardia and fever. There is tenderness and guarding in the abdomen which is either generalized or confined to the upper abdomen. Bowel sounds may be reduced or absent. Severe retro-peritoneal bleeding may manifest as bruising in the flanks or around the umbilicus. Pleural effusions occur in 4–6% of patients, as may ascites. These serous reactions are frequently bloodstained. Severe hyperglycaemia and diabetic acidosis may be a presenting feature; a fall in serum calcium may be sufficient to cause tetany. Mental confusion may be prominent particularly in the alcoholic. Cardiac failure, pulmonary oedema and acute respiratory failure are encountered. Diffuse interstitial inflammation, haemorrhage and microatelectasis, the 'shock lung', contribute to the respiratory failure and acidosis. A low platelet count suggests as associated disseminated intravascular coagulation. Uncommonly fat necrosis in the subcutaneous tissues manifests as painful areas, particularly in the legs. Arthralgia and mild eosinophilia are associated findings.

Biochemical abnormalities include leucocytosis, anaemia, glycosuria and an elevated serum amylase concentration at the height of an attack. Occasionally raised amylase levels are seen in other acute abdominal diseases such as acute cholecystitis, perforated peptic ulcer and a perforated colonic diverticulum. The serum amylase level may also rise after an injection of morphine. In general values which are five-fold greater than normal strongly favour pancreatic inflammation. The urinary output of amylase is a less reliable test, presenting problems of collection and inter-pretation. However, the finding of an abnormal amylase in the urine may be of diagnostic value in a mild attack or after the serum amylase levels have returned to normal. The renal clearance of amylase expressed as a percentage of creatinine clearance (amylase/creatinine clearance ratio) is characteristically increased in acute pancreatitis. Serum amylase levels usually return to normal within a week. Persistent hyperamylasaemia suggests that the inflammation is continuing, the development of a pseudocyst or renal damage. A rare cause is the binding of the amylase in the serum to a 7S globulin, thereby forming a complex which is too large to be excreted by the kidneys. Under these circumstances there will be an elevated serum amylase but no amylase in the urine. Normally a raised serum amylase is accompanied by amylase in the urine because this is the route of amylase excretion. Amylase estimation in the pleural or ascitic fluid is a valuable guide to the presence of an underlying pancreatitis.

Other biochemical changes include elevation of the serum trypsin and lipase levels, hyperglycaemia or frank ketosis, hyperlipaemia and hypocalcaemia which has been ascribed to marked fat necrosis with the formation of calcium soaps. Hypocalcaemia is so constant a feature in acute pancreatitis that a search should be made for hyper-parathyroidism if the calcium concentration remains normal throughout an attack of severe pancreatitis. About one-third of patients will have a slight increase in serum bilirubin values. Variable electrolyte changes occur depending on the severity of the shock, vomiting and fluid loss.

The plain radiograph of the abdomen may reveal a local ileus either as a loop of small bowel overlying the pancreas ('sentinel loop') or in the transverse colon ('colon cut-off sign'). Gall stones or pancreatic calcification may be visible. A barium meal has little place in the diagnosis of the acutely ill patient but in those less ill the conventional barium study or hypotonic duodenography may indicate a swollen head of pancreas because the duodenal mucosa appears oedematous and rigid. Angiography, pancreatic scanning and formal tests of pancreatic function have no place in the diagnosis of acute pancreatic inflammation and are possibly harmful. Flattening of the T waves may be detected on the electrocardiograph.

The differential diagnosis includes other causes of acute abdominal disease, especially acute cholecystitis and a perforated peptic ulcer. Diaphragmatic pleurisy, myo-cardial infarction and porphyria will require consideration at times. The diagnosis may be most perplexing and may become apparent only after a laparotomy. If there is any doubt about the diagnosis a laparotomy is advised. In favourable circumstances there is no increase in the mortality rate following a diagnostic laparotomy in pancreatitis. No further surgical procedure is undertaken once the abdomen has been opened and the diagnosis verified and operations on the biliary tract are avoided unless the patient's condition is satisfactory. If the diagnosis of pancreatitis appears reasonably certain clinically then there is nothing to be gained from a laparotomy for operative intervention may be associated with a high complication rate.

Conventional therapy for acute pancreatitis includes adequate analgesia, restoration of the fluid and electrolyte balance, nasogastric aspiration and intravenous feeding. Morphine and its derivatives are contraindicated because they cause spasm of the sphincter of Oddi and may worsen the inflammation. Anticholinergic therapy (propantheline bromide 15 or 30 mg by intramuscular injection) is effective in controlling pain in some patients. A broad spectrum antibiotic is frequently recommended during the first 14 days of the illness in the belief that it may prevent pancreatic abscess formation but there is little satisfactory evidence to support its use. Trypsin and kallikrein inhibitory agents have little to offer and are of no benefit. Other methods of therapy include glucagon (1 mg intravenously over 6 hours), carbonic anhydrase inhibitors and hypothermia but these have not been sufficiently evaluated clinically. The introduction of 20 units insulin/litre 5% dextrose and water is said to reduce the pain within 4 hours.

Once the acute phase subsides the patient is fed orally and attempts are made to determine the cause of the inflammation. The patient is advised against alcohol for at least 3 months and if the pancreatitis is thought to be alcohol-induced there should be total and permanent abstinence. If gall stones are present they are removed. Biliary tract surgery during the acute episode has a high mortality. There is no indication for performing a sphincterotomy or sphincteroplasty after a single attack of acute pancreatitis.

The prognosis is variable depending upon the age of the patient and the cause of the inflammation. Mortality is greater in patients over 55 years, when there is marked elevation of the white blood count, urea and glucose, and low levels of haemoglobin and calcium. The mortality rate may be around 20% but figures as high as 40% are published for patients over the age of 70 years. About 20% of patients may have a recurrence, particularly those who have an alcoholic aetiology. The mortality rate is greatest in the first attack of acute pancreatitis. Alcoholic patients with recurrent disease progress to chronic pancreatitis rather than relapsing acute pancreatitis. The pancreas has a considerable capacity to regenerate and severe insufficiency during the acute phase will revert to normal endocrine and exocrine function.

Complications include the development of diabetes mellitus, diabetic ketosis, severe tetany, circulatory collapse and a pancreatic abscess or pseudopancreatic cyst. A pancreatic abscess is a serious but uncommon complication. The main clinical features are continuing abdominal pain and tenderness, severe backache, the presence of a mass, fluctuating fever, leucocytosis and prolonged elevation of the serum amylase concentration. An abscess requires external drainage. A pseudopancreatic cyst follows the release of pancreatic ferments and oedema fluid into the lesser omental sac. There is sealing off of the foramen of Winslow and the encystment of the fluid within the lesser sac. The patient complains of pain and a mass is palpable in the upper abdomen. Other features are nausea, vomiting, fever, pleural effusion and jaundice. The serum amylase remains elevated. The mass may be demonstrated by a plain radiograph of the abdomen by a barium meal which shows a widened duodenal loop and displacement of the stomach or by ultrasonic scanning of the pancreas which is proving to be the most useful of the diagnostic techniques. The cyst is managed by performing internal drainage between the anterior wall of the cyst and the posterior wall of the gastric antrum. Pseudocysts of the pancreas must be distinguished from other forms of true pancreatic cyst including a retention cyst following obstruction of the main pancreatic duct, neoplastic cysts and congenital cysts.

Relapsing Acute Pancreatitis

Attacks of relapsing acute pancreatitis do not differ in any way from those of acute pancreatitis. Thus during and immediately after an isolated attack of acute pancreatitis it is not possible to predict whether the patient will have further attacks. By definition patients with relapsing acute pancreatitis do not develop chronic pancreatic insufficiency. The condition is most likely to develop in the absence of an obvious cause of pancreatitis or when the pancreatitis is of the inherited variety or associated with metabolic disease. Males appear to be affected more frequently than females. This form of pancreatitis is uncommon in the United Kingdom.

The diagnostic procedures and management are similar to those for acute pancreatitis. The best results seem to be obtained with strict adherence to a medical regimen of regular light meals, no smoking, total abstinence from alcohol, avoidance of morphine derivatives and regular anticholinergic therapy. If the attacks become more persistent there will be increasing pressures to embark on some form of surgical therapy. Unfortunately the overall impression is that surgery has little to offer in the way of lasting benefit. Sphincterotomy and sphincteroplasty have not found general acceptance. A diagnosis of stenosis or spasm of the sphincter of Oddi is very difficult to substantiate and requires cinecholangiography. It is probable that the majority of operations which are performed on the basis of a single film obtained at operative cholangiography do little to alter what is probably normal sphincter function. Other surgical procedures which have been undertaken include retrograde pancreatic drainage and pancreatic resection.

Patients with idiopathic pancreatitis who have had one recurrence are more likely to have a second. The interval is usually 1–2 years but may be 10. By comparison with acute pancreatitis relapsing acute pancreatitis is a benign condition with a mortality rate of 1.5%.

Chronic Pancreatitis

Chronic pancreatitis is uncommon in the United Kingdom but is encountered more frequently in those parts of the world where much alcohol is consumed, such as the United States, France and South Africa. It rarely follows gall stone disease and frequently no cause is apparent. The possibility of an underlying neoplasm of the gland must always be considered. Gross calcification occurs in many of the glands; this is called *calcific pancreatitis* and is associated particularly with an increased alcohol intake. There is evidence that alcoholic chronic pancreatitis is increasing in the United Kingdom. The glands show sclerosis with varying degrees of inflammation and necrosis affecting both exocrine cells and the islets of Langerhans. Damage to ductules and larger ducts is apparent. The main duct is often dilated and tortuous with cyst formation. Mucous plugs are present and these may become calcified. Rarely families are recorded in which pancreatitis occurs with a high frequency. Such patients often have calcified glands and an accompanying aminoaciduria.

Pain is usually present but occasionally a patient will present with either calcification or painless pancreatic insufficiency. The pain is recurrent rather than continuous and is subject to acute exacerbations. It is felt in the epigastrium although occasionally in the right or left hypochondrium. Back pain is usual and typically is relieved by bending forward. Loss of weight is a constant feature. Jaundice may occur briefly during acute crises and in such patients the possibility of a neoplasm must always be considered. The features of exocrine and endocrine insufficiency will become apparent. Steatorrhoea occurs in less than 20% of patients and is more likely to be found in patients with a calcified gland. Almost 95% of pancreatic exocrine function has to be lost before faecal fat values increase above normal. The steatorrhoea is often gross yet is unassociated with the other nutritional deficiencies such as tetany, haemorrhage and hypoalbuminaemia which usually accompany enterogenous steatorrhoea. Starch maldigestion is rare because amylase output is usually adequate even when there is extensive pancreatic damage. It is claimed that iron absorption is increased in chronic pancreatitis. Some patients have decreased vitamin B_{12} absorption for reasons which have not been clarified but this association adds to the difficulty in determining the cause of steatorrhoea. There has been much argument over the frequency of peptic ulcer disease. Current evidence suggests that in chronic pancreatitis the secretory capacities of the stomach and pancreas are both reduced and that peptic ulcer disease is not a significant feature. Chronic ascites is a rare manifestation of chronic pancreatitis and the patients are usually young alcoholic subjects who complain of abdominal pain, swelling and weight loss. Persistent hyperamylasaemia is associated with elevated enzyme levels in the ascitic fluid. Cirrhosis of the liver may complicate alcoholic pancreatitis but it is surprising how seldom these two diseases coexist.

The serum amylase values are usually normal and the most helpful investigations are a faecal fat estimation, a glucose tolerance test and more particularly a test of exocrine pancreatic function. Pancreatic stimulation can be achieved directly by hormones using secretin, either alone or in combination with cholecystokinin, or indirectly by feeding a test meal (Lundh test). The duodenal aspirate is measured for volume, bicarbonate output and enzyme output in response to the hormonal stimulus but only the enzyme output is measured after the test meal. The pancreatic response in chronic pancreatitis is a reduction in volume, bicarbonate output and enzyme output. There is a reduction in the enzyme output in response to the test meal. Although the distinction between normal and diseased glands appears to be reasonably accurate using exocrine pancreatic function tests the response to both direct and indirect stimulation is not sufficiently precise to permit unequivocal differentiation between pancreatitis and pancreatic cancer.

The plain radiograph of the abdomen may show pancreatic calcification. Barium meal studies are generally unhelpful. Hypotonic duodenography may be informative. In this technique the duodenum is paralysed enabling the mucosal appearances of the medial margin of the duodenum to be clearly demonstrated. In pancreatitis there is stiffness, straightening and oedema of the folds. Arteriography is not helpful. Radioisotope scanning using ^{75}Se selenomethionine demonstrates an abnormal pancreatic scan in 75% of patients. There is usually a diffuse reduction of isotope uptake but at times a filling defect is observed. The distinction between cancer and inflammation is made with difficulty from the scan. A combination of radiological tests is often valuable and the nature of the tests will depend upon the suspected lesion. A useful combination is hypotonic duodenography and isotopic scanning. Endoscopic retrograde cholangiopancreatography (ERCP) enables the duct and ductular morphology to be visualized radiographically and has proved of considerable diagnostic value. It has the added advantage of also outlining the biliary tract. Another new and helpful diagnostic technique is grey-scale ultrasonic pancreatic scanning.

The differential diagnosis includes the various causes of steatorrhoea, abdominal pain and diabetes mellitus. The diagnosis is particularly perplexing when the major problem is pain and there is no functional or radiological evidence of pancreatic disease. Genetic diabetes mellitus is suggested by a positive family history, the presence of vascular disease and elevation of the serum cholesterol concentration. Once the steatorrhoea is shown to be of pancreatic origin it is still necessary to determine the nature of the pancreatic disease—whether inflammatory, cancer or cystic fibrosis. There are a variety of disorders of nutrition which are complicated by reversible and temporary pancreatic exocrine insufficiency including kwashiorkor and the various intestinal malabsorption syndromes such as coeliac disease, postgastrectomy malnutrition and intestinal resection.

The treatment of chronic pancreatitis is taxing and unsatisfactory. Relief of pain is difficult and the patients require large and frequent doses of analgesics. Drug dependence and addiction become real problems. Diabetes mellitus requires control either with oral hypoglycaemic agents or insulin. The steatorrhoea is managed with a low fat diet and pancreatic extracts. A variety of preparations are available; pancreatin B.P. or the stronger Pancrex V are useful. There are many proprietary preparations, one of which, Cotazym, is lipase-enriched. Trypsin and lipase activities are destroyed by contact with pepsin at acid pH and therefore the pancreatic extracts must be administered with food and an antacid to buffer the gastric pH. Pancreatin is inactivated by hot food. The dose is very variable and must be adjusted to individual needs. Probably one or two capsules with each meal are a good start but larger doses taken more frequently may be required. Alcohol is contraindicated.

Many surgical procedures have been suggested for chronic pancreatitis, particularly when the condition is associated with intractible pain. No single procedure has found universal acceptance and indeed it is unlikely that any such operation could be devised, for the nature of the operation will depend on the extent of the disease. Operative pancreatography often demonstrates dilated ducts with cyst formation and segments of narrowing. Sphinctero-plasty, distal pancreatectomy, pancreaticoduodenectomy and total pancreatectomy have all been attempted. The essential feature of these various operations is an attempt to improve pancreatic drainage. Operations on the biliary tract may be necessary. Claims have been made for the value of splanchnicectomy for the relief of pain. But on the whole the results of surgery are usually disappointing and the management is devoted to the pharmacological relief of pain, attention to nutrition, attempts to boost the morale of the patient and injunctions to abstain from alcohol.

Tumours of the Pancreas

About 80% of pancreatic tumours are adenocarcinomas which arise from ductular epithelium. Less common but of interest are the endocrine tumours since their bizarre symptomatology may direct attention away from the pancreas. The great majority of the hormonally active tumours arise from the cells of the islets of Langerhans.

CANCER OF THE PANCREAS

Cancer of the pancreas accounts for 0.5% of all hospital admissions and for 1–2% of all malignant tumours found at autopsy. The cause is unknown and although there is an association between pancreatic cancer, chronic pancreatitis, particularly of the calcific variety, and alcoholism it is unlikely that this has aetiological significance. About 80% of the tumours are adenocarcinomas of ductular origin, 13% arise from the acinar tissue and the remainder are of indeterminate origin. Tumours arising in the anatomical head of the gland account for 50–70% of the growths. The cancer may have a multicentric origin. The pancreas has no limiting capsule and has a rich lymphatic and venous drainage so that extrapancreatic extension of the growth is early and widespread. This is particularly striking in tumours of the body and tail. Cancers of the head show early involvement of the bile duct, the duodenum and the regional lymphatics. Distal metastases involve particularly the liver. Males are affected twice as commonly as females and the tumour is most frequently encountered between the ages of 50 and 70 years, although all age groups and even children are at risk.

The major clinical features are weight loss, pain and jaundice. Loss of weight occurs in most patients; it may be rapid, amounting to as much as 20 kg in a few months. Pain occurs in 60% of patients with cancer of the head of the pancreas and in 80% of tumours of the body and tail. The nature and site of pain depends on the site of the growth. Characteristically there is epigastric pain that bores 'through' to the back in the lower thoracic region and is relieved by leaning forwards. The pain may be more vague or it may resemble the pain of peptic ulcer disease. Jaundice occurs in 85% of cancers of the head and in 20–40% of growths arising from the body of the gland. Painless jaundice occurs in under 30% of patients. There is associated pruritus which rarely may be the first sign of disease. Other symptoms include fatigue, anorexia, nausea, vomiting and a change in the bowel habits with constipation being more frequent than diarrhoea. The vagueness and variability of the symptoms is frequently perplexing to both patient and doctor and the average duration of symptoms prior to hospital admission is 6 months.

There are frequently no abnormal physical signs. The patient may show weight loss and icterus and an enlarged liver may be palpable. The gall bladder is felt in 50% of icteric patients but Courvoisier's law is mainly of interest to the pathologist and has little clinical relevance. It may be possible to feel a large pancreatic mass. Other features include ascites, splenomegaly and distant metastases. There are a number of unusual clinical manifestations which may obscure the diagnosis of a cancer. Well recognized is the presentation of the tumour by an episode of acute pancreatitis. Occasionally the first manifestation is a large gastrointestinal haemorrhage and more rarely there is subcutaneous fat necrosis. The patient may first appear with the symptoms of diabetes mellitus. In 10–25% of patients the cancer manifests with peripheral venous thrombosis particularly in the femoral veins. This presentation is a late sign and usually accompanies growths in the body or tail. A neuropsychiatric syndrome of anxiety and agitated depression is claimed to be a feature in some patients and this may occur early in the disease.

The laboratory diagnosis is frequently impossible until the tumour has reached a large size. Routine tests of liver function show evidence of cholestasis without any indication as to the cause. There is elevation of serum bilirubin, alkaline phosphatase, 5′nucleotidase and cholesterol concentrations while transaminase levels are normal or near normal. At times the only biochemical abnormality is a raised serum alkaline phosphatase level. The serum protein profile shows an elevation of α_2- and β-globulins. Patients with prolonged jaundice have steatorrhoea, vitamin K malabsorption and a prolongation of the prothrombin time which is readily shortened by the administration of vitamin K. Serum concentrations of the pancreatic digestive enzymes are rarely of diagnostic value. Steatorrhoea occurs in less than 20% of patients and frank diabetes mellitus in 30%. The presence of carcino-embryonic antigen is detected in the serum of some patients but is not specific for cancer of the pancreas.

Plain radiology of the abdomen has little to offer in the diagnosis; about 25% of patients with calcific pancreatitis will develop a cancer of the gland. The conventional barium meal is helpful in detecting pancreatic disease in less than 50% of patients and is not helpful in the identification of the aetiology. Features to be looked for include a widening of the duodenal loop, depression of the duodeno-jejunal flexure, distortion of the antral area, forward displacement of the stomach and irregularity of the duodenum.

The comment has been made that any duodenal abnormality in a diabetic subject should raise the suspicion of a pancreatic cancer. Hypotonic duodenography is more helpful in demonstrating rigidity and infiltration of the medial and occasionally the lateral wall of the duodenum. Percutaneous transhepatic cholangiography outlines the bile duct system in the icteric patient and in pancreatic tumours the obstructed duct is seen to be tapered or to have a sharp 'cut-off' point (Plate XI). Arteriography has not proved to be as helpful as had been anticipated. Pancreatic cancers show pathological vessels, neoplastic arterial stenosis and displacement and venous compression and displacement. The ^{75}Se selenomethionine scan is abnormal in over 80% of patients, the tumours being indicated by either a filling defect or the diffuse failure of the gland to take up the isotope. Endoscopic retrograde cholangiopancreatography, grey-scale ultrasonic scanning of the pancreas and computerized axial tomography are newly introduced techniques. Unfortunately by the time the patient presents the growth is usually large and non-resectable.

Secretin stimulation of the gland characteristically shows a reduction in the volume of pancreatic juice to less than 2 ml/kg body weight with normal bicarbonate and amylase concentrations; however, one large series has demonstrated a significant reduction of bicarbonate concentration. Duodenal tryptic activity as tested by the Lundh test meal has shown a marked reduction of pancreatic enzyme output to 2 μmol/ml/min with an upper limit of 5.0 μmol/ml/min. The value in normal subjects is a mean of 22.8 with a lower limit of 11.2. A cytological examination can be made on the duodenal aspirate at the time of the secretin test and in good hands this gives positive results for malignant cells in just under 90% of patients.

The major problems in the diagnosis of pancreatic cancer are first that the patient presents to the medical practitioner at a stage when the disease is so advanced that successful removal of the growth is rarely feasible, and secondly the frequency with which some degree of pancreatitis develops so that the radiological, isotopic and function tests are equivocal in distinguishing between a tumour and inflammation. The differential diagnosis includes the various causes of epigastric pain, extrahepatic cholestatic jaundice and diabetes mellitus. The essential steps in making the diagnosis are to consider pancreatic disease as the cause for the patient's ill health, to demonstrate pancreatic dysfunction and to differentiate tumour from inflammation. The distinction between ampullary growths and cancers of the head of the pancreas is particularly important because of the better prognosis with ampullary tumours.

Treatment is surgical, the usual exercise being to relieve the biliary obstruction. Curative surgery is rarely possible; at times a growth in the tail is resected by a distal pancreatectomy and rarely total pancreatectomy is undertaken for a tumour in the head of the gland. Cancers in the head may be treated by a Whipple's operation—a pancreatico-duodenectomy in which the head and part of the body of the pancreas are removed together with the pyloric antrum and the entire duodenum. Total pancreatectomy is advocated under certain circumstances. But 90% of patients have metastases at the time of laparotomy and the usual procedure is a palliative choledochojejunostomy or cholecystjejunostomy with an enteroanastomosis. Some authors advise a gastroenterostomy in addition thereby avoiding the difficulties which might arise from duodenal obstruction. Non-surgical treatment includes relief of pain, control of diabetes mellitus and treatment of intractable pruritus and diarrhoea. Therapy with the various antimitotic agents is rarely effective. The prognosis is dismal and the survival of patients either unoperated or after a palliative procedure is 6 to 9 months. At least the quality of life is better after the palliative operation. The 5-year survival for a pancreaticoduodenectomy is under 5%.

AMPULLARY CANCER

Cancers arising in the region of the ampulla of Vater may originate from the duct epithelium or less frequently from duodenal mucosa or other cellular elements in this region. Because of its situation the growth gives rise to jaundice at an early stage so that it is frequently possible to operate on the patient before extrapancreatic spread has occurred. The characteristic clinical features are painless, fluctuating jaundice unaccompanied by fever or signs of cholangitis. Anorexia is frequent and rarely melaena stools occur. An ampullary cancer is treated by a pancreatico-duodenectomy and the 5-year survival is 30–50%. It is necessary both clinically and prognostically to distinguish between ampullary cancers and cancers of the head of the pancreas and this may be achieved by hypotonic duodeno-graphy and pancreatic scintiscanning, but at times the final arbiter can only be the pathologist who examines the resected specimen.

TUMOURS OF THE ISLETS OF LANGERHANS

Islet cell tumours may be functionally active or inactive and arise from the α, β or δ cells. The majority of tumours are found in the body and tail of the gland which is a reflection of the distribution of the islets. In 10% of patients the tumours are extrapancreatic, being situated in the duodenum of splenic hilum. The tumours may be benign or malignant, single or multiple. Malignant tumours are generally slow growing.

Zollinger–Ellison Syndrome (Gastrinoma) (p. 50)

This is the syndrome of gastric acid hypersecretion and peptic ulceration which accompanies a tumour arising from the argyrophil–metachromatic δ cells. The syndrome reflects the excessive gastrin production by tumour cells.

Pancreatic Cholera (Watery Diarrhoea and Achlorhydria Syndrome, WDHA Syndrome)

In this uncommon syndrome the growth possibly arises from the non-β cells. The clinical features are profound watery diarrhoea, hypokalaemia and achlorhydria. Peptic ulceration is not a part of this syndrome. Other features include hypercalcaemia, hyperglycaemia, episodes of flushing and hypotension. The patient may die from dehydration and shock. The syndrome arises from the excessive secretion of vasoactive intestinal polypeptide (VIP) by the tumour. This hormone stimulates adenylate cyclase and the production of cyclic AMP. There is marked secretion of intestinal water and electrolytes in a manner similar to the effect of the cholera toxin. The diagnosis can be made by demonstrating elevated plasma levels of VIP. The main differential diagnosis is from a villous tumour of the colon (p. 165) and from laxative abuse. Removal of the tumour results in dramatic cessation of the diarrhoea. Streptozotocin therapy may also be effective.

Insulinoma

This tumour arises from the β cells of the islets. About 10% are malignant and 30% are multiple. There may be diffuse hypertrophy of the islets rather than an actual tumour. The clinical features are the result of the excessive and unrestrained production of insulin which induces spontaneous hypoglycaemia. The patients present with restlessness, tremor, palpitations, elevated blood pressure, sweating, hunger and abnormal and aggressive behaviour. If the hypoglycaemia persists coma ensues and is followed by permanent cerebral damage. The hypoglycaemia may revert spontaneously but many patients may require to eat glucose or some other carbohydrate and excessive weight gain is a feature in a few patients. The recurrent episodes of low blood sugar levels are a stimulus to gastric acid secretion and peptic ulcer formation may complicate the clinical picture. A characteristic triad is periodic mental disturbance in the fasting state, a blood sugar less than 50 mg/100 ml (2.7 mmol/litre) and immediate relief of symptoms following the administration of glucose.

The essential feature of the illness is normal or high plasma insulin concentrations which accompany hypoglycaemia. The diagnosis requires first the demonstration that the symptoms are due to hypoglycaemia and secondly an elucidation of the cause of the low blood sugar. The most reliable test is a fast for 24–48 hours during which time only water is permitted. Two-thirds of patients with an insulinoma will develop hypoglycaemia with inappropriate insulin secretion within 24 hours and the remainder do so within 48 or 72 hours. An intravenous injection of tolbutamide can induce an excess release of insulin with a fall of blood glucose to below half of the fasting value but this test is not without hazards. Similarly intravenous

TABLE XXII. *Classification of Hypoglycaemia*

Reactive	*Fasting*
Functional	Pancreatic islet β-cell disease
Alimentary hypoglycaemia	Non-pancreatic insulin-producing tumours
Secondary to mild diabetes mellitus	Anterior pituitary hypofunction
	Adrenocortical hypofunction
	Severe liver disease
	Alcohol and poor nutrition
	Leucine sensitivity
	Infantile hypoglycaemia without leucine sensitivity
	Glycogen storage disease
	Iatrogenic: insulin or sulphonyl-urea administration

glucagon can be used to demonstrate a fall of blood sugar. Unfortunately these tests give normal values in 20–30% of insulinoma patients. The glucose tolerance test is of little diagnostic value.

Because of their small size insulinomas are difficult to detect by barium studies or radioisotope scanning. Angiography shows a tumour capillary blush and irregular tumour vessels but only about 20% of growths are detected by this method. The differential diagnosis includes the various causes of fasting hypoglycaemia in Table XXII.

Once the diagnosis has been established an attempt is made to remove the tumour. Because it is often a small growth the tumour is identified with difficulty and the whole gland including the anterior and the posterior surfaces must be explored. When no obvious tumour is demonstrated, or where there appears to be diffuse islet cell hypertrophy, resection of the body and tail is advocated, but this should not be undertaken before an adequate exploration has been made of the likely sites of extra-pancreatic tissue. Failure to identify or remove the tumour leaves the patient with the problem of severe recurrent hypoglycaemic attacks. Intravenous glucose is required and injections of glucagon may increase the blood sugar. Corticosteroids and diazoxide have been used. A promising treatment is the intravenous administration of strepto-zotocin, an antibiotic derived from *Streptomyces chromo-genes*. The usual dose is a weekly intravenous infusion of 0.6 to 1.0 g/m^2 body surface area to a total dose of 4 g/m^2 body surface area. The drug is toxic to the liver and the renal tubules.

A variety of other islet cell tumours have been described with varying hormonal effects. These include Cushing's syndrome, carcinoid tumours, ACTH-secreting tumours and tumours secreting parathyroid hormone and melano-cyte stimulating hormone and ADH. These hormones may be secreted singly or in combination thereby producing varied and at times puzzling clinical syndromes.

GLUCAGONOMA SYNDROME

In this uncommon disorder hypersecretion of glucagon by pancreatic α-cell tumours is accompanied by a clinical syndrome of stomatitis, weight loss, diabetes mellitus and a characteristic skin eruption: necrolytic migratory erythema.

Cystic Fibrosis (Mucoviscidosis)

Cystic fibrosis of the pancreas affects children, adolescents and young adults and is a generalized disorder involving all the exocrine glands. The disease is transmitted as an autosomal recessive trait and has been called the most frequent lethal genetic disease of childhood. The gene carrier frequency is $1:25$. Homozygotes present the features of the syndrome but there is no evidence of any ill health in their parents. The disease affects Caucasians and is rare in African Negroes and Mongolians. The abnormalities include markedly viscous mucus secretions which obstruct ducts, an increase in the concentration of the sodium, chloride and potassium in sweat and an increase in calcium and phosphorus levels in saliva. The primary genetic abnormality remains to be identified and there are many, and as yet unsuccessful attempts to provide a single hypothesis to explain all the biochemical disturbances. A basic error of glycoprotein metabolism has been suggested and the precipitation of relatively insoluble calcium–glycoprotein complexes may be important. The abnormality of glycoproteins may also influence the function of the cell plasma membrane so that there is inhibition of the movement of water and ions through the secretory cells of the affected glands. Failure to remove the secretions results in obstruction to the bronchioles and pancreatic ducts. Atelectasis and pulmonary infection occur and progress to obstructive pulmonary disease, pulmonary hypertension and cor pulmonale. Pancreatic ductular obstruction causes destruction of the exocrine cells and eventually of the islets of Langerhans.

In 10% of the patients the disease presents in the new-born as meconium ileus. It is likely that the intestinal obstruction is due to the abnormal composition of meconium rather than any pancreatic insufficiency. Occasionally there is meconium peritonitis and ileal atresia. The 'meconium ileus equivalent' syndrome occurs at a later stage and may even affect young adults. Hard firm mucofaeculant masses accumulate in the colon causing abdominal pain, vomiting and the signs of intestinal obstruction.

Older children present with pulmonary and pancreatic complications. There are recurrent respiratory infections and the patient may have a persistent or paroxysmal cough. Eventually acidosis, hypercarbia and hypoxia supervene. About 80% of the patients have progressive loss of pancreatic exocrine function. The triad of failure to thrive, good appetite and loose stools should suggest cystic fibrosis. Clinically the patients may appear well with few physical signs. However, at an advanced stage of the disease, when severe cardiopulmonary and pancreatic insufficiency have supervened, there is wasting, clubbing, cyanosis, purulent sputum and greasy stools. Other features are nasal polyps, rectal prolapse and enlargement of the submaxillary salivary glands. Diabetes mellitus, and uncommonly cirrhosis of the liver and portal hypertension occur in older children. An increase in iron absorption may cause iron overload. Males who survive to adult life have been shown to be sterile because of absence of the vas deferens. Females have a reduced fertility but produce normal children.

Many methods have been suggested to establish the diagnosis and the most widely accepted is the estimation of the sodium content of the sweat following electrophoretic stimulation. Values below 50 mmol/litre exclude the diagnosis of cystic fibrosis; values greater than 60 mmol/litre are diagnostic. Intermediate values are inconclusive and indicate that the test must be repeated. A neonatal screening test based on the increased albumin content of meconium in cystic fibrosis is currently under evaluation.

The differential diagnosis includes bronchiectasis, the various causes of steatorrhoea and cirrhosis in childhood.

Treatment requires careful attention to the physical, mental and emotional health of the child. Unstinted parental cooperation is necessary. Bronchial obstruction and chest infections are managed by a combination of antibiotic therapy, physiotherapy, breathing exercises and postural drainage. Pancreatic extracts (p. 315), a low-fat diet and supplements of medium-chain triglycerides and vitamins are helpful. Modern supportive and replacement therapy and particularly the use of antibiotics are proving effective and more patients are enjoying increasing longevity but in a variable state of health.

Further Reading

Broder, L. E. and Carter, S. K. (1973) Pancreatic islet cell cancer. *Ann. int. Med.*, **79**, 101–107; 108–118.

Fajans, S. S. and Floyd, C. R. jr (1976) Fasting hypoglycemia in adults. *New Engl. J. Med.*, **294**, 766–772.

James, O. et al. (1974) Chronic pancreatitis in England: a changing picture? *Br. med. J.*, **ii**, 34–38.

Mitchell-Heggs, P. et al. (1976) Cystic fibrosis in adolescents and adults. *Q. Jl. Med.*, **45**, 479–504.

Olsen, H. (1974) Pancreatitis. *Am. J. dig. Dis.*, **19**, 1077–1090.

Ranson, J. H. C. (1974) Prognostic signs and the role of operative management in acute pancreatitis. *Surgery, Gynec. Obstet.*, **139**, 69–81.

Rovner, A. J. and Westcott, J. L. (1976) Pulmonary edema, and respiratory insufficiency in acute pancreatitis. *Radiology*, **118**, 513–520.

Said, S. I. and Faloona, G. R. (1975) Elevated plasma and tissue levels of vasoactive intestinal polypeptide in the watery-diarrhoea syndrome due to pancreatic, bronchogenic and other tumors. *New Engl. J. Med.*, **293**, 155–160.

Saunders, J. H. B. and Wormsley, K. G. (1975) Pancreatic extracts in the treatment of pancreatic exocrine insufficiency. *Gut*, **16**, 157–162.

Trapnell, J. E. and Duncan, E. H. L. (1975) Patterns of incidence of acute pancreatitis. *Br. med. J.*, **ii**, 179–183.

Warren, K. W. et al. (1975) Results of radical resection for periampullary cancer. *Ann. Surg.*, **181**, 534–540.

Warshaw, A. L. and Fuller, A. F. jr (1975) Specificity of increased renal clearance of amylase in diagnosis of acute pancreatitis. *New Engl. J. Med.*, **292**, 325–328.

Youngs, G. R. et al. (1973) A comparative study of four tests of pancreatic function in the diagnosis of pancreatic disease. *Q. Jl. Med.*, **42**, 597–618.

Zimmon, D. S. et al. (1974) Endoscopic retrograde cholangiopancreatography (ERCP) in the diagnosis of pancreatic inflammatory disease. *Radiology*, **113**, 287–292.

Disorders of the biliary tract, together with appendicitis, peptic ulcer disease and malignant neoplasms, are among the most common digestive disorders which require hospital admission. It is estimated that diseases of the gall bladder and biliary tree are responsible for the loss of about 0.8 million working days a year. Extrahepatic biliary disease is the most frequent reason for upper abdominal surgery. The most important factor responsible for gall bladder and bile duct disease is the presence of gall stones.

Gall Stones

The prevalence of gall stones in the community is unknown. A conservative estimate is that around 10% of males and 20% of females in the age group 55–65 years have gall stones. There is marked geographical variation; gall stones are frequent in the Western Hemisphere but rare in Africa. In Asia and Japan the frequency of gall stones is related to the prevalence of biliary tract infection.

Gall stones may be classified in a variety of ways but the most meaningful categorization is by composition. The major component of gall stones in the Western Hemisphere is cholesterol, which accounts for between 40 and 80% by weight of gall stones. Other components include calcium carbonate, calcium phosphate, calcium palmitate and mucus. Many stones contain a well-defined nucleus and this is not necessarily of the same composition as the rest of the stone. Not all gall stones are of mixed chemical composition and nearly one-third comprise a single crystalline substance such as cholesterol, calcium palmitate, calcium carbonate or calcium bilirubinate.

The aetiology of gall stones is complex and almost certainly multifactorial. Because of the importance of the cholesterol component in Western gall stones most research has concentrated on those factors which influence cholesterol solubility in bile; but this can be only part of the problem and while there is now an understanding of why cholesterol precipitates out of bile there is still incomplete information regarding the process whereby the stone grows.

Cholesterol is present in bile in the free, non-esterified form. There is no relationship between bile and serum cholesterol concentrations and the serum cholesterol level gives no guide to the presence or absence of gall stones. Cholesterol is virtually insoluble in water and is maintained in solution in bile by being incorporated into a mixed micelle. The mixed micelle is a polymolecular aggregate composed of cholesterol, phospholipids and bile salts. The bile salts and to a lesser extent the phospholipids have both polar and nonpolar end groups and are able to form micelles which enable cholesterol to be solubilized. The precise mechanism for the excretion of biliary lipids and the site of micelle formation remains uncertain. Probably lecithin and cholesterol are coupled in their movement into the canaliculi where they meet the bile salts and form the mixed micelles characteristic of bile. It is postulated that the source of lecithin and cholesterol is from the plasma membrane of the canaliculus that has been solubilized in the process of secreting the bile salts which have a powerful detergent action. The other possibility is that biliary cholesterol and phospholipids are not derived from the canicular membrane but from another source within the liver cell.

Both hepatic and gall bladder factors operate in the formation of gall stones. Bile secreted by the liver contains an excess of cholesterol relative to the amount of bile salts. This comes about either because of an increased hepatic synthesis of cholesterol or from a reduced pool size of bile salts, or a combination of the two. It is the last mechanism which appears to operate in the majority of individuals with gall stones. The effect of an imbalance of cholesterol relative to bile salts is to produce hepatic bile that is supersaturated with cholesterol which can precipitate out as crystals.

Normally there is a phasic, diurnal variation in biliary cholesterol saturation. During postprandial periods, when the gall bladder has contracted and there is an effective enterohepatic circulation of bile salts, there is a rich flow of bile which is undersaturated with cholesterol. During fasting, and particularly at night, the gall bladder is filled with bile; most of the bile salts lie in the gall bladder, and there is a relative break in the enterohepatic circulation so that the newly secreted hepatic bile becomes supersaturated with cholesterol. Because this is a normal event a reason must be found why most people do not form gall stones. There may be stone-promoting and stone-inhibiting factors in bile and almost certainly the gall bladder has an important role to play in this. Gall bladder contractility, mixing, mucous secretion and infection are all significant although only 30–50% of bile samples from gall stone patients contain bacteria. Nucleating factors must be present which enable cholesterol to precipitate out as crystals and then coalesce as stones. The process is multifactorial, complex and poorly understood.

A number of clinical relationships are associated with gall stones although none provides useful insight into the mechanism of gall stone formation. Gall stones are twice as common in females as in males and the disease increases in frequency with age. Stones are more common in Caucasians than Negroes and have a remarkably high prevalence in some American Indian tribes. No certain relation has been established between diet and gall stone disease. Reports from different parts of the world are conflicting and an association has been claimed for an increase in total calories, an increased intake of fat, a low fat diet and a diet low in fibre. Gall stones occur with increased frequency in hepatic cirrhosis, disease or resection of the ileum and diabetes mellitus. There is inadequate evidence to support any special association between gall stones and coronary artery disease, peptic ulcer, gastric surgery, diverticular disease of the colon and hiatus hernia. Pigment gall stones are more frequent in haemolytic disorders and occur in 50% of patients with hereditary spherocytosis, 35% of patients with sickle cell anaemia and 25% with thalassaemia major.

Gall stones may be single or multiple. They may be unassociated with symptoms—the 'silent stone'—or they may initiate disease in the gall bladder or bile ducts. It is not clear why some stones cause symptoms and others do not. Thus there may be acute or chronic cholecystitis and a stone impacted in the cystic duct may cause a mucocele or an empyema; internal fistulas may form to the stomach, duodenum or colon. Stones which migrate to the common bile duct cause colic, obstructive jaundice and cholangitis. The presence of gall stones may be associated with gall bladder cancer and acute pancreatitis. There is considerable debate as to whether gall stones cause flatulence, fatty food intolerance and nausea. The suggestion has been made that associated duodenal reflux causes gastritis and gastric hyposecretion which may be responsible for some of the symptoms. An argument against any special association between gall stones and these gastric and oesophageal symptoms is that cholecystectomy does not necessarily relieve the symptoms. Gall stones which occur in haemolytic disorders, ileal disease and cirrhosis of the liver seldom give rise to symptoms; when such patients become jaundiced a cause other than the gall stones should always be sought.

The diagnosis of uncomplicated gall stone disease can be made by plain radiograph of the abdomen in the 15% of patients who have radio-opaque stones. An oral cholecysto-gram is an extremely accurate technique for demonstrating gall stones and gall bladder disease (Plate X. Fig. 1). Non-opacification of the gall bladder, in the absence of any technical problems, is a strong indication of gall bladder disease and usually implies the presence of gall stones. Intravenous cholangiography may be tried if the oral technique fails but it is not as successful in demonstrating the gall bladder even in the absence of disease. Endoscopic retrograde cholangiopancreatography (ERCP) is a valuable technique particularly if the patient is icteric (Plate X. Fig. 2).

Once gall stones have caused symptoms they should be removed unless there are strong contraindications to surgery. The operation of choice is a cholecystectomy with or without common bile duct drainage, depending on whether there are stones in the duct. Operative cholangio-graphy is advised by many as a routine procedure in all patients with gall stones. The morbidity and mortality from uncomplicated elective operations are very low and the mortality rate is around 0.1% in patients less than 60 years old. The older the patient the more likely there are to be complications, so that once gall stones have given rise to symptoms they should be removed. There is no solution to the problem of the truly silent stone, that is a gall stone which has been discovered by pure chance. Two opposing views have been expressed: on the one hand it is recommended that the gall bladder should always be removed because of the fear that symptoms will develop, particularly when the patient is older and infirm, and on the other hand it is held that the gall bladder should be left alone because there may never be any trouble.

There have been many attempts to treat gall stones by medical means; only one has stood the test of time. Chenodeoxycholic acid, the primary dihydroxy bile salt, has been shown to be effective in dissolving gall stones in an oral dose of 10–15 mg/kg body weight. It is only effective when there are radiolucent stones in a functioning gall bladder. Stone dissolution takes from 6–24 months depending on the size and number of stones. The mechanism of action is primarily to reduce cholesterol output from the liver. Further experience with this agent is necessary before a precise role for it in the management of gall stones can be defined.

Cholecystitis

Cholecystitis may present as an acute, subacute or chronic illness. It is more common in females and increases in frequency with age. However, all age groups are affected and acute cholecystitis has been described in infants and children, when it is frequently secondary to an anomaly of the cystic duct. Cholecystitis is usually associated with and ascribed to cholelithiasis; but between 10 and 30% of patients will have inflammatory changes in the absence of gall stones. Other factors implicated include chemical irritation by the bile, reflux of pancreatic juice and localized arteriosclerosis and ischaemia. Bacteria may be cultured from the bile in less than 50% of patients and include coliform organisms, *Streptococcus*, *Staphylococcus*, *Clostridium* and *Salmonella*. The gall bladder mucosa shows varying degrees of inflammation and destruction of the surface cells. There is goblet cell hyperplasia and occasionally hyperplasia of the mucous membrane. In chronic cholecystitis all the elements of the gall bladder wall become thickened and there is much fibrosis.

Acute Cholecystitis

Acute cholecystitis presents with the sharp onset of epigastric and right upper quadrant pain which radiates round the right costal margin. There may be pain in the renal angle or the right shoulder tip and rarely on the left side of the upper abdomen. The pain usually starts abruptly and persists until therapy is instituted. The acute episode is accompanied by headache, nausea and vomiting. A few patients complain of intolerance to fatty food before the attack. On examination the patient is febrile, there is a rapid pulse and peritoneal irritation is indicated in the right upper quadrant by tenderness, guarding and muscle rigidity. Occasionally there is tenderness and hyper-aesthesia in the right subscapular region. A mass may be felt and this represents either adherent omentum around an inflamed gall bladder or a gall bladder which is distended with mucus (mucocele) or pus (empyema). A reflex bradycardia may occur. Cholecystitis may be complicated by acute renal failure. Jaundice is usually absent and if present is suggestive of a stone in the common bile duct and is therefore an indication for exploration of the common bile duct. Jaundice and abnormal liver function tests, in the absence of common bile duct stones, have never been explained satisfactorily but the usual reason given is that there is oedema and temporary compression of the common bile duct by a stone which has impacted in Hartmann's pouch. Uncommon complications include free perforation and massive bleeding from the gall bladder which presents as haematemesis and melaena. Adherence of the inflamed gall bladder to the stomach, duodenum or colon can result in internal biliary fistulas and these are found in 1–5% of patients at operation. Their presence may be suspected by the finding of gas in the biliary tree on a plain radiograph of the abdomen. Steatorrhoea may develop. Rarely a gall stone which has passed from the gall bladder into the gut causes obstruction; the usual site for hold-up is at the terminal ileum but the stone may impact in the duodenum.

The stones may be seen on a plain radiography of the abdomen. If the patient is not severely ill a cholecystogram is performed and this will show non-functioning of the gall bladder. The radiology may be performed at a later occasion if the patient is acutely ill. The differential diagnosis includes a perforation of a peptic ulcer, acute pancreatitis, right lower lobe pneumonia and myocardial infarction. Acute appendicitis can cause confusion in children.

The treatment of acute cholecystitis is to control the pain once the diagnosis has been established, counteract shock and electrolyte imbalance and undertake a cholecystectomy. About 30–50% of the patients who are left unoperated after an attack of cholecystitis associated with a gall stone will develop serious symptoms within 10 years. These patients then have to undergo an operation when they are older and consequently there is an increase in the morbidity and mortality. There are two bodies of opinion regarding the timing of the operation. The 'conservative' attitude is to manage the patient with analgesics, antibiotics and intravenous therapy if necessary, until the inflammation subsides and then after an interval of 4–6 weeks to perform a cholecystectomy. The other view favours an early cholecystectomy even during the acute phase of the illness. Advances in surgical care, surgical technique and anaesthesia have reduced the risks of cholecystectomy in the presence of acute inflammation and there is now a tendency to operate within a few days of the onset of illness. Antibiotics lessen the duration of the acute illness and reduce the incidence of wound infection which is frequently caused by the same organism which can be cultured from the bile. Antibiotics of value are tetracyclines, ampicillin and rifamide.

The morbidity and mortality rate of acute cholecystitis increases with age and the presence of complications.

While the mortality rate is 0.1% in patients under 60 years who undergo elective uncomplicated operations it rises to around 5% in patients above the age of 60 who have stones in the common bile duct.

CHRONIC CHOLECYSTITIS

Chronic inflammatory disease of the gall bladder usually accompanies gall stones. A variety of mucosal changes are described in patients without gall stone disease and this has led to the introduction of the term 'cholecystoses', which includes cholesterolosis (strawberry gall bladder), cholecystitis glandularis proliferans and adenomyomatosis. In adenomyomatosis there is epithelial proliferation with protrusion of the mucosa into or through the muscularis layer. These diverticula are called Rokitansky–Aschoff sinuses.

The symptomatology of chronic cholecystitis is similar to acute cholecystitis but the severity of the pain and the presence of the physical signs are less marked. Such patients are treated with cholecystectomy.

Many more problems are presented by the patient with flatulence, fatty food intolerance and a vague ache in the right upper quadrant and in whom a non-functioning gall bladder is demonstrated but no gall stones. The radiology may show the presence of adenomyomatosis which is recognized as small filling defects within the gall bladder or an irregular outline to the gall bladder wall. In such patients it is difficult to be sure that the symptoms are of gall bladder origin and a search for other diseases is necessary, including hiatus hernia, diverticular disease of the colon and peptic ulcer disease. The problem is that these conditions may coexist with undoubted gall bladder disease. The final decision regarding the type of operation is difficult and requires careful judgment.

Common Duct Stone and Cholangitis

Common bile duct stones occur in 10–15% of all patients with gall stones. The gall bladder stones migrate into the common bile duct where they impact, the usual site being the sphincter of Oddi. Stones rarely form de novo in the bile ducts and when they do they are invariably a complication of a biliary stricture or parasites in the biliary tree. The stones cause jaundice and cholangitis and it is rare for a stone to be in the common bile duct without clinical evidence of biliary obstruction. Small stones may be passed with little or no evidence of obstruction. The distension of the extrahepatic and intrahepatic biliary tree is variable and if there is much biliary 'mud' and debris there is relatively little intrahepatic duct dilatation. In longstanding obstructive jaundice reabsorption and alteration of the bile pigments may occur and the gall bladder ducts are filled with 'white' bile. Choledocholithiasis is common in older patients and the disease carries a greater risk to life than does cholelithiasis.

Stones in the common bile duct usually present with pain, jaundice and fever. Pain is felt in the epigastric region or to the right of the midline and radiates round the costal margin to between the shoulder blades. It is of varying severity and is usually constant. The pain is not characteristic of true colic and the term biliary 'colic' is a misnomer. The common bile duct in man has few, if any, muscle fibres and the pain is probably due to distension of the duct. Jaundice is of the cholestatic variety with conjugated hyperbilirubinaemia, elevated serum alkaline phosphatase and cholesterol values and a prolonged prothrombin time. Pruritus may be marked if the obstruction is complete and longstanding. At times an elevated serum alkaline phosphatase level is the only biochemical indication of bile duct obstruction. The jaundice is not necessarily persistent; fluctuating jaundice, recurrent bouts of pain and fever are classical accompaniments of a stone which intermittently obstructs the common bile duct (Charcot's intermittent biliary fever). A stone may impact and cause obstructive jaundice in the absence of pain. The liver is moderately enlarged and slightly tender. It is unusual to feel the gall bladder but a palpable gall bladder does not exclude gall stone disease or a stone in the common bile duct.

Superadded infection of the biliary tree is a frequent complication of choledocholithiasis. It is a clinical observation, as yet unexplained, that extrahepatic biliary obstruction due to malignant disease is rarely complicated by bacterial contamination and overgrowth. Cholangitis is accompanied by a bacteraemia and the patient is febrile and has rigors. Fulminating septicaemia, particularly with coliform organisms, may supervene. Bacterial overgrowth in the bile may contaminate the upper small intestine causing vitamin B_{12} malabsorption and bile salt deconjugation leading to fat malabsorption (p. 103).

The diagnosis can usually be made on clinical grounds and will be supported by the demonstration of gall stones in the gall bladder and/or the common bile duct by cholecystography or cholangiography. Tomography undertaken at the time of biliary radiology is of help. The technique for demonstrating the bile ducts is intravenous cholangiography. Neither cholecystography nor cholangiography is of value once the serum bilirubin concentration is greater than 70 μmol/litre. However, variations in the technique of administering the dye such as the 'dribble' method with the oral tablets and an infusion method for the intravenous agents have occasionally enabled stones to be identified when the serum bilirubin is slightly higher than 70 μmol/litre. Percutaneous transhepatic cholangiography is useful for outlining the ducts when the bilirubin is elevated and demonstrates both the presence and the nature of the extrahepatic biliary obstruction. However, failure to enter the ducts does not necessarily imply that the ducts are normal for they may not be dilated when there is much biliary mud, intrahepatic stones and cholangitis. Where available the use of endoscopic retrograde cholangiopancreatography (ERCP) is the method of choice. The technique has the added advantage of being able to visualize the ampulla of Vater and can detect tumours in this region which might be causing jaundice. A negative antimitochondrial antibody test (p. 225) is helpful and a pancreatic scan and hypotonic duodenography may provide useful information.

The diagnostic exercise is first to determine whether the cholestatic jaundice is of extra- or intrahepatic origin and then to decide upon the nature of the pathology (Table XV, p. 216). The most frequent diagnostic difficulty is to decide between cholestatic viral hepatitis or drug jaundice on the one hand and choledocholithiasis or pancreatic neoplasm on the other. In this situation a liver biopsy may be the only method of arriving at a conclusion. There is an understandable reluctance to undertake a liver biopsy in extrahepatic obstructive jaundice but it must be realized that an unnecessary laparotomy on a patient with hepatitis carries a much higher morbidity and mortality than a liver biopsy on a patient with obstructive jaundice. In skilled hands the procedure carries little added risk and has a high degree of diagnostic accuracy.

It is important in adopting an expectant approach to the differential diagnosis of cholestatic jaundice and choledocholithiasis that the patient remains under careful clinical and biochemical observation. Extrahepatic biliary obstruction is not harmful in the short term, hence the acceptability of this policy. However, the clinician must be aware of the danger that the patient may develop cholangitis and septicaemia which increase the morbidity and mortality rate. Blood cultures are taken when there is evidence of infection in the biliary tree and antibiotic therapy (ampicillin, tetracycline or rifamide) is instituted immediately. The eventuality of cholangitis strongly suggests that the cause of the cholestasis is choledocholithiasis and an urgent operation is indicated in order to confirm the diagnosis and to decompress and to drain the biliary tree.

Choledocholithiasis is treated surgically by exploration of the common bile duct, removal of the stones and the gall bladder and T-tube drainage of the duct. An operative cholangiogram should be undertaken routinely. If this is performed it is probably unnecessary to obtain a post-operative T-tube cholangiogram; but the T-tube cholangiogram must be undertaken if there has been no operative radiology. It is essential to demonstrate the intrahepatic ducts on the cholangiogram if no stone is found at operation. In this way cancers of the bile ducts will not be overlooked. Another important function of cholangiography is to assess the termination of the bile duct and the flow of bile into the duodenum. The biliary tree is dynamic and the flow of bile into the duodenum is episodic, determined mainly by duodenal contractions. Thus the significance of narrowing of the duct in the region of the sphincter of Oddi is difficult to interpret when only a single radiograph is available. Ideally cinecholangiography should be employed to demonstrate that a narrowing of the terminal segment of the duct is indeed permanent. Great care must be exercised in the diagnosis of spasm or stenosis of the sphincter of Oddi. Undoubtedly these conditions are diagnosed too frequently and many unnecessary sphinc-terotomies are performed. When there is convincing evidence for narrowing of the common bile duct termina-tion a transduodenal sphincteroplasty is probably the best operation.

Operations on the bile ducts are associated with an increased morbidity in 40% of patients and the mortality rate is 5%. The chief causes of death are overwhelming cholangitis, septicaemia and pancreatitis.

Postcholecystectomy Syndromes

The great majority of patients operated upon for gall stone disease have a satisfactory result and enjoy good health and normal digestion. A few patients persist with their symptoms or develop new complaints after biliary tract surgery and they are classified as having the postcholecystectomy syndrome. The syndrome occurs more frequently in patients who have had a cholecystectomy in the absence of gall stone disease. It has also been shown that the longer the preoperative history the higher the frequency of postcholecystectomy distress. The prevalence of symptoms following cholecystectomy varies greatly, depending on how thorough a search is made. The usual complaints are flatulence, fatty food intolerance and pain in the epigastrium and right upper quadrant. The causes can be grouped as follows:

1. *Mistaken diagnosis.*

2. *Common duct stone.* The incidence of retained and recurrent stones in the common duct is believed to be around 4%. They may present within weeks, months or years after the original operation.

3. *Injury during surgery.* This may take the form of a leak of bile immediately after the operation with consequent bile peritonitis. Of more importance is bile duct stricture. There are many causes of a bile duct stricture of which operative damage is the most important. Other causes include trauma, periductal fibrosis, severe cholangitis, severe postoperative adhesions, sclerosing cholangitis and malignant disease. The patient presents with pain, jaundice and cholangitis. Features of bacterial overgrowth in the small bowel (p. 103) may be prominent. The management is resection of the stricture and reconstruction of the continuity of the duct system. This may prove to be one of the most difficult of operations.

4. *Overlooked malignancy.* This includes tumours in the bile ducts, pancreas and duodenum.

5. *Cystic duct remnant*. The cystic duct may harbour concretions with accompanying infection. The cystic duct stump dilates and this may be so great as to simulate a gall bladder.

6. *Stenosis of the sphincter of Oddi*. This presents as narrowing of the sphincter and dilatation of the bile ducts. Jaundice and pain are frequent and cholangitis may supervene. Great care must be exercised in making the diagnosis and ideally it should be made on the basis of cinecholangiography which demonstrates a permanent narrowing of the duct.

7. *Biliary dyskinesia*. There is no good evidence that functional derangement of the biliary tract follows cholecystectomy. Fat digestion and absorption is adequate. Furthermore there is no evidence that the common bile duct dilates following removal of the gall bladder. Thus if the width of the duct is greater than 10 mm it must be assumed that there is organic obstruction to the flow of bile. This is usually due to a retained gall stone and less commonly to a stricture of the duct or stenosis of the sphincter of Oddi.

Primary Sclerosing Cholangitis

Sclerosing cholangitis may occur secondarily to infections of the biliary tree, particularly when this occurs in association with gall stones and common bile duct strictures. Primary sclerosing cholangitis is a rare disorder in which there is diffuse inflammation of the extra- and intrahepatic duct system in the absence of gall stones or previous biliary surgery. The aetiology is unknown but the disorder may occur in association with ulcerative colitis, retroperitoneal fibrosis, thyroiditis, mediastinal fibrosis and retro-orbital tumours. The ducts demonstrate a chronic fibrosing inflammatory process with plasma cell infiltration.

Males and females are equally affected and the age range is between 20 and 40 years. Jaundice is present in 100% of patients although in 75% it is intermittent. Pain occurs in the majority of patients, usually in the right upper quadrant. Other features include pruritus, anorexia and weight loss. The duration of symptoms prior to diagnosis is from 1 to 5 years.

The diagnosis is difficult to establish but may be suspected from a liver biopsy when there are inflammatory changes around the ductules. Cholangiography shows a characteristic beaded appearance of the extrahepatic biliary tree. Other radiological signs include strictures and a deficiency of the intrahepatic biliary system. At operation the common bile duct is found to be narrowed and thickened and a biopsy demonstrates the chronic inflammatory changes.

Once gall stones have been excluded the main differential diagnosis is between a primary bile duct cancer and primary biliary cirrhosis.

Treatment is unsatisfactory and comprises operative decompression of the biliary tree and T-tube drainage. There is no evidence that medical treatment is helpful although corticosteroids and immunosuppressive agents have been tried. The patient is treated for chronic cholestasis on the same lines as for primary biliary cirrhosis (p. 260). The prognosis is poor because the patients eventually develop a secondary biliary cirrhosis. The average length of life from the time the diagnosis is established is 6 years.

Tumours of the Biliary Tract

Benign tumours of the gall bladder and bile ducts are rare and the clinically important tumours are cancers which arise from the gall bladder and hepatic ducts.

Primary Cancer of the Gall Bladder

Cancer of the gall bladder accounts for 1% of all cancers in the United Kingdom and occupies fifth or sixth place in the frequency of gastrointestinal cancers. The tumour is usually an adenocarcinoma. It is commoner in females and this probably reflects the association between the tumour and gall stone disease. About 45–85% of patients have gall stones. The disease is commonest in patients over the age of 70 years. The presenting feature is usually painless jaundice but cramping right upper quadrant and epigastric pain may occur. The tumour is occasionally discovered accidentally at the time of elective cholecystectomy. A mass is palpable in 50% of the patients and 60% have elevated serum bilirubin or alkaline phosphatase concentrations. The radiological findings vary widely and include the demonstration of gall stones, calcification of the gall bladder, non-visualization of the gall bladder, displacement of the duodenum and internal fistulas. At the time of laparotomy there is usually extensive local spread to the liver, stomach, colon and omentum. Cholecystectomy can be undertaken in 30% of the patients but it may be possible only to take a biopsy or to relieve obstruction in the common bile duct, stomach or duodenum. The operative mortality rate is 37% and patients who survive the operation live for an average of 5 months.

Because of the hopeless outlook for this cancer prophylactic surgery has been advocated for non-functioning or gall stone-containing gall bladders. Such a policy must be viewed with caution: the great majority of gall bladder cancers occur in the very old at a time when the life expectancy is short. It is at this age that cholecystectomy has an appreciable morbidity and mortality. It is probable that elective surgery for gall bladder or gall stone disease would reduce the number of deaths from cancer of the gall bladder but only at the expense of a lessened expectancy of life.

CANCER OF THE HEPATIC DUCTS

Cancer developing along the course of the common bile duct is a well-recognized cause of obstructive jaundice.

However, cancers arising at the junction of the main hepatic ducts are of particular importance for although uncommon they present a puzzling clinical picture and are frequently misdiagnosed.

The tumour is usually an adenocarcinoma which is only locally invasive; it has rarely spread at the time of diagnosis. More than half of the growths occur in the upper one-third of the bile duct. The age distribution is from 35 to 75 years and both sexes are equally affected. An association with ulcerative colitis has been claimed. The usual clinical features are persistent jaundice, pruritus, diarrhoea, anorexia and marked weight loss. Mild epigastric pain occurs in 50% of patients. Liver enlargement is marked and the gall bladder is not palpable. The laboratory findings are those of cholestatic jaundice with elevated serum bilirubin, alkaline phosphatase, 5′nucleotidase and cholesterol concentrations. The liver biopsy shows the features of extrahepatic bile duct obstruction (p. 291) but the most valuable investigations are either the percutaneous transhepatic cholangiogram or ERCP which reveals a blunt or nipple-like termination at the point where the hepatic ducts are obstructed. The obstruction may be partial or complete.

The main differential diagnosis is between the other causes of cholestatic jaundice (Table XV, p. 216) including primary biliary cirrhosis, drug jaundice and pancreatic cancer.

A collapsed gall bladder is usually found at laparotomy and the surgeon may overlook or fail to palpate the tumour. It is essential to perform an operative cholangiogram and great care must be taken to visualize the intrahepatic duct system. Failure to outline the intrahepatic biliary pattern despite good radiological technique should always arouse the suspicion of a hepatic duct tumour. The cancer is resistant to radiation or cancer chemotherapy and is best managed by local resection with some form of bypass operation. Tumours at or near the confluence of the hepatic ducts are treated by the palliative procedure of inserting a tube into the duct above and below the obstruction; tumours in the lower portions of the duct can be resected en bloc. Hemihepatectomy or even hepatic transplantation has been attempted. The survival after a palliative procedure is surprisingly good and averages over 1 year with some patients living for 3 or more years. Medical treatment of the pruritus and other features of biliary obstruction are required (p. 260).

Congenital Abnormalities of the Biliary Tract

There are a great variety of rare malformations which affect the extra- and intrahepatic biliary tree.

Congenital Biliary Atresia

Congenital biliary atresia may involve both the extra- and intrahepatic ducts. The aetiology is unknown but there is a relationship with giant cell hepatitis. Indeed it has been suggested that biliary atresia and giant cell (neonatal) hepatitis may be variations of a common disease process. An appearance similar to giant cell hepatitis is seen in 15% of patients. Icterus may be present at birth but in half the infants it manifests only after 2–3 weeks. Unless relieved there is marked cholestasis, hepatomegaly, malnutrition, growth retardation and eventually cirrhosis of the liver. The differential diagnosis is from other causes of neonatal jaundice (Table XXI) and in particular between neonatal hepatitis and biliary atresia. Over 90% of infants with extrahepatic biliary obstruction have biliary atresia.

A liver biopsy helps to differentiate between atresia and hepatitis although there may be certain features in common including bile duct proliferation, fibrosis and giant cells. Other causes of neonatal hepatitis need to be excluded. An intravenous [131]I Rose Bengal faecal excretion test will show the failure of bile flow. Once the diagnosis is suspected an operation is undertaken within 10–16 weeks. In some

3–15% of patients it is possible to anastomose either the gall bladder or common bile duct to the small intestine using a Roux-en-Y loop. Other patients may benefit from hepatic portoenterostomy in which a loop of bowel is anastomosed to the porta hepatis without any attempt to link bile ducts directly to mucosa. Cholangitis is a frequent complication requiring regular antibiotic therapy. Liver transplantation has been advocated. In those many children in whom adequate bile flow is unobtainable management is along the lines of a low fat diet, added medium-chain triglycerides, cholestyramine (6–16 g/day), and parenteral supplements of the fat-soluble vitamins.

Congenital dilatation of the biliary tract may involve the extrahepatic portion of the duct system and rarely the intrahepatic radicles. The commonest manifestation is a *choledochal cyst* which usually presents in children and teenagers with the characteristic triad of abdominal pain, jaundice and an abdominal mass. Internal drainage procedures are undertaken such as choledochocystoduodenostomy and a Roux-en-Y choledochocystojejunostomy. More radical surgery may be attempted by excising the cyst.

Congenital dilatation of the intrahepatic biliary tree is usually associated with *congenital hepatic fibrosis* in which there is fibrosis of the liver with hypoplasia of the interlobular portal venules. The main features are portal hypertension or cholangitis and hepatocellular function is well preserved. The dilated ducts are often the site of microcalculi and gall stones. The diagnosis is most readily established by a surgical wedge biopsy of the liver. The cystic dilatation of the intrahepatic bile ducts may be demonstrated by intravenous cholangiography or percutaneous transhepatic cholangiography. In 80% of patients there is coexistent medullary sponge kidney but this is seldom of clinical significance. The renal changes are accompanied by recurrent urinary infections and occasionally kidney stones.

Congenital hepatic fibrosis, cystic dilatation of the intrahepatic bile ducts and medullary sponge kidneys must be distinguished from *polycystic liver disease* which is associated with polycystic kidneys. This is inherited as a dominant trait; the hepatic cysts are large and visible on the liver surface and portal hypertension is rare. The prognosis is determined by the polycystic kidneys and death in renal failure is the rule.

Further Reading

Bodvall, B. and Overgaard, B. (1967) Computer analysis of postcholecystectomy biliary tract symptoms. *Surgery Gynec. Obstet.*, **124**, 723–732.

Bouchier, I. A. D. (1975) Gall stones. In *Modern Trends in Gastroenterology*, A. E. Read (ed.). pp. 203–230. London: Butterworths.

Bouchier, I. A. D. (1976) Gall stones. *Br. med. J.*, **12**, 870–872.

Donaldson, L. A. and Busuttil, A. (1975) A clinicopathological review of 68 carcinomas of the gall bladder. *Br. J. Surg.*, **62**, 26–32.

Foulk, W. T. et al. (1971) Congenital malformations of the intrahepatic biliary tree in the adult. *Gastroenterology*, **58**, 253–256.

Kaye, M. D. and Kern, E. (1971) Clinical relationships of gall stones. *Lancet*, **i**, 1228–1230.

Longmire, W. P., jr et al. (1973) Carcinoma of the extrahepatic biliary tract. *Ann. Surg.*, **178**, 333–345.

Ritchie, J. K. et al. (1974) Biliary tract cancer associated with ulcerative colitis. *Q. Jl. Med.*, **43**, 263–279.

Wenckert, A. and Robertson, B. (1966) The natural course of gall stone disease. *Gastroenterology*, **50**, 376–381.

The intestinal microflora is radically altered during an episode of acute diarrhoea. The pathogens are found in large numbers but in addition there is a marked reduction in the normal anaerobic flora which may be related to rapid transit of contents through the bowel. There are at least 3 mechanisms whereby pathogenic bacteria can induce acute diarrhoea:

1. The bacteria elaborate an exotoxin which causes abnormal secretion of salt and water into the lumen of the bowel. The organisms do not penetrate the bowel wall. Examples of this include *Vibrio cholerae* and *Escherichia coli*.

2. There is direct penetration of the epithelium causing ulceration and mucosal destruction. This is seen with strains of *Shigella* and some *Escherichia coli*.

3. There is direct mucosal injury as well as alterations in fluid transport. This is mainly observed in experimental salmonellosis but may also apply to man.

Acute Infective Gastroenteritis

There are many organisms which cause acute infective gastroenteritis including a variety of strains of *Salmonella*, *Escherichia coli*, certain phage types of *Staphylococcus aureus*, type A strains of *Clostridium perfringens* and viruses such as hepatitis, measles, poliomyelitis and the ECHO types 11, 20, 8, 19. *Salmonella* infection is commonly derived from animal sources. Food stored in warehouses may be contaminated by *Salmonella* from rodents. Infection is confined to the digestive tract and the incubation period is 6–24 hours. The pathogenic strains of *Staph. aureus* produce an enterotoxin. This is ingested with precooked foods and manufactured meat dishes which have been contaminated by staphylococci from the nose, throat or skin of food handlers. This form of infection has an incubation period of less than 4 hours.

The illness is of sudden onset with nausea, vomiting and diarrhoea. Pyrexia is a feature of salmonellosis but not of staphylococcal enterotoxin. Gross loss of water and electrolytes may cause hypotension prostration and collapse. The treatment will depend upon the severity of the illness. Mild attacks lasting less than a day are managed with warmth and oral fluids containing electrolytes. More severely affected patients need to be admitted to hospital; their fluid and electrolyte status must be carefully assessed and appropriate intravenous therapy instituted. Antibiotics have no place in the management as they may induce antibiotic resistance in normal bowel organisms, or induce a carrier state, and the antibiotics themselves may aggravate the diarrhoea. An antidiarrhoeal agent such as codeine phosphate or mist. kaolin et morph. is useful. Attention to the public health aspect of the illness must not be overlooked. Vomitus or faeces must be cultured, contacts and sources traced and where necessary the patient screened for the carrier state.

Infantile gastroenteritis still accounts for 400 deaths annually among children under the age of 2 years in the United Kingdom. In other areas of the world it is a major cause of death in infancy and childhood. In the United Kingdom a causal agent cannot be isolated in the majority of patients; enteropathic strains of *E. coli* have been detected in only 25% of the patients. A variety of viruses has been implicated. Outbreaks of gastroenteritis tend to occur in rest centres, children's nurseries and hospitals. The epidemics are indistinguishable from those caused by *Salmonella*. Most of the fatalities occur in children under the age of 3 months and death may be sudden enough to be described as a 'cot death'. Infants with gastroenteritis require particular attention to fluid balance. Milk or solid feeds are withdrawn and replaced by a salt-containing clear fluid preparation. This is given orally hourly or two-hourly over 48 hours. Antidiarrhoeal agents and antibiotics have no place in therapy. Once recovery is under way the normal feeding routine can be introduced gradually until the appropriate diet for the patient's age is given. After an attack of gastroenteritis many infants have a temporary reduction in their tolerance to dietary glucose and fat.

Traveller's diarrhoea is a common worldwide illness lasting 1–3 days. A variety of agents may be responsible including enterotoxigenic *E. coli*, invasive *E. coli*, *S. sonnei*, *S. flexneri*, *G. lamblia*, *Salmonella* and neovirus-like agents. Enterotoxigenic *E. coli* is the most important of these but in one-third of patients no cause, as yet, is identified. The condition has been called Aden gut, Basra belly, Delhi belly, Hong Kong dog, Montezuma's revenge, Aztec two-step and *turista*. The illness presents acutely with diarrhoea, nausea, vomiting and abdominal cramps and is seldom more than a nuisance during the first few days that the victim is in the strange country. Most patients recover with the use of antidiarrhoeal agents only. The use of antibiotics in the treatment of this condition is discouraged and the role of prophylactic antibiotic therapy is uncertain.

Typhoid and Paratyphoid Fevers

Typhoid fever is caused by *Salmonella typhi* and is endemic in Africa and other underdeveloped areas. In England and

Wales between 100 and 200 patients with typhoid fever and 300 and 400 with paratyphoid fever (usually paratyphi B) are notified annually and the majority of these are isolated infections contracted abroad. Typhoid is spread mainly by water or food contaminated by infected water, whereas paratyphoid fever spreads after multiplication of bacilli in food, particularly cream and synthetic cream. The bacteria enter the host via the mesenteric lymphatics. The Peyer's patches become swollen and necrotic. The ulcers heal without scarring. The necrosis of the ulcers is responsible for the haemorrhage and perforations which may occur during the third week of the illness.

The usual mode of onset is with headache, anorexia and malaise. Other symptoms include cough, abdominal pain, diarrhoea or constipation, vomiting and a sore throat. Pyrexia is a constant feature and may be the only manifestation of the infection. Abdominal tenderness and bradycardia relative to the fever are commonly encountered. Splenomegaly and rose spots are less frequently seen. In paratyphoid fever the rash is less common but when present may be quite profuse. In general paratyphoid fever is a milder illness than typhoid fever but the clinical distinction between the two is difficult. Important complications include intestinal perforation, severe bleeding, pulmonary infection, cholecystitis, osteomyelitis and renal failure.

The diagnosis is established by culture of the organism from the blood, faeces and urine. A rise in the Widal reaction takes some time to develop and is less easy to interpret. The mortality rate for typhoid fever varies from 5–25% and elderly patients do poorly.

The patient is isolated and given a high calorie, low residue diet. Chloramphenicol remains the most effective therapy and is administered orally in doses of 1 g 8-hourly until the patient is afebrile and then 0.5 g 6-hourly. Treatment is continued for 3 weeks. Other antibiotics such as ampicillin and co-trimoxazole have been used but are not superior to chloramphenicol. The disadvantages of chloramphenicol include the time taken for the fever to subside, the presence of toxic features even when the patient is afebrile and the tendency for the disease to relapse. Prednisolone (15 mg 6-hourly) is used in severely ill and toxic patients. The patient remains in isolation until the stool cultures are negative.

The chronic carrier is defined as one carrying the organism after 12 months and poses many public health problems. About 85% of chronic carriers have Vi agglutinins in a titre of 1:5 or more. Chemotherapy is ineffective in the carrier state but cholecystectomy has proved curative in a few well-established carriers.

Cholera

Cholera is caused by *Vibrio cholerae*. The bacteria do not invade the body but are limited to the gut lumen. The *Vibrio* toxin causes an outpouring of chloride from the intestinal wall. It is believed that the toxin is responsible for increased adenyl cyclase activity, thereby enhancing the conversion of adenosine triphosphate to cyclic AMP. The higher AMP level causes the intestinal cell to secrete sodium, chloride and water into the intestinal lumen. There is a coincident decrease in the net absorption of sodium which increases the fluid loss. The disease is endemic in Asia. An outbreak caused by the El Tor strain has currently acquired pandemic proportions and has extended as far west as Western Europe.

The illness is characteristically afebrile and begins with vague fullness in the abdomen and anorexia. Profuse diarrhoea and slight vomiting ensue and the patient rapidly becomes hypovolaemic. The stools are initially brown in colour but soon becomes the typical rice water stool which is opalescent, watery and flecked with mucus. The patients may rapidly lose 25–50% of the extracellular fluid volume. Treatment consists of replacing fluid and electrolytes and if this is undertaken promptly the mortality can be cut to less than 1%. Adequate fluid, sodium, potassium, chloride and bicarbonate must be supplied intravenously. An oral solution has been used with success and reduces the amount of intravenous replacement by 80%. The solution contains electrolytes with the addition of glucose to increase the transport of sodium into the intestinal cells. An antibiotic such as tetracycline reduces the duration of the illness by half but it is not a substitute for the life-saving therapy: adequate and rapid fluid and electrolyte replacement.

Abdominal Tuberculosis

The incidence of gastrointestinal tuberculosis in the Western Hemisphere has declined markedly during the past 25 years. It is usually secondary to pulmonary tuberculosis but rarely the bovine strain is responsible for ileocaecal lesions particularly when unpasteurized milk is consumed. In abdominal tuberculosis the intestines, liver and peritoneum are the main structures to be involved.

Tuberculosis enteritis follows lymphatic spread of the bacilli and is classified as ulcerative, hypertrophic and ulcerohypertrophic. Tuberculous ulcers are circumferential in distribution. They are accompanied by diarrhoea and there may be gastrointestinal haemorrhage or perforation. Less common is the hypertrophic form of the disease which affects the ileocaecal region, causing diarrhoea, malabsorption and intestinal obstruction. Other sites to be affected are the colon and rectum. The main differential diagnosis is between Crohn's disease and malignant disease. The diagnosis can be difficult to establish, particularly in those unusual situations when there is no active pulmonary lesion.

Tuberculous peritonitis follows invasion of the peritoneum by the bacilli. The organisms reach the peritoneal cavity via the lymph nodes or, in the case of females, via the fallopian tubes or ovaries. Alcoholic patients are at particular risk. The illness presents as fever, abdominal pain and swelling and weight loss. Usually the condition is chronic but an acute syndrome is encountered. Ascites is the usual manifestation. There is a plastic variety in which there is fibrous obliteration of the peritoneal cavity. This is rare and is probably a late stage of the disease; at this time the abdomen may have a 'doughy' feel. Half the patients with tuberculosis peritonitis have normal chest radiographs. The diagnosis is made by culturing the ascitic fluid and by peritoneal biopsy and peritoneoscopy.

Local tuberculous disease of the liver is rare whereas miliary tuberculosis of this organ is not unusual, being spread from a pulmonary or lymph node infection. There is abdominal pain and tender hepatomegaly and in one-third of patients there is also jaundice and splenomegaly. The usual biochemical abnormality is an elevated serum alkaline phosphatase concentration but the serum bilirubin may be raised and abnormal bromsulphthalein retention occurs. The diagnosis is established by liver biopsy.

The antituberculous drugs are highly effective in the management of abdominal tuberculosis and surgery can usually be avoided. However, ulcerative or obstructive lesions may require surgical intervention and an operation under antibiotic cover can be undertaken with satisfactory results.

Yersiniosis

Human infection with *Yersinia enterocolitica* and *Y. pseudo-tuberculosis* is common in Europe but is being recognized as a worldwide infection. The major clinical features are acute diarrhoea, abdominal pain, erythema nodosum and arthritis. Patients of all ages are affected. The abdominal pain varies in severity and may be severe enough to indicate a laparotomy. At operation mesenteric adenitis and acute inflammation of the terminal ileum are found. Moderate fever may persist up to 2 weeks. The joints involved are usually the knees, ankles and tarsal and patients with arthritis have an elevated erythrocyte sedimentation rate.

Diagnosis is established by demonstrating an increase in agglutination titres which are at their maximum after 1–2 weeks and then gradually decline. *Y. enterocolitica* can be isolated from the stools during the first 2 weeks of the illness. The organism is also isolated from the appendix or the mesenteric lymph nodes. The differential diagnosis includes Crohn's disease, *Shigella* and *Salmonella* infections and the other causes of erythema nodosum. The abdominal symptoms usually subside spontaneously within 1–2 weeks, although fever, joint pains and erythema nodosum may persist for longer. The organism is sensitive to sulphonamides, streptomycin, tetracycline and chloramphenicol but there is no evidence that the use of antibiotics is of value in managing the diarrhoea, arthritis or erythema nodosum.

Leptospirosis (Weil's Disease)

This infection is due to *Leptospira icterohaemorrhagiae* and is acquired by contact with the urine of infected rats. The spirochetes enter the body via skin abrasions. There is haemorrhagic necrosis of the liver, kidney and muscles in particular but the skin and lungs are also involved. The illness is heralded by fever, rigors and abdominal pain. There are severe muscular pains, conjunctival suffusion and pneumonitis, and jaundice becomes apparent by the end of the first week of the illness. At this stage the urine contains albumin, bile and urobilin; there is a leucocytosis and thrombocytopenia; the biochemical tests show elevated serum concentrations of bilirubin, transaminase, alkaline phosphatase and urea. The electrocardiogram shows evidence of myocarditis. Clinical improvement begins during the third week and resolution of the hepatic, renal and cardiac damage occurs without permanent disability.

The diagnosis is established by isolating the spirochetes from the blood and urine and by the leptospiral agglutination test which is positive after the first week of the illness. The differential diagnosis includes viral hepatitis and infectious mononucleosis. The mortality is around 16% and death is due to renal failure. Treatment is with penicillin but it is probable that if administered after the fourth day of the illness the antibiotic is ineffective.

Bacillary Dysentery

Bacillary dysentery is acquired by ingesting food contaminated with faecal material and the disease is therefore an indication of defective hygiene and sanitation. In the United Kingdom the commonest organism is *Shigella sonnei* and disease due to *Sh. flexneri* and *Sh. shigae* is unusual; but this is not so in other areas of the world. The shigellae invade the colonic mucosa causing intense inflammation. In severe involvement the mucosa becomes necrotic and sloughs leaving raw ulcerated areas. These are most prominent in the rectum but they may extend along the whole of the colon and even into the terminal few feet of the small intestine. Healing is usually complete, although in severe involvement the mucosa may be replaced by fibrous tissue.

Sonne dysentery is usually a mild disease and causes moderate diarrhoea. There may be as many as a dozen stools during the first 24 hours but the diarrhoea usually settles within 72 hours. The stool is watery and flecks of blood may be present, although frank bleeding is rare. The patient is afebrile, vomiting is unusual and abdominal pain is absent. The illness may be more severe in infants when it may be confused with meningitis. Flexner and Shiga dysentery are usually much more severe illnesses. Diarrhoea and dehydration are marked, there are severe abdominal cramps, pyrexia is prominent and the stools may consist of frank blood. Diarrhoea persists for one week. The gangrenous form of the illness is accompanied by severe intestinal colic and the stool comprises altered blood and mucosal sloughs; this form has a high mortality rate. The patient may develop an acute arthritis which is a manifestation of the associated septicaemia.

The diagnosis is established by cultures of blood and stool. The more severe forms of bacillary dysentery mimic ulcerative colitis and the sigmoidoscopic appearances are virtually identical. Other conditions to be considered in the diagnosis are mesenteric infarction in elderly patients and intussusception and appendicitis in infants and children.

Mild infections require oral fluid replacement and an antidiarrhoeal agent. It is not necessary to admit the patient to hospital and an antibiotic is probably not indicated. A more severe attack necessitates hospitalization and intravenous fluids are administered. An antibiotic is usually prescribed. Shigellae are sensitive to sulphonamides and sulphadimidine, 2 g initially followed by 1 g 6-hourly is used. Co-trimoxazole, streptomycin and neomycin have also been advocated. Sensitivity varies and resistance develops rapidly. It may be necessary to change the antibiotic during treatment if a resistant strain appears. The stool must be cultured to demonstrate that a bacteriological cure has been achieved. Three negative cultures are regarded as satisfactory evidence of cure.

Amoebic Dysentery

A large proportion of the world's population suffers from amoebiasis and a still larger number of people are carriers of the parasite. *Entamoeba histolytica* exists primarily as a commensal in the large bowel and the clinical manifestations of the infection appear when the amoebae invade the mucosa and ulceration develops. The amoebae are dependent on bacteria for their growth. The classic lesion is a flask-shaped ulcer with undermined edges which extends into the submucosa and muscularis mucosa. Intervening mucous membrane is normal.

The majority of patients experience a chronic low grade illness with 1–4 loose stools daily containing some blood and pus. Other complaints include vague abdominal pains, weight loss and fever. On examination the colon may be tender and sigmoidoscopy shows small yellow ulcers with normal intervening mucosa. Chronic infection can lead to the production of a large mass of granulation tissue in the caecum or rectum, known as an amoeboma. This must not be confused with a carcinoma. Occasionally the illness assumes an acute form and the patient has profuse bloody diarrhoea and becomes dehydrated and hypovolaemic.

The most important extracolonic manifestation of amoebiasis is a hepatic abscess. The complication is heralded by vague symptoms and followed by fever, weight loss and pain in the right upper quadrant of the abdomen. Jaundice is rare, as are other gastrointestinal symptoms such as diarrhoea. On examination there is usually a smooth tender enlarged liver. It is rare to palpate the abscess as it is usually situated in the upper aspect of the right lobe of the liver. A sympathetic right pleural effusion is common. This must be differentiated from an amoebic pleural effusion and amoebic lung abscess in which there is actual lung disease after rupture of the abscess across the diaphragm.

Laboratory findings include anaemia, leucocytosis and an elevated serum alkaline phosphatase concentration. It is uncommon to find amoebae in the stool. The site of the abscess can be ascertained by a liver scan and this information can be used as a guide for a diagnostic and therapeutic liver aspiration. The abscess typically contains brown-red necrotic material which is sterile, having no parasites.

Other manifestations of amoebiasis include pericarditis, peritonitis and the very rare meningoencephalitis. A syndrome of amoebic hepatitis is described in which there is a diffusely tender liver but no actual abscess formation.

The diagnosis is established by culture of a fresh warm stool or material obtained by biopsy from an ulcer or amoeboma. It is necessary to examine a warm stool sample so that the parasites can be seen to be motile. A number of serological reactions are in use including the gel-diffusion precipitation test and a rapid amoebic latex agglutination test. A negative test excludes the diagnosis of active amoebic disease but false positive results occur. The main value of the serological tests is in extra-intestinal amoebiasis; examination of a fresh, warm stool is the best diagnostic method for amoebic dysentery.

Patients with moderate infections are treated with metronidazole, 800 mg thrice daily for 5–10 days. Tetracycline, 250 mg 6-hourly for 10 days may be added. In severe infections emetine hydrochloride is used additionally: a daily subcutaneous injection of 65 mg for 4 days. Attention to fluid and electrolyte balance and anaemia is required. Liver involvement is treated with chloroquine, 300 mg of base twice daily for 2 days, thereafter 150 mg twice daily for a week. Diloxanide furoate 0.5–1 g thrice daily for 10 days is used to treat cyst passers.

Recovery from an episode of amoebic dysentery is usually complete. The postdysenteric irritable colon follows both bacillary and amoebic dysentery. The patient has mild intermittent diarrhoea and cramps for many years after the initial infection. Stool cultures are negative. The condition must be distinguished from ulcerative colitis. The management is symptomatic and the patient will need to be reassured.

Intestinal Schistosomiasis (Bilharzia)

Intestinal schistosomiasis affects approximately 80 million people in the Orient, Middle East, a wide area of Africa and parts of the Caribbean. It is caused by the trematodes *Schistosoma mansoni* and *S. japonicum*. Ova are deposited in the small tributaries of the portal vein and may be lost in the stool, or remain in the bowel wall or they may be carried to the liver.

The initial features of the infestation are itching and urticaria. One or two months later a generalized allergic response occurs and this is accompanied by fever, chills, cough, abdominal pain, urticaria, lymphadenopathy and hepatomegaly. Clinical manifestations at a later stage of the disease are the result of a fibrous reaction in response to the deposition of the ova. In the intestinal wall the fibrosis occasionally leads to abdominal pain, diarrhoea and rectal prolapse. Sigmoidoscopy shows the mucous membrane to be reddened and granular and small pinpoint yellow elevations with surrounding hyperaemia are characteristic. Of more clinical significance is the hepatic reaction in which there is fibrosis round the portal tracts, the so-called pipe-stem fibrosis, which is histologically distinct from a cirrhosis. The effect, however, is to produce presinusoidal portal hypertension in that there is an elevated intrasplenic pressure with a normal wedge hepatic vein pressure. The patient presents with hepatomegaly, splenomegaly, ascites and oesophageal varices.

The diagnosis is established by finding ova in snips of rectal mucosa. The complement fixation test is reliable. At a late stage the ova may be detected on a liver biopsy. Niridazole is the treatment of choice given orally in a dose of 25 mg/kg body weight in two divided doses daily for 7–10 days.

Echinococciasis (Hydatid Disease)

Hydatid disease is caused mainly by *Echinococcus granulosus* and has its highest incidence in Africa, Australia, Central Europe, South America and Wales. The human infection is acquired by ingesting the ova of the parasite. The embryos penetrate the intestinal wall and are carried to the liver where the brunt of the infection occurs; the lungs and other organs are involved to a lesser extent.

Once deposited in the various sites the embryos mature into hydatid cysts.

Symptoms are produced when the cysts expand in size. Thus they may be present, unnoticed, for many years in the liver and then cause hepatomegaly. Rupture into the peritoneal or pleural cavities causes severe anaphylactic shock. The passage of daughter cysts down the biliary tree causes intermittent obstructive jaundice. The diagnosis is suggested by a calcified mass in the liver. Angiography or isotopic liver scans may be used to locate the cysts in the liver. There may be an eosinophilia. The Casoni skin test and the indirect haemagglutination reaction can be used to establish the diagnosis. Therapy is unsatisfactory and the cysts are either drained or excised. Considerable care is required to avoid spilling the hydatid fluid at the time of operation, and the cyst should be sterilized with 10% formalin before attempting any surgical manoeuvre.

Giardiasis

Giardia lamblia is a common parasite in man and inhabits the duodenum and proximal small bowel. The infestation may be asymptomatic but is liable to be severe in children causing nausea, vomiting and epigastric discomfort. Heavy infestation is associated with marked loss of the villus architecture of the intestinal cell and there is malabsorption of fat and carbohydrate. The diagnosis can be made by examination of the stool, duodenal aspiration intestinal biopsy and an impression smear of intestinal mucosa. The last method is a quick and easy way to detect parasites. Metronidazole 200 mg thrice daily for 7 days or as a single daily dose of 2 g for 3 days is the treatment of choice.

Ascariasis (Round Worm Infestation)

About 25% of the world's population is infested with *Ascaris lumbricoides*. Infestation follows ingestion of the ova and after an early pulmonary phase there follows a prolonged intestinal phase. Adult worms may cause no symptoms but heavy infestation is associated with anorexia, nausea, vomiting, intestinal colic and even intestinal obstruction. Worms may pass up the common bile duct to cause intermittent biliary obstruction; pancreatitis has been recorded. The diagnosis is made by finding either the adult worms or their ova in the stools. The piperazine salts (piperazine citrate, 4.0 g as a single dose on one or two occasions) are safe and effective therapy.

Ancylostomiasis (Hookworm Disease)

Hookworm infestation is a most important cause of ill health for many millions in tropical and subtropical areas. In Europe and the Middle and Far East the cause is *Ancylostoma duodenale*, whereas in the Americas and tropical Africa the offending parasite is *Necator americanus*. The adult worms live in the upper small intestine attached to the mucous membrane from which they suck blood. During the initial phase of the disease there may be abdominal pain, diarrhoea and eosinophilia. Far more important is chronic hookworm infestation in which there is iron deficiency anaemia, hypoalbuminaemia and fat malabsorption. The diagnosis is made by detecting the ova in a fresh specimen of stool. The most satisfactory treatment for *A. duodenale* is bephenium given as a single dose of 5 g after an overnight fast and repeated for 2 days. Tetrachloroethylene is of value against *N. americanus*. No laxative is necessary. Nutritional deficiencies and anaemia must be corrected.

Strongyloidiasis

Strongyloides stercoralis has a geographical distribution similar to hookworm. The infection can be most chronic and persist for as long as 40 years. A local pruritic eruption at the site where the larvae penetrate the skin is followed by pulmonary manifestations of cough, dyspnoea and haemoptysis. The intestinal phase is characterized by nausea, vomiting, diarrhoea, flatulence, epigastric tenderness and probably fat malabsorption. The diagnosis is made from an examination of a fresh stool where the larvae can be identified. Treatment is with thiabendazole, 25 mg/kg twice daily for 3 days.

Tape Worm Infestation

Tape worm infestation is from either the beef tape worm, *Taenia saginata*, or the pork tape worm, *T. solium*; the clinical picture is similar for both worms. The infestation is frequently asymptomatic but there may be epigastric discomfort, diarrhoea, weight loss and irritability. Tape worm infestation acquires greater significance in the case of *T. solium* because man can act as the intermediate host for this worm. Cysticerci develop in the muscles and viscera causing muscle pains, weakness and epilepsy. Treatment of the adult worm is with niclosamide, 1 g followed after 1 hour by a second dose of 1 g, before breakfast. Dichlorophen, 6 g in divided doses on two successive days is also effective.

Enterobiasis (Pin Worm, Seat Worm, Threadworm Infestation)

This is probably the commonest infestation in man, affecting particularly children and family groups. It is caused by *Enterobius vermicularis*. The eggs are deposited on the perianal skin at night and self infestation is usual. The commonest manifestation of the infestation is pruritus ani which is most troublesome at night. The diagnosis is made by using a 'sticky tape' swab which is applied to the perianal skin in the morning before the bowels have been emptied. Occasionally the adult female worms, which are 10 mm long, may be seen. Treatment is either with viprynium in a single dose of 5 mg/kg body weight followed by a second dose two weeks later, or piperazine. The whole family should be treated and advice given regarding personal hygiene. Wearing of gloves at night may be used to prevent reinfestation.

Further Reading

Ahvonen, P. (1972) Human yersinosis in Finland II. Clinical features. *Ann. clin. Res.*, **4**, 39–48.

Geddes, A. M. (1973) Enteric fever, salmonellosis, and food poisoning. *Br. med. J.*, **i**, 98–100.

Hendrickse, R. G. (1973) Dysentery including amoebiasis. *Br. med. J.*, **i**, 669–672.

Ironside, A. G. (1973) Gastroenteritis of infancy. *Br. med. J.*, **i**, 284–286.

Kamath, K. R. and Murugasu, R. (1974) A comparative study of four methods for detecting *Giardia lamblia* in children with diarrhoeal disease and malabsorption. *Gastroenterology*, **66**, 16–21.

Merson, M. H. et al. (1976) Traveler's diarrhea in Mexico. *New Engl. J. Med.*, **294**, 1299–1305.

Index

Abdominal pain 197
Abetalipoproteinaemia 109
Abscess
  amoebic 360
  appendicular 121
Absorption
  calcium 83
  carbohydrate 109
  fat 80
  iron 254
  mechanisms 79
  protein 113
  xylose 86
Acanthocytosis 109
Achalasia of cardia 4
Acid output 25
  in diagnosis of peptic ulcer, 25, 32, 51
Acute fatty liver of pregnancy 299
  infective gastroenteritis 350
  liver atrophy 277
  liver cell failure 277
Adenitis, acute non-specific, mesenteric 122
Adenoma
  complex, multiple endocrine 49
  villous 165
Adenomatous polyp 164
Adult coeliac disease 87
Adult hypertrophic pyloric stenosis 190
Afferent loop syndrome 55
Alcohol, effect on oesophagus 9
Alcoholic cirrhosis 250, 255

Alcoholic fatty liver 248
Alcoholic hepatitis 249
Alcoholic hepatomegaly 248
Alcoholic liver disease 247
Alcoholic sclerosing hyaline necrosis 249
Allergic gastroenteropathy 117
Alpha$_1$-antitrypsin deficiency 263
Alpha-chain disease 99
Alpha-fetoprotein 158, 225, 270, 277, 288
Amoebiasis 359
Amoebic abscess 360
Amoeboma 360
Ampulla of Vater, cancer 321
Amyloidosis 108
Anaemia
  pernicious 67
  postgastrectomy 57
Anal continence 204
Anal fissure 207
Anal fistula 208
Anal haematoma, external 206
Anal skin tag 207
Ancylostomiasis 364
Aneurysm of abdominal aorta 155
Angina, intestinal 153
Anicteric hepatitis 274
Antibody
  antimitochondrial 225, 261, 291
  gastric 65
  parietal cell 65
  smooth muscle 225, 252, 261, 270
Anticoagulants 155

Antigen
  carcinoembryonic (CEA) 158, 161, 318
  hepatitis A 269
  hepatitis B 251, 267
Antimitochondrial antibody 225, 261
Antinuclear factor 225
Aorta, aneurysm 155
Appendicitis 120
  chronic 124
Appendicular abscess 121
Ascariasis 363
Atresia, congenital biliary 347

Bacteria, intestinal 103
Barrett's ulcer 13
Belching 2
Bile constituents 223
Bile formation 222
Bile micelles 330
Bile reflux 27, 63
Bile salts
  absorption 220
  fat absorption 100, 104
  metabolism 218
  in small intestinal disease, 100, 127
Bilharzia 361
Biliary atresia, congenital 347
Biliary cirrhosis, primary 260
Biliary dyskinesia 343
Biliary fever, Charcot's intermittent 339
Biliary tract
  congenital abnormalities 347
  tumours 344
Bilious vomiting
Bilirubin metabolism 213
Bleeding, gastrointestinal 40, 181, 234
Boerhaave's syndrome 14
Bone disease, postgastrectomy 59
Brunner's glands, hyperplasia 68
Budd–Chiari syndrome 295

Caeruloplasmin 259
Calcific pancreatitis 312
Calcium absorption 83
Cancer (see *Tumours*)
Carbohydrate absorption 109

Carcinoid syndrome 171
Carcinoid tumours 170
Cardia, achalasia 4
Carminatives 2
Charcot's intermittent biliary fever 339
Cholangitis 338
  sclerosing 130, 141, 343
Cholecystitis
  acute, 335
  chronic 337
Cholecystokinin 2, 175, 303
Choledochal cyst 348
Choledocholithiasis 338
Cholera 354
Cholestatic hepatitis 275
Cholestatic jaundice 217, 226, 291, 299, 340, 346
Chronic active hepatitis 251, 276
Chylomicrons 81
Cirrhosis of liver 213, 228, 230
  aetiology 246
  alcoholic 250, 255
  and fluid retention 242
  and gastrointestinal bleeding 234
  and jaundice 245
  neuropsychiatric complications 239
  posthepatitis 276
  primary biliary 260
Coeliac axis compression 155
Coeliac disease 87, 131, 188
Colitis
  granulomatous 125
  ischaemic 149
  ulcerative 131, 136
    extracolonic complications 140
Colon
  cancer 140, 159
  Crohn's disease 128
  diverticular disease 162, 179
  motility 175
  polyps 159, 164
  spastic 176
  strictures 133
  toxic dilatation 139
Colostomy 202
Congenital biliary abnormalities
  atresia 347
  hepatic fibrosis 348

Constipation 192
Contaminated bowel syndrome 103, 188, 339
Continence, anal 204
Contraceptives, oral and the liver 285
Corrosive oesophagitis 12
Crigler–Najjar syndrome 294
Crohn's disease 93, 122, 125, 144
  extraintestinal features 129
  involving colon 128
  involving small bowel 126
Cronkhite–Canada syndrome 169
Cruveilhier–Baumgarten syndrome 231
Cryptitis 208
Curling's ulcer 48
Cushing's ulcer 49
Cyst
  choledochal 348
  pseudopancreatic 310
Cystic fibrosis of pancreas 325

Defaecation 204
Delayed hypoglycaemia and dumping 57
Dermatitis herpetiformis 107
Dermatogenic enteropathy 107
Dermatomyositis 186
Descending perineum syndrome 206
Diabetes mellitus 9, 187
Diaphragmatic hernia 20
Diarrhoea 188, 191
  postgastrectomy 60
  traveller's 352
Disaccharidase activity 110
Diverticular disease of colon 179, 181
Diverticulitis 179
Drugs, effect on liver 281
  malabsorption due to 108
Drug jaundice 281
Dubin–Johnson syndrome 295
Dumping syndrome 56
Duodenal ulcer 28
Duodenitis 68
Dysentery 191
  amoebic 359
  bacillary 358
Dyskinesia, biliary 343

Dyspepsia, non-ulcer 68
Dysphagia 3

Echinococciasis 362
Encephalopathy, hepatic 239
Endocrine adenoma complex, multiple 49
Endoscopic retrograde cholangiopancreatography 291, 314, 319, 333, 340
Enteritis, regional 125
Enterobiasis 365
Enterocolitis
  haemorrhagic 153
  pseudomembranous 183
Enterohepatic circulation 219, 331
Enteropathy
  dermatogenic 107
  gluten-induced 87, 131, 188
Enzymes
  intestinal 76
  pancreatic 302
Errosive gastritis 63
External anal haematoma 206
External haemorrhoids 206
Extrahepatic cholestatic jaundice 291
Extrahepatic portal vein obstruction 292

Faecal fat 85, 86
Faeces 175
Familial Mediterranean fever 187
Familial polyposis coli 159, 166
Fat
  absorption 80
  faecal 85, 86
  malabsorption 83, 101, 104, 107, 186, 188, 313
    in liver disease 221
    mechanisms 79
Fatty liver
  acute, of pregnancy 299
  alcoholic 248
Ferritin 254
α-Fetoprotein 225, 246
Fever
  Charcot's intermittent biliary 339
  familial Mediterranean 187

Fever *continued*
  paratyphoid 352
  typhoid 352
Fibrosis
  congenital hepatic 348
  cystic, of pancreas 325
  retroperitoneal 189
Fissure, anal 207
Fistula, anal 208
Fluid retention in cirrhosis 242
Fulminant hepatitis 277, 284, 286

Gall bladder cancer 344
Gall stones 329
  in common bile duct 338
Gardner's syndrome 168
Gastric acid output 23
  in diagnosis 25, 51
  measurement 25
Gastric antibodies 65, 67
Gastric atrophy 66
Gastric cancer 61, 69
Gastric cytology 71
Gastric emptying 22
Gastric function 22
Gastric motility 22
Gastric mucus 26
Gastric outflow obstruction 44, 190
Gastric peristalsis 22
Gastric polyp 73
Gastric tumours 69
Gastric ulcer
  acute 63
  chronic 27
Gastrin 3, 24, 51, 67, 175, 189, 303
  effect on lower oesophageal sphinc-
      ter 2
Gastritis
  acute 63
  chronic 65
  errosive 63
  haemorrhagic 63
Gastroenteritis 350
  acute infective 350
  infantile 351
Gastroenteropathy
  allergic 117
  protein-losing 113

Gastrointestinal bleeding 40, 63, 181, 234
Gastrointestinal–polyposis syndromes 165
Giant rugal hypertrophy of gastric mucosa 68
Giardiasis 99, 363
Gilbert's syndrome 293
Glucagon 2, 325
Glucagonoma 325
Glucose–galactose malabsorption 113
Gluten 87
Gluten-induced enteropathy 87
Glycocalyx 26, 76
Granulomatous ileocolitis 125

Haematoma
  external anal 206
  intramural 154
Haemochromatosis 254
Haemorrhagic enterocolitis 153
Haemorrhagic gastritis 63
Haemorrhoids
  external 206
  internal 205
Halothane hepatitis 284
Heartburn 4
Hepatic (see also *Liver*)
Hepatic duct cancer 345
Hepatic encephalopathy 239
Hepatitis
  alcoholic 249
  anicteric 274
  cholestatic 275
  chronic 276
      active 251, 276
  fulminant 277, 284, 286
  halothane 284
  hyperbilirubinaemia 274
  infectious 266
  relapsing 275
  serum 266
  viral 266
Hepatitis-associated antigen 251, 267
Hepatolenticular degeneration 257
Hepatoma 287
Hepatomegaly, alcoholic 248

Hernia
  diaphragmatic 20
  hiatus 6, 17
Hiatus hernia 6, 17
Hookworm 364
Hormones
  intestinal 78
  pancreatic 303
Hydatid disease 362
Hyperamylasaemia 307
Hyperbilirubinaemia
  posthepatitis 274
  unconjugated 217, 293, 297
Hyperplasia
  of Brunner's glands 68
  nodular lymphoid 99
Hypertension, portal 228, 362
Hypogammaglobulinaemia 99
Hypoglycaemia 323
  delayed 57

Idiopathic steatorrhoea 87, 131, 188
Ileitis
  acute 126
  terminal 125
Ileocolitis, granulomatous 125
Ileostomy 199
Immunoglobulin(s) 91, 97
  in coeliac disease 91
  deficiency states associated with
    steatorrhoea 97, 224, 261
  in liver disease 224, 261
Indicans 106
Infantile gastroenteritis 351
Infarction, mesenteric 151
Infectious hepatitis 266
Insulin test 54
Insulinoma 322
Internal haemorrhoids 205
Intestinal absorption 79
Intestinal angina 153
Intestinal bacterial flora 103, 176
  overgrowth 103
Intestinal cell turnover 75
Intestinal enzymes 76
Intestinal gas 176
Intestinal histology 74
Intestinal hormones 78

Intestinal immune system 97
Intestinal ischaemia 151
Intestinal lymphangiectasia 100, 115
Intestinal motility 79
Intestinal polyps 164
Intestinal resection 100
Intestinal transport 77
Intestinal tumours 158
Intramural haematoma 154
Intrinsic factor 25
Iron absorption 254
Irradiation 184
Irritable bowel syndrome 176
Irritable colon syndrome 176
  post-dysenteric 278
Ischaemia, intestinal 151
Islet cell tumours 50, 321

Jaundice 217, 245
  cholestatic 217, 226, 291, 299, 340,
    346
  drug 281
  neonatal 296, 347
  postoperative 300
  in pregnancy 299
Jejunoileitis 127
Juvenile polyps 170

Kayser–Fleischer ring 258

Lactase deficiency 111
Lactose intolerance 111
Laxative abuse 195
Laxatives 193
Leptospirosis 357
Leukaemia 188
Liver (see also *Hepatic*)
  acute fatty, of pregnancy 299
  atrophy, acute 277, 284, 286
  and blood coagulation 226
  cancer, primary 246, 287
  cell 212
    failure, acute 277, 284, 286
  cirrhosis (see *Cirrhosis*)
  in Crohn's disease 129
  disease, alcoholic 247
  disease, polycystic 349

Liver *continued*
  and drugs 281
  function 213, 226
  necrosis, massive 277, 284, 286
  protein metabolism 224
  and renal dysfunction 227
  tumours
    benign 286, 290
    primary 246, 287
    secondary 289
  in ulcerative colitis 140, 252
Lupus erythematosus, systemic 186
Lymphangiectasia, intestinal 100, 115
Lymphoma 172

Malabsorption, carbohydrate 109
  fat 85, 97, 99, 101, 186, 188
    due to drugs 108
    in liver disease 221
    mechanisms 79
  glucose–galactose 113
  in liver-disease 221
  in newborn infants 108
  in pancreatic disease 313
  and skin disease 107
  sucrose–maltose 113
  sugar 109
  vitamin B_{12} 67, 100, 108, 127
Mallory–Weiss syndrome 13
Malnutrition, postgastrectomy 58
Mastocytosis 109
Mediterranean fever, familial 187
Menétrier's disease 68
Mesenteric adenitis, acute non-specific 122
Mesenteric infarction 151
Metabolism
  bile salt 218
  bilirubin 213
Micelles, bile 220
  fat absorption 80
Monilial oesophagitis 12
Mucosa, gastric, giant rugal hypertrophy 68
Multiple endocrine adenoma complex 49
Muscoviscidosis 325
Myotonia dystrophica 100

Necrosis
  alcoholic, sclerosing hyaline 249
  massive liver 277, 284, 286
Neonatal jaundice 296
Neuropsychiatric complications of cirrhosis 239
Nodular lymphoid hyperplasia 99
Non-specific mesenteric adenitis, acute 122

Oesophagitis
  corrosive 12
  monilial 12
  reflux 10, 18, 185
Oesophagogastric junction 1
Oesphagus
  cancer 5, 14
  effect of alcohol 9
  emetogenic injury 13
  lower, lined by columnar epithelium 13
    ring 6
    sphincter 1, 2, 20
  peristalsis 3
  reflux 2
  rupture 14
  spasm, diffuse 8
  stricture 11, 18, 185
  ulcer 13
  upper sphincter 1
  web
Osteomalacia 59
Osteoporosis 59

Pancreas
  cancer 316
  cholera 322
  cystic fibrosis 325
  enzymes 302
  function 313, 319
  hormonal control 302
  insufficiency 313, 326
  secretion 302
  tumours 316
    islet cell 49, 321
Pancreatitis
  acute 305
    relapsing 311

calcific 312
chronic 312
classification 304
Papillitis 208
Paratyphoid fever 352
Parietal cell antibodies 65
Paterson–Brown–Kelly syndrome 7
Pepsin 25
Peptic ulcer 22
    acute 48
    complicated by gastric outflow ob-
        struction 44
    haemorrhage 40
    malignancy 48
    penetration 47
    perforation 46
    recurrent 53
    treatment 33
Peristalsis
    gastric 22
    oesophageal 3
Pernicious anaemia 2, 67
Peutz–Jeghers syndrome 169
Pinworm 365
Plummer–Vinson syndrome 7
Polyarteritis nodosa 186
Polycystic liver disease 349
Polyposis coli, familial 159, 166
Polyps
    adenomatous 164
    colonic 159, 164
    gastric 73
    intestinal 164
    juvenile 170
Portal hypertension 228, 362
Portal vein obstruction, extrahepatic
    292
Portasystemic collateral circulation
    229, 232
Postbulbar ulcer 31
Postcholecystectomy syndrome 342
Post-dysenteric irritable colon 361
Postgastrectomy
    anaemia 57
    bone disease 60
    diarrhoea 60
    malnutrition 58
    problems 52
    surgical complications 61

Posthepatitis cirrhosis 276
Posthepatitis   hyperbilirubinaemia
    274
Posthepatitis syndrome 274
Postoperative jaundice 300
Pregnancy
    acute fatty liver of 299
    jaundice in, 299
Presbyoesophagus 9
Primary biliary cirrhosis 186, 260
Proctitis, ulcerative 141
Protein absorption 113
Protein-losing gastroenteropathy 113
Protein metabolism 224
Pruritus ani 210
Pseudomembranous enterocolitis 183
Pseudopancreatic cyst 310
Pyloric stenosis 44, 190
Pyoderma gangrenosum 140

Rectum
    cancer 159
    solitary ulcer 209
Reflux oesophagitis 10, 18, 185
Regional enteritis 125
Relapsing hepatitis 275
Relapsing pancreatitis 311
Renal disease 189
Renal dysfunction in liver disease 227
Retroperitoneal fibrosis 189
Reye's syndrome 298
Rheumatoid arthritis 186
Rotor syndrome 195
Roundworm 363

Schatski ring 6
Schistosomiasis 361
Scleroderma 2, 9, 185
Seat worm 365
Secretin 2, 303
Serum hepatitis 266
Skin disease and malabsorption 107
Skin tag, anal 207
Smooth muscle antibody 225, 252,
    261, 270
Spastic colon 176
Splenic flexure syndrome 178

Sprue, tropical 94
Steatorrhoea, idiopathic 87, 131, 188
Stenosis
    adult hypertrophic 190
    pyloric 44
Stomal ulcer 53
Stress ulcer 48
Stricture colon 133
Stricture oesophagus 11, 18
Stronglyloidiasis 364
Sucrose–maltose deficiency 113
Sugar intolerance 109
Sugar malabsorption 109
Systemic lupus erythematosis 186

Tapeworm 365
Terminal ileitis 125
Tertiary contractions 3, 4, 18
Threadworm 365
Toxic dilatation of colon 139
Traveller's diarrhoea 352
Triglycerides, medium-chain 81
Tropical sprue 94
Tuberculosis 355
Tumours
    ampulla of Vater 321
    biliary tract 344
    carcinoid 170
    colonic 140, 159, 164
    gall bladder 344
    gastric 69
    hepatic duct 345
    intestinal 158
    islet cell 50, 321
    liver 287
    oesophageal 14
    pancreatic 316
    rectal 159

Turcot syndrome 169
Typhoid fever 352

Ulcer, Barrett's 13
    Curling's 48
    Cushing's 49
    duodenal 28
    gastric 27
    oesophageal 13
    peptic (see *Peptic ulcer*)
    postbulbar 31
    solitary rectal 209
    stomal 53
    stress 48
Ulcerative colitis 131, 136, 252
Ulcerative proctitis 141
Unconjugated   hyperbilirubinaemia
        217, 293, 297

Veno-occlusive disease 296
Villous adenoma 165
Viral hepatitis 266
Vitamin B_{12}
    deficiency 58, 67, 108
    malabsorption 67, 100, 108, 127
Vomiting 196
    bilious 55

WDHA syndrome 322
Weil's disease 357
Whipple's disease 96
Wilson's disease 257

Xylose absorption 86

Yersinosis 131, 356

Zollinger–Ellison syndrome 2, 50, 321